ESSAYS IN HONOUR OF AUBREY BURL

PREHISTORIC RITUAL AND RELIGION

EDITED BY
ALEX GIBSON &
DEREK SIMPSON

SUTTON PUBLISHING

First published in 1998 by
Sutton Publishing Limited · Phoenix Mill
Thrupp · Stroud · Gloucestershire · GL5 2BU

British Library Cataloguing in Publication Data
A catalogue record for this book is available from the British Library.

ISBN 0-7509-1597-8 [hardback]
ISBN 0-7509-1598-6 [paperback]

The royalties from this book are being donated to the Diane Fossey Gorilla Fund, 110 Gloucester Avenue, London.

™ ALAN SUTTON™ and SUTTON™ are the
trade marks of Sutton Publishing Limited

Typeset in 10/13 pt Bembo.
Typesetting and origination by
Sutton Publishing Limited.
Printed in Great Britain by
WBC Ltd, Bridgend.

CONTENTS

CONTENTS

LIST OF
CONTRIBUTORS

Patrick Ashmore is Principal Inspector of Ancient Monuments at Historic Scotland. He is the author of numerous works on Scottish archaeology including *Neolithic and Bronze Age Scotland*.

John Barnatt is Senior Survey Archaeologist for the Peak District National Park Authority. He has a first degree in Fine Art and taught in an art school for several years before studying for his doctorate at Sheffield University, researching the design and distribution of stone circles. He has written several books and numerous papers on the Neolithic and Bronze Age in Britain, often with the emphasis on the Peak District, where he has worked for the last fourteen years.

Richard Bradley has been Professor of Archaeology at the University of Reading since 1987. His main interests are in landscape archaeology, rock art and the interpretation of monumental architecture. Recent publications include *Altering the Earth* and *Rock Art and the Prehistory of Atlantic Europe*. He is co-author of *Interpreting the Axe Trade*. A new book, *The Significance of Monuments*, will appear in 1998.

Bryony Coles is Professor of Prehistoric Archaeology and Director of the Centre for Wetland Research at the University of Exeter. She is the author of *Anthropology for Archaeologists* and *Wetland Management: A Survey for English Heritage*. She is co-author of *Sweet Track to Glastonbury: the Prehistory of the Somerset Levels, People and the Wetlands* and *Enlarging the Past: the Contribution of Wetland Archaeology*.

Tom Condit studied at Queen's University, Belfast and now works for the National Monuments Service in Dublin. He has published numerous articles on the history and archaeology of Ireland and is currently also a regular contributor to and editor of *Archaeology Ireland*.

Gabriel Cooney is a Statutory Lecturer in Archaeology at University College, Dublin and is director of the Irish Stone Axe Project. He is the co-author of *Irish Prehistory: A Social Perspective* and has written numerous papers on different aspects of the Irish Neolithic.

Mary Davis is a conservator specialising in archaeological artefacts. Currently working at the National Museums and Galleries of Wales, she has also worked for the National Museums of Scotland, Norwich Castle Museum and the Museum of London. Her publications include several articles on the analysis, sourcing and conservation of jet and jet-like artefacts.

Alex Gibson was educated at the Universities of Newcastle, Leicester and Amsterdam and is currently projects manager with the Clwyd–Powys Archaeological Trust. He has excavated and published widely on neolithic and bronze age sites, and is author of *Neolithic and Bronze Age Pottery* and co-author of *Prehistoric Pottery for the Archaeologist*.

Miranda J. Green is Reader in Archaeology and Head of the SCARAB Research Centre at the University of Wales College, Newport. Her books include *The Gods of the Celts*, *Symbol and Image in Celtic Religious Art*; *The Sun Gods of Ancient Europe*; *Celtic Art: Reading the Messages* and, most recently, *Exploring the World of the Druids*. She is archaeology and art editor of the University of Wales Board of Celtic Studies Journal *Studia Celtica*.

Barrie Hartwell is Senior Research Officer at the Department of Archaeology and Palaeoecology at the Queen's University, Belfast. He is curator of the Department's teaching collection and has interests in field survey techniques and excavation. He is joint editor of the *Ulster Journal of Archaeology*.

Jan de Jong is senior consultant at the Rijksdienst voor het Monumentenzorg, Netherlands. He is the author of a thesis on the mathematical principles of Greek and Roman temple design and of several articles on the history of architecture and the relation between architectural designs and mathematics. He is co-editor of *Munus non Ingratum* (Babesch suppl. 2) and of *Archeologie en Bouwhistorie in Zwolle* vols 1–3.

Ian Kinnes is Assistant Keeper in the Department of Prehistoric and Romano-British Antiquities at the British Museum. His research interests lie in the Neolithic of Britain and France and he is author of *Non-megalithic Long Barrows and Allied Structures in the British Neolithic* and *Round Barrows and Ring-ditches in the British Neolithic*.

Roy Loveday teaches part time in the Department of Adult Education at the University of Leicester. Returning to archaeology from history, he completed his doctoral thesis on *Cursus and Related Monuments of the British Neolithic* and has written a number of articles on aspects of ritual monuments.

Frances Lynch lectures in archaeology at the University of Wales, Bangor. She has excavated religious monuments of the Neolithic and Bronze Age, notably at Newgrange and the Brenig Valley, North Wales. She is author of *Prehistoric Anglesey* and has dabbled in some of the shallower pools of cognitive archaeology now and again.

Roger Mercer was formerly Reader in Archaeology at the University of Edinburgh and is now Secretary of the Royal Commission on the Ancient and Historical Monuments of Scotland. He has been an active archaeological field surveyor and excavator for many years and has published many papers on the Neolithic and Bronze Age.

Graham Ritchie is an archaeologist with the Royal Commission on the Ancient and Historical Monuments of Scotland. He has measured many standing stones in the course of the Commission's survey work in Argyll and elsewhere and has excavated two stone circles – Balbirnie, Fife, and the Stones of Stennes, Orkney. He has a particular interest in the historical aspects of the recording of field archaeology in Scotland.

Clive Ruggles is Senior Lecturer in Archaeological Studies at Leicester University. His research interests centre upon archaeoastronomy and computer applications in archaeology. He has edited or co-edited several books, including *Astronomy and Society in Britain during the Period 4000–1500 BC; Records in Stone, Archaeoastronomy in the 1990s* and *Astronomies and Cultures* as well as writing numerous articles. His *Astronomy in Prehistoric Britain* will be published in 1998.

Alison Sheridan is the Assistant Keeper of Archaeology in the National Museums of Scotland and is currently working on the new Museum of Scotland (opening 1998). Her research interests have focused on the Neolithic and Bronze Age of Scotland, Ireland and Wales. She has co-edited *Vessels for the Ancestors* and has written numerous articles on neolithic and bronze age artefacts and on the Scottish 'Treasure Trove' system.

Andrew Sherratt teaches archaeology and anthropology at Oxford where he is Reader in Archaeology, and also Senior Curator in the Ashmolean Museum. His first volume of collected papers, *Economy and Society in Prehistoric Europe*, has just been published by Edinburgh University Press.

Derek Simpson is Professor of Archaeology at Queen's University, Belfast. He has published widely on various aspects of neolithic and bronze age archaeology in Britain and Ireland and is co-author of *An Introduction to British Prehistory*.

ACKNOWLEDGEMENTS

The editors would like to thank all the contributors for the prompt submission of their papers and to Rupert Harding and Sarah Fowle of Sutton Publishing for their enthusiasm for the project and their patience with the editors. Judith Burl has been a constant help throughout the preparation of this volume and Jane Gibson has been more patient than most.

INTRODUCTION

*Today the interior [of the Muir of Ord] has been levelled for one of the greens on a golf course . . .
As the players engage in the ritual of depositing a chalky white ball into a hole carefully positioned
inside the henge, one wonders if they sense faint mocking laughter somewhere on the green.*

(Burl 1991b, 56)

As the first contributor to this volume of collected essays by colleagues and friends has
commented, Aubrey Burl's first book, *The Stone Circles of the British Isles*, has remained the
primary source on the subject for twenty years. This is no mean feat in a time when
archaeological books are being published in increasing numbers, when old ideas are being
challenged and when the theoretical tides seem to change with seasonal, if not lunar, regularity.
Yet, despite the lasting value of *Stone Circles*, it is not true to say that Aubrey's ideas have
remained static. They have not, and indeed a second, revised, updated and reconsidered edition is
currently in preparation, doubtless to take its place as the new standard work well into the third
millennium (AD!).

While it is with stone circles that Aubrey Burl is invariably connected, these megalithic rings
do not form the only focus of his attentions as a glance at his bibliography will show. Henges and
stone rows have also come under his scrutiny while Stonehenge, in the present writer's view the
epitome of timber circles (despite being built of stone), has been studied in minute detail. In *The
Stonehenge People*, Aubrey concentrated on contemporary society, constantly reminding us that
without people there would have been no monuments and that while archaeologists classify and
quantify the archaeological resource, it is people who were responsible for it.

To return to the beginning, *Stone Circles* was written at a time when archaeological ritual,
and in particular megalithic sites, was receiving increased attention from scholars within
archaeology and those from other disciplines. Alexander Thom had produced plans of many
sites to a level of accuracy that was almost unprecedented within the archaeological fraternity
and perhaps even beyond the intentions of the monuments' creators. Thom's plans made
apparent the complexity of stone rings, the variety of their architecture, geometry, dimension
and orientation. A standard unit of measurement, the megalithic yard, had been proposed and
accepted unquestioningly by some, but refuted by others. Archaeoastronomy, long since
recognised at Stonehenge, was being increasingly applied to other sites both in Britain and
abroad but the results of these applications varied considerably in their degree of archaeological
credibility, far less acceptance. A combination of the geometry and orientations of stone circles
and alignments lead to the formulation of complex theories regarding archaeoastronomy, the
prehistoric calendar, a society governed by astronomer-priests and a level of numeracy among
prehistoric populations far in excess of previous preconceptions and preceding Pythagoras by
many centuries.

In 1976 there was a clear split between the earthfast archaeologists, who thought that the archaeomathematicians were all completely mad, and the latter, who regarded the archaeological fraternity as intellectual Luddites incapable of seeing beyond the horizons of their own excavation trenches.

In *Stone Circles*, Aubrey Burl demonstrated that both camps were right. Archaeoastronomy had been too liberally applied to many sites using inaccurate data, such as natural or relocated stones as siting posts or astral bodies which had long since moved across the sky and were no longer in the positions in which they would have been observed by prehistoric peoples. Calendrical interpretations were often so complex as to be certainly beyond the ken of a society which exhibits little evidence for advanced numeracy. And the megalithic yard was often decimalised, sometimes to three decimal places, to facilitate its application to nationally, even internationally, distributed monuments.

Nevertheless, there was a growing body of evidence – from Stonehenge, Newgrange and Maes Howe, for example – to demonstrate that megalith builders were indeed aware of the positions of at least the major solar and lunar events. Many stone circles, when carefully scrutinised, also demonstrated orientation on major solar or lunar events at times of the year which were important to agrarian societies and which would later become the major Celtic festivals. There was also variation in the architecture of circles, sometimes by design and sometimes not.

By critical analysis, using his sound archaeological background and an unprejudiced approach, Aubrey was able to stand astride the chasm between the two bitterly opposed camps and while he may not have completely united them, he did at least provide a platform for peace talks and fostered mutual tolerance. Most serious scholars now accept a centre line between the depths of the blinkered and the heights of fanciful hypothesis.

Within conventional archaeology, and aside from the archaeoastronomers and archaeogeometricians, until the end of the 1960s archaeologists strove to make clear-cut distinctions between the ritual and domestic, sacred and profane, in the archaeological record. Settlements were treated separately from the religious or sepulchral sites and the ritual practices of prehistoric populations were interpreted very much from a Judaeo-Christian perspective – a distinct, yet inaccurate, dichotomy between that which was sacred and that which was mundane. While settlement debris had been found beneath sepulchral sites, this was always attributed to an earlier phase of activity, the settlement having gone out of use prior to the construction of the sepulchro-ritual monument.

Increasingly in the 1970s, however, with the growth of interpretative archaeology, it became more difficult to draw this clear distinction. One particular example is the large Wessex henge excavations – Durrington Walls, Mount Pleasant and Marden – where the size and architecture of the henges demanded a ritual explanation while the vast quantities of ostensibly midden material – pottery, lithics, food remains – were more indicative of settlement.

Even less monumental domestic sites are now capable of ritual interpretation. For example, burnt mounds may represent the detritus from trance-inducing sweat-houses, ostensibly domestic structures may in fact be connected with mortuary ritual, and even the humble rubbish pit may well be a receptacle for the structured deposition of material of ritual purpose and potency – if ultimately of domestic derivation.

This, in retrospect, is hardly surprising and we do not need to search for exotic ethnographic parallels to demonstrate that ritual and domestic are inevitably intertwined. While ethnography cannot be denied as a useful tool for the archaeologist (though, it would appear, it is hardly ever

Lundin Links, Fife, Scotland. (Photo: Alex Gibson)

used *vice versa*), in Britain our own (mainly) Judaeo-Christian background reminds us of the inseparability of the domestic and religious. Religious symbolism may be worn as jewellery even by people who do not practise the beliefs they appear to profess. Crossing oneself is a religious ritual while shaking hands is purely ritual in a secular sense. Fruit in a fruitbowl is essentially utilitarian, but the same fruit at a harvest festival takes on a whole new meaning. Eggs have enhanced significance at Easter (the spring festival), corn is intricately woven at Harvest (the autumnal festival), while overtly utilitarian candles remind us of Advent in the winter months and about the time of the winter solstice – each modern festival relates in some way to those of our Celtic and even neolithic forebears. All major religions, while possessing specific religious paraphernalia, unite in the occasional enhancement of mundane objects to positions of high religious significance.

Surely, and as other writers have demonstrated, this inextricable interplay between the religious and the mundane must similarly have existed among primitive communities. In European prehistory, we need look no further than the stone axe, a tool which must have been fundamental to an agrarian society within a largely forested landscape yet often made of exotic materials, involving intensive craftsmanship, and frequently buried, in pristine condition, in non-domestic contexts. Complex trade networks appear to have been built around the exchange of axes, a trade in which stone circles appear to have played no small part, and it is therefore not surprising that it is as axe ingots that the new copper and copper alloys were initially traded.

However, and at the risk of stating the obvious, some clear distinctions may be drawn between life's religious and domestic facets. Architecture, for example, produces building forms which are

Stonehenge – the epitome of timber circles. (Photo: Alex Gibson)

not overtly domestic. Thus churches differ from vernacular buildings, and stone circles differ from huts, yet the link between non-megalithic long barrows and the Linear Bandkeramik houses of the European landmass serves to remind us that even this aspect is fraught with difficulties of interpretation. Should we therefore see a dichotomy between religion and domesticity, the two united by ritual and with only the priesthood truly combining the two? Is the question answerable?

In his studies of prehistoric religion and ritual, Aubrey has constantly reminded us that we should not underestimate the conviction with which religion is held by many, that society may be divided between those who practise religion and those who control it, and that the distinction between sacred and profane is rarely easy to define. Importantly, it is fundamental to remember that, whichever aspect of life we study, it is people who are the ultimate focus. Stone circles, henges, cursus monuments, stone rows, all were caused to be built by people and actually constructed by people. Religion was practised by people, probably under the guidance or instruction of others. Axes were made for people by other people and probably traded and deposited by yet others. Religion was fundamental to the ordering of society, Marxist opiate or not.

This volume of essays, written in honour of Aubrey Burl, was commissioned in his 70th year and is presented to him in recognition of his substantial contribution to the study of prehistoric ritual and religion. The contributors, all colleagues and, above all, friends, have each dealt with aspects of prehistoric ritual which they have made their own yet which owe much in their initial conception and direction to Aubrey's work. Thus, in the first section, monuments form the focus

– their architecture, setting and functions. In the second section the roles of artefacts in prehistoric ritual are considered, while in the third section, attention is given to the antiquarian records of prehistoric sites, a source of information well used by Aubrey and which can often shed important light on sites, in particular by highlighting elements which are the result of nineteenth-century romanticism yet on which, on occasion, astronomical alignments were proposed. Finally, the fourth section deals with aspects of prehistoric ritual from a more theoretical viewpoint.

To conclude, the short quotations with which this introduction begins and ends are typical of the humour, eloquence and observation of Aubrey Burl, who has contributed so much wisdom to the study of ritual and ritual monuments of the third and second millennia BC. His works, ranging from the popular to the profoundly academic, are united in the depth of their observation of archaeological, topographical and literary minutiae. His particular attention to detail, context and architecture is second to none, and should serve as an example to future generations. It is hoped that Aubrey derives as much pleasure from reading this book as the editors did from compiling it.

The gritstone crag of Robin Hood's Stride rises jaggedly with two stubby piles of boulders jutting up at either end of its flat top like the head and pricked-up ears of a wrinkled hippopotamus.

(Burl 1995, 53)

Alex Gibson, Montgomery
Beltane, 1997

PART ONE

MONUMENTS

CHAPTER ONE

STONE CIRCLES AND PASSAGE GRAVES – A CONTESTED RELATIONSHIP

RICHARD BRADLEY

INTRODUCTION

It was Cyril Connolly (1938) who suggested that an author's ambition should be 'to write a book that holds good for ten years afterwards'. Aubrey Burl achieved this at the first attempt, which is why, twenty-two years after it was first published, *The Stone Circles of the British Isles* provides the starting point for this chapter.

In chapter seven of that book, Aubrey considered the complex relationship between passage graves and the stone circles which occasionally enclose them. Writing about the recently excavated monument at Newgrange, he said: 'It seems likely that [its] outer circle is no later than the passage grave and therefore the earliest stone ring yet recognised' (Burl 1976, 242). It is this interpretation that has become so contentious. Were the first stone circles associated with megalithic tombs, or were they a later development? Were there composite monuments of the kind that he suggests, or were the two forms built at different times and used in entirely different ways?

In this chapter I would like to consider these questions in the light of more recent research at Newgrange and other sites. All of these monuments were considered in Aubrey's book, but in every case their interpretation has become more complicated over the years. I shall concentrate on four main sites: Newgrange, where this discussion began, Ballynoe, Bryn Celli Ddu and Balnuaran of Clava. Two other important sites, Millin Bay and Callanish, are not considered here. There are several reasons for this. The strange composite monument at Millin Bay has neither a passage grave nor a stone circle, although it does include an oval mound bounded by standing stones (Collins & Waterman 1955). Callanish presents a very different problem. Although excavation has shown that a tiny passage grave was built inside an existing stone circle, neither monument is at all characteristic of wider developments in Britain and Ireland. The circle has a centre stone and is approached by four avenues – features which are not found together on any other site – while the passage grave is quite exceptionally small. It overlies a structure associated with sherds of Grooved Ware and may be among the last tombs of this kind to be built (Ashmore 1996, 73).

In any case enough controversy surrounds the other sites. In two cases, Newgrange and Ballynoe, Aubrey was unable to draw on the results of excavation, for these were not available when he was writing his book. Both have now been published, although there is disagreement over the interpretation of the evidence (M. O'Kelly 1982; C. O'Kelly 1983; Groenman-van-Waateringe & Butler 1976). The same applies to Bryn Celli Ddu where Aubrey refers to Clare O'Kelly's reconsideration of the excavation report (C. O'Kelly 1969). Since 1976 her interpretation has been questioned by George Eogan (1983). In the case of Balnuaran of Clava, the difficulties of understanding the monuments were only increased when the results of a hitherto unknown excavation became available for the first time (Barclay 1990). In that case the problems of interpreting this material led to fresh fieldwork on the site (Bradley 1996).

This chapter considers each of these monuments and the light that they shed on the problematical relationship between stone circles and passage graves. I shall outline the main debates surrounding Newgrange, Ballynoe and Bryn Celli Ddu, before turning to the evidence from my own work at Clava.

NEWGRANGE

The evidence from Newgrange epitomises the character of the debate. Here a setting of monoliths encloses an enormous passage grave. An early excavation suggested that the two structures were contemporary with one another, for one of the monoliths had been erected before any material had slipped from the surface of the mound (Ó Ríordáin & L'Eochaldhe

The entrance to Newgrange. (Photo: Alex Gibson)

Newgrange. (Photo: Alex Gibson)

1956). Aubrey reported this observation in 1976, and Brian O'Kelly followed the same interpretation when he published his own work on the site (M. O'Kelly 1982). This seemed to show that the front face of the cairn had not collapsed until the stone circle had been built, for some of the debris had come to rest against the base of the uprights. It was possible, though hardly likely, that the stone circle was constructed before the passage grave, but the results of these two excavations were enough to show that it belonged to a very early phase in the history of the monument. Most probably, Newgrange was a composite structure, combining a ring of monoliths with a chambered tomb. There the matter might have rested, but in fact this interpretation has been challenged. It may have happened because the reports on O'Kelly's excavation are not sufficiently detailed. Some of the most important sections were not illustrated and it is difficult to relate a number of the artefacts to the contexts in which they were found. This is probably because the project was prepared for publication when the excavator's health was failing. In any case these comments need have no bearing on the quality of the fieldwork itself. More serious are the criticisms advanced by a recent excavator of the site, who suggests that one of the monoliths was erected after the tomb was built and was later in date than a trench associated with the Beaker occupation of the same site. There was a massive timber setting beyond the limits of the passage grave, and David Sweetman (1985) suggests that this was the immediate precursor of the stone circle. In his view the sequence might be the same as that in England and Scotland, where timber monuments were often replaced in stone during the Beaker period.

The results of these excavations are incompatible with one another. There are plausible explanations – the monolith in question might have been re-erected, or the underlying feature

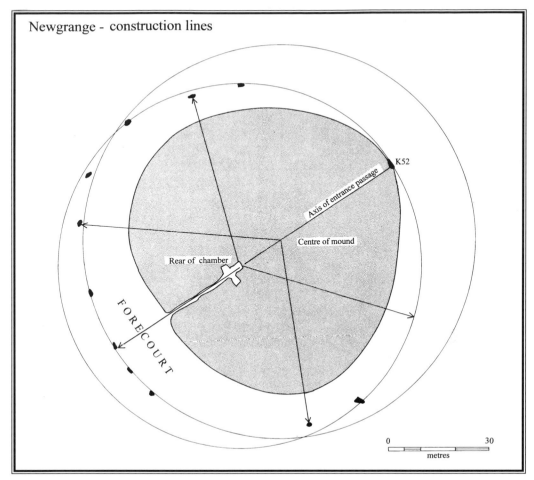

Newgrange - construction lines

1.1 The suggested layout of the stone circle at Newgrange.

might predate the tomb – but at present it is hard to decide between the two versions of the sequence. One of the excavators may have been mistaken, and it is impossible, using the written record, to suggest a convincing solution. This is especially unfortunate as the crucial area of the site was investigated on such a large scale.

There may be a further clue in Aubrey's discussion of this monument, written before the controversy began. In his account of Newgrange he suggests that 'it appears that both mound and circle share a common centre' (Burl 1976, 241). This simplifies the situation since both depart from a circular outline. The kerb is flattened on either side of the entrance and the monoliths are not a consistent distance from the kerb. It was an 'egg-shaped' circle. The course of the stone setting follows two distinct arcs. In front of the entrance it may have a point of origin at the centre of the mound, but behind the monument it follows a quite different course, apparently laid out from the position occupied by the back of the chamber. That second arc intersects the edge of the monument at the decorated kerbstone 52 which is directly in line with the entrance passage (Fig. 1.1). If this projection has any validity (and it could be tested by locating the sockets for further monoliths), it would mean that the entire design was conceived before the monument was built. Unfortunately, this interpretation has to be backed by fieldwork if it is to be taken any further.

BALLYNOE

When Aubrey was writing in 1976, there seemed little prospect that the results of van Giffen's excavation at Ballynoe would ever appear in print. The work had been carried out nearly forty years before and the excavator had died. Fortunately, a report on the work has since been published, but the evidence proves to be just as controversial as the excavation of Newgrange (Groenman-van-Waateringe & Butler 1976).

The site has three basic components: a long cairn with stone chambers at either end; a circular or oval mound partly revetted by a kerb; and a stone circle which encloses the entire site, taking the long cairn as its diameter (Fig. 1.2). As we shall see, the sequence of the two mounds is controversial, and there is no stratigraphic relationship between either of these and the stone circle. There is virtually no dating evidence, although the site produced Carrowkeel Ware, the ceramic style normally associated with passage tombs, but it did not come from reliable contexts.

The excavation report, which was compiled from an unsatisfactory record after the excavator's death, includes an unusual feature. After a review of the work carried out on the site, the authors provide a brief discussion of the sequence. There follow two commentaries on this evidence by leading students of Irish megalithic tombs, George Eogan and Brian O'Kelly, who disagree

Ballynoe stone circle. (Photo: Alex Gibson)

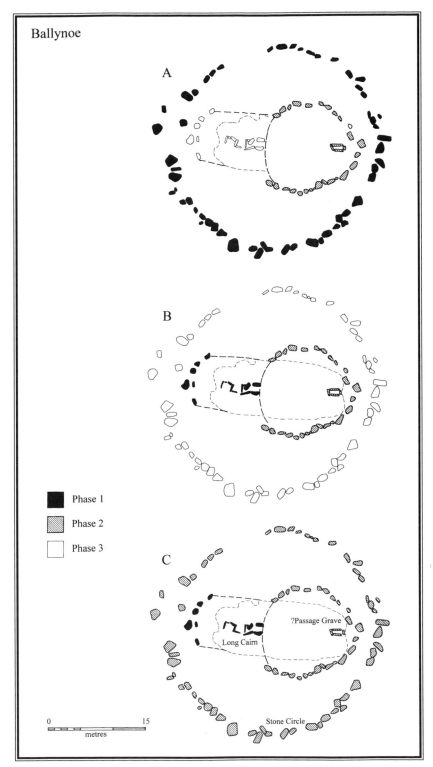

Phase 1
Phase 2
Phase 3

Ballynoe

A

B

C

?Passage Grave

Long Cairn

Stone Circle

0   15
metres

1.2 Three interpretations of the sequence at Ballynoe. A: O'Kelly's interpretation;
B: Eogan's interpretation; C: the interpretation favoured in the present chapter.

completely. For O'Kelly the primary monument was the stone circle. An oval mound was built inside it during a secondary phase, with a single chamber at one end. This mound was later lengthened and a series of chambers constructed at its western limit. These were probably built in succession to one another. O'Kelly makes it clear that he favours an early date for the stone circle because of his work at Newgrange. The authors of the excavation report quite rightly respond that Van Giffen's section drawings seem to show that a round mound, delimited by a kerb, was superimposed on an already existing long cairn.

This observation provides the starting point for Eogan's commentary on Ballynoe. He suggests that the primary monument was a long cairn with chambers at either end, and he relates this to the well-known tradition of court tombs. Alternatively, the eastern chamber might be a secondary development contemporary with the construction of the round mound, in which case it might represent the remains of a damaged passage grave. The stone circle may be a still later development, enclosing the entire monument. In suggesting this, Eogan refers to the possibility that the ring of monoliths at Newgrange belonged to the Beaker period. The authors of the report express their reservations on this point and quote Aubrey's own suggestion that the stone circle might be of an early type.

Again the evidence is inconclusive, although there is nothing in the excavation record to support O'Kelly's interpretation. Eogan's version of events is more consistent with what is known about the site, but there is no compelling reason to argue that the stone circle is later than the round mound. The fact that they are not concentric is surely due to the presence of an earlier long cairn. Unless the stone circle cut across that cairn, destroying the burial chambers in the process, it would only have been possible to build a ring of monoliths with the round barrow at its centre if people had been prepared to construct a larger monument. This would have involved the use of 50 per cent more stones.

BRYN CELLI DDU

Bryn Celli Ddu (Fig. 1.3) is a rather earlier excavation than Ballynoe and the work was not carried out to the same high standard as van Giffen's project (Hemp 1930). None the less, the published report raises very similar problems. These have been addressed in a paper by Clare O'Kelly (1969). There were three main components to the chambered tomb at Bryn Celli Ddu, although other features were recorded which are not relevant to this account. There was a passage grave, which had seen at least two phases of construction, as witnessed by changes to its kerb. The latter defined the outer edge of a round mound or cairn, the remains of which had been largely removed, and overlay the filling of a ditch which appeared to mark the limits of a circular enclosure. Inside this earthwork and buried beneath the mound were the remains of fourteen upright stones. Several of these were associated with cremated bone.

O'Kelly argued that there had been two successive monuments on the site. The earlier one was a stone circle, enclosed by the earthworks of a henge. In a later phase this was replaced by a passage grave which was built over the surviving remains of the stone circle, its outer kerb being bedded in the ditch of the older monument. At first sight the sequence at Bryn Celli Ddu resembles that at Callanish, and seems to provide support for Aubrey's view that stone circles originated alongside henge monuments during the Neolithic. An equally close link between passage graves and stone circles was also evidenced at Newgrange, and O'Kelly emphasised that point in her article.

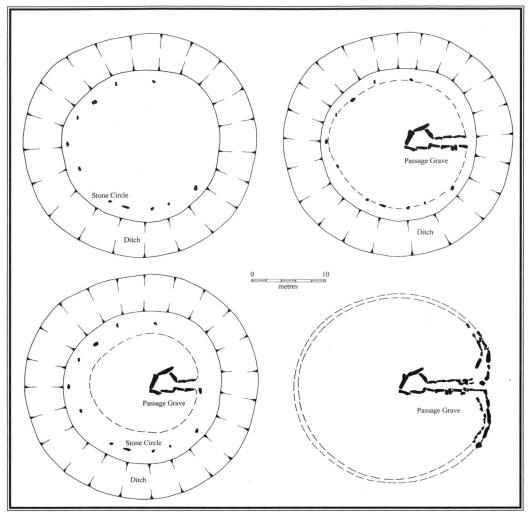

1.3 Possible interpretations of the sequence at Bryn Celli Ddu. A: C. O'Kelly's interpretation; B: Eogan's interpretation; C: the interpretation favoured in the present chapter; D: the final phases of the monument as agreed by all three authors.

Ironically, it was that same work at Newgrange that prompted a different interpretation of this evidence. George Eogan (1983) has drawn attention to one of the satellite tombs at Newgrange which was built in two separate phases (M. O'Kelly *et al.* 1978). The first of these involved a circular mound with a passage grave, surrounded by a ditch. At a later stage this mound was enlarged so that the passage itself was extended and a new kerb was created beyond the outer edge of that earthwork. The ditch itself was buried beneath the newly built monument. Eogan suggested that a similar sequence might have taken place at Bryn Celli Ddu.

This would entail a significant revision to the interpretation put forward by O'Kelly and accepted by subsequent writers, including Aubrey himself, and in effect would question the very existence of a henge monument on the site. There are certainly some difficulties with O'Kelly's interpretation, although these may result from the limited extent of the excavation. There is no evidence of an external bank and no trace has been found of any entrance through the ditch. Any bank could have been destroyed by ploughing, but this does not explain how a post setting and an animal burial in front of the entrance to the tomb had escaped destruction by the same process. Eogan's interpretation is supported by the fact that the passage was certainly lengthened on at least one occasion. A second kerb was built at the same time. Could this have been only the latest in a series of modifications to the monument?

The weakness of the new interpretation is that it assumes that the circle of monoliths formed a kerb around the earliest tomb. This does not seem likely, for small uprights of this kind could hardly have retained the edges of the mound. The fact that several of these stones were associated with cremations suggests that they were regarded as separate entities. On the other hand, there is no reason why an early mound should have possessed any kerb at all – such classic passage graves as Fourknocks lacked this feature altogether (Hartnett 1957). One way of reinterpreting the sequence at Bryn Celli Ddu is to suggest that in its first phase it consisted of a circular unrevetted mound about 15m in diameter, containing a passage grave. Around the edge of this structure was a stone circle, and beyond that there was a quarry ditch. When the monument was enlarged, not on one occasion but twice, the passage was extended as far as the earlier ditch and a significantly larger mound was bounded by kerbstones. The weakness of this interpretation is that the primary mound is so small.

Again the field evidence is inconclusive, although there is one point of similarity with Newgrange which seems to have been overlooked. The early stone setting at Bryn Celli Ddu is not exactly circular. Like its counterpart at Newgrange, it is actually 'egg-shaped': it is flattened towards the side where the passage was built and stretched from a perfect circle on the opposite side of the monument. If we follow my own interpretation, another component of this setting may be identified, for the projected course of this enclosure intersects the entrance passage where two of the orthostats are set sideways on to the passage. Might these originally have belonged to a freestanding setting of monoliths? It is impossible to tell without fresh excavation, but it would be hard to account for the similarities between this site and Newgrange if the passage grave at Bryn Celli Ddu was not built until a later period. At the moment it is enough to say that the clear-cut sequence identified by O'Kelly raises as many problems as it solves.

BALNUARAN OF CLAVA

The difficulty with the monuments described so far is that they provide few indications of the stratigraphic relationship between passage graves and stone circles. The evidence from Newgrange is confusing and contradictory. Bryn Celli Ddu does nothing to resolve the argument, and there was no relevant stratigraphy at Ballynoe. Fortunately, the evidence from Balnuaran of Clava (Fig. 1.4) is less ambiguous.

The two surviving passage graves on this site (there may once have been two more) take an identical form. Each is defined by a ring of kerbstones which are higher towards the entrance and lower at the rear of the monument. Each of the cairns appears to sit on a rubble platform whose outer edge is marked by a circle of monoliths. These stones are graded by height and echo the changing proportions of the kerb (Henshall 1963, chapter 1).

The relationship between these three elements has always been controversial. There has been no way of showing whether the stone circles are earlier or later than the tombs, nor has it been possible to establish the relationship between the platforms and the rings of stone. Instead there has been more discussion of how the platforms are related to the cairns. Two possibilities arise. Audrey Henshall has argued that one of the functions of these platforms was to retain the kerbstones in position so that they would not be disrupted by the mass of the cairn (ibid.). She based her interpretation on the results of Stuart Piggott's excavation at Corrymony where the kerb had given way (Piggott 1956). The other possibility arose from Gordon Barclay's publication of a previously unknown excavation at Balnuaran of Clava in 1930–1. The results of this work seemed to suggest that the platform was a secondary blocking, piled up against the structure of the cairns when the tombs went out of use (Barclay 1990). My own excavations in 1994 and 1995 were designed to test these interpretations and to relate the passage graves to the stone circles that surround them.

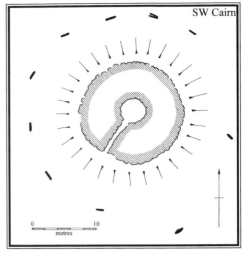

1.4 Outline plan of the south-west passage-grave at Balnuaran of Clava.

The basic stratigraphic relationships were not difficult to establish (Bradley 1996). As Henshall had foreseen, the kerbstones had very few sockets and would not have withstood the pressure from the cairn for any length of time. They survive because they were buttressed by the platforms built against them. On the north-east cairn at Balnuaran of Clava, the stone circle

Balnuaran of Clava. (Photo: Alex Gibson)

Corrymony Clava cairn. (Photo: Alex Gibson)

marked the outer limits of the rubble platform. The same material provided the packing for one of the monoliths which had no socket at all. It follows that the platform and the stone circle must have been built together. Although that platform was secondary to the erection of kerbstones, they would have slipped out of position once the material of the cairn had stabilised. It follows that both the platforms and the stone circles forming their outer boundary were either built simultaneously with the passage graves or so soon afterwards that the difference is unimportant. My own view is that the kerbs were exposed for a very short period before the platforms were constructed. This would have given access to the passage graves and would also have allowed the carved decoration on the kerbstones to be seen for a brief interval before it was obscured. On a prehistoric timescale, however, these elements are contemporary with one another. Given the very stereotyped character of Clava passage graves, we might expect a similar sequence to be found on other sites.

CONCLUSION

It would be quite wrong to use the Clava Cairns as a general model for the relationship between passage graves and stone circles, but that has not been my intention here. Rather, the evidence from these particular monuments helps to substantiate the position that Aubrey adopted in his discussion of Newgrange over twenty years ago. As we have seen, the situation has become more complicated over those two decades, but nothing has happened to upset his original conclusion. Some of the earliest stone circles were built at the same time as passage graves. To return to Cyril

Connolly's dictum, quoted at the beginning of this chapter, every author would like to write a book which lasts ten years. Aubrey Burl has certainly done so, but more than that, he has given us many ideas that have lasted twice as long.

ACKNOWLEDGEMENTS

I am most grateful to Margaret Mathews for providing the figure drawings.

CHAPTER TWO

DOUBLE ENTRANCE HENGES – ROUTES TO THE PAST?

ROY LOVEDAY

As Aubrey Burl has often demonstrated (1969, 1991), however we attempt to classify, or declassify, henge monuments (Atkinson 1951; Clare 1986; Harding & Lee 1987; Barclay 1989), certain types remain obstinately obvious – notably that type with two entrances. Whereas the single entrance form (type I) could be dismissed as self-creating – simply the need to access an enclosure – the same argument could only be advanced for the double entrance form (type II) if its causeways were randomly disposed. They are not. Moreover, these sites are frequently ovate, elongated along the axis of their opposed entrances; almost as frequently, this axis highlights a pronounced asymmetry. Clearly this is not an accidental by-product of the decision to add an extra causeway. Deliberation is indicated in a common formula for layout which resulted in recurrent 'banana and tea bowl' plans.

STRUCTURE AND RITUAL

Architecturally, this design seems ill-suited for a ritual site: on entering, the celebrant would appear to have been greeted with a view straight through the monument (Harding 1987, fig. 26). Blocking devices or central foci can, of course, be invoked to nullify this, yet in neither case particularly satisfactorily. Post rings as potential supports for such devices have been comparatively infrequently recorded as elements of class II henges (Gibson 1995), while the posts recorded at the butt end of one of the Stanton Harcourt ditches remain unparalleled (A. Barclay et al. 1995).

Coves, such as those at Cairnpapple and Arbor Low (Piggott 1948, Gray 1903) suggest a central focus. Extensive excavations at North Mains, Milfield North and Stanton Harcourt (G. Barclay 1983; Harding 1981; A. Barclay et al. 1995) have, however, failed to locate either these or comparable substantial features; the possible post structure at the latter site is of uncertain date and decidedly insubstantial. Nor have they emerged as cropmarks. In view of this we might conclude that opposed entrances were neither ancillary to some central focus nor routinely reduced to single entrance type by employment of a blocking device.

The vista through the opposing gap may itself have furnished a *raison d'être* yet skylines in the vicinity of henges are rarely dramatic and frequently all but flat (Harding 1987, 35–6). Even

The view out from the collapsed cove at Arbor Low. The blanking effect of the bank is obvious. The entrances lie at 90° to left and right.

when this is not the case monuments often ignore obvious features. At Dorchester on Thames, for instance, where the twin peaks of the Sinodun Hills mark the skyline, the Big Rings henge alignment is perversely deflected from them by some 20°. Nor are causeways suitable for astronomical sighting, being too wide to permit any degree of precision and overwhelmingly orientated along north–south axes wholly divorced from solar and lunar skyline phenomena (Harding 1987, fig. 27b).

Arbor Low exemplifies the problem. If the central stones are correctly interpreted as the remains of a cove, this would have opened to the south–south–west (Gray 1903; Burl 1976, 279), a direction blocked within 30m by the considerable bulk of the henge bank. Nor do the causeways frame a skyline: since the monument was placed on gently sloping ground the southern entrance reveals only open sky while the northern one opens into a valley and lower land beyond. It is in fact easier to explain the choice of location in terms of external visibility – like so many barrows the henge is sited on a false crest. Yet even this is problematical since it only applies across an extremely restricted area. We might be driven to hypothesise that the monument's entrance vistas served to link the settled lowlands with the sky beyond but this cannot be consistently claimed of type II henges elsewhere and they do appear strikingly standardised monuments, however variable their 'furniture and fittings' (pit, post, and stone circles; coves; pits; and graves). Individual cases can be made; overall explanations that match their standardised ditch plan prove illusory.

Why then was the opposed entrance plan so commonly adopted? Barrett has argued for the

The view through Arbor Low from the northern entrance.

The view through Arbor Low from the southern entrance.

need to consider ritual monuments in terms of the sequential experiences that they presented to those entering and passing around them (1994). Here there seems little to discuss: unless we envisage two separate groups entering by the opposed entrances and meeting at the centre, the logic of these monuments is of passage **through** them, whether directly or cyclically. This notion of thoroughfare encouraged Harding's advancement of procession as an explanation of henge clusters in the Milfield basin (1987, 34, 62–3). There the Coupland henge uniquely possesses a formalised routing of such activity through its confines – the irregularly laid out ditches of the so-called avenue. Although Bradley (1992, 119) has recently questioned its prehistoric date, preferring to see it as a manifestation of the Irish 'royal road' phenomenon (Wailes 1982), here linked to the Anglo-Saxon complex of Melmin, this fails to explain its extension equidistant from each henge entrance. Another example, although in stone, may have existed at Broomend of Crichie (Ritchie 1920b). Whatever the date of the Coupland feature it effectively emphasises the potential of Harding's 'classic' type II sites for movement to and then across, rather than around, their interiors.

Does this in any way further understanding of orientation and siting? Movement to and through a monument should make certain detectable practical demands: clearance of vegetation at each extremity and the adoption of topographically accessible (though, given the reversals inherent in ritual, not necessarily advantageous) ground. Proof of the former would of course require a series of sealed contexts ideal both in terms of location and preservation which it is most unlikely any site could furnish. Topography on the other hand is readily available for examination.

The Ring of Brodgar, Orkney. (Photo: Alex Gibson)

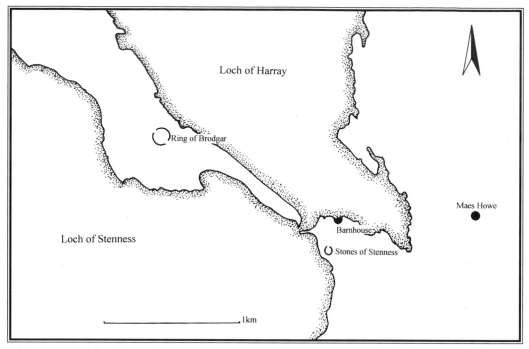

2.1 Location of the Ring of Brodgar.

LOCATION IN THE LANDSCAPE

Disappointingly, type II henges are overwhelmingly located on flat undifferentiated terrain but one site where immediate topographic influence can be tested does present itself – the Ring of Brodgar in Orkney (Fig. 2.1). On the narrow isthmus between Lochs Harray and Stenness the orientation of this site eschews the dramatic skyline of Hoy to the south and the distant view of Maes Howe to the east. Instead it is aligned like the modern road along the isthmus. Nor is this an accidental by-product of alignment on the presumptively earlier Stones of Stenness – the causeway axis of Brodgar misses them by a considerable margin, as it does the Watch Stone. Practical considerations appear paramount here as they do at Stenness where the class I henge opens towards the Barnhouse settlement (Richards 1993).

Elsewhere, while the influence of topography on alignment is far less compelling, the pattern can still often be discerned, as Aubrey has long emphasised with regard to stone circles and rows. The causeways of Llandegai B are aligned along the length of the coastal plain edging the Snowdonia Massif and parallel to the Menai Straits. At Milfield in Northumberland the sites at Coupland, North Milfield, Akeld and Ewart Park broadly mirror the course of the River Till in its locally wide valley, while that at Yeavering is aligned along a natural dryland route (Hope Taylor 1977, fig. 2) into the narrow tributary valley of the Glen – both historically well-used and fought-over routes to and from the Firth of Forth. In an area of gentler relief the henge at North Mains points into the valley of the Mahany Water where it leaves the wider expanse of Strath Earn, and at Broomend of Crichie the henge again lies parallel to the river. In the latter case it is

The Kennet Avenue at Avebury, one of the two routes into the great circle marked by stone avenues.

The false crest siting of Arbor Low. The figures are standing on the eastern arc of the bank and the northern entrance is behind the third fence post from the right.

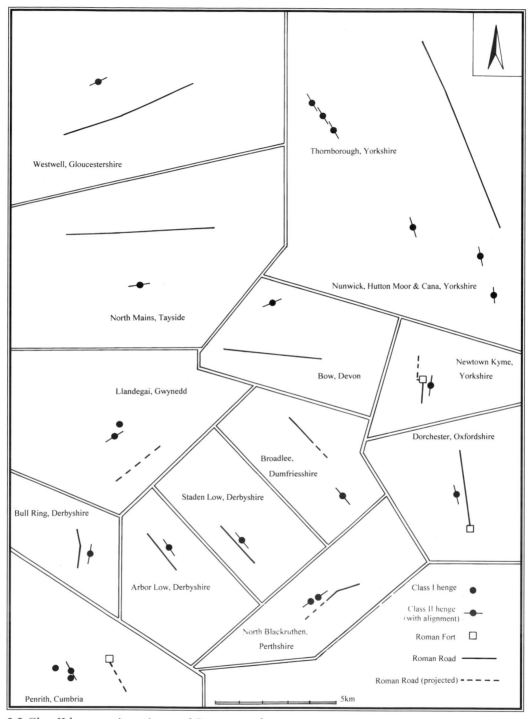

2.2 Class II henge orientations and Roman roads.

noticeable that the adjacent road and railway adopt the same alignment, confirming its topographic advantages. This pattern is repeated in the Peak District at the Bull Ring which lies at the entrance of the easiest north-western approach to the limestone plateau. Thus it could be claimed that several henges were sited with a view to ease of movement, and over distances considerably in excess of the 1.6km of the Coupland 'avenue'.

Of course, not all 'classic' type II henge monuments in areas of pronounced topographic relief are neatly aligned along natural lines of communication. At Ballymeanoch near Dunadd on the Kintyre peninsula for instance, the henge entrances are perversely aligned some 10° away from the entrance to the Kilmartin valley, despite the fact that this is the obvious route north from Loch Crinan. The delusion of seeking straight lines of communication from a site must be avoided though, particularly when this involves the approach to a major ritual complex such as that in the Kilmartin valley. Here impact may have depended upon sudden not progressive revelation (cf. the Kennet avenue as it approaches Avebury – Burl 1979). Moreover, the henge is aligned along the corridor between the Kilmartin Burn and its easterly neighbour – the most straightforward route prior to peat formation at the head of the loch.

No such special pleading is convincing in the case of Arbor Low. Lying, as detailed earlier, just off the crest of a local rise in the gently undulating limestone plateau, its siting furnishes no hint of paths towards its confines. The presence of a Roman road just 400m away indicates that some two and a half millennia later the location lay on a well-frequented route but Roman motives and context were clearly fundamentally different from those of the Neolithic.

CAUSE OR COINCIDENCE?

It is all the more disconcerting then to discover that the alignment of this road coincides closely with that of the entrances of the henge. Nor, even more worryingly, does this appear to be an isolated coincidence. It recurs at similar distances, with variations of alignment of between 5° and 25°, at Dorchester, Broadlee, Hutton Moor and Newton Kyme, and North Blackruthen – the latter sites omitted from Harding's 'classic' category (1987, 419) but conforming closely in opposed entrance plan (Barclay 1982 & pers. comm.). Even at sites such as the Bull Ring which reassuringly seemed to break the pattern, work since Margary (1967) has established the existence of an adjacent Roman road mirroring its axis (Wroe & Mellor 1971). More surprisingly the pattern remains broadly evident at distances of 2km: for example, at Westwell, North Mains, Llandegai, and Bow. Even at Thornborough and Nunwick in Yorkshire divergence from the line of Dere Street at distances of up to 5km is not great. (Fig. 2.2). Wherever it seems one of Harding's 'classic' double entrance henges lies within 5km of a Roman road there is a strong probability that there will be a broad similarity in their alignments.

Such a relationship, however imprecise, is absurd: absurd because of the distances involved – physical and chronological – and absurd because of the fundamental gulf of purpose. But while one or two cases can be dismissed as a coincidence, and three or four as an aberration, seventeen cases (77 per cent of Harding's 'classic' and probable double entrance henges lying within 5km of a Roman road) is a pattern, however uncomfortable. Inclusion of the sites at North Blackruthen and Staden Low (VCH 1905, 373–4 & 385) increases this figure to 79 per cent. Even restriction of the sample to those sites exhibiting an alignment coincidence of some 10° or less leaves a figure of 59 per cent (Table 2.1). This cannot be dismissed and a sane answer must exist.

The interest of certain aerial archaeologists in Roman military sites has increased the

Table 2.1: Class II henges lying within 5km of a Roman road.

SITE	APPROX SEPARATION (KILOMETRES)	APPROX SEPARATION (DEGREES)
North Mains	2.3	14
Normangill	1.2	10
Weston	5.0	35
Broadlee	0.5	8
King Arthur's Round Table	1.6	8
Thornborough North	5.0	8
Thornborough Centre	5.0	8
Thornborough South	5.0	8
Nunwick	3.5	4
Hutton Moor	1.0	13
Cana	1.2	16
Newton Kyme	0.22	6
Ferrybridge	3.0	70
Maiden's Grave	4.6	70
Bull Ring	0.4	8
Arbor Low	0.4	10
Llandegai B	1.5	10
Condicote	2.5	?40
	5.0	?5
Westwell	1.8	8
Big Rings	0.25	8
Bow	2.0	25
Castilly	1.2	70

('Classic' and probable sites after Harding 1987)

North Blackruthen	0.18	6
Staden Low	0.4	17

likelihood of discovery of henges near Roman roads, but can hardly influence their alignment! Nor could henges have influenced road layout – in most cases they were probably all but invisible by the Roman period and in no case does a road pass closer than 180m anyway. Obvious topographic features can also be dismissed as determinants, except perhaps at the Bull Ring and Staden Low; the cases quoted earlier lay mostly away from Roman roads. Alignment along subtler topographic corridors may explain some instances, such as the Vale of York henges which mirror the River Ure (Burl 1991b), but fails to account for sites such as Newton Kyme set at right angles to the Wharfe or Westwell and Arbor Low lying in evenly undulating landscape. It could be argued that, where enthusiasts have sought them, minor roads are so numerous that they represented a rich bran tub from which a coincidence of alignment could always be plucked. This is particularly true of the south–east midlands but no henge–road coincidence is claimed there and only in the possible case of the Bull Ring can the road in question be dismissed as a minor local route. Alternatively a statistical aberration could be claimed, created by the known north–south axis preference of type II henges (Harding 1986, fig. 27b), their clustering in the Vale of York and the selection of this as the route for Cerealian and Agricolan advance. However, removal of the Vale of York sites from the calculations still leaves a figure of 54 per cent coincidence – significant enough to attract attention. Sites as far apart as Bow and North Mains

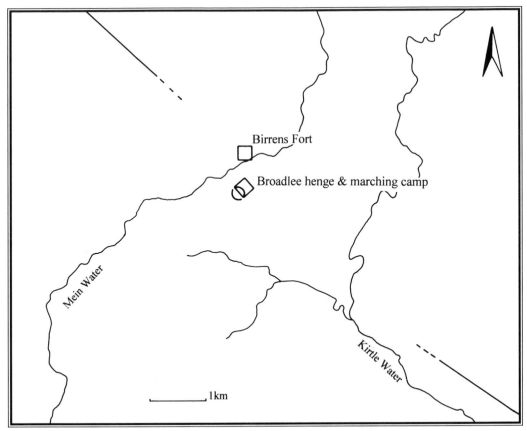

2.3 Location of Broadlee.

lay 90° from this preferential axis yet retain the pattern, as do Westwell and Broadlee which lie some 45° respectively to east and west.

In the last case it is perhaps of interest that although the henge is aligned at right angles to its adjacent river valley (Mein Water) it extends the alignment of the lower valley of the Kirtle Water which runs down to the Solway Firth (Fig. 2.3). This was apparently selected as the line of Roman advance, a marching camp being constructed through the entrance gaps of the henge (Harding 1986, 346–8), and later a fort placed nearby at Birrens. The road constructed to link Birrens and forts further along the chain mirrored the henge alignment which in turn reflects the route from the lower Kirtle Water to the Annan valley.

Does an answer then lie in the process by which Roman military control was established? An army on campaign does not cut through uncleared woodland and cross line after line of hedgebanks, it follows existing tracks in so far as intelligence confirms that they accord with its line of advance. Only later, after the establishment of forts at strategic points, would the line be rationalised to the straightest possible route between distant extremities and deflected accordingly. Hence the Newton Kyme henge adjacent to a crossing of the River Wharfe is immediately juxtaposed by Roman road, fort and vicus (St Joseph 1980, pl xviii; Ramm 1980, fig. 4), while the Thornborough and Ripon henges to the north lie up to 5km to the west of the road.

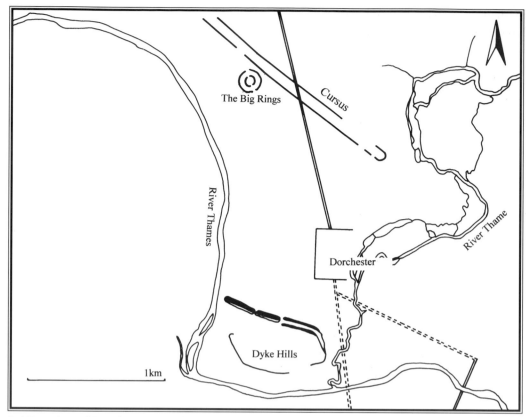

2.4 Location of Dorchester on Thames.

But is it remotely conceivable that routes related to henges were still in use at the time of the Roman conquest? We would naturally dismiss such longevity. Yet as our green lanes and footpaths testify, once a route has been established it is likely to endure, apart from a tendency to drift, whatever its change of status.

Perhaps the greatest difficulty we face in accepting major, as against purely local, routes of the earliest date is that our concept of a road is determined by those constructed by Roman and turnpike surveyors – single well-established lines. But as Taylor (1979) and Hindle (1993) have demonstrated, turnpike surveyors rationalised routes which had previously followed a number of different, parallel tracks, often as much as two miles apart even when the topography was neutral (e.g. the Icknield Way and the Great North Road: Taylor 1979, figs 30 & 57). Such a braided course is fossilised for us today on the ultimate 'flat' – Newmarket Heath – where across some two miles the various original routes of the A11 (Icknield Way) have left gaps in the great barrier of the Devil's Dyke. Only in 1763 was the road channelled to a single line, and even then only after considerable dispute (Taylor 1979, 157–8). Andrews and Dury's mapping of Salisbury Plain in 1773 furnishes a similar picture of the route from Bulford to Lavington in the area of Robin Hood's Ball.

It is highly probable that just such a pattern of braided routes existed prior to Roman rationalisation and that among these were some which had, millennia earlier, originated as routes through, or parallel to, class II henges. A hint that this was the case is furnished by the sites at Dorchester upon Thames (Fig. 2.4). There, when the great cursus–henge complex went out of use, a field system associated with pottery of Deveril Rimbury type was laid out, cutting the cursus. As Bradley and Chambers noted (1988) this strikingly retained the axis of the Big Rings henge. Since no respect for the earlier ritual monuments is evident, this might best be explained in terms of a residual ancillary element of the landscape such as a track. Even more remarkable is the fact that the same general axis is evident in the Roman road just 250m to the east. This could be coincidental, resulting from the establishment of the Dyke Hills oppidum and later the Roman town to the south, but it is arguable that the Dyke Hills location, like that of similar oppida elsewhere, was selected as much to control the river crossing of an existing routeway as for its defensive potential (Cunliffe 1995a, 69). This element we might hypothesise had determined landscape development over two millennia.

Ultimately, of course, the existence of such tracks is archaeologically unprovable unless they are defined by ditches or by empty linear bands within dense settlement zones. Monuments will always be uncertain indicators even in areas where there can be some confidence that near totality of the data is available. The proximity of round barrows probably tells us little (Taylor 1979, 36–7) and while the capacity of long barrows to point may be topographically suggestive, and hence of greater value (Tilley 1994), the fact that these monuments are most impressive in the landscape when approached from the side (for example, those associated with the Gussage and Amesbury cursus monuments) introduces a major element of ambiguity into any argument linking their alignments with those of putative paths. Class II henges on the other hand clearly prescribed directional approach. Cumulatively the circumstantial logic of their architectural form, their alignment along topographic corridors and their frequent enigmatic mirroring of Roman routes provides perhaps the most convincing case for an association with tracks, or at least some of the braided courses which we can hypothesise passed through their confines.

'Thoroughfare' and Ritual

Parallels for ritual activity that might give rise to this pattern are scarce. It could be considered to have been pre-figured by cursus monuments whose parallel sides and frequently greatly elongated dimensions appear specifically designed for linear movement. It should not be forgotten, however, that sites of cursus type descend to minimal lengths while retaining a notably greater width than is appropriate to an 'avenue' – a good example is Barford, with dimensions of 185m x 40m (Loveday 1987). Indeed, most classic cursus sites approximate to the widths of two motorways (some could accommodate three!) and close definition of their confines precludes acceptance of this as a consequence of braiding and trackway drift (Loveday 1985). A small group including Sarn-y-Bryn-Caled, North Stoke and Llandegai (Gibson 1994; Case 1982; Houlder 1968) appear specifically designed for human directional movement yet even here the probability of internal mounds in the latter two cases, and the certainty of closed terminals or blocking devices in all three cases, present a further obstacle to easy acceptance of 'thoroughfare' as their *raison d'être*.

By contrast, causeways were clearly pivotal features of class II henges – frequently emphasised by the monuments' ovate plans and set apart by details of their adjacent ditches. Fires were lit successively in the ditch terminals flanking the entrances to the Devil's Quoits henge at Stanton Harcourt (A. Barclay *et al.* 1995) and ditches had been widened at this point at North Mains (G. Barclay 1983). The latter is a recurrent feature and is accompanied, where earthworks survive, by commensurate heightening of banks (Topping 1994). Causeways in henges, it seems, functioned both as a bridge and as a psychological barrier to those moving into the enclosure. Recent discussion of the movement within post structures and great henge enclosures has also emphasised exclusivity (Pollard 1992; Gibson 1994; Barrett 1994) through reduced physical space, high banks, stones and even conceivably screens. We are thus faced with a paradox. Plan, location and the circumstantial evidence of later routes emphasise movement; architecture emphasises exclusion.

Punctuation of movement is of course a common feature of ritual architecture although invariably this is related to the monument's confines and immediate periphery; punctuation of movement along paths too long to be considered mere processional ways, as hypothesised here, is of a quite different order. An echo is perhaps to be found in the form of the pilgrimage, a practice of great religious antiquity (Renfrew 1985, 255–6; Bradley 1996, lecture at York) and one invariably involving prescribed ritual procedures, such as movement to and past shrines, at fixed points along a route. The Hindu experience probably equates most closely to any hypothesised prehistoric practice since it lacks a centralised priesthood, a single deity and a single sacred text; it also has demonstrable antecedents in second millennium BC hymns composed in an Indo-European tongue (Rig Veda). Here the expression used to describe the process of pilgrimage is *Tirthyatra*, a compound of *yatra* (travelling) and *tirtha* (a complex Sanskrit term encompassing the notion of fording, or a safe crossing point between human and divine realms) (Coleman & Elsner 1995, 137–8). Each tirtha represents a propitious location – a node in the sacred geography traversed by the Hindu pilgrim. Movement to and across a class II henge could well have been considered in similar vein to an act of fording the divine. The European pilgrim was encouraged to experience just such feelings during the early medieval period when corridor crypts were constructed to take them through dark, highly charged passageways past the divine, secret world of the shrine (Woodward 1993) – a classic example of harnessing both movement and exclusivity.

Along the roads which led pilgrims to these meeting points with the divine, distinctive long-distance patterning can often be observed. It is notable, for instance, that the shrine churches built to punctuate each of the pilgrimage roads crossing France closely resemble each other (Conant 1959, 93). Their model is hundreds of miles away at the pilgrims' goal – Compostella. In thus strikingly transcending the architectural localism of the period they recall the long-distance patterning observable in classic henge plans from Bow to Cairnpapple (type II), and from Dorchester upon Thames to the Vale of York (type IIA). This likewise presupposes movement. The alternative – down the line passage of an idea – would lead almost inevitably to fairly gross results at the extremities of distribution. The important implication is that, like the roads to Compostella, the hypothetical paths seem likely to have been in existence prior to the henges which punctuate them.

Tilley (1994) has emphasised the pivotal importance of paths for hunter-gatherer communities and drawn attention to evidence for an association between mesolithic activity and those earlier neolithic monuments which might be taken to delineate paths. Certainly causewayed enclosures had demonstrably attracted people, artefacts and materials from considerable distances to what, it is increasingly recognised, were peripheral locations (Sharples 1991) – facts which have led Barratt to declare that 'these sites did not occupy the centres of territories as much as lie at the end of one path and the beginning of the next' (1994, 149). Their polydirectional plans, with suggestions of unimpeded access, contrast, however, with those of henges. Since both can

The eastern entrance to the Avebury circle. The track on the right is the eighteenth-century Bath Road, and was before that a Saxon herepath. As its route from the western entrance to the circle is marked by the Beckhampton Avenue, can a prehistoric origin also be postulated for the eastern approach?

plausibly be linked to tracks we are left to enquire what caused such fundamental change? The sudden appearance of totally contrasting, fully formulated plans might suggest the imposition of a novel belief system centred around exclusive access, were it not for the evidence of Flagstones and Stonehenge (Woodward & Smith 1987; Cleal *et al.* 1995) where a more evolutionary development towards a henge plan is indicated. Similar phases may well have preceded formalised henge plans elsewhere. Earlier post phases at North Mains, Milfield North and probably Cairnpapple and Bow (Barclay 1983; Harding 1981; Piggott 1948; Griffith 1985) similarly suggest longer developmental sequences at henge loci.

An alternative explanation may lie in the changing role of the attendant hypothetical routes. Since Houlder's discovery of a mint condition group VI axe and a group XVIII polishing stone in henge A at Llandegai (1978), it has been a commonplace that henges were intimately associated with the movement of axes. Complexes like Penrith are at nodal points on historically long-established routeways (Topping 1992) and, like Llandegai, adjacent to stone source areas. Further flung complexes like Thornborough appear ideally suited as 'staging points' on the axes' journey (Manby 1979; Bradley & Edmonds 1993). And as the trade moved into top gear in the later Neolithic it was accompanied by the manufacture and movement of other prestige items that Bradley has linked to ranked spheres of exchange (Bradley 1982). The floruit of these

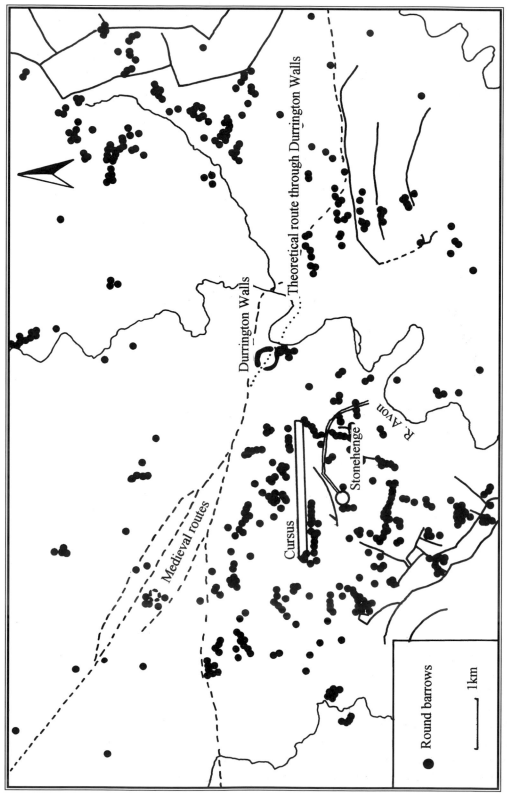

2.5 Medieval east–west routes north of Stonehenge (dotted line represents the hypothetical route through Durrington Walls).

Round barrows

1km

R. Avon

Stonehenge

Cursus

Durrington Walls

Theoretical route through Durrington Walls

Medieval routes

exclusive prestige goods appears to coincide with the construction of double entrance henges. Thus the contradictory elements indicative of movement and exclusion built into the monuments might be resolved: travel along existing linked routes being conceivably restricted, beyond a seasonal agricultural radius, by elites whose position depended not only on possession of prestige goods but also on close control of their movement. Ritual would furnish the obvious mechanism in establishing such control. With this possibility in mind the position of the great henge enclosures deserves brief review.

Great Henge Enclosures and Historic Routes

If earlier arguments about the potential longevity of routes adopted for Roman advance are entertained, the location of Roman marching camps directly adjacent to the Walton (St Joseph 1980a; Gibson 1995) and Meldon Bridge (Burgess 1968) enclosures may not be altogether insignificant. Absence of such camps from Wessex (RCHM 1995), however, deprives us of this circumstantial line of enquiry and, with the exception of the Avebury avenues, there is little in fact to suggest movement through the great Wessex henge enclosures.

Nevertheless it is worth noting their relationship to historically attested routes. A herepath mentioned in an Anglo-Saxon charter (Grundy 1918, 79) and long surviving as an alternative westerly route to that along the Kennet valley (Taylor 1979, 192), runs from the Marlborough region across Overton Down to pass through the east and west entrances of Avebury. A similar situation may once have existed at Durrington Walls – in essence a huge type II henge with entrances aligned along a short dry valley leading up from a possible crossing of the River Avon. It lies immediately adjacent and parallel to another medieval east–west route, conceivably deflected from the henge by a new crossing at Bulford (Fig. 2.5). Its popularity is demonstrated both by the deep hollow ways which mark its descent of Beacon Hill en route to Bulford (Beresford & St Joseph 1958, fig. 106) and by the care taken by the trustees of the Amesbury Turnpike to control it, thus avoiding toll evasion on their main routes past Stonehenge (Chandler 1970). Andrews and Dury's map of 1773 details its divided course once on the west side of the Avon: north-west past the Robin Hood's Ball causewayed enclosure, and west to Shrewton and then Heytesbury on the River Wylye, where, perhaps significantly, an isolated series of rich Wessex burials with no obvious focus was centred (Upton Lovell G1 and 2e). A hint that the route was of some antiquity is furnished by its correspondence with the only substantial opening in the linear ditch system of the eastern Plain (Bradley et al. 1994).

On Cranborne Chase, the maps of Ogilby and Speed in the seventeenth century reveal Knowlton/Brockington, almost as clearly as Cranborne, as the node of the main pre-turnpike routes heading south to Poole and south-west to Dorchester – the former route still bisecting the great enclosure. Marden for its part lay along the general line of the Ridgeway where it crossed the Vale of Pewsey, its descent of the Marlborough Downs near Knap Hill being dominantly visible from the enclosure's northern entrance. A charter appears to place the route about 800m to the east during the Anglo-Saxon period (Grundy 1918, 79–80). Finally the Mount Pleasant enclosure lay on the southern bank of an obvious crossing of the River Frome – Stinsford – and to judge by recent discoveries along the east–west ridge line (Sparey Green 1994) could be hypothesised to have lain at an intersection of paths corresponding to its entrances. Coincidence perhaps, and as direct evidence, of course, valueless, but it does serve to demonstrate that just a couple of centuries ago several of these enclosures were a great deal less isolated than they are today. A *raison d'être* in the ritual control of routeways might go some way to explaining their largely unprepossessing locations.

Sherratt has recently reasserted arguments about the riverine location of Wessex henges, likening them to hillforts as links in a transport network: one based on ritual control, the other on defended portage points (1996, 220–2; n. 48). Without denying the importance of substantial rivers, it must be doubted whether the winding, narrow, shallow upper reaches of the Avon or Wylye rivers would ever have been more attractive as routes than simple paths, and seriously questioned whether the Wylye's headwaters in particular could ever have justified the huge effort of constructing Battlesbury and Scratchbury hillforts. Their location close to the crossing of the medieval Beacon Hill–Heytesbury route is probably significant though, as may be the isolated placing of Yarnbury, Bratton and Sidbury. Each lies some distance from water but intriguingly adjacent to routes to Bath and Marlborough which were already old when Andrews and Dury mapped the area. Hillforts and henges could indeed have performed similar control functions but surely primarily in relation to movement by land rather than by water. The double opposed entrance form of early Wessex hillforts is particularly noteworthy in this regard, the more so since the roadway shown to link the entrances at Danebury passes straight through the interior in a manner suggesting its priority and importance (Cunliffe 1995b, 19–20).

ROLE IN NEOLITHIC SOCIETY

The events acted out in 927AD at another early nodal point marked by henges – Eamont by Penrith – furnish a possible analogy, albeit on a larger scale, for the use of such monuments in the Neolithic. There Athelstan called all the rulers of northern and western Britain to a meeting to accept his rule and . . . 'they established peace with pledges and oaths . . . and renounced all idolatry' (Whitelock 1961, 68–9). 'Safe', peripheral locations on well-established tracks would appear to have been prerequisites for ritual, homage and gift-giving in both societies. On the other hand these monuments were clearly more than elite stadia or ritual customs posts.

The antecedents of double entrance monuments in single entrance forms and their close echo at small sites such as Corporation Farm, Abingdon (Harding 1987, 235) and site E, Llandegai (Houlder 1968) locates them in a long tradition of small-scale, and undoubtedly local, ritual observance. Regional orientation patterns which Aubrey long ago emphasised (1969) are in some instances so close (e.g. Stanton Harcourt, Westwell and Corporation Farm: A. Barclay et al. 1995, fig. 35) as to call into question the whole thesis of on-site, route-led orientation advanced here. The same problem, however, arises when suggesting that specific local skyline views acted as the determinants of henge orientation (Harding 1987, 36). Neither appears to furnish the key to unlock the 'mental template' of regional orientation patterns, while solar and lunar horizon phenomena have already been discounted by virtue of the clustering of alignments around a north–south axis.

Does an answer perhaps lie in a process already observed in the pilgrimage phenomenon – replication? Parallels abound from Greek temple architecture and the great churches of the pilgrimage roads to the establishment of lesser Benares (Coleman & Elsner 1995, 143–4). The initial site in an area is likely to have served as a paradigm and should the rituals enacted within it have involved reference to seasonally specific celestial alignment, this would undoubtedly also constitute a key element for replication. Stellar risings are notoriously faint but appearance of a constellation that had been accorded particular significance over a hill or path directly aligned with the initial henge monument could well have established the regional pattern. Transposing the qualities of such a path to a new location would be straightforward; transposing those of a hill or horizon pattern fraught with difficulty, particularly as many henges lie in flat or at best gently undulating terrain. 'Following a star' along a path highly charged with significance might thus, upon imposition of a henge monument, be transformed into local orthodoxy and give rise to confusing regional variations in orientation.

If the association of class II henges with paths (whether pre-existing or ritually replicated) has been correctly identified, it underlines their role in late neolithic society. Substantial movement is implied by the evidence of artefacts and monument plans but is unlikely to have been unimpeded. The appearance of individuals in the funerary record accompanied by high status artefacts and weaponry suggests jealous territorial delineation and the need for movement to be sanctioned, whether the passage was from commonly held to ancestral land, from profane to sacred areas or from one territory to another. If henges are accorded this function it follows that they must be viewed as peripheral rather than central to ritual observance. What could then be seen as the primary foci?

Bradley (1993) has championed archaeologically less tangible aspects of the natural landscape and more venerable but less formalised ritual constructs. From the navel of the earth at Delphi and the black rock in the Ka'aba at Mecca to the sacred Ganges, this accords better with recorded religious practices. Could it then be that the Watch Stone and its neighbours on the Isthmus between Lochs Harray and Stenness was the real subject of interest to the Orkney henge builders; the Rud Stone the objective of those constructing the Maiden's Grave; and, at a greater distance, those most neglected of prehistoric ritual accomplishments, the Devils Arrows (Burl 1991a), that focused the efforts of the builders of the Thornborough, Ripon and Newton Kyme henges? Perhaps most intriguingly, routes through the Bull Ring, Staden Low and Arbor Low would appear to have led towards the warm spring where Buxton now stands — an area possessing the clearest evidence of earlier neolithic occupation (Garton 1987) and one which, like that adjacent to the Bow henge (Griffith 1985), carried a nemeton (Celtic sanctuary) name into historic times — *Aquae Arnemetiae*.

Could this explain a strange feature of the much later recorded ritual activity with which Aubrey has often tantalised us? — its concentration not on obvious monuments but predominantly around standing stones and springs. Rather than reflecting Celtic religious reorientation, might this simply result from collapse of a society which had employed monuments as control mechanisms? The legacy would be abandoned henges, accessible primary foci (stones and springs) and, as Conrad recalled from the Congo basin, unrestricted 'paths, paths, everywhere; a stamped-in network of paths spreading over the empty land, through long grass, through burned grass. . . .' (*Heart of Darkness*, J. Conrad 1899).

Only in Ireland, which in many ways appears anachronistic at the close of the first millennium, is there a faint hint of continuity. In one of the oldest tales we hear that when Conare, the hard-pressed king, is forced to seek shelter in the mysterious hostel of the Derga he learns: '. . . the road we are on goes to it, for the road goes *through* it' (*The Destruction of the Derga's Hostel*, Gautz 1981, 69).

ACKNOWLEDGEMENTS

The author wishes to express his particular thanks to Gordon Barclay for his encouragement to continue with this article, and to Richard Bradley, Tony Brown, Alex Gibson and Aubrey himself (who saw it in an earlier form) for similar encouragement and advice. They are not of course responsible for the wilder ideas expressed here.

CHAPTER THREE

THE BALLYNAHATTY COMPLEX

BARRIE HARTWELL

INTRODUCTION

The townland of Ballynahatty covers 100ha of the Lagan Valley in Northern Ireland. From the north it is dominated by the basalt hills of the Antrim Plateau which overlay chalk strata rich in flint. The present valley floor is a drift landscape, covered by mixed glacial sands, gravels and clays with sandy ridges providing a light, easily cultivated soil. The River Lagan, 20m wide, flows past the western side of Ballynahatty and discharges into the Irish Sea at Belfast, some 8km to the north-east. At Shaw's Bridge, on the northern corner of Ballynahatty, the river becomes shallower and in the Neolithic it was probably the lowest fording point and therefore a focus of north-south routes. On the other three sides it is defined by steep slopes, streams and ancient peat-filled hollows to form a discrete but irregular plateau about 40m high. Three archaeological sites survive as relief features on this plateau: a large earthen enclosure called the Giant's Ring; a partially destroyed passage grave; and an isolated stone standing in a field fence.

The first archaeological record of a site in Ballynahatty was that of an 'ancient sepulchral chamber' described by members of the Belfast Natural History and Philosophical Society in 1856 (MacAdam & Getty 1855, 358–65). This account showed that many other sites had been destroyed in the preceding century in the lands surrounding the Ring as it was being developed for agriculture. These sites included two flat cemeteries from which vast quantities of human bones were removed; a cemetery mound containing several cremations in stone cists; at least five cists containing urns and either cremations or unburnt bone and some with flint grave goods; a megalithic tomb containing an urn and some bones; and a standing stone and a deep pit filled with burnt stone and charcoal. Similar cists were found in at least three adjacent fields. Therefore the area around the Giant's Ring acted as a magnet for possibly hundreds of burials through the Late Neolithic and Early Bronze Age. The full extent of the cemetery may only be limited by the steep sides of the plateau (Fig. 3.1). In 1990 a programme of excavation was initiated on the site of a large palisaded enclosure to the north of the Ring, based on the results of aerial survey (Hartwell 1991, 1994 & 1995). Three aspects will be discussed here: the passage grave tradition, the hengiform and the palisaded enclosures.

THE PASSAGE GRAVE TRADITION

The earliest occupation of the area is represented by the passage graves. The megalith (BNH2) within the Giant's Ring has been denuded of its mound and survives as five orthostats enclosing a

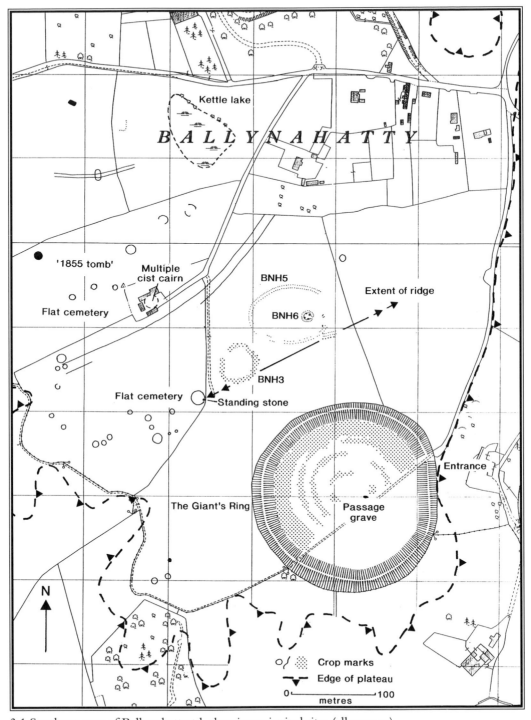

Kettle lake

BALLYNAHATTY

'1855 tomb'

Multiple
cist cairn

BNH5

Extent of ridge

BNH6

Flat cemetery

BNH3

Flat cemetery

Standing stone

Entrance

The Giant's Ring

Passage
grave

N

○⌒ ∷∷ Crop marks

▼ Edge of plateau

0 ⌞_____⌟ 100
metres

3.1 Southern area of Ballynahatty td. showing principal sites (all sources).

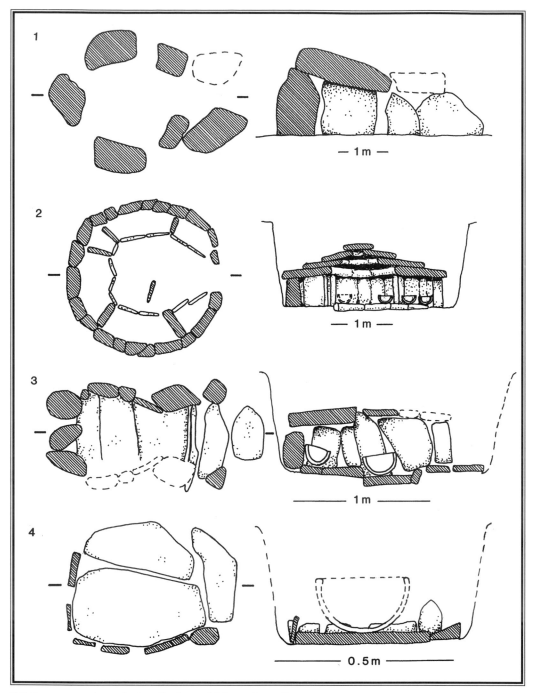

3.2 Passage-tombs and cists. Scale variable to show form.

chamber 1.5m across (Fig. 3.2, 1). One massive capstone is in place and another has slipped and now blocks the remains of a short entry passage defined by one surviving orthostat. Harris reported the existence of a stone kerb (Harris 1744, 200) though this has been disputed by later commentators (Benn 1880, 257–8). In 1917 Lawlor excavated beneath the chamber and found burnt bone in an area of modern disturbance (Lawlor 1919, 19). Though incomplete and much abused, this site does demonstrate the main attributes of a simple passage grave. A chamber is defined by a series of orthostats and roofed by overlapping capstones, often corbelled. There is a distinct entrance which may be developed into a passage and the covering mound may be retained by a kerb of stones. The burial may take the form of a cremation, often in association with heavy, poorly fired, round bottomed 'Carrowkeel Ware' decorated with stab and slash decoration.

In their account of 1855, MacAdam and Getty describe in detail a cist which was radially segmented, stone lined, and had a corbelled roof (MacAdam & Getty 1855, 364). The chamber was 2.15m across and lined by a number of worn flagstones, 60cm high and leaning towards the centre (Fig. 3.2, 2). There was an entrance 60cm wide to the east. The interior had been divided into six peripheral compartments by upright flags and sills. The first two compartments to the left of the entrance contained three, possibly four, Carrowkeel Ware bowls with cremations (Hartwell 1991, 13; Herity 1974, 227 & 281). The next compartment was vacant but the one opposite the entrance contained human ribs and a humerus, some animal bone, two complete human skulls and three more jaws sitting in a bed of sand on some burnt bone. Parcels of burnt human bone were also found in the remaining two compartments. Two mortuary practices are in evidence here. The primary context is represented by the corbel-roofed, compartmented chamber containing at least nine cremated individuals, possibly many more, and the Carrowkeel bowls. The top of the structure was 45cm below ground level and the floor depth and entrance at 1.4m. This seems to be constructed in the passage grave tradition though its sunken position is anomalous. Access had to be achieved on a number of occasions in its initial phase of use and then again when it was reused for secondary inhumations. This is not an uncommon practice and may represent an attempt to promote legitimacy of occupation by associating the burials of one social group with the ancestral remains of another (Thomas 1991, 40). The cist was described as having been covered by small stones as though to form a cairn. This would have functioned as a marker for the tomb and allowed access by preventing the entrance from collapsing. MacAdam and Getty reported that another compartmented cist had been found in a neighbouring field earlier in the century.

A burial cist was found in 1994 during the excavation of Ballynahatty 5. It is situated 100m north of the Giant's Ring near the eastern end of a prominent natural ridge which runs across the field to the standing stone. Though smaller and different in shape, this tomb shares some features with the compartmented cist and passage graves in general (Fig. 3.2, 3). The chamber was sub-rectangular, 80cm by 40cm, and the walls defined by a line of rounded field boulders, 50cm high. The floor and roof, however, were of split stone slabs. The western end of the structure had a clearly defined entrance of two specially selected, pillar-like miniature orthostats of a different rock type, joined by a narrow lintel. This entrance was approached from the outside by a short paved passage, 50cm long, terminating in a threshold stone laid on end from which there was a drop of a few centimetres to the floor of the chamber. The capstones were found immediately below plough depth, so both chamber and passage were originally constructed as a buried cist. Between the walls and the cut edge of the pit many small pebbles survived as evidence for a covering cairn. Part of one side of the cist had been destroyed in antiquity by a post hole and this had resulted in most of the chamber and passage being filled with soil. This activity also damaged the contents of the tomb – two Carrowkeel bowls containing cremations. The reason for the subterranean nature of these two graves is probably prosaic. Demand for large glacial erratic stones may have outstripped supply. Smaller field boulders, rarely longer than 50cm and present everywhere in the soil, would have been the obvious substitute, with the flagstones brought in for roof and flooring. Every occurrence of flat or split stone in the excavated area is in a built context.

The 'passage grave cist' can be seen in its minimalist form in four partially destroyed cremation deposits representing at least two adults and a juvenile. In the best surviving example, a flat stone only 30cm long was placed on the floor of a pit of about the same depth (Fig. 3.2, 4). An edging of split stones, no more than 4cm high, formed the symbolic walls of the chamber which was just wide enough to hold a Carrowkeel Ware bowl containing burnt bone. This 'chamber' was clearly not meant to be accessed at a later stage. Indeed the relationship of these four cremations is atypical in that they are equally spaced 1m apart in a straight line with a north-east orientation. This group contrasts with the other four passage tombs in Ballynahatty which are found in an apparently random scatter across the southern part of the townland with east or west orientations. MacAdam describes some cists as having a stone slab at the base and another as a lid, being 'shorter than a man' and containing urns and these may also be in the passage grave tradition (MacAdam & Getty 1855, 364–5).

One characteristic of these passage grave cists is their human scale. They seem to be the tombs of known individuals whose cremated remains were carefully placed in pots or discrete, orderly packages. The variable fill of the compartmented cist, one section of which was vacant, suggests that occupancy may have been predetermined, perhaps for a family group. The cists became a small but persistent element of the landscape and any ritual associated with them was presumably on a much more personal scale. Could this represent a democratisation of the passage grave complex? BNH2 had greater physical impact and as the founder tomb its importance would have been enhanced. This status was later confirmed when it was selected as the nodal point of one of the largest neolithic embanked enclosures in Ireland and the focal point of the community.

THE GIANT'S RING EMBANKED ENCLOSURE

The Giant's Ring is the best preserved and most accessible of the large, hengiform, embanked enclosures in Ireland. The bank still survives to a height of 4m and probably originally enclosed an area about 190m across (Fig. 3.3). It has received relatively little attention since its first extensive excavation in 1917 by Henry Lawlor (Lawlor 1919). In 1954 A.E.P. Collins addressed many of the unanswered questions by excavating selected areas, including another section through the bank (Collins 1954, 47). Lawlor had excavated 540m of trenches (but only to a width of 45cm), radiating out from the centre, including a section three-quarters through the bank, but he found little evidence of occupation. His interpretation of the bank as having been built over many years by workers bringing rounded pebbles from the surrounding countryside (Lawlor 1919, 21) was not supported by his own evidence. Collins' excavation showed conclusively what Lawlor's had hinted at – that the bank material was derived from a broad, shallow, 1m deep quarry ditch on the inside of the bank. Subsequent erosion gives the interior the appearance of an upturned saucer. This feature is characteristic of a number of other Irish enclosures, such as those at Dowth Hall in the Boyne Valley, Co. Meath, and at 'Rath Maeve',

1km south of the Hill of Tara (Stout 1991, 257, 259). These similarities can be found elsewhere in the Irish Sea province in south-west Wales (Burl 1969, 10, 17–18).

Up to five entrances have been postulated in the past but most of these can be explained as farming access from surrounding fields. Taking the surviving evidence of the quarry ditch, the only area where a causeway across it can be demonstrated is adjacent to the present entrance and car park. This would place the single entrance east-north-east and the enclosure can be classified as a type IC henge (Burl 1991b, 15). Entry to the enclosure is prevented from the south and east by a steep slope. Organised entry, for example a procession, would be guided from the north along the edge of the plateau, being highly visible to all the land to the east, until it disappeared through the bank and into the enclosure. The northward extension of this route leads to a natural amphitheatre along the bottom of which flows a stream, the Minnowburn, which in turn discharges into the Lagan near the fording point at Shaw's Bridge. The area is therefore readily accessible from both north–south (land) and east–west (river) routes.

Why should the enclosure be constructed on the eastern side of the plateau when there is ample room for it to have been placed on the western side where it would have been visible from the River Lagan itself? The reason is the passage tomb, BNH2. It has been argued elsewhere that the enclosure bank was deliberately laid out using this megalith as the nodal point (Hartwell 1991, 14). The diameter was considered immutable to the extent that the enclosure had to be distorted to fit the space available between the megalith and the steep edge of the plateau. The importance of the tomb and the size of the enclosure were therefore prime considerations in its location and layout.

A narrow trench cut through the bank by Collins showed something of the structure and provides us with the best opportunity of reconstructing an Irish henge bank (Fig. 3.3). Resting on the original ground surface was a low bank which probably served both as a marker and subsequently as a retainer for the material dug from the internal quarry ditch. The inner face was retained by a boulder revetment leaving a berm of 1m at the edge of the quarry and a bank width of 16m. If the revetment were projected, it would be inclined back at an angle of 70°. The outer slope is at present inclined at an angle of 30°, which is the natural angle of rest. There is a relatively small fan of displaced material on this side suggesting that this may have been close to the original angle of slope. Using these two angles and an estimate of the amount of material that has slumped back into the quarry area, the original bank can be reconstructed as 4m in height with a flat top 8.5m across. Even if the angle of the boulder revetment was less, it would be

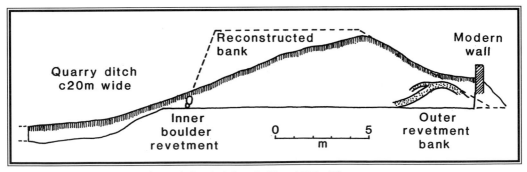

3.3 Giant's Ring. Section through bank (after Collins 1954, 47).

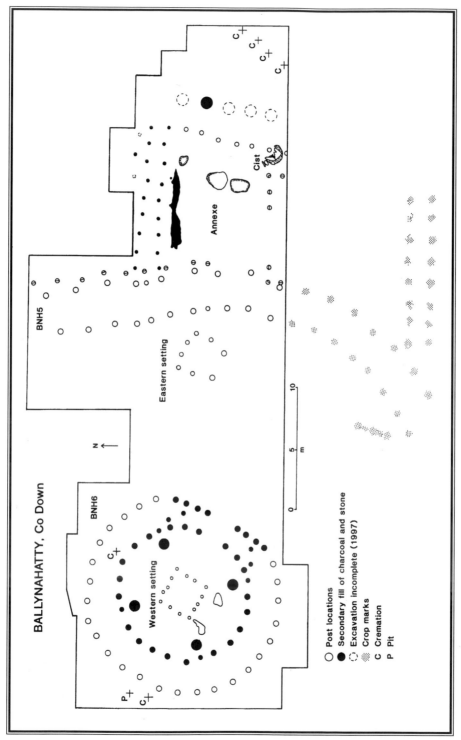

3.4 BNH5 and 6: location of posts and features.

difficult to escape the flat top. This, and the quarrying of bank material internally, is a characteristic feature of the Irish embanked enclosures (Stout 1991, 246–7). The angle of rest of boulders within the bank showed that it had been constructed by dumping quarried material along the central axis. The implication of the flat top and shallower outer slope is that the bank was designed not so much to exclude observers as to facilitate them. However, the steep inner slope and revetment would have prevented participation in any central activity, which signifies divisions within the community. Although the sequence of passage grave followed by enclosure can be demonstrated, the time frame is more problematic. Without radiocarbon dates it is only possible to attribute the Giant's Ring to the Late Neolithic or Early Bronze Age. A similar relationship between a passage grave and an enclosure, but with better dating, can be shown by returning to the excavations which have been continuing since 1990 in the fields to the north of the Giant's Ring.

BALLYNAHATTY 6 TIMBER ENCLOSURE (BNH6)

Extensive crop-marks appeared in the dry summer of 1989 in the Lagan Valley. In Ballynahatty they manifested themselves as a series of circles and blotches representing the remains of barrows and cists. The most extensive marks, however, were two palisaded enclosures, Ballynahatty 5 and 6 (Fig. 3.4). With a diameter of only 16m, BNH6 is by far the smaller of the two enclosures. It is situated 100m north of the Giant's Ring on a levelled platform on the north slope of the east–west ridge. At ground level the view to the south over the Ring is blocked but a few metres away on the top of the ridge is the only vantage point from which the passage grave and the interior of the Ring can be seen from outside. These structures await a comprehensive interpretation but an outline of their probable history follows. Because any linking stratigraphy has been damaged by ploughing, it is sometimes difficult to establish the exact relationships between the various elements.

The initial phase was of a single circle of posts, 11m in diameter, probably enclosing a square setting of four posts. An entrance gap was placed to the south-east and a small annexe constructed to emphasise or restrict entry. This is based on the survival of three otherwise anachronistic post holes on either side of the entrance of the later structure. They are stratigraphically earlier and morphologically different to the later enclosure postholes. In plan it would have been virtually identical to the structure found outside the eastern passage at Knowth (Eogan & Roche 1994, 223; 1997, 104) which was excavated at about the same time. The two sites differ in the existence of a central structure at Ballynahatty. The postholes of the 'western setting', are only 30cm deep, sufficient to keep these much smaller posts upright while the structure, 3m square, was being braced. It was given an orientation by using five posts on each side parallel to the south-east axis which runs through the entrance of BNH6. The other two sides each have four posts. As there is no door space it could be a support for a platform. A cremation deposit of a woman in her thirties was found in a setting of split stones to the north-east beyond the inner ring of posts. On a projection of the main axis to the north-west, beyond the outer circle, there was a pit containing a 'hoard' of split stones and close by a cremation of a child. The cremations would seem to be foundation deposits whereas the significance of the split stone pit is that it occupies one of the three nodal positions from which the BNH6 complex was laid out.

The following phase is one of enlargement of both area and height. Still retaining the diameter of 11m, the posts are removed and the holes of the central four posts are excavated to a depth of 2.4m to take free-standing posts of nearly 1m in circumference and over 9.5m in length. This is estimated by the height of a free-standing post above ground level being approximately three times the depth of the posthole (Mercer 1991, 150). Radiating ramps had been excavated from each hole to facilitate the erection of these prodigious timbers. These posts would have towered 7m above ground level. The twenty-three postholes of the enclosing ring were similarly enlarged to a depth of 2m to take posts of about 50cm diameter, thereby obliterating much of the earlier phase. The ramps of the two postholes closest to the north-east cremation show its primary position and integration within the structure by diverging to avoid damaging it. The postholes on either side of the entrance were joined by slots which, together with the evidence of a charred oak plank, suggest that it had been defined and emphasised by a planked facade. The whole structure was then enclosed by a similar ring of thirty-three posts. The ramps of the nearest two postholes diverge to avoid the split stone pit, acknowledging its primary position. The entrance is again emphasised by a planked facade but this time with six panels. To create some visual order, the individual posts of the concentric rings may have been connected by lintels as has been demonstrated at the Sarn-y-Bryn-Caled complex in Wales (Gibson 1994, 212). There is no evidence that it was ever roofed.

If the axis of BNH6 is projected 10m beyond the entrance to the south-east, it passes between two settings of postholes. The one to the north-east, the 'eastern setting', has been excavated and its mirror image to the south-west found by geophysical survey. These postholes are 80cm deep and the settings are oriented at right angles to the BNH6 axis, with the nearest side open and the back wall curved. They have been laid out as opposing sectors of a circle with the curved rear walls falling on to the arc and the sides conforming to the rays. The centre of the circle is at the intersection of the setting's axis with that of BNH6. This, however, is more than just a convenient method of laying out. It means that this intersection is the one crucial point from which the full contents of the settings can be seen as well as providing an unimpeded view through the facade and entrance to the full width of the central platform (Fig. 3.6, position B). In a ceremonial context, the participant is being induced to stop during his or her approach in order to observe these three views before continuing into the interior of BNH6. The planked facade may have provided a support for various motifs and symbols and a view of the interior from other directions may have been blocked by wicker panels. Towering over the enclosure would have been the four main posts. The massive nature of these would have been an ideal support for carvings. The approach to this building was calculated to inspire awe (Fig. 3.5).

The functions of these three enclosures were clearly linked. Their position within a ceremonial landscape and the primary association of the cremations strongly suggest a mortuary function and they may be regarded as mortuary enclosures. BNH6 is clearly the focus for active ritual. If the interpretation of the central platform is correct then this may have been an excarnation site involving the exposure of cadavers and defleshing. However, there is no direct evidence for this in the form of bone remains. The eastern setting and its counterpart could have taken a more passive role as ossuaries for the storage of bone material. The absence of unburnt bone from this site may be the result of soil conditions.

This unified and conceptually advanced building was designed and executed with great skill and precision. The post positions as recorded in the bottoms of the post holes, where they were

3.5 Reconstruction of BNH6, phase 2.

not subjected to displacement by settlement, show that the structure is remarkably symmetrical along a line passing through the entrance. The whole of BNH6 can be laid out by generating a series of concentric lines from three fixed points on a straight line using a unit of measurement of 1.3m, close to twice Burl's theoretical 'beaker yard' (Burl 1991b, 49). Although the plan appears to be based on a standard formula, it is the product of a skilled practitioner and must reflect established rituals (Fig. 3.6).

This phase ends with the deliberate firing of the structure. A bell-shaped pit was excavated around the burnt, earthfast stump of each of the main four posts and they were then levered out of the ground. This was a practice noted at the Dorchester upon Thames pit circles (Gibson 1992). The inner ring of posts and the entrances were treated in the same way. The charcoal remains of the conflagration were then scraped together and deposited in the open holes. In some cases burnt stones were deliberately incorporated in the secondary fill in layers alternating with the loose ash and charcoal. The position of the main posts were marked by low cairns of burnt boulders and cobbles. The stumps of the outer ring were allowed to rot *in situ*.

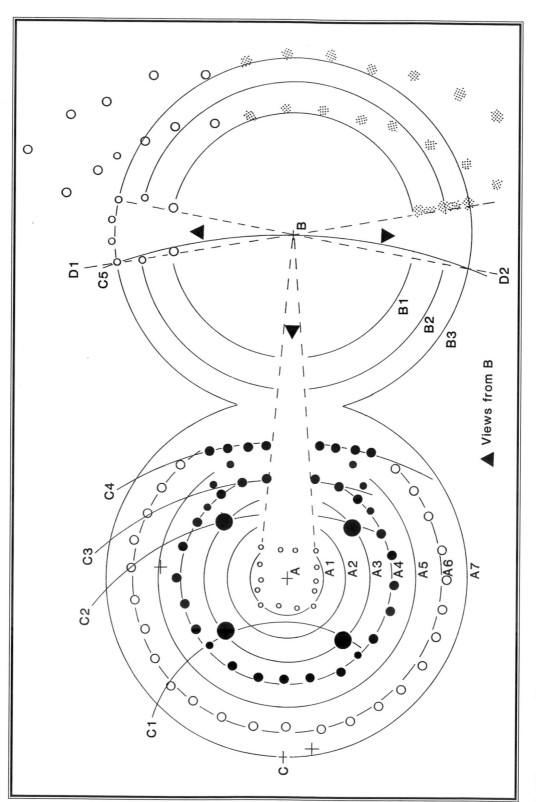

3.6 Construction of BNH6, phase 2.

BALLYNAHATTY 5 TIMBER ENCLOSURE (BNH5)

BNH5 consists of a double line of ramped post holes, averaging 1.8m deep, which probably held free-standing posts approximately 6m high and 30cm in diameter. The earthfast lower section had rotted *in situ* but scatters of surface charcoal suggest that the posts had been burnt. At least 260 mature oak trees were felled and hauled to the site and each posthole would have taken one person about twenty-six hours of digging with an antler pick to reach the required depth. The eastern end of BNH5 has been distorted slightly in order to enclose the 'eastern setting' of the BNH6 complex which therefore precedes it (Fig. 3.4). Here, the south-westerly sweep of the palisade runs up to and along the top of the east–west ridge to overlook the Giant's Ring. At this point, where BNH5 straddles the approach to BNH6, an annexe consisting of two adjacent cells, 10m square, was constructed. The alignment was not taken from the BNH6 axis but from that of the ridge which had by then become an important element in the ritual landscape. Although the annexe is only partly excavated, it is clear that one of its main functions was to create a focal point for an approach from lower ground beyond the eastern end of the ridge. This coincides with the postulated principal approach to the Giant's Ring along the eastern edge of the plateau. To facilitate this, the eastern side of the annexe was constructed of massive posts, 140cm in diameter and 6m high. These posts were eventually burnt and the stumps extracted by digging out the rotten wood and refilling it with charcoal and burnt stone. To the west of this line was at least one series of relatively narrow posts about 4m high which rotted *in situ*. The cells were enclosed to north and south by similar sizes of posts set in pairs but containing a secondary fill of layers of charcoal and burnt stone. A similar cycle of activity is therefore evident to that found in BNH6. It is not yet known if there is an entrance through the annexe and BNH5 in line with the main approach to BNH6.

Only a brief discussion of the finds from the Ballynahatty excavation is possible here. Considering the amount of timber that was used on the site it is remarkable that 'heavy' cutting equipment is represented by only two polished axes. There was much opportunistic use of glacially derived flint from the soil. The 65 cores and 1,220 reduction flakes found totalled 11.5kg. In addition there was 4.3kg of burnt flint. Of the tools, there were 87 scrapers and 32 blades and points. Together with some burnt animal bone, probably pig, this provides abundant evidence of feasting. Some of the burnt flint is identifiable as reduction flaking or artefacts and the possibility remains that it was being deliberately burnt as part of a ritual. Distribution of artefacts within BNH6 show a concentration in the secondary fill of the post pits on either side of the entrance. The main concentration of pottery was found within the annexe and consisted of 218 sherds of Grooved Ware representing twenty-six vessels.

CONCLUSION

Two charcoal samples from BNH5 gave a combined date range of between 3018 and 2788 Cal BC (2 σ). However, this early date may have been affected by the nature of the charcoal which was derived from mature oak (see Gibson 1994, 202–3 for comparison with other timber circle dates). The Grooved Ware association ties in well with the Knowth timber structure which produced evidence of thirty pots (Eogan & Roche 1994, 326). Here the sequence runs: passage tomb settlement, passage tombs/Grooved Ware complex, Beaker settlement with the relationship between the middle two uncertain. At Ballynahatty, the passage tomb (BNH2) is simple in form and could therefore be assigned to stage 1 or 2 of Sheridan's scheme of passage grave development (Sheridan 1985/6, 19). This would give an end date of about 3050 cal BC with the 'passage grave cists' being constructed at any time afterwards. BNH5 and 6 post-date the passage grave occupation because one of the post holes of the annexe cuts through the edge of the cist containing Carrowkeel Ware. Although Sheridan warns against the traditional equation of 'Carrowkeel pottery = passage tombs = passage tomb people' (Sheridan 1995, 11), at Ballynahatty, Carrowkeel Ware only occurs in a mortuary context, that is, as a receptacle for cremations and in a primary relationship with passage grave or related structures. None of the cremations associated with BNH5 and 6 has any ceramic element.

A relative sequence of building has been outlined above. The sequence of BNH6, BNH5, Annexe, is probably part of a continuous building programme. Some indication of length of use is provided by one of the four main posts of BNH6. The bottom metre seems to have become detached and remained earthfast when the remainder of the stump was extracted. The most likely explanation is that it was rotten and broke at this point. The duration of use was therefore determined by the condition of the oak posts. At Newgrange, a large pit enclosure was excavated by Sweetman (1985) which provides a more complex model for the larger enclosure of BNH5. Though much more extensive, the Boyne Valley provides close parallels for many of the developments in Ballynahatty.

The ritual function that underpins these monuments does strongly suggest some form of spiritual leadership, either imposed or inherited. The crucial importance of death rituals in a traditional agrarian society has been discussed by Thomas (1991, 105). Death of the individual can be seen as ultimately affecting the survival of society as a whole. Mortuary rituals promote links between the changing present and what must have been perceived as society's immutable past. Over time, however, the past becomes subject to reinterpretation and power becomes concentrated in those who are able to intercede between the living and their ancestors and to manipulate these links. This authority must have been sufficient to motivate society to produce these extraordinary earth and timber structures in the later Neolithic. Ballynahatty should therefore be seen as a focus of community ceremony and death rituals in the Late Neolithic and Early Bronze Age of the Lagan Valley. The traditions of cremation, inhumation and excarnation can be viewed as strategies for the transformation and purification of bone which provided a tangible link with the past. In the same way, the timber posts were not destroyed by fire but were cremated and deliberately transformed and then replaced in their sockets. They continued to exist beyond the ravages of decay.

CHAPTER FOUR

IRISH HENGIFORM ENCLOSURES AND RELATED MONUMENTS: A REVIEW

TOM CONDIT & DEREK SIMPSON

INTRODUCTION

The first of what would now be considered as Irish henge monuments was excavated at Dun Ruadh, Co. Tyrone, in 1935 (Davies 1936) although its significance in terms of broader relationships was not recognised at the time (Simpson 1993; Simpson *et al.* 1994). Ó Ríordáin (1953) first suggested that the enclosures at Micknanstown and Dowth belonged to the British series of henge monuments. Burl (1969) listed seven certain and five possible henges from Ireland. He first recognised the Boyne Valley monuments as one of the significant concentrations in the two islands and suggested a second North Channel coast group with two Irish sites and seven Scottish monuments, curiously including Cairnpapple Hill, West Lothian (Piggott 1958). In the same year Wainwright (1969) listed thirteen Irish sites, a number of which were labelled as doubtful by Burl. The first general study of the Irish enclosures was by Hicks (1975), regrettably unpublished, and the major concentration of such monuments in the Boyne region was highlighted by Stout (1991). She also drew attention to nine other monuments which bore similarities to those in the Boyne region. Since then other henges have been located from the air, notably in the Boyle area, Co. Roscommon (Condit 1993).

This review deals with a variety of sites, some certainly hengiform enclosures, others more problematical but nevertheless, in our view, worthy of consideration. Aubrey's pioneering paper of 1969 drew together the Irish and British monuments and stressed the inter-regional relationships. This chapter is offered as an update of his work on the Irish material. This will be considered under seven headings: earthen embanked enclosures; internally ditched enclosures; embanked stone circles; circle henges; timber circles; 'royal' enclosures; and, finally, ritual ponds.

EARTHEN EMBANKED ENCLOSURES

The term earthen embanked enclosure is used by Ó Ríordáin (1953) to refer specifically to a type of ceremonial site which consists of a large earthen bank, without an obvious ditch, forming an enclosure around an area from which the bank material was scraped, thus creating a lower

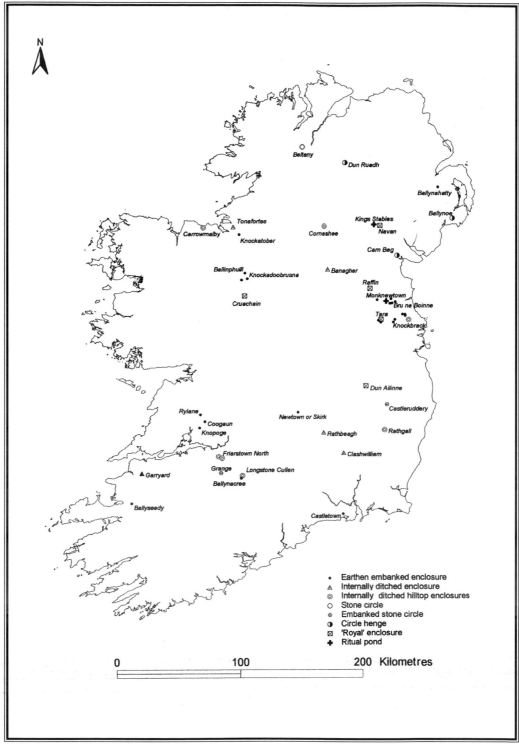

Distribution map of henges and related sites in Ireland. (B. Masterson, The Discovery Programme)

surface inside the monument than outside. The principal observations concerning the distribution of earthen embanked enclosures in the Irish landscape are that they are a lowland, river valley phenomenon, they are closely associated with passage tombs, and their distribution seems to be related to copper resources, at least in Co. Meath (Stout 1991, 253, fig. 5).

Grouping is a feature of the earthen embanked enclosure monuments. Of the thirteen examples in the greater Boyne Valley region, four distinct groups can be identified. The best known of these groups is in the vicinity of the three great passage tombs at Brú na Bóinne. The best preserved is the example at Dowth; it is sited on gently sloping ground overlooking the River Boyne at the east of the complex. Two further examples are Site A, which encompasses a burial mound presumed to be a passage tomb, and Site P on the alluvial gravel terrace to the south of the Newgrange mound, immediately beside the Boyne overlooking Roughgrange ford. The Monknewtown enclosure excavated by Sweetman is located to the north of the Brú na Bóinne complex near the River Mattock. This complex also contains three timber circles, two to the north east and south west of Newgrange itself, and the timber circle at Knowth outside the entrance to the eastern tomb in Site 1. Another noteworthy monument within this complex is the cursus located to the east of Newgrange (Condit 1995).

Tara also contains a number of hengiform monuments, two of which are of the earthen embanked enclosure type. South of the summit of the Hill of Tara is the site known as Rath Maeve, a particularly large example, and to the west is Ringlestown, a much-degraded example which, like Rath Maeve, is sited on sloping ground. Kilbrew and Irishtown, located on the crest of a low ridge close to the River Hurley (which is a tributary of the River Nanny), consist of two enclosures only 110m apart. Finally in the greater Boyne area are three enclosures within the Fourknocks group, located on the north-facing slopes of the ridge on which the Fourknocks passage tomb is located, overlooking the River Delvin. A further significant concentration has been identified in the vicinity of the town of Boyle in north Co. Roscommon, two on the hill named Knockadoobrusna and another at Ballinphuill, 1.8km to the north (Condit 1993). This group of enclosures is notable for the fact that two of them are situated on hilltops. One is contiguous with a mound which crowns the summit of the hill at 122m. The other is located to the south-east on a terrace of the hill. At least one bivallate barrow and an enclosure of unknown function are sited nearby. A conical mound is located on the summit of a neighbouring hill. There may be a final possible grouping in Co. Armagh. There is a ditched enclosure, 12m in diameter, with an entrance on the south-south-east producing sherds of Carrowkeel Ware, at Scotch Street, Armagh (Hamlin & Lynn 1988), and three further earthworks recorded on the OS maps as 'forts' or enclosures which, from their size – 90–100m in diameter – and their low-lying situation, might also be considered as ceremonial monuments.

All of the groups are associated with mounds in the near vicinity and most can be clearly associated with known passage tombs. Furthermore, those which occur in ritual landscapes are close to other monuments with henge characteristics. It can also be stated that, based on current evidence, the discrete earthen embanked enclosures may be associated with other ritual monuments which can be identified as subsurface features such as those found close to the Giant's Ring by Hartwell (1994).

Outliers from these main concentrations of earthen embanked enclosures are known. The most impressive is the Giant's Ring, Ballynahatty, Co. Down, again with a bank scraped up from the interior (Collins 1957). Another well-preserved enclosure on the gently sloping sides of a valley is located in the townland of Ballynacree near the town of Cullen in Co. Tipperary. In Co.

4.1 Aerial photograph showing ritual complex and earthen embanked enclosures at Knockadoobrusna, Co. Roscommon. (CUCAP)

Sligo, aerial photographs have helped to identify another apparently isolated enclosure at Knockatober. Sweetman *et al.* (1996) recorded an interesting example apparently reused as a motte and bailey in the townland of Newtown or Skirk, Co. Laois. The work of the Discovery Programme in the north Munster area has uncovered and recorded two examples in south-east Clare at Coogaun and Knopoge (Grogan & Condit 1994). A further example, some 46m in diameter, has been identified by Ms Ines Hagen near the town of Tulla in Rylane (unpublished). The OS maps indicate two possible megalithic tombs, now destroyed, to the south-west of the site. Another intriguing example with a diameter of over 40m has recently been identified at Ballyseedy, south of Tralee, Co. Kerry. This discovery follows the recent excavation of a passage

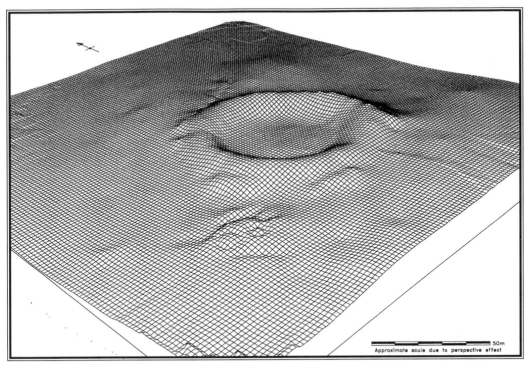

4.2 Digital terrain model of earthen embanked enclosure at Ballynacree, Co. Tipperary. (B. Masterson, The Munster Project, The Discovery Programme)

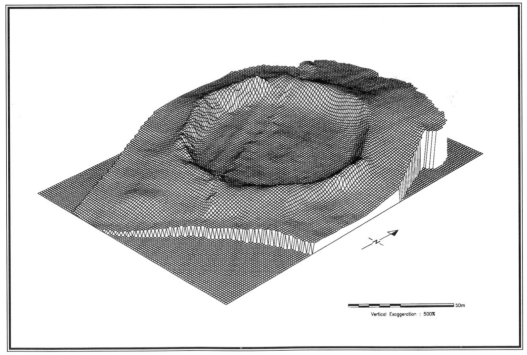

4.3 Digital terrain model of earthen embanked enclosure at Coogaun, Co. Clare. (B. Masterson, The Munster Project, The Discovery Programme)

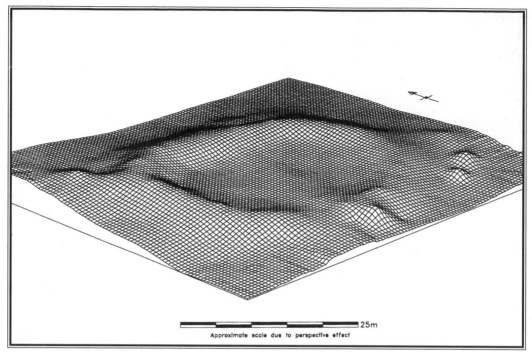

4.4 Digital terrain model of earthen embanked enclosure at Knopoge, Co. Clare. (B. Masterson, The Munster Project, The Discovery Programme)

tomb in advance of a proposed road development (Connolly 1996). Other examples are known in Co. Waterford, near Tramore at Castletown (Condit and Gibbons 1988), and a smaller example measuring 24m in diameter in the recently identified ritual landscape complex in the Araglin Valley, Co. Waterford (Moore 1995).

INTERNALLY DITCHED ENCLOSURES

These are the so-called classic British henges but there are only a limited number of examples in Ireland (Harding 1988). The first Irish site was excavated at Dun Ruadh, Co. Tyrone (Davies 1936). A number of the 'royal sites' also fit into this category (see below). Some have been identified from aerial photographs which clearly show the configuration of the internal ditch with external bank. Part of the difficulty in classifying the field remains is in differentiating between large barrows and ritual sites which are likely to have functioned as henges. A further problem is discriminating between hillforts and hilltop henges. The royal sites described below are obviously of ritual significance. However, there are other hilltop sites which have previously been described as hillforts although the internal ditch/external bank configuration clearly signals the likelihood that such sites were constructed for a ritual purpose.

Three internally ditched henges have been identified in Co. Kilkenny (Gibbons 1990) at Rathbeagh close to the River Nore, at Annamult near Bennetsbridge and at Clashwilliam. Furthermore, at Carran townland aerial photographs have pinpointed a large circular crop-mark

4.5 Internally ditched hilltop enclosure at Carrownrush/Carrowmalby, Co. Sligo (CUCAP)

which surrounds a central cairn. In Co. Kerry, a number of henges have been published in the *North Kerry Archaeological Survey*. They are at Garryard, Gullane East, Knockenagh North and Ballynorrig. The author has classified them firmly as 'henges (embanked enclosures)' but has also indicated that some at least may be large ring barrows. The Garryard example, some 77m in diameter and with a single entrance on the south-east, can be confidently classified as a henge (O'Donovan 1985).

Aerial photography has helped to identify a hengiform enclosure at Tonafortes, south of Sligo town and 2km east of the megalithic cemetery at Carrowmore (Condit & Gibbons 1991). This

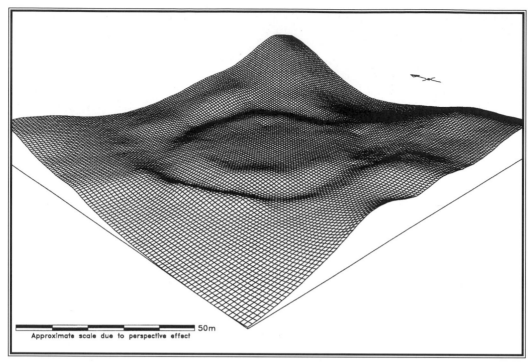

4.6 Digital terrain model of henge monument at Tonafortes, Co. Sligo. (B. Masterson, The Munster Project, The Discovery Programme)

site, with an overall diameter of 80m, is located on low-lying ground surrounded by moraines which immediately overlook it. The site has been recorded by digital terrain model (DTM) survey which highlights the presence of a causeway on the east. From this low location there are fine views of Knocknarea to the west. A small pond, which would expand extensively, is located to the south-west of the henge, and was most probably formed by a small spring.

Excavations on hillfort sites have also uncovered monuments which could sit easily within the henge category. At the multivallate fort of Rathgall, Co. Wicklow, Raftery (1976) excavated an internally ditched enclosure 35m in diameter, at the centre of which was a structure 12–15m across which he interpreted as a house. Within this structure was a pit filled with organic material which contained a penannular gold ring. Raftery noted that the internally ditched enclosure did not have a causeway and may have been crossed by means of planks. He felt that the ditched enclosure was an outwork for the house. A single example of an internally ditched henge, with an internal diameter of 42m, has also been identified in Banagher townland, Co. Cavan (O'Donovan 1995).

There are also other enclosures, usually classed as hillforts, which are more likely to belong to the henge class. At Clomantagh Hill near Johnstown, Co. Kilkenny, a large stone-revetted enclosure, c. 200m in diameter, surrounds at its centre the remains of what is likely to be a passage tomb (Condit & Gibbons 1987). At Croghan Hill, Co. Donegal, a hilltop cairn suspected to be a passage tomb is surrounded by a stone-built enclosure (Lacy 1983). This site looks across to Beltany Hill (see below) opposite and overlooks the passage tomb cemetery at Kilmonaster.

4.7 Aerial photograph of ritual enclosure at Longstone Cullen, Co. Tipperary.

Excavations have taken place at another hilltop henge at Longstone Cullen in Co. Tipperary. This site has a standing stone in its interior and incorporates a number of barrows. Beaker pottery was found during the excavations but the site has yet to be published. Interestingly, this site overlooks the valley in which the earthen embanked enclosure, Ballynacree, is located.

If we try to understand some of the internally ditched hilltop sites, certain intriguing interpretations become apparent and there are close similarities with the more conventional henges both in Ireland and Britain. As stated above, some sites which have been classified as hillforts can be sensibly discussed within the context of henge monuments. We know that hilltops were used in prehistoric times for both ritual and defensive purposes and the coincidence of cairns (many presumed to be passage tombs) has been noted (Raftery 1994). In an earlier study of Irish hillforts Raftery (1972) also indicated that (in addition to Navan, Dún Ailinne and

Tara) Clogher, Co. Tyrone, and Cornashee near Lisnaskea, Co. Fermanagh, should be considered as hillforts of ritual significance on the basis of their internal ditch/external bank configuration. Both Cornashee and Clogher contain mounds and are associated with inauguration sites mentioned in historical texts (Manning 1976).

Further sites have been added to the archaeological record in recent times. A recently identified hillfort at Knockbrack, Co. Dublin, encloses a hilltop mound and other mounds are located on the lower terraces of the hill. The enclosure, however, consists of an internal ditch and external bank. The site itself lies 7km south-east of the Fourknocks landscape referred to above (Keeling 1983). At Ballylin, Co. Limerick, Cody identified an extremely large bivallate (possibly trivallate) hillfort near the town of Ardagh (Cody 1981). This site consists of internally ditched banks c. 300m in diameter. An interesting pair of hillforts are located on a hill at Friarstown north, also in Co. Limerick. Both can be shown to have internal ditches and one contains the possible remains of a mound. Like the earthen embanked enclosures, these occur in close proximity and are likely to be henges rather than hillforts.

Two sites are worth mentioning because of the amphitheatre effect produced by the modification of naturally occurring terraces around them. One is the site known as Magh Adhair in the townland of Toonagh in south-east Clare, where there is a large, 4m high, flat-topped mound surrounded by a ditch and outer bank. It is considered to be the inauguration site of the

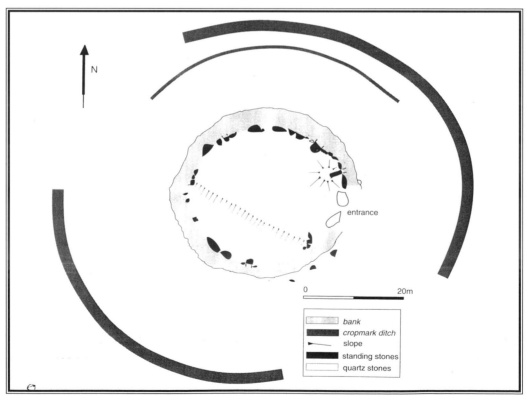

4.8 Plan of Castleruddery stone-lined enclosure showing cropmark enclosure on exterior. (Grogan and Hillery 1993)

O'Briens of Dal gCais referred to in the early Irish annals. A number of standing stones are located in its immediate vicinity and a large conglomerate 'basin stone' is situated on the surrounding level ground to the north of the mound (Westropp 1896). The name 'Cregnakeeroge' is used by the Ordnance Survey to refer to the rocky terrace which surrounds the mound on the north and east, providing a natural amphitheatre (Manning 1976, 110). Portions of this terrace appear to have been scarped to provide a smooth gradient. At Magh Adhair a turlough appears in winter, filled with water which floods from holes in the limestone in a small cave in the surrounding limestone crags. The Magh Adhair complex lies 2km north of the Coogaun earthen embanked enclosure. At Lisnalurg, just north of Sligo town, there is a large circular enclosure, 150m in diameter, the bank standing up to 5m above the interior. The enclosing bank appears to have been constructed from material scooped up from the interior. Centrally placed within the site is an earthen enclosure 75m in diameter; a gap in the bank corresponds to a similar gap in the outer enclosure (Condit & Gibbons 1993).

EMBANKED STONE CIRCLES

True embanked circles, in which the stones are set against the inner face of the enclosing bank, are not common in Britain or Ireland. Burl (1976, 259) suggests a total of some thirty sites for the two islands. Six, or possibly seven, examples occur in Ireland. The best known and largest is the Great Circle at Grange, Co. Limerick, which has a diameter of 64m and a clearly defined entrance on the north-east (Ó Ríordáin 1951). Sherds of Grooved Ware were found within the circle and beneath the bank (Eogan & Roche 1994, 328). North of the Great Circle in the adjacent field is an oval setting of fifteen stones set into an earthen bank with a maximum diameter of 22m. An entrance exists on the south-west. Set centrally is a low mound (Ó Ríordáin 1951). Grooved Ware was also recovered from this site.

Two other sites occur in Wicklow. The larger, Castleruddery, encloses an area 30m in diameter, its eastern entrance marked by two large quartz boulders (Leask 1945). Beyond this entrance are seven prostrate stones which may have formed an avenue or row. A resistivity survey of the site revealed a ditch outside the bank (Churcher 1985). The smaller site at Boleycarrigeen, or the Griddle Stones, is 14m in diameter. The stones are graded in height and there is a possible entrance on the east. Burl (1976, 221) drew attention to the fact that on the south-east coast of Ireland several embanked circles are in hilltop situations reminiscent of many Irish passage tombs. In Banagher townland, Co. Cavan, a complex of burial and ceremonial sites occupies a patch of uneven elevated pasture 150m by 130m at 700–800 OD. These include an embanked stone circle with seven surviving stones, a free-standing circle surrounding a ruined passage tomb, and an embanked enclosure with internal ditch (O'Donovan 1995, 13). Far to the west is a small cluster of four circles at Cong, Co. Mayo. The southern monument is 33m in diameter with four surviving stones built into the inner face of the bank (Burl 1995, 241; Evans 1966, 162). The seventh and more doubtful candidate for inclusion in this category is Beltany, Co. Donegal (Lacy 1983, 72–3). This is a ring of near-contiguous stones 50m in diameter. Gaps exist in the ring but none is an obvious entrance. A cup-marked stone occurs on the north-east; another stands 20m to the south-east of the circle. The interior of the monument has been considerably disturbed, with large numbers of stones and small boulders piled up against the inner face of the circle; indeed Evans (1966, 85) suggested that the whole monument might represent a despoiled cairn. There is a suggestion of an external bank (Burl 1995, 229).

The Irish embanked stone circles have in general greater diameters than their British counterparts. Notable exceptions are the two large circles at Pobull Fhinn and Loch a Phobuill on North Uist in the Outer Hebrides (Burl 1976, 259).

CIRCLE HENGES

Burl (1976, 274; 1991, 35) identified a distinctive group of monuments within the general category of henges which were distinguished by the erection of circles of standing stones or other settings in their interiors. In general, members of this category occupy a narrow zone where eastern henge and western stone circle traditions overlap. Examples extend from Orkney to Cornwall and westwards into Ireland. In this chapter a more rigid application of the term circle henge will apply. Only those enclosures demarcated by an earthen bank, with or without a ditch, and having free-standing stone uprights erected within them are included. This is to distinguish this group from the embanked stone circles where the stones are set against the inner face of the bank. It would be reasonable to consider the latter as single-period monuments, the bank and its juxtaposed circle forming an integral structure. With the circle henges, on the other hand, it is impossible to establish the chronological relationship between the earthwork and the stone structures erected inside it (Burl 1976, 275). Circle henges in the context of this chapter are again uncommon in Ireland, as are embanked stone circles (Burl 1976, 274).

Six sites may be included in this category. Beginning in the north of the island, a first tentative candidate is Dun Ruadh, Co. Tyrone (Davies 1936; Simpson *et al.* 1994), the first 'true' henge to be excavated in Ireland (Simpson 1993) in terms of the British definition of such monuments (Atkinson *et al.* 1951). As Davies demonstrated, the site was of multi-period construction, perhaps involving an early period of neolithic settlement or activity associated with Lyles Hill pottery but with no built features. His second phase was the ditch with external bank and an entrance on the south-west. Phase 3 was the multiple cist cairn with cists and cremations accompanied by food vessels, again with an approach to the cairn which shared an entrance with the pre-existing earthwork, thus forming a ring cairn. What is interesting in terms of sequence is the horseshoe-shaped setting of standing stones considered as a revetment to the cairn. An alternative interpretation is that this was a free-standing horseshoe erected within the henge. Such settings are known elsewhere in Britain if not in Ireland (see Burl 1995 for examples). Ballynoe, Co. Down (Groenman-Van Waateringe & Butler 1976), is a more convincing candidate for a circle henge, with a setting of close-set stones enclosing an area 96m in diameter. Van Giffen suggested the presence of a ditch outside the main circle but the results were not conclusive. He hoped to confirm its existence in a third season of

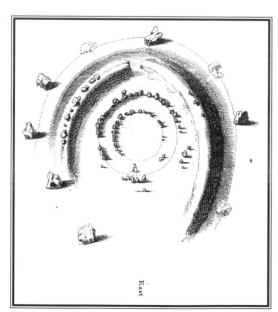

4.9 Thomas Wright's drawing of the stone-built henge at Ballynahattin, Co. Louth.

excavations but this was never achieved. Geophysical survey of the site in 1993 does appear to confirm the presence of such a ditch (O'Keefe 1994), although only further excavations can verify this supposition.

Further to the south, a vanished monument at Carn Beg, Ballynahatne, near Dundalk, Co. Louth, certainly belongs to the circle henge category (Buckley 1988). An eighteenth-century engraving shows a massive circle of stones surrounding an earthen bank with a double circle of smaller stones within it. The site of this monument has recently been rediscovered as a crop-mark 130m in diameter, with two smaller concentric rings in the interior. In Cork and Kerry are three further sites which might qualify for inclusion in the circle henge category. All are on a considerably smaller scale than the previous sites, as indeed are the unenclosed circles in the south-west. The largest is at Lissyvigeen, Co. Kerry (Ó Nualláin 1984, 25), where a circle of seven stones is enclosed by a bank 20m in diameter with entrance gaps on the north-east and south-west. At Glantane East, Co. Cork, a ruined circle of six stones stands within a surrounding ditch 10m in diameter with faint traces of an external bank (Ó Nualláin 1984, 11). The final example, also in Cork at Reanascreena South, was a circle of thirteen stones surrounded by a ditch 18m in diameter with an external bank. Excavation failed to produce any significant or datable finds (Fahy 1962). These three monuments appear to be diminutive versions of circle henges, just as the recumbent stone circles in the same region are smaller versions of the very similar monuments in north-east Scotland.

TIMBER CIRCLES

Henges comprising timber circles are a relatively new phenomenon in the Irish landscape. All, with the exception of Ballynahatty, Co. Down, have been identified in the course of excavations. One other likely example has been discovered through the use of geophysical investigations at the Rathcroghan Mound in Co. Roscommon (see below). Not surprisingly, these timber circles have been discovered at the well-known archaeological complexes of Brú na Bóinne, Navan, Dún Ailinne and Cruachain. The Ballynahatty circle was identified along with a series of other subsurface features in the vicinity of the Giant's Ring earthen embanked enclosure. Two of the Brú na Bóinne timber circles were excavated close to the Newgrange passage tomb (Sweetman 1982; 1984), while another was located outside the entrance to the east chamber at Knowth, Site 1. All three sites date to the late neolithic period, while the Knowth timber circle has a significant quantity of Grooved Ware in the fill of the post pits.

Sweetman showed clearly that the larger Newgrange timber circle, located to the south-east, pre-dated the stone circle which encompassed the perimeter of the mound. Recent aerial photographs suggest that the timber circle may be elliptical in shape and may actually be contiguous with the cursus monument east of Newgrange.

The smaller Newgrange timber circle is located 30m to the west of the main site in close proximity to the two passage tombs which are sited on the summit of the ridge at that point. It is interesting to speculate that this timber circle is related to one or both of the passage tombs rather than to Newgrange, with which the larger timber circle is associated.

The Knowth timber circle, about 9m in diameter and located close to the entrance of the eastern tomb, is on a similar scale to that of the smaller Newgrange circle. The presence of four post holes in the centre of the site is reminiscent of the structure at the centre of the Ballynahatty timber circle. Passage tomb settlement is overlain by the Knowth circle and the latter is covered by Beaker material, indicating a clear date in the later neolithic period (Eogan & Roche 1993).

Radiocarbon and dendrochronological dating have placed two other timber circles firmly in the Iron Age. At Navan Fort, the multi-ringed timber circle with its central post indicates an unequivocal building date of 98 BC for the Forty Metre Structure which was covered in its entirety by a cairn before being ritually burned. Analogous with this feature is the timber circle from Dún Ailinne which was radiocarbon-dated to the Iron Age. Geophysical evidence from Rathcroghan Mound is indicating the likelihood that a double-ringed timber circle also exists there.

Based on the above evidence, there are clearly two phases of construction of timber circles in the Late Neolithic and in the Iron Age. Like the earthen embanked enclosures the timber circles are closely associated with areas where passage tombs were built. The Iron Age timber circles are found within the large royal henges at the provincial capitals.

'ROYAL' ENCLOSURES

In discussing the results of his excavations at Dún Ailinne, Co. Kildare, Wailes (1990, 19) described the principal earthwork as a henge and noted the hengiform characteristics of the other sites at the heart of the royal landscapes in Ireland – Navan, Co. Armagh, Rathcroghan (Cruachain), Co. Roscommon, and Tara, Co. Meath, all linked with the earliest historical documents. At Dún Ailinne there was no dating evidence for the main enclosure with its internal ditch. Within the major earthwork there was a considerable quantity of neolithic finds (Johnson 1990) including a stone bead and fragments of two elaborately decorated pots in the Drimnagh tradition from a pit which Herity (1982, 309) suggested may have been a burial. At Navan, again the earthwork cannot be precisely dated although coring of the ditch's lowest deposits indicates a high pine pollen count, suggesting a neolithic date (Weir 1987, 41). Navan may therefore be a classic henge equal in dimensions to those of the great Wessex monuments (Simpson 1989) although only excavation of the major earthwork can confirm or refute this supposition. Archaeological evidence for neolithic activity is slight – a scatter of pottery and flint flakes in the area which was excavated in the interior. The only feature which could be related to this period was an ill-defined hollow (Lynn 1986, 14).

Navan, Tara and Dún Ailinne share much in common in that they are large hilltop, internally ditched enclosures. These enclosures are on a spectacular scale. At the Cruachain complex the great mound known as Rathcroghan Mound is surrounded by a large circular enclosure over 300m in diameter (Waddell 1985). East of this mound is another large enclosure with a barrow in its interior. These complexes are often discussed in the context of the Irish Iron Age (Raftery 1994) but their initial beginnings are uncertain.

It is interesting to note that the enclosures at Navan and Rath na Ríogh at Tara contain large mounds. At Tara in the north-east of the enclosure is the Mound of the Hostages which contains a passage tomb subsequently used as a major cemetery mound in the Bronze Age. At Navan, the hilltop henge encompasses the large mound (Site B) which covered the Forty Metre Structure which has been firmly dated to the Iron Age by means of dendrochronology (Baillie 1986). The chronological relationship with Navan Fort itself has yet to be demonstrated. What is unusual about this site, something which takes us into the realms of 'hazardous speculation', is that the Forty Metre Structure itself, if found in isolated circumstances, would be approximate to a timber circle-type henge. Similarly at Dún Ailinne was a series of palisade enclosures overlying one another, including Wailes's Phase 3 which comprised a 25m diameter single timber circle of Iron Age date.

A programme of geophysics is currently being carried out at the Cruachain complex where the large enclosure around Rathcroghan Mound has been clearly traced by geophysical techniques (Waddell & Barton 1995). Although this enclosure does not share the hilltop location of the other royal sites, the fact that it encircles a large mound would seem to indicate that it is analogous with the Navan and Tara hilltop henges. Of further interest is the apparent revelation, again through geophysics, of a multiple pit circle on the summit of the mound.

With the exception of Dún Ailinne, all of the above royal sites can be associated with other sites in the near vicinity and form components in complex archaeological landscapes. At Navan, research has shown that a late Bronze Age hillfort, Haughey's Fort (Mallory 1988), crowns the hill to the west. Numerous ring-ditches and linear earthworks have also been discovered (Hartwell 1991, 6). North-east of Haughey's Fort is the embanked pond known as the King's Stables (Lynn 1977; see below). Two possible ruined passage tombs may also form part of the complex (Warner 1986). Tara also has a significant associated landscape, both on the Hill of Tara itself and in its immediate hinterland (Newman 1997). Ring-ditches and barrows abound, and sites such as the Sloping Trenches, impressive barrows designed to 'hang over the edge' of the ridge of the hill, show that highly individualistic monuments are a vital part of such royal landscapes. A particularly noteworthy monument is the 'Banquet Hall', which has been suggested as a cursus monument, the construction of which is similar to that of the earthen embanked enclosures described above (Condit 1995). Furthermore, a long double-banked earthwork, analogous with the linear earthwork discovered at Navan, has been located at the foot of the hill separating Tara from the enclosure at Ringlestown (Condit 1993).

At Cruachain an extensive landscape extends in all directions around Rathcroghan Mound. Again this includes numerous mounds and barrows, ritual roadways and a major linear earthwork, The Mucklaghs. Also within the complex are enclosures not readily classifiable which are likely to be related to the henge class (Waddell 1985).

As mentioned above, Dún Ailinne is often perceived as being unassociated with a ritual landscape. However, it does overlook the Curragh plain to the north-west which contains a significant number of mounds, barrows and hengiform monuments (Ó Ríordáin 1950). Here on the Curragh can also be found linear earthworks called 'the Race of the Black Pig'.

Raffin Fort, Co. Meath, was considered by the excavator to be a minor 'royal' site comparable with the above but on a considerably reduced scale, representing a centre for a smaller political unit (Newman 1993a & b). Unlike the other major sites, where a neolithic presence is either ephemeral or problematical, Raffin has produced substantial evidence for neolithic activity. The primary structure on the site is a ditch of U-shaped profile as yet of uncertain diameter. This may have enclosed a multi-ring timber structure composed of at least five concentric post settings. This may be compared with the post circles at Knowth (Eogan & Roche 1993; 1994), Newgrange (Sweetman 1993; 1987) and Ballynahatty (Hartwell 1994).

RITUAL PONDS

Within the archaeological record are two sites, the King's Stables and a lesser-known site at Monknewtown, which on the basis of their morphology should be included as being directly related to henge monuments, in particular the earthen embanked enclosures, which themselves can be shown in some instances to encircle ponds and springs or to be otherwise located close to streams and rivers like many of the related British monuments. The King's Stables is the name for the ritual pond in the Navan complex excavated by Lynn (1977). The site in its original condition consisted of a man-made hollow surrounded by a bank of earth, similar in construction to the earthen embanked enclosures. This intriguing site, dated by radiocarbon to the Late Bronze Age, has been interpreted as having a 'ritual axis' in relation to Haughey's Fort, a trivallate hillfort to the west of Navan Fort, the ramparts of which have also provided dating evidence of the same period. On excavation the pond, which is fed by a small stream deliberately diverted into it, was shown to contain numerous fragments of clay spear moulds and a portion of a defaced human skull. These were interpreted as dedicatory offerings. Another possible related monument is the site located to the south-west of the Monknewtown earthen embanked enclosure excavated by Sweetman (1976). To date it remains unexcavated but bears strong similarities to the King's Stables. It consists of a circular earthen bank surrounding a waterlogged area and is noted by Moore (1987) as possibly dating to the prehistoric period. The 2m high bank of the enclosure measures 15m wide at its base and 4m wide on top. There are also traces of an external ditch, but no evidence for any entrance features. Its location in the Monknewtown 'zone' of the Brú na Bóinne complex reinforces the likelihood that the site served a ritual purpose.

There are many ponds, small lakes and bogs which are considered to have been used as locations for ritual deposition. However, few of them have been demonstrated to be either man-made or significantly modified. The King's Stables and the Monknewtown site are rare examples of totally artificial 'ritual reservoirs'. The dating evidence for the King's Stables shows that it is clearly of Late Bronze Age construction and Cooney and Grogan's interpretation of its ritual axis in relation to Haughey's Fort is persuasive, particularly in the context of the argument of ritual continuity which they felt was also demonstrated by the relationship of the Loughnashade trumpet deposit to Navan Fort. The monuments in the Monknewtown complex suggest a Late Neolithic/Early Bronze Age date and the proportions of the enclosing bank are similar to those of the earthen embanked enclosures, four of which are sited in the Brú na Bóinne complex. Also in close proximity to the earthen embanked enclosure is a mound presumed to cover a passage tomb.

The association of ponds and water bodies with hengiform monuments is quite distinctive. At Knockadoobrusna a pond is located in the south-east quadrant of the interior of the site. At Ballinphuill the embanked enclosure seems to have been constructed around a small spring which is located at the centre of the site. At Ballynacree, Co. Tipperary, the interior of the earthen embanked enclosure even to this day fills with water. Among the monuments on the Hill of Tara are at least three wells in the environs of Rath na Ríogh. Furthermore, on the terraces below Newgrange there are two ponds, at least one of which has the appearance of being shaped or modified by the hand of man. It is also interesting to note that the linear earthworks at Tara, Navan, Cruachain and 'the Race of the Black Pig' on the Curragh either run directly into waterlogged terrain or are in close proximity to such terrain. At Longstone Cullen, Co. Tipperary, there are a number of natural ponds occupying hollows in the nearby undulating terrain. The site overlooks the 'Golden Bog of Cullen' where, from the seventeenth century onwards, numerous finds of gold and other objects were found during peat-cutting and reclamation. Also located close to a natural pond is the low-lying Tonefortes site in Co. Sligo.

Excavated evidence points to the presence of clays at Grange and at Monknewtown. While the primary purpose of importing the clay into the interior of these sites may have been to provide an artificial 'floor', it is interesting to speculate that clay may also have been selected for its water retention properties. The broken pottery at Grange in particular may be evidence that containers of 'ritual liquids' may have been deposited in an already watery environment. It should also be noted that many of the earthen embanked enclosures identified from aerial photography have been noticed because of the differential vegetation, reeds and flaggers which now grow on the sites' waterlogged interiors, perhaps not just a by-product of the removal of the topsoil in the interior to construct the bank but a deliberate attempt to retain water within the enclosure.

CONCLUSIONS

As can be seen from the above survey, a great variety of monuments in Ireland can be encompassed within the henge category. Major problems are the lack of excavation, scarcity of dating evidence, and regrettably the absence of publication, in particular of the royal sites. There is no doubt that further hengiform monuments will be identified in the course of fieldwork and aerial photographic analysis. What is interesting is that some of the recent discoveries fit the patterns observed in previously identified sites. The distribution is widespread but with a clear tendency to occur in focal complexes of other ritual monuments. The variation in size of the earthen embanked enclosures outside the Boyne Valley may reflect smaller contemporary communities or are possibly associated with smaller-scale ritual monuments of a later period. While few sites have been excavated it is clear that a number were in use throughout the prehistoric period, with the Iron Age timber circles, in particular, echoing the form and associations of their Late Neolithic counterparts. Interesting also is the grouping of henges of the same type and scale such as at Friarstown and Kilbrew. More knowledge of the chronology of these variant monuments is needed to understand the grouping of henges, such as the relationship between Rath Maeve and Rath na Ríogh on Tara.

The re-use of sites as places of gathering and inauguration also displays the longevity of ritual association of some of the complexes attested in the earliest historical documents. Such continuity would appear to be less apparent in Britain, other than the construction of a number of Christian churches in or adjacent to a henge or stone circle (Burl 1976, 13). In Ireland it is also interesting to speculate that the henge complexes with their related monuments may point to other, later, gathering and inauguration sites which have not found their way into the surviving historical record, as has been suggested for Raffin Fort, Co. Meath (Newman 1993). Perhaps prehistoric archaeology can point the way to other minor 'royal sites' in terms of their antecedents.

The further discussion of hilltop henges will lead to a better understanding of the relationship of hillforts with cairns in their interiors, many of which are considered to cover passage tombs. Upland henges are not a feature of the British landscape with two notable exceptions: the Priddy Circles in the Mendips in Somerset (Burl 1970, 12) and Arbor Low and the Bull Ring in Derbyshire (Burl 1970, 16). British causewayed enclosures in some cases in hilltop situations have been interpreted as the precursors of henge monuments, the latter assuming some of their functions. Potential and proven henges in Ireland do appear in more cases to occupy upland situations. Upland early neolithic sites such as Donegore (Mallory & Hartwell 1984) and Lyles Hill (Evans 1953) may provide antecedents for such hilltop ceremonial enclosures.

Finally, what must be stressed in the Irish situation is the location of wells and ponds within and close to henges, in particular the earthen embanked enclosures, which project back into prehistory what is normally considered to be a feature of Celtic ritual. This is a subject to which all students of henge-like structures might address themselves.

CHAPTER FIVE

COLOUR IN PREHISTORIC ARCHITECTURE

FRANCES LYNCH

The last few decades have seen an increasing appreciation of the aesthetic qualities of ancient architecture, not just in the sun-drenched world of marble columns but even in the silhouettes of unhewn boulders glimpsed through native mists. Aubrey Burl's work on the British stone circles has done much to foster this new view and has increased our understanding of the sophistication of their builders, so it gives me the greatest pleasure to offer him this small lateral comment on an aspect of design which has seldom been discussed in this context.

The physical form of monuments of all kinds has long been a major preoccupation of archaeologists who have studied their morphology, development and change in an effort to extract from them some understanding of their history and of their purpose. A concern with their setting within their contemporary landscape is a feature of more recent writing which tries to encompass both the built structure and the natural setting as a single human artefact designed to reflect and to influence social and cultural behaviour. Some of these attempts to look into the soul of prehistoric man seem more successful than others and my ambitions in this chapter are much more modest.

The impact of these monuments within their landscape has largely been considered in grey and white terms. Perhaps, like the architecture of the mid-twentieth century which, it is said, was designed to look good in the black and white photographs of *The Architects' Journal*, this monochrome viewpoint is the product of the fact that the monuments are all weathered and grass grown as we see them today, their effect softened by the passing millennia.

When new, chalk mounds, like the gleaming castles shown in thirteenth-century miniatures and seen in reality at white-plastered Conwy, must have been startling and arresting; even grey stone, when fresh and unweathered, can stand out to challenge the passer-by. This was vividly brought home to me on first seeing the reconstructed Platform Cairn in the Brenig Valley from a nearby hilltop. Before and during excavation this monument had seemed positively self-effacing from nearby, a neatly built but flat low platform no more than half a metre high (Lynch 1993, 107). When reconstructed, with unweathered stones formerly in the lower levels of the cairn used on the surface, it shone like some alien spacecraft!

Such effects, of course, are automatic, an inevitable result of using certain materials which, as in the case of chalk mounds, may be not a matter of choice but of necessity. The effect would certainly have been welcomed, for the careful positioning of monuments shows that their builders intended them to be seen and seen, one imagines, from some distance. Again the Brenig Valley can provide some evidence of this: here the turf barrows were each capped with a layer of pale clay providing contrast with the moorland background and emphasising to those living in the valley below the presence of the protective cemetery (Lynch 1993, 48, 84). Ploughing on other barrows on Hiraethog shows that this pale clay cap was a regular feature of barrows in that region.

The presence in significant positions within and around a monument of conspicuous stones like quartz, which retains its whiteness even today, demonstrates that colour could be used in a detailed and deliberate way, the product of careful planning. The best-known examples of such use must be the black and white stone wall at Newgrange (O'Kelly 1982), the great quartz blocks at the entrance to Castleruddery embanked stone circle in Co. Wicklow and the white pillar in the centre of Boscawen Un, Cornwall (Burl 1976, Fig. 41; 124). There are, however, many other less spectacular examples, such as the concentration of shattered quartz in the semi-circle cairn at Brenig 51 (Lynch 1993, 110), scattered on the top of the ring cairn at Cefn Caer Euni II (Lynch 1986a, 95) and at numerous neolithic, Bronze Age and even early Christian graves, as noted by Fleure and Neeley in their discussion of those found at Cashtal yn Ard in the Isle of Man (1936, 388–9).

These examples are the traditional black and white effects, frequently commented upon. But, just as the original polychrome surfaces in classical, medieval and renaissance buildings and sculpture are now being restored in a search for authenticity, and are being welcomed by a changed taste, it is surely time to consider whether a more colourful veneer can be given also to prehistory.

Shortly after I had begun to prepare this chapter an article appeared drawing attention to the red and white stones used in the construction of Clyde tombs on Arran (Jones 1997). These stones are used in the chambers, covered by the cairn and therefore dark inside, making colour variation difficult to see. Disappointingly, the sparkling mica- and garnet-encrusted stones of Baldoon must also have languished beneath a covering cairn (Henshall 1972, 566). It is suggested by Jones that such colours had a symbolic rather than aesthetic role. The fact that several megalithic chambers were built of stones brought from some distance away even though adequate rock, superficially indistinguishable, was available close by might reinforce the idea that symbolic factors were paramount in the selection of building stone (Patton 1992; Kalb 1996).

These considerations are not this chapter's primary concern, however; instead, it aims to look at the use of coloured stone for visible artistic effect, without prejudicing the notion that there might have been an additional – or even primary – symbolic role. Attention will focus therefore upon the external features of neolithic tombs and on Bronze Age monuments where the structural stones remain visible.

Whereas Newgrange is strikingly black and white, its quartz wall embellished with dark Newry granite (granodiorite), possibly arranged in geometric patterns, the mound at Knowth was decorated not only with quartz and granodiorite but also with blue and white striped siltstone cobbles. These colourful cobbles were collected from near Dundalk and were found near the entrance to the eastern and western tombs (Eogan 1986, 48, 65; Mitchell 1992). It is not clear exactly how they were used but evidently they were chosen for their attractive colour.

The effective use of colour and texture is found at several significant points at Knowth. Circular settings outside the entrances to the eastern and western tombs in the main mound and to Satellite 4 consist of carefully matched smooth pebble kerbs with rough quartz cobbling in the centre. Whatever they were used for, great care had been taken to create the contrast of texture and colour at this focal point.

The decorated stones at both sites rely mainly on the play of light and shade for their effect. Inside, this could be manipulated by torches; outside, around the kerb, this would be more difficult to contrive: some colour differentiation between pecked and unpecked stone may have aided visibility. At Knowth, where the decoration is often formed with broad shallow pecking, the colour distinction could have been quite strong. Since the kerb has been protected from weathering during the last two millennia or more, one might have expected this to be visible today. However, a trawl through my colour photographs has not produced good examples.

Passage graves in northern Iberia have, however, made extensive use of colour even in their internal decoration (Shee 1974; Devignes 1992). The colours used are black, white and red, this last in several distinct shades, the paint being produced by a mixture of ochre, charcoal, kaolin and eggwhite. Normally a white background would be applied to the whole of the stone to provide an enhanced contrast; occasionally the background was entirely red. The majority of the designs are in red but black may be used to echo the patterns, as at Antelas (Albuquerque e Castro *et al.* 1957). The painting often covers all the stones of the chamber and gives the impression of a tapestry-hung room. This effect suggests two things; first, the problem of visibility may be irrelevant since the decoration was for the benefit of the dead and, secondly, the houses of the living may have been equally colourfully embellished with real hangings or painted walls. Unfortunately such elusive evidence has not been recognised – nor is it likely to survive – in damper northern climes where the demonstration of an interest in colour has to be based on geological variation and selection.

One neolithic monument where the use of variously coloured stones on the exterior is clearly the result of careful and deliberate planning is the Jardin aux Moines in the Forêt de Broceliande, Brittany (for colour view see Briard 1987, 78). Here the long rectangular mound is bounded by a kerb in which slabs of red schist alternate with blocks of white quartz which must have been brought from at least 3km away. The mound was built in three segments; the quartz was used in all three but the carefully contrived alternation of colour belongs to the Late Neolithic phase.

Excavators of Bronze Age cairns seldom comment on the appearance of the stones used, but Oliver Davies, working at Carnagat, Co. Tyrone, makes specific note of the variety of colours among the stones used in that small monument (Davies 1938). These are the small stones of the cairn and it is not clear how obvious this kaleidoscope would have been to the passer-by. Similarly the use of small pieces of pink granite to infill the grey kerbed cairns at Cullerlie, Aberdeenshire, may be predominantly a matter of availability (Kilbride Jones 1935). Such assortments may represent a ritual need to gather contributions from many communities or localities, as is argued for the megalithic tombs constructed of varied rocks and the mounds composed of differing soils, rather than a simple enhancement of the appearance of the cairn. Both concerns, no doubt, could have been operating simultaneously.

The use of different coloured rocks to enhance the appearance and probably also the symbolic power of a monument would seem to be a regular feature of religious architecture in north-east

Scotland. The Clava cairns and ring cairns and the recumbent stone circles of Aberdeenshire have several architectural refinements, such as the careful gradation of the height of the kerb and circle stones and an unusual consistency of orientation, which indicate that they were most meticulously planned and built (Henshall 1963, 12–39; Burl 1976, 160–90). Consequently it is not surprising that they should also exhibit the most sophisticated geological selection for colour variation.

The significant use of white quartz in the platforms around the Clava cairns has been noted by many writers, including Aubrey Burl himself (1976, 164) but recent work by Richard Bradley at Clava has added a further element of deliberate colour choice to emphasise the religious content of the monuments. He has suggested a link between the orientation of the group as a whole, and of the individual entrances towards the sunset, and the position of red quarried sandstone blocks. These occur in the chamber walls facing the entrance and might be illuminated by the sun, despite the roof, and in the south-western arc of the circles and the kerbs. They contrast with the glacial erratics, grey, white or quartz-veined, which face the sunrise at the back of the monument. The validity of this symbolism, with the warm red stones picking up the glow of the declining sun and the cooler, shining boulders reflecting the dawn, is believed to be reinforced by the observation that the code is most strictly adhered to in the focal, south-westerly cairn of the group (Bradley 1996, 142 & pers. com.).

The Aberdeenshire recumbent stone circles which have been so extensively studied by Aubrey Burl (1970) share many of the architectural refinements of the Clava cairns, including this interest in the colour of the stones used, though I would hesitate to suggest a motivation for their builders' concern in this matter. The monuments consist of a circle of spaced upright stones often set in a low bank and usually graded in height, with a large recumbent stone between the two tallest stones in the ring. This distinctive arrangement of a huge, carefully levelled recumbent stone with tall flankers invariably lies on the south-western arc of the circle. Frequently the centre is occupied by a low ring cairn which may be linked to the recumbent stone and its flankers. The recumbent stones are often exceptionally large and it has been noted that they have frequently been brought to the site from some distance away. This effort has normally been explained by the need to find a stone of appropriate size and shape (Burl 1976, 174). While not denying that size and shape must have been very significant in these most carefully designed monuments, one can add another factor of important variation – colour – to the considerations of the builders.

It is notable that in ten out of the twenty-three circles where I can find the relevant information (Thom & Burl 1980) the recumbent stone is a different colour from those of the circle. Where this is the case – Tyrebagger, Garrol Wood, Tomnaverie, Raes of Clune, Whitehill and Auchquhorthies – the circle stones are of red or pinkish 'granite' and the recumbent is grey or whitish. At Auchquhorthies the recumbent and its flankers are all three grey; at other sites, such as the Mains of Hatton where the flankers are quartz or quartz-veined, the flankers differ in colour impact from the recumbent stone which they frame. At Balaquhain which is best known for its tall quartz outlier, the recumbent stone, which was brought from some distance, is very pale grey, while the flankers are noticeably darker. Such distinctions must have been much more striking when the stone was newly quarried.

At Castle Fraser (Fig. 5.1) the recumbent and its flankers are of the same grey, quartz-veined stone and the circle contains both grey and red stones (Thom & Burl 1980, 199). The circle has been damaged and it is now incomplete but the three remaining stones on the east side show an

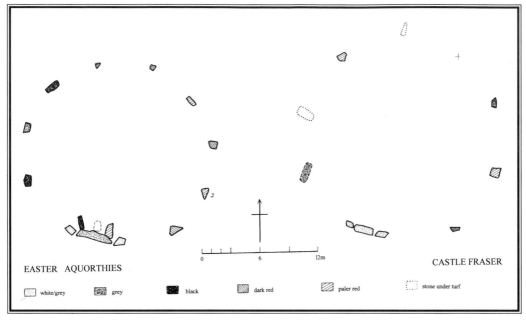

5.1 Plans of Easter Aquorthies and Castle Fraser showing colour variation. (Stones only shown, based on Thom & Burl 1980)

alternating arrangement of grey–red–grey which could have continued round to the remaining red stone on the north-west. However, if the spacing is regular, the pattern cannot have been maintained on the west side.

A better example of more complex colour patterns is Easter Aquorthies (Thom & Burl 1980, 163). This is a very well-preserved site where the circle is complete and the recumbent has two tall flankers and also two horizontal blocks projecting from it towards the centre of the circle (Fig. 5.1). I was lucky enough to visit this monument shortly after a latex mould had been made from it to re-create part of the circle for the *Symbols of Power* exhibition in Edinburgh. The lichen and dirt of ages had been peeled away with the latex and the stones were restored to their original glowing colours. This experience helped me to appreciate the striking effect that colour could have and to recognise the sophisticated way in which the different stones had been deployed here. The recumbent is grey; the two flanking stones are a whitish grey. The western projecting stone is black, veined with quartz; its eastern partner is a pink granite. The stones of the circle on the western side are alternately grey and black; on the eastern side they are pink, alternating in shade in the same way and including at the cardinal point a block of gleaming jasper.

This playing with colour is not obligatory. At Yonder Bognie all the surviving stones are the same material (Thom & Burl 1980, 185) and this must be true of the majority of sites. Significant colour variation is not as consistently found as the gradation in stone height, the horizontality of the recumbent or its orientation, so, if it is a matter of symbolism, as distinct from an architectural *jeu d'esprit*, it is not one that is essential to the religious function of the monument. Though we can never confidently interpret the motivation for

Recumbent stone and flankers, Easter Aquorthies, 1985.

such choices it is important that we should recognise them and, in doing so, increase our appreciation of the sophisticated aesthetic which lies behind the best architecture of all periods.

ACKNOWLEDGEMENTS

I am most grateful to Ian Shepherd for checking details of Aberdeenshire circles for me, to Richard Bradley for giving me information from his current excavations at Clava and to Aubrey Burl who, unbeknown to himself, has provided material for this article by generously over the years giving me photographs of circles and other monuments.

CHAPTER SIX

HINDWELL AND THE NEOLITHIC PALISADED SITES OF BRITAIN AND IRELAND

ALEX GIBSON

INTRODUCTION

Aubrey Burl's enthusiastic research, lectures and writings have always reminded his audience that in Prehistory we are dealing with the material remains of people. These remains range from the smallest of portable artefacts to field monuments of massive proportions. Each has its own story to tell about its creators and users. The smallest microlith and the largest hillfort each equally represents a tangible manifestation of the society responsible for them. Whether it be small open stone circles or large enclosed henge monuments, Aubrey Burl has always made us aware that they are the arenas for human ritual, religion and ceremony: they serve the specific purposes of the communities to which they belong – the Stonehenge *People* (Burl 1987, my emphasis). These less tangible aspects of prehistoric life, their meanings and attendant ceremonies, are more difficult to understand but, to their creators, are as important as the monuments, perhaps even more so.

As well as movers and shapers of large quantities of rock and earth, neolithic craftsmen were competent carpenters. A large variety of timber monuments are becoming recognised, some of strikingly intricate design (Wainwright & Longworth 1971; Behrens 1981; Gibson 1994; Becker 1996) involving complex ritual (Burl 1991b; Gibson 1994; Pollard 1992; 1995). Other sites, less informative about their specific functions, clearly involved substantial effort in their constructions and attest at the very least to the deep conviction of their creators. Palisaded enclosures of the later Neolithic fall into this category and it is these sites which form the subject of this chapter.

In 1994, during routine aerial photography for the Clwyd-Powys Archaeological Trust, a large arc of ditch (Powys Sites & Monuments Register No.19376; NGR SO250607) was discovered showing as a crop-mark in ripening barley (Gibson 1995; 1996). It lay on Hindwell Farm, in the Radnor Valley, Powys, and it described an arc from a circle of *c.*400m diameter (Fig. 6.1). The sheer size and shape of the monument immediately suggested a prehistoric date, and invited comparison with sites of the British, Irish and western European Neolithic (Palmer 1976; Burgess *et al.* 1988; Mallory 1993; Jeunesse 1996). Accordingly geophysical survey and a small excavation were mounted to investigate the nature of the site and to try to recover dating material from secure contexts.

6.1 First aerial photograph of the Hindwell palisaded enclosure. (Photograph by
Alex Gibson, by permission of the Clwyd-Powys Archaeological Trust. Copyright reserved.)

This excavation (Gibson in prep.) proved the site to be a palisaded enclosure comprising closely spaced intersecting post-pits a little over 2m deep. The excavated post-pits each contained a single oak upright measuring 0.7–0.8m in diameter (Fig. 6.2). The posts had been inserted from the outside of the enclosure and their erection was facilitated by the excavation of post-ramps, 4m long, allowing access to each pit. All four posts had been partially carbonised prior to their erection. The lack of *in situ* burning indicated that this had taken place outside the pit, at an unknown location, and was presumably done to provide some waterproofing to the post. Each postpipe, therefore, was visible as a cylinder of fine-fractioned silt ringed by intermittent charcoal within the replaced gravel filling of the post-pit (Fig. 6.2).

In 1995 further aerial photography produced evidence for a ditch of similar character in the field known as Berrymeadow at SO257607 (Fig. 6.3). This ditch appeared to be coming out from beneath the modern track which described a peculiar curve at this point. It was regarded as a distinct probability that the track fossilised the line of the earthwork and that the Berrymeadow ditch was indeed part of the same site. If this were the case, then the ditch described an oval some 800m x 400m. This hypothesis was proven by a second season of geophysical survey and excavation in 1996.

Subsequent air photography and geophysical survey in 1996 located further arcs of ditch comprising the southern perimeter of the enclosure, with the result that almost 75 per cent of the circumference can now be traced (Fig. 6.3). The site is now known to have had a circumference in the region of 2.3km and to have enclosed some 34ha.

6.2 The area of the Hindwell palisaded enclosure. Part of the perimeter is showing in clover within grass to the lower right of the photograph. (Photograph by Alex Gibson, by permission of the Clwyd–Powys Archaeological Trust. Copyright reserved.)

Four radiocarbon dates were obtained from the excavations on Hindwell II. These dates are statistically similar and may be combined to produce a date of *c.* 2700 cal BC (Gibson in prep.), a date comparable with the Grooved Ware activity located below a barrow mound at Upper Ninepence (Gibson 1995) some 500m to the north and conforming to the broad trend of dates from late neolithic palisaded enclosures (Gibson 1996). From an admittedly small sample, the radiocarbon evidence seems to suggest a developmental sequence of these sites from widely spaced post hole examples through close-set post hole types like Hindwell, and finally to palisades of contiguous posts such as at Mount Pleasant (Fig. 6.4). This sequence occupies approximately a millennium from 3000 to 2000 cal BC (Gibson 1996, Fig. 4).

6.3 Hindwell palisaded enclosure: post pipes during excavation. (Photograph by Alex Gibson, by permission of the Clwyd-Powys Archaeological Trust. Copyright reserved.)

PALISADED SITES OF BRITAIN AND IRELAND

Typology

There are three main types of palisaded enclosure in neolithic Britain (Fig. 6.5). The first type consists of enclosures with a perimeter of individual post holes such as at Walton, Radnorshire (St Joseph 1980; Gibson 1996); at Meldon Bridge, Peeblesshire (Burgess 1976); Forteviot, Perthshire (Harding & Lee 1987, 409–11); Dunragit, Dumfries (Mercer 1993); Newgrange, Co. Meath (Sweetman 1987) and Ballynahatty, Co. Down (Hartwell 1991; 1994). The Aubrey holes at Stonehenge, if indeed they originally held posts, would also fit into this group. The site is admittedly small, at under 90m in diameter, but the likely association with Stonehenge I (Cleal *et al.* 1995) agrees with the early dates for individual post hole palisades.

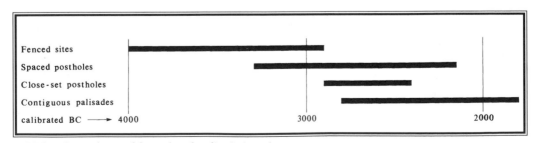

6.4 The chronology of fenced and palisaded enclosures.

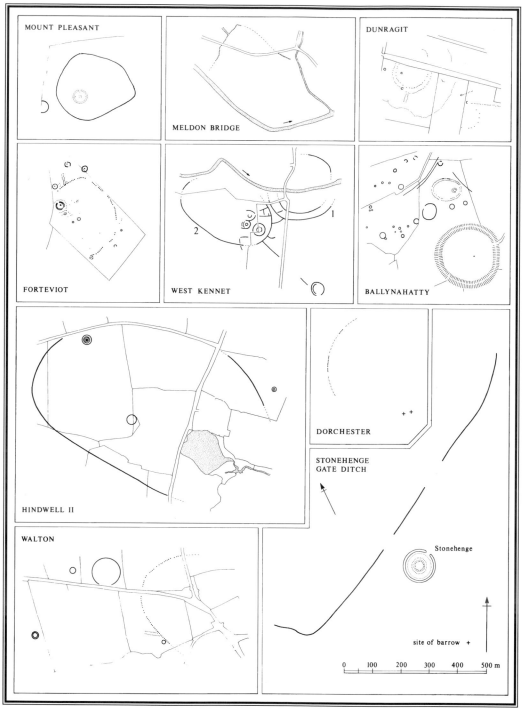

6.5 Comparative plans of palisaded enclosures.

The second type are those with perimeters composed of closely spaced postpits like Hindwell and Greyhound Yard, Dorchester, Dorset (Woodward *et al.* 1993). The third type comprises sites with perimeters with uprights set in bedding trenches such as at the Palisade (or Gate) Ditch, Stonehenge (Walker & Montague in Cleal *et al.* 1996); West Kennet 1 and 2 (Whittle 1991; 1992); Orsett, Essex (Hedges & Buckley 1978); Mount Pleasant, Dorset (Wainwright 1979); Haddenham, Cambridgeshire (Evans 1988); Knowth, Co. Meath (Eogan 1984, 219); Donegore, Co. Antrim (Mallory 1993) and possibly Lyles Hill in the same county (Simpson & Gibson 1989) though the exact nature of this latter palisade cannot yet be determined.

The Orsett, Haddenham, Knowth, Lyles Hill and Donegore sites differ greatly in their construction and date from the others. They comprise comparatively small palisades with narrow posts standing up to a maximum of 3m high (Fig. 6.6). They may be termed fenced sites to distinguish them from the larger monuments. They are associated with earlier neolithic monuments and ceramics and thus pre-date the sites under consideration here. An exception to this rule is the outer palisade from Lyles Hill (Simpson & Gibson 1989) which has a late neolithic date. Such a small portion of this site was excavated, however, that the true nature of this feature remains unresolved.

The association of palisades or fences with causewayed enclosures will be considered again below, but suffice it to say that the Aubrey Holes at Stonehenge are also broadly associated with an essentially causewayed ditch, while at Dunragit the outer palisade has a markedly scalloped effect. Perhaps these sites provide the link between causewayed enclosures and the palisades of the ensuing period, thus supporting the tentative typology already suggested (Gibson 1996).

Size

In terms of size, the areas of these enclosures can at best be estimated since the only sites with fully known circumferences are Ballynahatty, Forteviot and Mount Pleasant (Fig. 6.7). Of the rest, about 75 per cent of the Walton perimeter is known and the area can therefore be estimated; this is true also of West Kennet 1 and 2, and Dunragit, where the perimeter can be rounded off to provide a rough estimate. Dunragit has been broken into two sites: an outer pit circuit with a scalloped effect and no entrance corridor, and an inner site marked by a more regular double palisade; the extent of both enclosures may be guessed from the aerial photographs. At Walton and Meldon Bridge the riverine location of each site suggests that the river course was utilised in closing the site. The perimeter of Greyhound Yard is less certain but, when combined with similar pits found in Church Street in 1982/3, the area of the enclosure can be tentatively estimated (Woodward *et al.* 1993, 30). The Gate Ditch at Stonehenge is neither dated nor known in its entirety and remains something of an enigma.

These estimations show that the average area for neolithic palisaded sites (excluding Hindwell) is approximately 4.5ha but that there is a large variation in the areas of individual sites (Fig. 6.7). At over 34ha, Hindwell is far bigger than any other neolithic palisaded site yet known in Britain and it even dwarfs the causewayed enclosures (Palmer 1976) of which Haddenham, covering some 8.5ha, is one of the largest (Evans 1988). Greyhound Yard and the Gate Ditch at Stonehenge remain rivals to Hindwell. The estimated area of Greyhound Yard is conservative for it presupposes a circular design. The Church Street and Greyhound Yard arcs, however, do not share a common centre (Woodward *et al.* 1993, fig 172) and thus the true outline may be more oval, like Hindwell's. At the Gate Ditch, Stonehenge, some 1.3km of ditch have been traced but this is essentially a straight line running south–

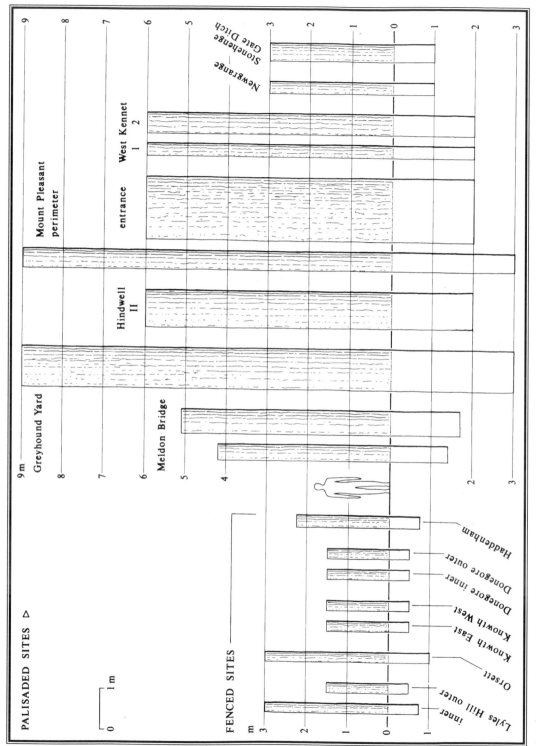

6.6 Comparative post size-estimates for fenced and palisaded sites.

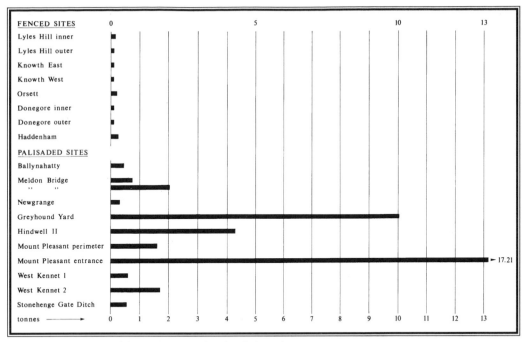

6.7 Estimated areas of fenced sites and palisaded enclosures.

west–north–east with a return at each end. Whether the site represents an enclosure or an elaborate screen is a matter for debate (Cleal *et al*. 1996, 482). For comparative purposes, it is worth pointing out that the internal area of the hillfort at Maiden Castle is only some 17.22ha (Sharples 1991, 38).

Despite its huge area, the posts at Hindwell would not appear to have been as imposing as those from Greyhound Yard or Mount Pleasant (Fig. 6.6) but nevertheless they compare favourably with the other sites' and completely dwarf the posts of the earlier fenced enclosures. The palisades at Lyles Hill, Newgrange, Knowth, Haddenham and Orsett are much flimsier than those at the other sites, even allowing for erring on the side of generosity in estimating the post dimensions, and this further suggests a difference in function. The Newgrange site is problematic in its interpretation since many post holes were later reused for other purposes of ritual deposition.

In terms of weight, Mercer (1981) gives the weight for 1cu. m of green oak as approximately 1.07 tonnes. Using the 1:3 ratio for the below ground:above ground lengths of the posts and by using data from preserved postpipes, the volume of each post may be estimated (Fig. 6.8). For the sake of comparison, it is assumed that all the timbers involved were indeed oak, an assumption confirmed where the information survives. These calculations demonstrate that fenced sites are remarkably uniform in their selection of posts, but that palisaded sites show considerable variation – ranging from 0.3 tonnes at Newgrange to 10 tonnes at Greyhound Yard. The remarkable entrance posts at Mount Pleasant, almost 2m in diameter and set 2m deep in the ground, are estimated at a staggering 17 tonnes; the other palisade posts, at 1.61 tonnes, are far more modest.

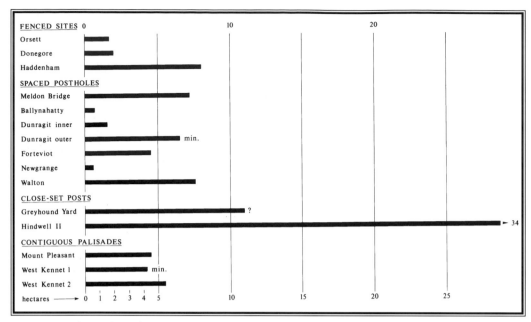

6.8 Estimated weights of posts utilised at the fenced sites and palisaded enclosures.

Reconstruction and Function

In the study of the remains of palisaded sites, we are dealing with a small fraction of the original data. The majority of the sites survive as crop-marks, therefore any associated earthwork evidence has been obliterated. Even if these sites were not earthwork-associated, agricultural degradation may well have obliterated shallow structural features complementing the more massive posts. Reconstruction, therefore, beyond the minimalist approach of free-standing timbers, must rely greatly on speculation.

Sites with contiguous timbers clearly form a solid barrier. This is less certain at the post hole sites but Meldon Bridge provided evidence for more slender pairs of intermediate posts suggesting extra supports for some sort of planking closing off the gaps between the uprights. So even here, where widely spaced posts were encountered, a solid barrier may be envisaged. The similarity between the Meldon Bridge, Forteviot, Walton and Dunragit sites may invite a similar reconstruction. If this is accepted, then at either end of the proposed sequence we have sites with solid barriers. It may be logical, therefore, to envisage the middle sites in the sequence, the sites like Hindwell with close-set post holes, as supporting similarly solid barriers through the use of horizontal planking.

These late neolithic palisaded sites would therefore appear to be enclosures in the strict sense: solid barriers enclosing often substantial areas. Movement in and out of these areas seems to have been severely restricted and rigidly controlled. At Meldon Bridge, Walton, Dunragit and Forteviot the entrance was formed by a post hole corridor (Fig. 6.5). Except at Dunragit, these do not emanate radially from the circumference, but are skewed at an angle to produce a peculiarly asymmetrical feature. These entrances are unlikely to have been defensive since it is not immediately obvious how they would have been defended. An in-turned entrance passage would have provided the defenders with an opportunity to harass attackers before they entered the enclosure proper, forcing them, in effect, to run the gauntlet. An external entrance passage would have simply presented the attackers with an opportunity to burn it down. At Mount Pleasant, the monumental gateposts also indicate that entrance to (and exit from) the enclosure was strictly controlled (Fig. 6.5). While this entrance could certainly have been defended from above, the size of the posts providing ample opportunity for an overhead internal platform, there is no direct evidence to suggest that it was.

Despite their apparent differences, the entrances of the Meldon Bridge-type enclosures and Mount Pleasant are indeed quite similar in that they would only permit single-file passage through the entrance. Indeed, despite its monumentality, the eastern entrance at Mount Pleasant was only some 0.7m wide. People seeking entry to the enclosure, therefore, would have to queue for entry and process in orderly fashion. That the Meldon Bridge-type entrances are not overtly defensive suggests that the entrants were not hostile but were welcome or at least tolerated.

The strange angle of the Meldon Bridge-type passages and the narrowness of the Mount Pleasant entrance are also similar in the fact that they severely restrict visual, as well as physical, access to the interior. In this respect it is interesting that Mount Pleasant, Ballynahatty, and possibly Forteviot contain hengiform monuments. Timber circles are present at Mount Pleasant and Ballynahatty and unexcavated pit circles are visible on the aerial photographs of Forteviot (Darvill 1996) and Hindwell. It has been demonstrated that timber circles appear to have involved restriction of access both physical and visual: the screens at Durrington Walls (Wainwright & Longworth 1971), the restricted sightlines in Woodhenge (Cunnington 1929; Burl 1991b), controlled access at Mount Pleasant (Pollard 1992) and the evidence for planking at some timber circles (Gibson 1994). Internal henge monuments are visible on the aerial photographs of Forteviot (Darvill 1996) and Dunragit (Mercer 1993). Henges, like palisades and timber circles, may define areas to which only a privileged few were admitted (*inter alia* Burl 1991b; Topping 1992) and since they do not share the same entrance orientation as the palisade, it suggests that visual access is further restricted and that visitors would not have been able to take a direct route to the inner monument; perhaps processing round the monument in a build-up to the final ritual.

Much has been written about the supposed festivals and rituals that may have taken place in henge monuments and timber circles, and it is not the intention to repeat those here. It is more important to point out that palisaded sites seem not only to have restricted access to their interiors but also to have *contained* sites offering further control and restrictions. In this respect Avebury and Durrington Walls bear close comparison with palisaded sites despite their different means of enclosure. We can thus envisage a grading of privilege within the community: those who were excluded; those who were allowed within the enclosure, perhaps only at certain times; those who were allowed into the inner enclosures and, finally, those who controlled access (see Chapter 16).

Construction

It is these power-bearing individuals who must have provided the impetus for the construction of these spectacular monuments. The size of the timbers involved has already been discussed but these numbers and statistics are in themselves meaningless unless translated into terms of human effort.

At Hindwell the spacing of the posts in the two excavated sections indicates that there were three posts every 5m; therefore, in a monument with a circumference of 2.3km, almost 1,400 posts would have been needed to complete the perimeter. Each post would have weighed about 4.3 tonnes, involving the manhandling of some 6,000 tonnes of freshly felled oak. Startin (1978) has calculated the labour involved in the cutting and felling of timbers for LBK houses and as the timber and technology was broadly the same, we may safely use his figures here.

Each post-pit was large enough only for a single individual while another could have been employed on the post ramp. Using antler to loosen the gravel and scapulae to remove it may have taken in the region of two days per pit – a figure reached independently by experiment at Ballynahatty (inf. B. Hartwell & B. Dunlop). The spoil would not have been moved far from the pit as it was quickly backfilled as packing around the post, but as the pit deepened so the spoil heap would have grown and two people may well have been present to minimise slippage and to manage the dump. Accordingly each pit would have accommodated four people for two days. The backfilling of the pit and post-ramp would have taken two people approximately two days, though it may well have been more rapid using larger numbers. With 1,410 pits being involved, digging and backfilling the pits would therefore have involved a total of 16,920 work days.

The trees involved were about 0.8m in diameter. Startin argues that a 0.3m diameter tree could be felled in approximately 20 minutes, but that this time would increase proportionately for larger timbers. A conservative estimate for an 0.8m diameter bole might therefore be two hours; assuming a ten-hour day, five trees could be felled per day, each requiring two axemen. Thus 1,400 trees or boles might occupy two people for 280 days, making a total of 560 workdays. The debarking and trimming of the tree might take three times as long as the felling, or 1,680 workdays.

Whether the trees were local or imported remains to be discovered. Assuming that they were local, then they would not have been transported far. Nevertheless, each timber weighed some 4 tonnes and, even assuming that oxen were used as traction, driving and hitching teams would have been needed. An absolute minimum may have been five people working for one day per tree to transport it to site, giving a total of 7,050 days. The same team and the same oxen may have been occupied for a similar amount of time in the erection of the posts.

Thus the erection of the main frame at Hindwell may have taken approximately 33,276 workdays. But it has been argued that these sites were intended to be solid barriers so the felling of trees for planking, the splitting of planks and the fixing of those planks to the uprights, presumably pegged, may have taken at least twice as long. In addition, ropemakers and repairers, tool sharpeners and providers, surveyors and supervisors would all have been required. Over 70,000 workdays may therefore have been involved.

The population of the Radnor basin in 2700 BC is not known. The basin is rich and fertile but may have been at least partly forested. The flint scatters suggest that settlement was largely restricted to the low ridge that bisects the valley. This small area and the exploitable land around it may well have been capable of supporting a community of 500 people (c.10 per sq. km) in scattered farmsteads. Not all members of this community would have been available for construction work, and if we assume that one in five were sufficiently able-bodied and mature to undertake this work, then a workforce of 100 people might have been available. Other tasks would still have had to be undertaken: harvesting, planting, everyday farm management and religious observance during major festivals. Many of these tasks could have been largely undertaken by the less able-bodied population – the elderly, immature and disabled – but some reliance on the fully able-bodied members of the community would still have been maintained. Weather may also have added a limiting factor to the project, particularly affecting the groundworks and log transportation. If we assume that some 200 days per year were available for the construction of Hindwell, then the entire project would have seriously committed the local population for approximately three and a half years (assuming 70,000 workdays needed and 20,000 workdays/year available). What is more intriguing is that, once completed, many of its builders may well have been excluded from it, thus ensuring the security of the secrets it contained.

THE WIDER CONTEXT

Palisaded enclosures are not restricted to Britain and Ireland. At Sarup, in Denmark, a middle-neolithic palisaded site covering some 6ha is associated with a bivallate causewayed enclosure (Andersen 1988). The palisade trench varies from 0.5 to 1.1m deep and contained posts of between 0.16 and 0.42m in diameter. These were widely spaced, averaging 0.65m apart. At Lønt, also in Denmark, a mid-neolithic palisade enclosing some 12–15ha was also associated with a double circuit of causewayed ditch (Madsen 1988). At Büdelsdorf, Denmark, the complex palisaded enclosure of some 6–7ha comprises both individual post hole and palisade trench circuits but the complexity of this site is not fully understood (Madsen 1988). Dating to the centuries prior to 3000 cal BC, these sites and their associated ditches bear closer resemblance to our causewayed enclosure sites, albeit they are rather more spectacular.

In France, too, palisades appear to be associated with causewayed enclosures (Mordant & Mordant 1988). But the largest of the French palisaded enclosures, Challignac (Charente), exceeds 18ha in area and is dated to the Artenac phase of the final Neolithic, c.2000 BC. At 2m deep and containing contiguous timbers some 0.3–0.4m in diameter, this double enclosure is more closely related in date and design to the large, Late Neolithic, British sites.

The largest neolithic palisaded enclosure so far discovered in Europe is at Urmitz, near Koblenz, Germany (Boelicke 1976); at over 60ha in area (an unknown, but presumably large amount having already been eroded by the Rhine), this dwarfs even Hindwell. The Urmitz site is associated with a double circuit of causewayed ditches and, like the French and Danish sites, is Early Neolithic in date, being associated with Michelsberg ceramics. An increasing number of ditched, probably palisaded, enclosures are coming to light in Germany through aerial photography (Meyer 1995; Braasch 1996) and are being subjected to sophisticated geophysical survey (Becker 1996). Many of these sites are producing middle neolithic artefacts and, more importantly, are being seen to enclose complex timber circles (Becker 1996). The site at Meisternthal (Niederbayern), covering between 2 and 3ha, enclosed a pit circle and an oval ditched enclosure, 46m x 37m, which had opposed entrances orientated on the equinoxes. These German enclosures, dating to the 5th millennium BC, are clearly much earlier than the British sites but the fundamental similarities are remarkable.

ACKNOWLEDGEMENTS

Information regarding palisaded enclosures was gratefully received from Claude Burnez, Barrie Hartwell, Jim Mallory, Michael Meyer and Graham Ritchie. The illustrations are from the skilled pen of Brian Williams.

CHAPTER SEVEN

TIMBER CIRCLES AT ZWOLLE, NETHERLANDS

JAN DE JONG

During and subsequent to the excavations of a Bronze Age settlement at Zwolle-Ittersumerbroek, some surprising discoveries have come to light (Clevis & Verlinde 1991; Verlinde 1993). For the first time in the Netherlands two circles, in a settlement context, have been identified and are interpreted as possible solar calendars (De Jong & Wevers 1994).

INTRODUCTION

Stone circles from the Neolithic and the Bronze Age are common in the British Isles. Archaeologists who study these stone circles, and in particular Aubrey Burl, can describe, catalogue, classify and sometimes ascribe a function to these circles on the basis of their structural remains. Furthermore, recent studies have emphasised the existence of many timber circles in Britain and Ireland (Gibson 1994).

However, when, as at Ittersumerbroek, the evidence for the circles comes from post holes within a settlement context, the interpretation becomes more complex. The excavations (and interpretation) were hindered by the strongly homogenised topsoil resulting from forestry operations, the irregular surface of the subsoil, the high level of groundwater and bad weather (Hamming 1991).

THE CIRCLES AND THEIR MEASUREMENTS

Description

A cluster of post holes came to light in Area 16 of the Zwolle-Ittersumerbroek excavations. A large number of these were variously attributed to dwellings, a cattle enclosure, granaries and sheds (Van Beek & Wevers 1993) but many unallocated post holes remained. While it was not possible to recognise any familiar structures among them, a certain patterning in two clusters of post holes was noted which suggested that we might be dealing with timber circles. Indeed, a round structure was then identified, consisting of fourteen irregularly spaced posts (Fig. 7.1).

7.1 View over the Zwolle-Ittersumerbroek site in 1992. Area 16, site of the south-west circle (black dots). (Photo: Archaeological Service Zwolle)

The distribution of the posts was such that various circles with irregularly spaced posts on their circumference could be constructed on the basis of an average distance from a hypothetical centre. In other words, there were so many post holes that it would have been possible statistically to identify round patterns anywhere. Whether this pattern consisted of six or fifteen posts would in the first instance be irrelevant. Nor is the diameter very significant: the literature presents evidence of an enormous variation in circle diameters. The suggestion that there might have been at Ittersumerbroek a circle consisting of fourteen irregularly spaced posts, with a diameter of c.11m and an unmarked centre, was at first hardly convincing.

However, 15m away, on the circle's (south-east/north-west) axis, a second circle was found (Fig. 7.2), which probably also consisted of fourteen posts. (Two posts are missing from both the south-east and the north-west circle.) Of the north-west circle, one post hole had been disturbed by a pit and the second by a post hole of a later granary. Of the south-east circle one post was situated outside the excavated area and again one post hole had been disturbed by a large pit. That we are probably dealing with intentionally made constructions becomes clear when we shift the plan of the south-east circle along the axis that connects the two centres, and project it on to the north-west circle. Then the two structures are found to be so similar in design that coincidence must be ruled out. Of the fourteen pairs of post holes that occupy corresponding positions on the circles, nine turn out to overlap completely or partially, while in one case they are touching and in another they are just 0.3m apart. The three other pairs are incomplete.

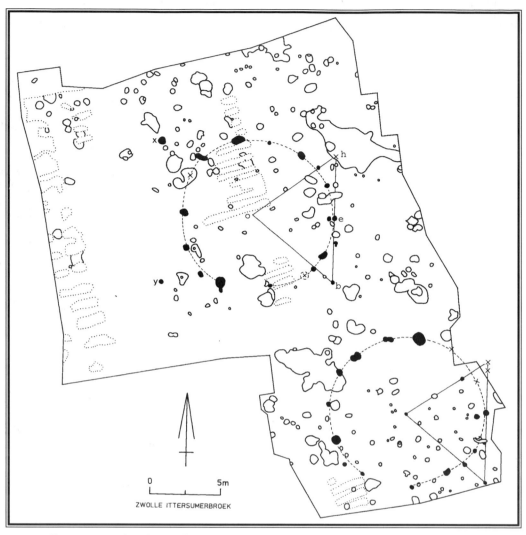

7.2 Zwolle-Ittersumerbroek. Circles with a possible calendrical function.

The most striking points of similarity are:

1. both circles have a diameter of 11m (measured from the post hole centres);
2. between the southern posts there is an extra wide space, and the next gap (clockwise) is extra narrow;
3. the pattern of the distances between the posts is very similar (Table 7.1).

The differences are:

1. the south-east circle has a post hole at its centre; no centre point was found in the north-west circle;
2. the axis of the south-east circle is rotated about 4° with respect to the north-west circle.

Table 7.1 Distance in metres from the centre of the circle to the centres of the post holes. Centre = O; gap 1–14 is southern entrance.

	SE circle	NW circle	Difference
O-1	5.30	5.30	–
O-2	5.70	5.75	– 0.05
O-3	5.50	5.50	–
O-4	5.60	5.30	+ 0.30
O-5	5.50	5.50	–
O-6	5.50	5.50	–
O-7	5.50	5.50	–
O-8	5.50	5.30	+ 0.20
O-9	–	5.50	–
O-10	–	5.50	–
O-11	5.75	5.75	–
O-12	5.50	5.50	–
O-13	5.00	5.45	– 0.45
O-14	5.25	5.50	– 0.25
Median	5.50 (6x)	5.50 (8x)	
Diameter	11.00	11.00	
Circumference	34.55	34.55	

At first sight the circles in Area 16 appear to be like the single, widely spaced post circles that are often found as peripheral structures around tumuli, but there is no evidence to suggest that either structure encircled or lay below a mound. As with many such structures, the circles at Ittersumerbroek are made up of dissimilar post holes and the circle diameters are close to the average given by Lohof (Lohof 1991, 162ff). However, the type of construction at Ittersumerbroek deviates in several respects from the barrow circles. For instance, while the Ittersumerbroek structures are basically circular, the difference between the greatest gap and the smallest gap exceeds the margins that Lohof allows for regular post circles. The widest opening in both circles is 3.65m, the narrowest 1.50m. This irregularity cannot be attributed to problems in positioning the final post, the last one to be put in place. It seems doubtful whether use was made of sightlines in the course of construction. For example, if lines are drawn between the cores of opposing post holes in the circles of Ittersumerbroek, these lines do not intersect at any one specific point. In such cases Lohof refers to a type of peripheral structure 'in which the posts were set at random around the circle's circumference' (Lohof 1991, 165–7). The depths of the posts also vary from 0.3m to 0.04m and since the topsoil here averaged 0.3m thick then the posts had been originally embedded some 0.34m to 0.6m below the present surface.

Differences in Depth and Diameter of the Post Holes

There are several explanations for the differences. The builders need not have dug the holes in the sand equally deep and wide; the topsoil may not have been equally thick everywhere. The excavator is not always able to create a level at the transition of the topsoil to the underlying coversand as was the case at Ittersumerbroek. More recent, wide and shallow pits may force the excavator occasionally to take the level considerably further down in search of even deeper post holes. This situation occurred quite frequently at Ittersumerbroek. And finally, not every post hole's depth was measured with a level. Such circumstances may explain the differences in depth and circumference of the post holes making up the circles.

Another question is why have no circles been found in the Netherlands before? This is probably because archaeologists have focused their attention exclusively on post circles surrounding barrows as monuments for the dead. Timber circles seem to have been the realm not so much of the dead as of the living, which may mean that they may also be found in a settlement context. Future research will show whether this idea is correct.

Laying Out the Circles

It is possible to lay out a circle using a length of rope. The positions of the posts on the circumference can then be determined (for instance by pacing). Irregularities may occur through this procedure. Yet at Ittersumerbroek rather large deviations in the spacing are found, with gaps varying from 1.50 to 3.65m. In the first instance, this suggests haphazardness. However, the widest and the narrowest openings occupy identical positions in the two circles (Fig. 7.2). In the construction of the second circle, simultaneously or subsequently, this haphazardness would have been copied. Indeed it is possible that, when the occupants of the settlement for some reason decided to lay out a second circle, they failed to remember whether the first circle had been designed thus for a particular reason, and simply copied it integrally.

However, the question arises why people should go to the trouble of copying a circle while laying one out anew is such a simple process. This is likely only if there was a specific design to start with. This suggests that the first circle was deliberately laid out in this way, with a particular purpose to the spacing of the posts. On the basis of this assumption, an attempt was made to gain insight into the design of the circles.

The Design

The method adopted here involves first calculating the proportions. Only 'logical' proportions are used, i.e. between elements that structurally relate to each other. For instance, it is not logical to assume a numerical relationship between the diameter of post 8 and the distance between posts 11 and 12, however neat the result might be. On the basis of the calculated ratios and any system that may emerge, inferences may be made about the unit of measurement used. However, so little is known about measures used in prehistoric Western Europe, that any outcome can only serve as a working hypothesis and must be corroborated or refuted by future analyses. A precondition for identifying a unit of measurement is that the system of proportions and the measurements in terms of this unit must bear a certain numerical relation to each other.

The centres of the two circles were determined by means of perpendicular bisectors. The radius was measured from this centre to the core of each post hole (Table 7.1). Also, the distances between the post holes (core to core) were measured. The calculations were based on the following starting points:

1. The measurements were carried out with an accuracy of 50mm for the positions and diameters of the post holes;
2. The positions of the posts (and even their thickness) could only be assessed within certain margins. The measurements are based on the position of the post hole: the position of the post

within the hole could no longer be determined. In the calculations, use is made of the measurements (without rounding up or down) made during the excavation, taken from the centres of the post holes. Given these uncertainties, a maximum margin of *c.*100mm is acceptable. Thus if the distance between the centres of two post holes is given as 2.30m, this is to be read as 'between 2.25 and 2.35m'.

3. Average measurements have the disadvantage of producing calculations based on measurements that do not occur in reality. It is preferable to work with the median (i.e. the most frequent measurement) as the measurement that was probably intended.

The tables show that the posts were set on the circumference of a circle. Whether the posts were simply a surrounding structure or whether a perfect geometrical figure (a circle) was aimed at, is a question on a different level. Only when mathematical analysis or finds demonstrate that we are dealing with a specific design at Ittersumerbroek, can inferences be made as to whether a circle was constructed or whether fourteen posts were somewhat haphazardly placed about a broadly circular site. For this it is necessary first to calculate the proportions of the elements of the circle.

Proportions

Circumference:diameter = 34.55m:11.00m = 22:7

This is the normal proportion between a circle's circumference and its diameter, the arithmetical value of π. This in itself is nothing remarkable. In this context it is interesting to note that Thom explains the slightly flattened circles in Britain as circles in which the proportion between the circumference and the diameter was taken to be 3:1.

Diameter: 'entrance' (posts 14–1) = 11.00m:3.65m = 3:1

Next to the 'entrance', 3.65m wide, is the smallest gap in the circle (posts 1–2) = 1.50m.

The distance between posts 14 and 2, i.e. the 'entrance' and the adjacent space, is 5.15m. The proportion of its subdivision is:

(posts 14–2):entrance = 5.15m:3.65m = 1.41:1 = 10:7

In the final column in table 7.2 the distances in the north-west circle have been added up in pairs. It will be seen that the wide entrance is compensated for by the narrow space of 1.50m. The column shows that the paired distances 6–8, 8–10, and 10–12 are clearly greater than the other four pairs. The sum of distances 6–8, 8–10, and 10–12 (lumped together as 6–12) is 15.40m; the arc is 15.70m.

Of the entire circumference of 66 'units', 30 units (the distance between posts 6 and 12) have now been accounted for, so that 36 units remain for the four other pairs. It seems that the circle was divided into three sets of 10 units and four sets of 9 units.

Table 7.2: Diameter: (posts 6–12) = 11.00m:15.70m = 1:1.427 = 21:29.97 = 21:30

Scheme:			
entrance	diameter	posts 6–12	circumference
7	21	30	66

Function

Until 1992 no other structures like those at Ittersumerbroek had been identified in the Netherlands. Post hole circles had been found around tumuli, but since no traces of graves or of former barrows have appeared at Ittersumerbroek, these circles must have had a different function.

In Britain there has been research into the possible functions of circles (Thom 1967). According to Burl, the circles were in the first place intended as ceremonial gathering places (Burl 1976). In some cases he identifies a calendrical function when some of the stones in the circle, or the entrance, relate to specific solar or lunar positions. But this so-called archaeoastronomy is fraught with problems.

There is clearly a preference for certain orientations, but to what extent any actual observations were made cannot be ascertained. Also it seems unlikely that prehistoric people intending to build an observatory would have chosen a circle. A row of stones with a fixed observation point is much more appropriate for observing the sun and the moon (Burl 1976, 53). If indeed these British circles had an astronomical function, this was only part of their overall function. This in itself is an interesting idea; Burl considers their shape and function separately, in order to eliminate speculation. Burl's line is adopted in this chapter: the structures' orientation towards certain sunrises is clearly evident, whereas other assumed relations are difficult to ascertain.

Calendar

To investigate whether the circles of Ittersumerbroek functioned as calendars or observatories, we looked at lines of sight – that is to say, whether any two or more posts were aligned with a significant position of the sun or moon. Yet so many lines could be drawn between posts that some sightline would always point towards some celestial body or sign of the Zodiac. At Ittersumerbroek, ninety lines can be drawn to connect the fourteen posts of either circle, i.e. one line for every 4° of the circle's arc. To make matters even more complicated, one could view along the sides of posts or across the centres (through a sight), and base one's observations on the top, bottom, or sides of the sun or moon. Moreover, connecting lines could be drawn between the posts of the two circles.

Description of the Calendar

To find out whether the post circles of Ittersumerbroek served in combination with a calendar, the directions from the centres of the circles to where the sun rises and sets at the beginning of spring, summer, autumn and winter were determined. There are two posts in the north-west circle which are due west and east of the centre, marking the beginning of autumn and spring. There is no evidence that either of the solstices was marked by circle posts. Keeping in mind Burl's remark about the shape, function and occurrence of outliers outside the British stone circles, attention was also given to post holes in close proximity to the circles.

It is remarkable that on the east–west line just beyond the east post there is an extra post (E). Running through this post and closely along the circle, there is a north–south line on which posts B and H are also situated (Fig. 7.2). The lines OB and OH point towards the midwinter and midsummer sunrises respectively. The principle is simple. From the observation point at the centre, sunrise is observed in its most northerly position at midsummer (21 June), and in its most southerly position at midwinter (21 December). At the equinoxes (21 March and 21 September) the sun rises on the east–west axis. The angle between the midwinter and midsummer sunrises is dependent on the observer's position in the northern hemisphere; at this latitude the direction is 50° from due north, and 51° from due south (calculated by Stichting De Koepel, Utrecht). The two 'legs' of the triangle, the two sightlines, both make an angle of 52° with the north–south axis. This deviation may mean that the point of measurement was the moment at which the entire sun had risen above the horizon, and not the point at which it first appeared. The angle between the legs thus is 180° − (2 x 52°) = 76°. Thus there are two lines that with the base, which runs parallel to the north–south axis, form an isosceles triangle (Fig. 7.2). Whether people in the Bronze Age employed the north–south axis we do not know. For the modern researcher it is a helpful aid in finding the solstice sightlines. The orientations of the lines forming the triangle indicate that its builders were able to record some calendrical events and therefore the accurate passing of the seasons. Therefore the structure can be regarded as a type of calendar.

Near the north-west circle there are posts X and Y at 8.40m from the centre, in the extensions of BO and HO (Fig. 7.2). The distance BX = 15.70m, with BX:circle diameter = 15.70:11.00 = 1.427:1 = 30:21. If the west post is included, this makes three observation points. These intersect at O, which therefore might have served as the sole observation point. Yet since there is no post hole at O, it seems that three other observation points were used instead.

The south-east circle features a fixed centre point, but since it lies on the extreme end of the excavation area there are too few calendar posts to confirm the hypothesis. In order to formulate a working hypothesis about the employed unit of measurement at Ittersumerbroek, some of the principal measurements in metres were divided by the 'units' from the proportion scheme (Table 7.3).

This points to the use of a measurement unit between 0.520 and 0.525m, referred to hereafter as an Ell. An Ell represents the length of the forearm (including the hand with stretched fingers). It is notable that Gericke, in a counter-analysis of one of Thom's circles, concludes that a unit of just over one metre was used. Gericke calls this the 'Double Ell' (Gericke 1990, 6). Of course the unit employed might equally have been half of a 52cm Ell; this would merely double the number of units, and produce a measure quite similar to a foot (Dilke 1987).

These calculations were made using 'our' twentieth-century methods. This has highlighted proportions resulting from the specific post arrangements used by the Bronze Age builders.

Table 7.3. Unit of measurement at Ittersumerbroek

	ratio	metres	unit
NW circle			
entrance	7	3.65m	0.5220m
diameter	21	11.00m	0.5238m
circumference	66	34.55m	0.5235m
posts 6–12	30	15.70m	0.5227m
NW calendar			
OE	11	5.75m	0.5238m
OB=OH	14	7.30m	0.5214m
BH	17	8.90m	0.5235m
BX	30	15.70m	0.5233m

However, this does not imply that in the Bronze Age calculations were made in the same way or were intentional (Angell 1978). The concept of 'number' will have been linked to concrete objects and distances. In an agrarian society, where it is necessary to maintain stocks and organise the required manpower, there must have been a conception of number (Damerow 1991). It was not an abstract concept since, as far as we know, such a thing was first developed by Greek mathematicians. People are unlikely to have thought along the lines stated above: 'Construct two line segments in the proportion of a:b . . .' but they would have been able to comprehend that from the observation point of the midsummer and midwinter solstices a triangle emerged with a base of 17 units and sides of 14 units. However, it is a fact that, in the analysis of buildings, numerical ratios of various kinds occur which the builders never consciously intended or were even aware of. On the basis of the above ratios it may be concluded that there was a number system linking the calendar and the circle. In other words, the two structures were part of the same design and there are clearly demonstrable ratios. It is possible to make further calculations, but this introduces the risk of the fortuitous effects of a particular choice coming to be regarded as intentional.

CONCLUSIONS

In summary, the following conclusions can be made:

1. the calendar was laid out in proportions which demonstrate that use was made of a numerical system;
2. the calendar and the circle fit into the same system and were designed together;
3. the simple proportions indicate that use was made of a numerical system;
4. the simplicity of the system means that it was transmissible.

This final conclusion implies that making circles with calendars could be performed at all times by means of an easily memorised system. It was not necessary to observe the sun throughout the year with all the inherent uncertainties such as overcast weather. In fact it would suffice to determine one of the four points of the compass or either of the two solstice orientations before laying out the calendar on the basis of the numerical system.

REVISITING ITTERSUMERBROEK

In 1995 the City Archaeological Service of Zwolle invited Professor H.T. Waterbolk to study the excavations and publish his interpretation (Waterbolk 1995). He concludes that the excavators missed several two- and three-aisled constructions in their interpretation. Concerning the timber circles he agreed on the interpretation of the two timber circles proposed by Wevers and De Jong (Fig. 7.4: circles e21 and e25). Besides that he reconstructed nine more circular or oval structures (Fig. 7.3) though doubts arise over circles h2 and o2.

The Ittersumerbroek circles did not surround barrows but are all found within a settlement context. The diameters range from 9.00 to 19.00 metres. The number of posts in the circles ranges from 6 to 16. There is no relation between the size of the circles and the number of posts.

The similarity in design of these Ittersumerbroek circles suggests that they all had a ritual function. As individual structures they are hard to recognise, but as a group they cannot be

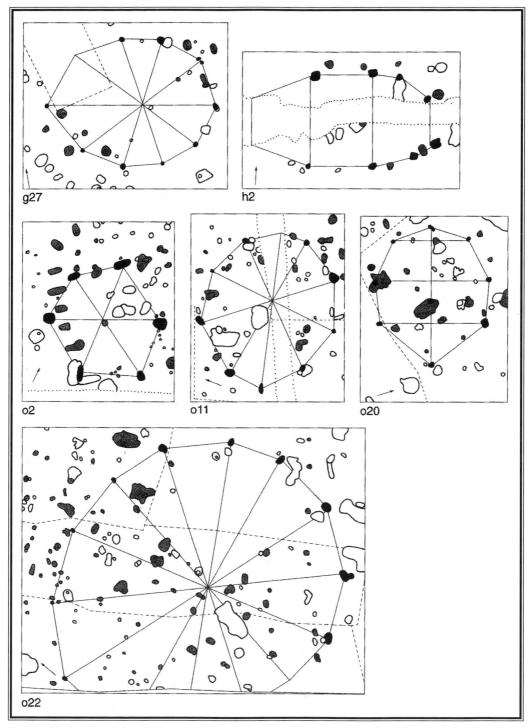

7.3 Zwolle-Ittersumerbroek. Six oval or circular structures as interpreted by Waterbolk. Scale 1:200.

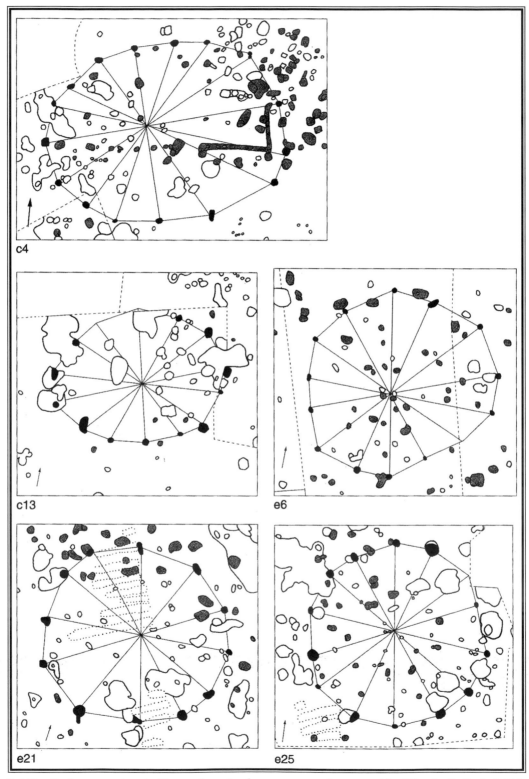

7.4 Zwolle–Ittersumerbroek. Five oval or circular structures as interpreted by Waterbolk. Scale 1:200.

denied. Waterbolk proposes more research within the context of other settlements to obtain more detail and certainty of the designs of these circular and oval structures in the Netherlands, but is not yet convinced of the combination of ritual (circle) and calendrical (triangle) functions of the structures as suggested by Wevers and De Jong. All except one seem to date from the Middle or Late Bronze Age; the exception is a six-post structure (Fig. 7.3: circle o2) which, on stratigraphical grounds, cannot be earlier than the Early Iron Age.

CHAPTER EIGHT

MONUMENTS IN THE LANDSCAPE: THOUGHTS FROM THE PEAK

JOHN BARNATT

When people build ritual monuments, what goes through their minds when choosing a site? Undoubtedly complex factors come into play since the monuments have to function on various levels, some with the participants' overt cognisance, others not. Some prehistoric decisions must remain unknowable, for example where siting was governed by an event or by an ephemeral object such as a sacred tree. However, many references to topographically permanent features, natural and made, and the form of the landscape itself, are re-examinable.

The placing of monuments in the landscape needs to be explained on a regional and often site-by-site basis, rather than viewing monuments of any one type as always functioning similarly. For example, at a socio-organisational level of explanation the small stone circles of the Peak District may be the equivalent of the Dartmoor stone rows (Barnatt 1989, 200). Round barrows on the East Moors of the Peak District have dichotomous locations, some built adjacent to settlement, others placed near to watersheds (Barnatt 1996a, 70–5), but never in large Wessex-type cemeteries.

This chapter looks at monuments which illustrate a variety of factors pertinent to their location within the landscape. It will stress visual and topographic factors. Thus, the view of the landscape from monuments (and vice versa) is considered, as is regional topography and the choices it presents. During assessment it is often vital to ask how a chosen site differs from others available but not used. It is not the aim to draw conclusions or overviews but rather raise issues which will stimulate further research.

As an aid to discussion, a series of oppositions are presented that may well influence site location. Some operate on socio-organisational levels:

mobile	sedentary
regional	local
central	peripheral

Further oppositions emphasise prehistoric people's engagement with the landscape at a more personal level. Those discussed are:

the natural	the made
close to 'home'	a place of pilgrimage
procession	arrival
the seen	the unseen
the everyday world	other worlds
the living	spirits and ancestors

This text draws heavily on the works of Barrett (1994), Bradley (1984; 1993), Tilley (1994) and, last but not least, Aubrey Burl (notably 1976; 1981a; 1987a; 1993), whose passion for prehistoric monuments and their interpretation inspired my own involvement. Here I expand upon one aspect of this interest, if not with Aubrey's familiar eloquence.

MONUMENTS IN TIME AND SPACE

Mobile/Sedentary

Neolithic and Bronze Age societies in Britain probably had differing lifestyles (Bradley 1984; Thomas 1991; Barrett 1994). While societies were doubtless changing within each period, with a time of transition, for simplicity's sake an opposition is drawn here. Neolithic peoples probably had much in common with their mesolithic forebears in that they were seasonally mobile, with shared tenure over pastures and other resources. In contrast, by the Bronze Age, people had begun to settle the land in a more sedentary way, individual 'family' groups concentrating their activities at 'permanently' laid-out farms and fields. When these radical changes took effect is debatable. It has recently been suggested that the critical point of change was part-way through the Bronze Age (Barrett 1994, 132–54). However, it may be that the transformation took place gradually over many centuries and was not necessarily synchronous across Britain; western and upland regions often developing 'permanent' fields (and all that went with them) in the later Neolithic and earlier Bronze Age (Barnatt 1996b, 54–5; in prep.).

These two lifestyles were concomitant with different views of the world and this will be reflected in the monuments built. Where people moved around the land, pathways between places would be emphasised, and monuments sited beside them. Given the scale of many neolithic monuments, they may also have been placed at locales where groups were in closer proximity at certain times of the year. At such times and places there was increased propensity for both social tension and cooperation; monuments may have been designed to both resolve and take advantage of these non-everyday situations.

In the Bronze Age, once people had settled in individual farms, there would have been a more bounded sense of place. In some ways this probably freed the monument users from the need to always cater for the wider community. While some communal monuments such as Stonehenge 3 (Cleal et al. 1995) were still in use in the earlier Bronze Age, others were built within specific areas of land whose use was no longer shared with other members of the larger community. Thus, more localised perceptions could be expressed at small monuments built by individual groups.

Regional/Local

Important in monument siting and design is the extent to which they expressed a sense of regional community or whether they served more local needs. Similarly, some monuments may have only been used by specific factions. Different monument forms display distinct distribution patterns which are likely to reflect both diverse functions and social practices changing through time (Garwood 1991; Bradley 1993; Barrett 1994; Harding 1995).

Interpretation of monuments as expressions of social organisation has come a long way since Renfrew explored their relationship to territorial division (Renfrew 1973; 1976). However, while the correlation of spatial patterning of monuments with types of social system in a territorial sense is now unviable, the complex but repetitive patterning of monuments across the landscape must have meaning (Barnatt 1989, 166–226). The regularity of the spacing of large neolithic monuments across large tracts of land must reflect the scales of movement by groups as part of their seasonal round. Similarly, the close correlation of small stone circles and barrows with specific agricultural areas, for example on the East Moors of the Peak District, suggests each local Bronze Age group built monuments for 'family' ceremonies.

While agreeing with Richards (1992, 75–6) that monuments were 'spatial representations which were built to be experienced visually, physically and imaginatively', his conclusion that 'it is highly unlikely that they would have thought of them [chambered tombs] as territorial markers or in terms of rights over resources' is debatable. Monuments will often operate on several levels. All too often we do ourselves and prehistoric populations a disservice by our tendency towards unicausal explanations of the past governed by fashions of acceptable interpretation. People built monuments for complex reasons, often in an attempt to resolve the irresolvable, to explain the contradictions of life and to make statements about their place in the land around them. While much has been written that emphasises the wholly different perceptions of the world held by past societies, perhaps inevitably our explanations are still presented in a twentieth-century compartmentalised way. With this caveat in mind, I discuss prehistoric monuments while being aware that other aspects of prehistoric peoples' life were probably all-embraced by ritual beliefs and codes of behaviour.

Many neolithic ritual monuments are sparsely scattered and are often relatively large structures. In contrast, Bronze Age monuments are often smaller and more common. Thus, the amount of labour put into monument building per generation was often equivalent to that expended in the Neolithic. This is one of the most telling differences between the two periods; people chose to do things differently in the Bronze Age by placing the emphasis on the local.

This over-generalisation should be modified to embrace regional differences and continuing activity at earlier monuments. Regional variation in the use of neolithic monuments and their different social histories has been reviewed elsewhere (Bradley 1984, 6–95; Barnatt 1989, 166–226; Harding 1995). Also, within most regions, there are often different monument forms, used contemporaneously, that contrast in scale, purpose and distribution. In some regions 'monument hierarchies' can be proposed (Barnatt 1989, 166–226). Dartmoor illustrates this well for here there are two distinct types of large communal stone circle, as well as local stone rows and barrows, all in a complex but apparently complementary set of locations. In contrast, there are no henges or other large communal sites in the fertile lowlands of Grampian, while there is an atypically large number of monumental but small-diameter recumbent stone circles (Barnatt 1989, 176–8). Long-term use of specific locales is illustrated by numerous monument complexes across Britain (Barnatt 1989, 151–5; Bradley 1993, 91–112). Often individual complexes evolve into important foci, combining structures of diverse form and date responding to changes in society and its beliefs.

Central/Peripheral

Many major neolithic monuments have been assumed to be central places. In the context of mobile populations this concept may have little relevance since people may have only been here at specific times of short duration. However, where tenure of the land was shared, and where sites were only periodically visited, it remains possible that some monuments still laid claim to the traditional use of land through the legitimation of ancestors or the use of the monument for communal ceremonies. Thus by fixing a place in the landscape a link was created between living people and their forebears, while at the same time influencing patterns of land use for future generations. This is not to say such places were located 'centrally'. It may be that land use was fluid from year to year and that monuments were placed to be convenient for various options. It is equally likely that other monuments were placed at ambiguous locales on the edge of areas usually frequented by different peoples where traditional claims needed emphasising. Some monuments may have been placed on 'neutral' or 'out of the way' ground allowing larger numbers of people to participate by avoiding issues of tenure. Other monuments may have been sited at transitional locales through which groups passed at specific times of the year.

The act of building and using a monument may also have led to a transformation of the perception of the location. At a once peripheral site, long-term use may have been instrumental in bringing about greater social cohesion and thus the place may have become central (Barnatt 1996b, 51–4).

Another possibility is that specific parts of landscape were reserved for ritual, for example at Stonehenge 3 and its surrounding barrow cemeteries (Burl 1987b; Richards, J. 1990; Cleal et al. 1995; Woodward & Woodward 1996). Unfortunately insufficient is yet known of the Bronze Age settlement in the immediate vicinity of Stonehenge; we do not know if the land between the henge and the barrows remained open pasture or whether it had been divided into fields by the Early Bronze Age (Cleal et al. 1995, 484). Given the postulated neolithic mobility, it perhaps becomes irrelevant to argue for areas of land reserved for ceremonial activity. While the interiors of monuments like henges were so used, people who camped around for short periods may have continued everyday activities in much the same way as elsewhere, if in greater numbers. Their whole lives, including the mundane, may have been imbued with ritual belief and action, thus the boundaries between overt ceremonial and ritual acts, feasting and exchange, and the everyday are blurred. On Orkney, where later neolithic people were living in 'permanent' houses in close proximity to the Stenness henge and the Ring of Brodgar, a range of architectural cross-references were made between settlement and monuments illustrating the close integration of everyday and ceremonial aspects of people's lives (Richards 1993).

Other monuments, often funerary, were sometimes set in a different type of peripheral location. Here distinctions can be drawn between 'the land of the living' and wild and isolated places.

MONUMENTS IN OTHER WORLDS

When studying the siting of monuments, it is important to recognise that different scales of choice were in simultaneous operation. It is axiomatic that, at the regional level, monuments were built within areas which were regularly or seasonally frequented. Within these locational parameters there may have been numerous suitable sites available. Which place was chosen was probably determined by both its convenience (or otherwise) and because its character satisfied the builders' beliefs. At one level, ease or difficulty of access, the availability of appropriate raw materials, the spatial relationship with other places, or the uses to which areas were put, may have a bearing on location. Equally important and probably the final arbiter, are factors such as proximity to pre-existing natural or made sacred places, or the topographical suitability of the site in regard to aesthetic or ideological considerations. Thus, the choice of site may reveal how the monument builders saw their place in the world.

The Natural/The Made

The building of neolithic monuments has much to do with the appropriation of the natural world (Bradley 1993; Tilley 1994). Points of reference were established which fixed prescribed patterns of behaviour as people moved through the land. While some monuments combine natural features with made structures, for example the tor cairns of Cornwall (Barnatt 1982, 82–3, 212; Bradley 1993, 28–9; Johnson & Rose 1994, 34–40), the majority are entirely made, though even here the distinction is blurred. To the builders, it was probably vitally important which natural materials were used, these having been manipulated or transformed rather than being wholly 'other', thus creating a dialogue with the natural world around them. Although the surrounding neolithic landscapes had been used and changed by people, for present purposes it is valid to see these as 'natural'. Thus, it is the contrasts and inter-relationships between monument and landscape that are of interest here.

As a sedentary lifestyle developed, a second set of contrasts come more forcibly into play, distinguishing between the made landscape with its settlements and fields and the land beyond.

Close to 'Home'/A Place of Pilgrimage

Some monuments may have been sited at locales where 'everyday' activity took place not for convenience but because the associated rituals were pertinent to the acts of the living. In contrast, many societies place monuments at a distance to emphasise the sense of liminality or otherness of place and the specialness of the rites; the difficulties of the journey augmenting the experience. In practice, many monuments combine both extremes, creating and resolving dichotomies between the 'sacred and the profane'. Monuments close to 'home' architecturally emphasise otherness, for example the creation of 'underground' places for ritual at chambered tombs, or by bounding the space at stone circles and henges. Monuments distant from everyday life may refer to 'the land of the living' by careful siting so that this was visible or topographically signposted.

Procession/Arrival

That procession to and within a site, gradually unfolding its mysteries, is of equal significance to the acts performed upon 'arrival' has been illustrated at monuments in Wessex (Bradley 1993, 47–57; Thomas 1993a, 28–44; Barrett 1994, 13–20). At Stonehenge and Avebury avenues lead the participants along prescribed paths dictating the 'correct' way to experience the monuments. A site's impact can be emphasised both by architecture and by careful placing. Thus, although a distant monument is visible, sometimes spectacularly so as a skyline feature or because of strong colour contrasts with its surroundings, its interior is hidden by a bank or mound. At other monuments a careful choice of site makes them invisible until the participants approach, the impact emphasised by their sudden appearance.

The Seen/The Unseen

Monumental architecture and siting can govern what is seen and what remains unseen until the appropriate moment. While this is often visual theatre it can be much more. Neolithic monuments are often designed to distinguish between 'public' and 'private' space, as with chambers under mounds or the interiors of henges removed from the outside world by banks passed by restricted entrances, the interior in turn containing ritual foci defined by stone or timber settings. Perhaps only the initiated had access to the hearts of monuments, while a distinction must also be drawn between permitted participants and others who were excluded (*see* chapter six). Monuments in a chosen 'hidden' location may be equally important in excluding non-participants, literally rendering the rituals and ceremonies invisible.

Many small Bronze Age monuments no longer retain the element of visual exclusion, although contrasts are maintained between living and dead. The 'permanent' division of the land may have removed the need to distinguish between participant and stranger if the monuments were for 'family' use, there being less ambiguity over who had the right to be there.

The view from monuments was probably also important, either for the participants and/or the recipients (the ancestors or spirits). A broad view over the land may reinforce identity with it. In contrast, the removal from sight of 'the land of the living' heightens the places' otherness. Views of sacred hills or other natural places would have reinforced the dialogue between the people and the world they inhabited. Views also include astronomical events at such times as midsummer and midwinter; the specialness of a place being augmented by the sun or moon rising or setting above a significant point in the landscape.

The Everyday World/Other Worlds

Some rituals were probably concerned with the fecundity of people and their world. Others, dealing with the threatening or ambiguous, may have required distance, created architecturally or physically. Obvious examples are those which dealt with death. Different societies may have chosen different architectural or siting solutions when creating monuments used for rites of passage, social interaction, seasonal rites and communion with spirits. Thus, whether they chose to place monuments close at hand or at a distance will often remain ambiguous unless we have evidence locating everyday activities.

The Living/Spirits and Ancestors

While monuments were clearly built by the living for their own use, some were also visited or inhabited by spirits and ancestors. For the builders, the dead and the otherworldly may have had an active rather than passive role. Thus, for example, monuments where the ancestors overlooked the living or where spirits of the land were known to be present can be anticipated. While contact may sometimes have been sought, it is probable that this would have been seen as threatening or ambiguous and needing the mediation of shamen. The architecture and siting of monuments are probably as much about containment as about contact, hence the use of chambers and cists, or the building of banks or ditches to bound sacred areas. Monuments may be sited away from 'the land of the living' for the same reasons.

MONUMENTS IN DIFFERENT LANDSCAPES: FOR EACH A PLACE IN THE WORLD

A Variety of Sites

I shall illustrate the above with a few well-known sites before examining two regions in further detail. These are used to illustrate specific points rather than offering full interpretation of each.

Chun Quoit, Cornwall, is sited on the crest of a round-topped hill in the heart of the West

Penwith upland. It comprises a monumental 'closed-chamber' with a massive rounded capstone rising from a small circular mound that may never have fully enveloped the central setting (Barnatt 1982, 42–52, 124–6). The monument is not visible from the adjacent lower ground but is set apart, unseen high above the everyday world. The view is one of higher hilltops and the sea beyond. While, like other 'portal dolmens' in south-western England, its architecture tells of association with the dead, it may originally have contained no or only token burials. The shape of its dominant capstone echoes the granite tors thus linking the natural with the made. At this atmospheric site it is easy to imagine processions arriving from below and entering the world of ancestors and spirits for rituals associated with the closed box purposefully contained beneath the great weight of a 'tor'.

Castlerigg and Swinside stone circles in Cumbria are both large monuments clearly designed for communal ceremonies (Burl 1976, 55–97; 1988). However, even here their locations set them apart. Castlerigg lies on a flat ridge-top and is generally invisible from the surrounding valleys below, the latter radiating outwards and providing easy routeways through this mountainous region. Swinside is on a shelf, again hidden between the fells above and lowlands below. Both lie where mountainous panoramas create impressive backdrops, making them fine 'places of pilgrimage', removed from everyday life and long distance pathways, where ceremonies could be performed in a majestic setting.

The stone circles on Machrie Moor, Arran, contrast with those just discussed. Here six small diameter rings lie together on a low ridge at the western end of Machrie Glen, the main pass across the island (Burl 1976, 143–7; Barnatt 1989, 247–50; Haggarty 1991). The ridge and surrounding valley have plentiful evidence for prehistoric settlement. The circles are carefully sited so as to be seen from the surrounding landscape and also to have views up Machrie Glen where the sun would rise at midsummer (Barnatt & Pierpoint 1983). These monuments are in the heart of 'the land of the living', at a chosen site that takes cognisance visually and astronomically of one of the main features of the landscape, the one easy path across this mountainous island.

The siting of monuments relative to natural sacred features is again dramatically illustrated in the Peak District at the Nine Stone Close stone circle and the natural outcrop nearby known as Robin Hood's Stride (Barnatt 1978, 156–8; 1990, 28). This impressive crag, with two rock pillars rising over 3m from its summit, lies about 400m to the south-west of the circle. When viewed from the monument, the full midsummer moon would pass behind each pillar, framed between the two for several minutes.

Dartmoor

Numerous fine monuments survive on this granite upland (Burl 1976; 1993; Barnatt 1989; Fleming 1988; Butler 1991–4) better known for its exceptional Bronze Age boundaries and field systems (Fleming 1978; 1983; 1988). The stone circles, stone rows and barrows each have patterned distributions which complement and/or contrast with each other. Different topographic and spatial choices have been made.

Two types of large stone circle contrast strongly both in their architecture and locations. For example, in the upper Teign valley (Fig. 8.1), the Grey Wethers and the White Moor Down circle are carefully laid-out circular rings with stones of regular spacing and height. They lie high on the moor in isolated watershed locations, largely hidden from view, above the heads of the major valley systems. In contrast, Scorhill circle has many irregularly spaced stones of unequal height in a somewhat irregular ring. It, and the ruined Buttern circle, lie at the side of, and overlooking, a large upland basin scattered with prehistoric settlements. Thus, a dichotomy is formed between

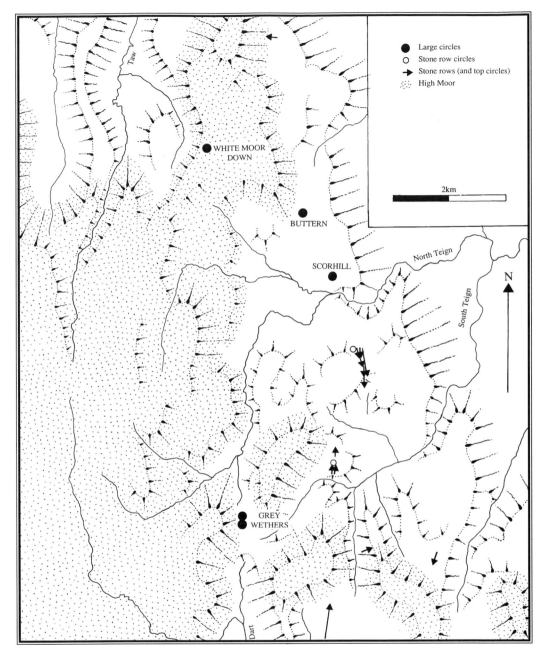

8.1 Dartmoor: the siting of stone circles on the north-eastern part of the moor.

monuments at the 'centre' and those at the 'edge'. The Scorhill circle is architecturally a highly visible monument within a focal area for grazing and settlement. The Grey Wethers and White Moor Down are topographically isolated, requiring special journeys to locations removed from the 'everyday world'. Significantly, they lie at the edge of the high north-west part of Dartmoor, an area which was probably viewed as a wild and bleak 'other world', and are sited at 'neutral points'

Scorhill stone circle. (Photo: Alex Gibson)

on paths between major valleys where different communities could gather for ceremonies. That the Grey Wethers comprises two juxtaposed near-identical rings (rather than one circle being sufficient) may indicate something of the tensions of such occasions.

The many single and double stone rows are distributed regularly across all more favourable areas of the moor suggesting that each local community built and used one. Both ends of the rows commonly have taller menhirs and/or terminal stones, while at the upper end there is usually a circular setting beyond. This normally comprises a cairn and/or a small stone circle. Often the two are combined, the cairn filling much of the interior of the circle making it impractical for the living to gather here for ceremonies.

Occasionally these monuments comprise multiple rows of up to eight parallel lines, and/or 'normal' rows that have been placed near each other, probably over time. The larger of these complexes also include free-standing stone circles, large barrows and small cairns with cists. In several cases the rows follow on from each other and as a result of crossing undulating land, some of their 'upper' ends point downslope.

A common characteristic of the Dartmoor stone rows is that their upper ends either point to locally high ground or to the heart of the moor. Thus, they lead to ambiguous parts of the landscape, either topographical boundaries or 'wild' places beyond where people normally lived (Fig. 8.2). This, combined with the rows' architecture, suggests a symbolic opposition between 'the world of the living' and that of spirits and ancestors. The double rows give clues here in that some are so closely spaced that it is difficult to walk between them. It may be that the rows were seen as spirit paths bridging the everyday world and the sacred places at the row tops and beyond.

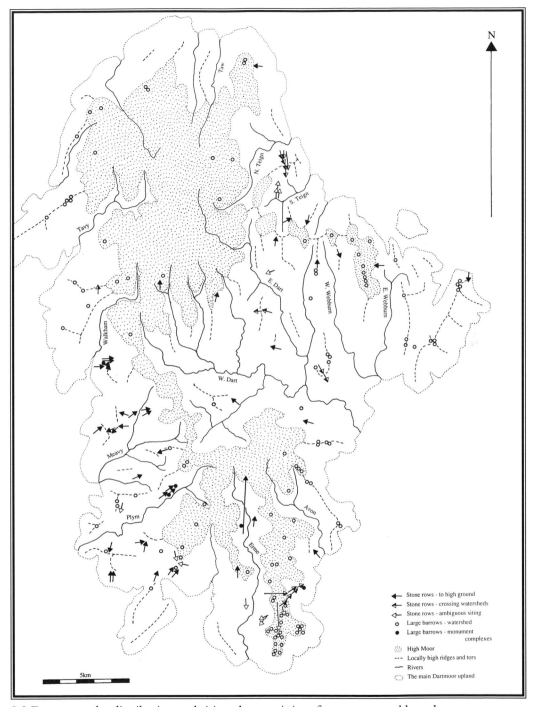

8.2 Dartmoor: the distribution and siting characteristics of stone rows and large barrows.

Thus, there is visual and architectural interplay between the made and the natural, the living and the dead, and everyday and other more uncertain realms.

Barrows of the region which are above about 15m diameter have a different distribution to smaller sites. The smaller barrows, including many distinctive examples with impressive kerbs and large internal cists, are randomly scattered in or close to settlement/grazing foci within each watershed. That many examples encase cists emphasises the funerary.

Larger barrows are mainly found in high locations at or near watersheds (Fig. 8.2). The exceptions are mostly at stone row complexes. It has been suggested that the watershed barrows acted as conspicuous indicators that the moor was occupied (Fleming 1983, 200–2, 216–17; 1988, 98–100). However, it may be that the primary concern was to distance them from the everyday world, with each local community choosing a nearby high place for its monument.

Taking a broader view, each of the main Dartmoor valleys which radiate from the upland core has subtle differences in that the architectural options are combined differently. For example, large regular stone circles are missing from the southern half of the moor while stone row complexes become more common. The most extreme case of local variation occurs in the Erme valley. Here the Stall Moor stone circle, of comparable design to Scorhill, is joined by an atypically long stone row which extends from the circle at the heart of the upper valley to a cairn at its head. Thus, 'the land of the living' is linked physically with that above. The Staldon row crosses the high ridge between the upper Erme valley and the lowlands to the south. Atypically it has tall stones and defines a sacred path leading into the hidden valley. The only other row on Dartmoor with many tall stones, on Piles Hill to the south-east of Staldon, leads eastwards out of the Erme valley to the Corringdon Ball row complex which focuses on the only large chambered long barrow of the Moor.

Taken together, such variation suggests that each valley community was discrete and, given that similar patterned division of the land can be seen in the reave systems, this is likely to have been so over an extended period. Even though movement to, from and within the Dartmoor upland was probably of great significance in both the Neolithic and the Bronze Age, either as part of a seasonal round or later as transhumant activity within a more closely bounded landscape, the strongly divided character of the landscape influenced where people chose to be.

The Peak District

This region has a varied suite of neolithic and Bronze Age monuments on its central limestone plateau (Barnatt 1990; 1996a; 1996b), whereas the eastern gritstone uplands have exceptionally well-preserved Bronze Age settlements in close association with monuments (Barnatt 1986; 1987; 1990; 1996a; in prep.). Although neolithic monuments cluster on the limestone plateau this need not imply that people concentrated their everyday activities here. Being at the heart of this upland region, this area is the one place where disparate groups that were moving seasonally are likely to have met and thus this was the obvious place to build monuments (Barnatt 1996b). That the remains of Bronze Age settlements still exist on the gritstone is a product of differential survival.

Minninglow is a large multi-phased neolithic mound with several chambers, sited on top of one of the highest hills along the spine of the limestone plateau. This is widely visible from a distance but, on approach, it disappears from sight as the hill is climbed, reinforcing the 'otherness' of the place. Upon arrival, the monument appears to sit above the world, from where the living and the dead alike could survey the extensive panorama. A smaller chambered site at Five Wells, sited above the precipitous northern edge of Taddington Moor, has panoramic views to the north over the broad shelves flanking the Wye gorge, an area which may have been one of the most favourable neolithic grazing areas in the region. If the monument had been sited a few metres further south, on slightly higher ground, the views would have disappeared. Because the monument is relatively small and has higher land behind, it is not readily made-out from the majority of the land that it overlooks. Thus, the views from the site appear more important than its visibility, indeed it may have been purposefully hidden from sight.

The one neolithic monument sited off the limestone plateau is the massive enclosure on Gardom's Edge, on the eastern gritstone upland (Ainsworth & Barnatt in press). The boulder-strewn interior is bounded to the east by a large but low rubble bank with several entrances, and to the west by the precipitous Gardom's Edge. From here the main valley of the region, that of the Derwent, is visible below. This monument appears to be an upland equivalent to the causewayed enclosures of southern England and as such may have functioned in similar ways (see Thomas 1991, 32–8; Edmonds 1993a; Harding 1995). Its location away from the limestone plateau, at the interface between the Derwent valley and the gritstone uplands, suggests it is at a transitional location between contrasting resource areas. Although sited high above the Derwent valley it is not visible from here nor from the limestone plateau beyond. Similarly, the enclosure bank is only seen from other directions upon approach. With a site such as this, with a low bank bounding liminal space, it may be that there was no need for it to be seen from a distance; everyone who participated knew where it was.

The two large henges, Arbor Low and the Bull Ring, are architecturally similar but topographically different (Barnatt 1990, 6–12, 31–41). Arbor Low lies high on the limestone plateau, to the north side of the crest of a prominent ridge. Its high bank is a skyline feature when approached from this direction, whereas the monument is largely hidden from elsewhere. The northern entrance is twice as wide as that opposite, suggesting that the monument was approached from the north. The southern entrance leads to other parts of the monument complex, including the earlier Gib Hill long cairn. Although the henge is an imposing sight from a few hundred metres away to the north, the bank obscures all view of the interior. As one comes nearer the monument it disappears from sight as the ascent steepens, reappearing as one approaches the entrance, revealing the site in all its glory, including a view into the interior with its once-tall stone settings. However, the interior of the central cove was carefully hidden from both entrances by its two massive side slabs. The rituals performed here were only to be seen by participants permitted within the sacred interior. Thus siting and architecture create ranked access and experience. Although open to the sky, the bank would have obscured all views of the outside landscape with the exception of distant hills to the north. Thus, when compared with chambered tombs for example, a much more private and exclusive space is created for the living.

The Bull Ring henge lies close to the north-west edge of the limestone plateau, at a low-lying spot above the heads of narrow valleys running north-west and south-east. The former valley is the only low-lying route out of the region leading to the Cheshire Plain and beyond. While the henge interior can be viewed from distant higher points, its bank again hides the interior during approach. The north-western part of the limestone plateau is generally high and uninviting and, as with Arbor Low, the location of the Bull Ring can be seen as 'neutral' ground. The henge lies at a point of transition between the path to the lowlands and others leading into the limestone plateau.

All small stone circles and many barrows on the eastern gritstone uplands, with the exception of those in zones of later destruction, have an intimate spatial correlation with the settlements, cairnfields and fields (Barnatt 1986; 1987; 1989, 189–92; 1996a, 70–5; in prep.). Each local community built small monuments within or near to its agricultural areas. The placing of barrows

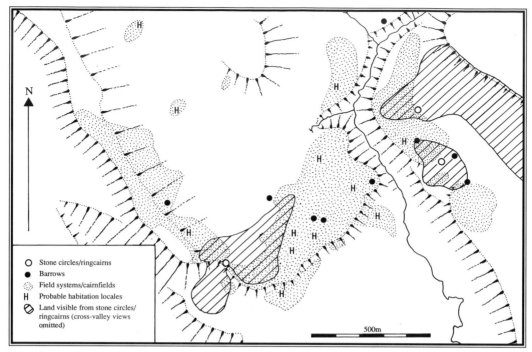

N

O Stone circles/ringcairns
● Barrows
.· Field systems/cairnfields
H Probable habitation locales
⬙ Land visible from stone circles/
   ringcairns (cross-valley views
   omitted)

500m

8.3 The Peak District: the spatial and visual relationships between stone circles, barrows and settlement on Big Moor.

and stone circles here is probably more than one of convenience, and may reflect identification of 'family' with traditional use of specific areas and with the well-being of this land. However, even though these monuments are placed 'close to home', their precise sites suggest that there was little attempt to emphasise this, but rather locations were often chosen to visually set them apart. This is illustrated here by the remains on Big Moor (Fig. 8.3). The three stone circles/ringcairns are all placed where views of the adjacent agricultural areas are not extensive and identified habitation locales are not seen. The monuments themselves are only clearly visible when stood close by; exclusion from view heightened in one case by placing the circle in a hollow between two agricultural areas. Equally, they are not sited in distinctive locations which lead people to them and to the settlement and agricultural areas beyond. Barrows are sited both central and peripheral to agricultural areas and views from them are sometimes more extensive, although again the impression is that visibility to and from settlement areas was not particularly important.

Not all barrows on the gritstones are sited in immediate proximity to settlement: some are placed near watersheds or other 'boundary' positions. For example, near the centre of Bamford Moor is a large barrow (Fig. 8.4: A) which, although relatively close to other monuments and fields to the south, is sited over the watershed with views north-westwards over land perhaps associated with known settlement on lower ground here. Similarly the barrows on the other side of the watershed (Fig. 8.4: B) overlook settlement to the south-east. Such siting suggests that these barrows were designed as 'private' monuments which overlooked particular pastures rather than commanding generally extensive vistas.

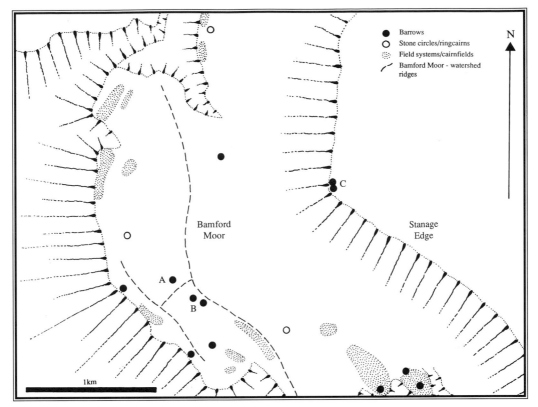

8.4 The Peak District: the location of monuments and settlement on Stanage Edge and Bamford Moor.

Two large barrows are placed together on the crest of Stanage Edge (Fig. 8.4: C), one of the most impressive topographic features of the region, a 5km long cliff which rises high over the land to the west. Bowl barrows built here would have been visible for miles. However, while there are extensive vistas from the site, both flat-topped mounds cannot be seen from the landscape below; they have been built on an imposing natural crag in an unseen 'other' place from where the dead can overlook the 'land of the living'.

Finally, to return to Arbor Low, the large barrow imposed on the bank of the henge in the south-east quadrant, at the optimal spot to dominate the interior of the monument, illustrates that not all barrows are the same. Here an overt political statement has been made at one of the main traditional centres that symbolised the Peak District communities' ceremonial and spiritual well-being.

ACKNOWLEDGEMENTS

Aubrey Burl provided much of the initial inspiration for my interest in the siting of monuments; many thanks to him for enthusiastic discussion and encouragement over many years. Thanks also to Mark Edmonds and Alex Gibson for commenting on drafts of the text. The information depicted in Fig. 8.3 is in part derived from a joint survey of this area by RCHME (Keele Office) and the Archaeology Service of the Peak District National Park Authority.

PART TWO
ARTEFACTS

Chapter Nine

Breaking Stones, Making Places: The Social Landscape of Axe Production Sites

Gabriel Cooney

Introduction

The deliberate deposition of stone axes in sacred places is well recognised as an aspect of neolithic life in Ireland and Britain. This can be seen as a clear indication of their significance as objects in ritual or ceremonial activity. Their symbolic importance is suggested by such actions as the placement of axes along with other material in the ditches of causewayed enclosures in southern Britain (Edmonds 1993b), the deposition of axes as part of grave-good assemblages, as at Caherguillamore, Co. Limerick (Hunt 1967), and the deliberate inclusion of axes as part of the blocking up of sites, as at the court tomb known as Dooey's Cairn, Ballymacaldrack, Co. Antrim (Evans 1938; Collins 1976). The cache of axes at Ferriter's Cove, Co. Kerry (Woodman & O'Brien 1993) indicates that complex ideas surrounding the use of axes may have pre-dated the formal beginning of the Neolithic. It is because of the ubiquity of axes in everyday life that they would have been seen as suitable for use in ritual (Cooney *et al.* 1995; Edmonds 1995). We know that axes of certain valued lithologies were moved considerable distances from their sources. Therefore we have to think of the axe as being a religious symbol, an item of exchange as well as a functional tool.

One of the most exciting aspects of stone axe studies in Ireland and Britain in recent years has been a renewed focus on the need to understand the processes involved in axe production as an essential component in looking at their uses and roles. Internationally, the approach taken towards research on axe production or quarry sites, however, has largely been from a functional perspective (Ericson & Purdy 1984). This is perhaps not surprising given that Ericson (1984, 2) has identified the character of the material record on such sites as 'shattered, overlapping, sometimes shallow, nondiagnostic, undatable, unattractive, redundant, and at times voluminous'. It is also to be expected that analysis would concentrate on understanding the processes of production and identifying diachronic changes in approaches to production (Bradley & Edmonds 1993). Accepting the fundamental importance of such an analytical standpoint, it is also relevant to point out that quarries or production sites are important not only because axes were produced there but because in the process the landscape was changed. We have become familiar with the term 'monumental landscapes' (Barber 1996) to describe the impact of humanly created structures. But at axe production sites monumental alteration of the landscape itself took place through the processes of extracting and working stone.

In this chapter I shall examine some aspects of stone axe production sites from a landscape perspective. My interest in this topic comes from the on-going work of the Irish Stone Axe Project (Cooney & Mandal 1995; Cooney et al. 1995) and the linked project on the survey and excavation of a quarry site on Lambay island, off the east coast of Ireland, where porphyritic andesite was exploited (Cooney 1993; 1996). Lambay is important because it is the first production site recognised in Ireland or Britain where pecking and hammering, rather than flaking, was the primary process of production. The site has produced hammerstones, grinding slabs and roughouts – the sort of evidence to be expected where this kind of axe production was carried out (Mercer 1986; Berridge 1994). It is clear that here grinding began earlier in the production sequence than in the case of flaked roughouts. Porphyritic andesite fractures very easily and it is difficult to create and maintain a predictable roughout shape. On the other hand our experimental work has shown that it can be ground and polished relatively easily. The presence of grinding and polishing slabs on the site, as well as hammerstones, a polished porphyritic andesite axe, and fragments of ground and polished porphyritic andesite, indicates that both secondary (grinding and polishing) as well as primary (pecking, hammering and some flaking) manufacture were taking place on site. What is also important about Lambay is the range of other material and structures that occur on the site. So there are unusual aspects to the quarry site on Lambay, such as the occurrence of all phases of the production process on-site. But there are also elements of the evidence that can be paralleled at other production sites. Hence this site has implications for our wider understanding of the cultural context in which axe production took place.

LANDMARKS

A basic assumption underlying this chapter is my agreement with Tilley's assertion of the symbolic, ancestral and temporal significance of the landscape for the type of societies that would have used stone axes in prehistoric Ireland and Britain. Tilley (1994, 67) states: 'the landscape is redolent with past actions, it plays a major role in constituting a sense of history and the past, it is peopled by ancestral and spiritual entities, forms part and parcel of mythological systems, it is used in defining social groups and their relationship to resources'. By naming places people transform their habitat from physical terrain into a pattern of experienced space and time that has a history (Weiner 1991, 32; Robinson 1996). If we see the landscape as a living entity, then the extraction of stone provides a mechanism for the appropriation of the land and its ancestral/spiritual meaning (Tacon 1991). More broadly, as Tacon (1994, 127) has argued, by connecting to the land at unusual, specially marked sites people gain a recognition of their own place in the world. This kind of connection to the earth could have surrounded any type of extraction and use of stone, for example in the case of the structural and decorative stones for megalithic tombs. One could speculate, for instance, that the incorporation of a range of lithologies from different areas into the passage tombs of the Boyne Valley in Ireland during the Neolithic (Mitchell 1992) was more than just about the use of local and more exotic stone.

Perhaps it served to literally draw the social landscape together and to underpin the sacred significance of these new landmarks.

Extracting stone from the earth can therefore be seen as providing a contact with the spirit or ancestral world. This not only imbued the stone with power but for the same reason it would have been seen as a dangerous activity for the people involved. The traditional avoidance of digging or disturbing the ground on certain days of the year in Ireland was attributed to the dangers of tampering with the ground on occasions when the links with the spirit world were perceived as being heightened (Danaher 1972, 87–8). Of course in axe quarrying there would have been an element of physical danger, but Burton (1984, 240), for example, records that in recent times in the Papua New Guinea highlands the Tungei people regarded quarrying as ritually dangerous, believing that it was important to keep on good terms with the spirit custodians of the stone. Human success in obtaining stone from the axe quarries was attributed to ritual purity and the correct axe-making magic (*see also* Pétrequin & Pétrequin 1993, 358).

As with the recent axe-makers in New Guinea I think we have to see prehistoric stone axe production as an activity permeated with ritual. The archaeological evidence from prehistoric quarries can be interpreted as exhibiting many of the classic signals of ritual activity (Parkin 1992; Renfrew 1994). The debitage is the result of multiple, repetitive and formal actions, and axe production frequently took place at formally defined locations. The functional element of this activity may be what is most apparent, but right from the beginning of the production process, whether it involved the creation of functional or ceremonial axes, there were symbolic overtones. This view is reinforced when we look at the other end of the life cycle of stone axes. We know that in archaeological contexts many axes were formally placed back in the earth in a range of contexts (Sheridan *et al.* 1992). Even axes broken during use may have been carefully treated. In a modern example from Langda, Irian Jaya, western New Guinea, recorded by Toth *et al.* (1992, 70) people deliberately collected broken axes and brought them back to the settlement rather than discarding the objects on the land, because they felt sorry for them and brought the axes home for final discard.

PLACES

The title of this chapter might be taken to suggest that it was the act of axe production which first brought places of production into the web of human relationships. But it is clear that at least in some cases part of the attraction of the place chosen for production was the nature of the location itself (*see* discussion in Bradley 1993). The dolerite axe production site at Le Pinacle on Jersey (Patton 1991; 1993) is at the foot of a massive outcrop of granite which has given its name to the location. Axes were produced on the neck of land linking Le Pinacle to the headland that forms the north-western corner of Jersey. As Patton (1993, 25) states, given the prominence of this landmark it seems likely that it was a significant feature of the sacred geography of the Channel Islands.

Bearing in mind this example of a focus on a spectacular location I have been struck by the broad visual and locational similarity between the axe production sites at Tievebulliagh, Co. Antrim (Fig. 9.1), the Pike of Stickle at Great Langdale in Cumbria (Fig. 9.2) and Killin in Perthshire (Fig. 9.3). In all three cases the sources exploited are on exposed locations on imposing peaks which form striking landmarks in the landscape. They are also, however, relatively easily accessible from lower-lying areas. These are the kinds of place that may well have

9.1 Tievebulliagh, Co. Antrim (from the north-east).

9.2 Pike of Stickle, Langdale, Cumbria (from the south).

9.3 Creag na Caillich, Killin, Perthshire (from the east).

been named and incorporated into mythology long before axe production began. Tievebulliagh is one of the two known sources for porcellanite axes, the other being at Brockley on Rathlin Island off the north-east corner of Ireland, over 25km distant from Tievebulliagh on the mainland (Jope 1952; Sheridan 1986; Mallory 1990). Porcellanite is by far the single most important lithology used in the production of stone axes in Ireland (Cooney & Mandal 1995). At Tievebulliagh thermal metamorphism of a ferruginous bauxitic clay in the vent of a volcano resulted in the formation of porcellanite with dolerite above and below it (Agrell & Langley 1958). Volcanic tuff or ash axes from the Langdale area are numerically the most important group of petrologically identified axes in Britain (Clough 1988). The source is a fine-grained volcanic tuff or ash which outcrops as an 18km long band in the Borrowdale volcanic sequence (Woolley in Claris & Quatermaine 1989). In contrast to Tievebulliagh and Langdale, Killin seems to have been worked on a small scale and only a restricted number of products are known. The worked outcrop was a calc-silicate hornfels created as the result of contact metamorphism of schist by an intrusive appinite sill (Edmonds *et al.* 1992).

A common feature of these three sites is that the exploited rock occurs as a band. At Tievebulliagh and Killin it can be argued that the limited extent of the suitable outcrops determined the location of the quarrying, but it seems clear that in the case of Langdale many good quality exposures were only partially utilised or not used at all, and the focus of production was deliberately placed at the Pike of Stickle. Furthermore the emphasis on the use of inaccessible locations seems to have increased over time (Bradley & Ford 1986; Bradley & Edmonds 1993). It seems plausible to suggest that while all three of these fine-grained rock types had qualities which made them suitable for working by flaking and grinding, these qualities may have been perceived as being enhanced by the special setting from which they came.

In many different societies peaks have a special quality as sacred places because they seem to touch the sky, and are seen as the seat of the gods (O'Connor 1992). In this sense they are between two worlds, places where the spirit world may be accidentally or deliberately encountered. In summarising the features of Minoan peak sanctuaries in Crete, Peatfield (1994, 23) makes the important point that they are very much part of the landscape from which the worshippers come. This is also an interesting perspective to use in relation to axe quarry sites. They are at a remove from the routine landscape but they also have to be accessible from areas of human settlement. Other places that could be regarded as liminal are small islands and it is interesting that two offshore island axe quarries have now been recognised in Ireland. Brockley on Rathlin Island, as stated above, is a source of porcellanite. The second site is Lambay, an island lying less than 5km off the east coast of Ireland to the north of Dublin. The source rock exploited for axe production is a porphyritic andesite or porphyry, a medium-grained rock which has distinct white/yellow phenocrysts (crystals) of feldspar set in a green groundmass. The outcrop at Brockley does form a local landmark but it is not on a par with Tievebulliagh. While the site on Lambay is in a strategic and visually commanding location in relation to the island, it certainly could not be defined as a spectacular location. What makes these sources special, however, is their island location. As with the use of spectacular mountains as sources, the location of quarries on islands raises the issue of whether this kind of exploitation is related to the question of control over a valued resource or the value placed on having an axe from a special place. The pattern of the use of island sources is known elsewhere, for example in Shetland (Ritchie 1968; 1992) and western Norway on the small island of Hespriholmen (Breun Olsen & Alsaker 1984). In the case of the latter it is suggested that the sources were exploited by foragers and that the quarrying and production of axes could have been an integrated part of annual inter-group gatherings, to the extent that the quarries may have been the focus of such gatherings, acting as sacred places and landmarks (Breun Olsen & Alsaker 1984, 100).

BREAKING STONES

The processes of quarrying and axe production have been, quite rightly, the foci of archaeological research at production sites. They may well have been perceived as dangerous activities (Tacon 1991, 203–4; Tilley 1994, 53). There was danger in both a physical and a metaphysical sense in working the rock surfaces, and perhaps even more so in the digging of pits or galleries to follow particular bands of valued rock – a point that has long been recognised in the case of flint mines (Clark 1952, 175). The danger in working by flaking or pecking and hammering was in the unpredictability of the stone itself. Of course people would have been skilled stoneworkers but accidents and mistakes would inevitably occur. As Edmonds has suggested (1995, 11) the tools and waste that we recover would have been entangled in a world of social practice. Thus it seems likely that problems such as rockfalls or low success rate in the production of roughouts would have been seen to reflect on the relationship between people and the live rock, or on inadequate ritual safeguards rather than on any analysis of the physical properties of the rock itself. Part of the ritual observances to keep danger and failure at bay may have involved deposition.

Two important instances of this have come to light from recent excavations at axe production sites. At Graiglwyd near Penmaenmawr in Gywnedd, north Wales, excavation at the southern (and undisturbed) end of the augite granophyre outcrop which had been used for axe production in the Neolithic (as well as being removed by modern stone quarrying) revealed a complete, finished roughout which had been placed resting against the base of a quarried rock face, and covered by debitage (Williams 1994, 36–8). At Lambay, during excavation of the debitage resulting from the prising of blocks from the porphyritic andesite outcrop and the subsequent pecking, hammering and grinding of these blocks, two discrete knapping clusters, one of flint and one of quartz, were found deliberately placed against a worked outcrop face (Cooney 1996).

Regardless of whether flaking or pecking/hammering was employed at axe production sites, the primary manufacturing processes normally involved considerable time expenditure (Boyston 1989). An important realisation that has come through the work of the Irish Stone Axe Project is that in the case of certain fine-grained sedimentary lithologies such as shale and mudstone, natural processes can produce what are in effect roughouts or literally preforms, with apparent flake-scar features on the sides. The most notable examples of this are the shale cobbles from the storm beach at Fisherstreet, Co. Clare, in south-west Ireland (Cooney & Mandal 1995). When first discovered (Knowles 1904), this site was described as an axe factory. However, the shale cobbles are ultimately derived from nearby coastal cliffs and because of the laminar structure of the shale when pieces are eroded and buffeted in the dynamic coastal environment, the cobbles that end up being deposited on the storm beach have a sub-rectangular cross-section and flake-scar like features on the sides. With minimum effort and time they can be edge-ground to provide serviceable axes. What would prehistoric people have made of these cobbles that must to them have looked like stone axes? Even in nineteenth-century Ireland and Britain people believed stone axes had dropped from the sky and were empowered to provide good luck (Evans 1872, 51; Burl 1976, 81–3), so it does not seem inconceivable that in prehistoric times people picking up shale cobbles at places like Fisherstreet would have seen them as having been provided by the living earth for their benefit. While these lithologies do not produce high-quality axes with a lasting edge, we can speculate that their use may have been predicated not only on the widespread availability of shale and mudstone sources in the west and south-west of Ireland (Mandal 1996) but also on this quality of being produced by the earth, not by people.

The working of stone on axe production sites is not solely a case of roughouts being produced – a lot of humanly created debitage is also created. This varies from large-scale debris from the initial quarrying process to smaller-scale replicated debitage resulting from the processing of stone for axe production. In effect we could view this debitage as a cultural deposit. It should not be regarded just as waste, but something which, in the same way as the roughouts, was culturally important. It also literally changed the nature and appearance of the sites. If we accept the debitage as a form of deposit and put it alongside the instances of deliberate deposition of particular objects referred to above, perhaps we should not be surprised that on at least a couple of sites there is clear evidence for the deliberate placement back in the ground of material associated with the working of the rock. The best known example of this in Ireland is at Goodland in Co. Antrim (Case 1973), where associated with the small-scale extraction of flint from a chalk surface was a small segmented ditched enclosure. In the ditch segments and in a large number of pits in the interior were deposits of flint and pottery with porcellanite and quartz also occurring (Fig. 9.4). In many of the pits these deposits were packed around boulders and were marked by low cairns.

While the excavations at Lambay are on-going, a striking feature is the occurrence of pits similar to those at Goodland on the floor of the small valley between the porphyritic andesite outcrops that were exploited in the Neolithic. One of these has been fully excavated and revealed a complex series of placed deposits of pottery and other material in a matrix primarily composed

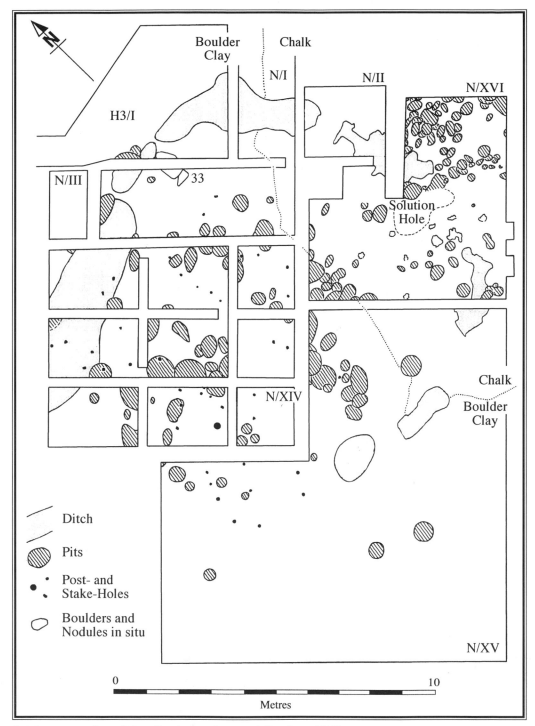

9.4 Summary plan of Goodland, Co. Antrim (after Case 1973).

9.5 Structured deposits in a pit from the axe production site on Lambay during excavation.

of porphyry debitage, but also with hammerstones and rubbers (Fig. 9.5). Particular parallels with Goodland include the provision of low cairns over the top of the pits, the deliberate placement of deposits within them, the presence of sherds of the Carrowkeel and Goodland styles of decorated globular bowls and the occurrence of the pits on sites where the primary concern appears to have been the extraction and working of stone. At Goodland, Case (1973, 193) suggested that this activity was concerned with ensuring the fertility of the earth to maintain a continued supply of flint nodules. Bearing in mind the evidence from Lambay it seems plausible to suggest that the deposition may represent a deliberate offering of material concerned with working stone and other activities back to the earth. This activity may have been carried out with both placation and dedication in mind. Such deposits would probably have been made at the beginning or end of a season or cycle of production.

CONCLUSION – LETTING IN THE LIGHT

The archaeological link between places of stone axe production and the spread of their products during the Neolithic has been achieved through programmes of petrological analysis. This has been the hallmark of the long-running programme of stone axe studies coordinated by the Implement Petrology Committee of the CBA (Clough & Cummins 1979; 1988) and is also a central aspect of the research programme of the Irish Stone Axe Project (Mandal *et al.* 1991/2; Cooney & Mandal 1995). Moving beyond the traditional reliance on petrological microscopic identification, geochemical analysis offers the potential to differentiate similar sources, as in the case of the two porcellanite sources in north-east Ireland (Mandal *et al.* 1997; Meighan *et al.* 1993). But a striking aspect of porcellanite is that it is recognisable in the hand. In the vicinity of the production sites the porcellanite is referred to as bluestone, because of its distinctive colour compared to the local dolerite. Similarly, the tuff axes from Langdale have distinct surface coloration and banding which makes them easy to identify. Many porcellanite (oblique butts) and tuff axes (faceted sides) also have distinct morphological features. Interestingly, research by Bradley *et al.* (1992) showed that the tensile strength of porcellanite was less than any other of the sources they considered. The tensile strength of the Langdale tuffs was higher but was matched by sources which were used to a much more limited extent. It would appear then that extent of use did not correlate simply with the quality of the stone but may have been related to the colour and appearance of the axe. Patton (1993, 26) came to a similar conclusion regarding neolithic Armorica. The most widely used sources are not those producing the best functional axes but those that are visually distinctive and easily recognised, particularly Type A dolerite axes from Plussulien in Brittany. The porphyritic andesite from Lambay is visually striking, particularly when it has been ground and polished (Fig. 9.6). This colour may explain the value of this type of rock (for comparison see Pétrequin & Pétrequin 1993, 18). Sources of similar rock were exploited elsewhere in neolithic Europe, as in central Sweden (Welinder & Griffin 1984). In the case of the recent use of stone axes in the New Guinea highlands it appears that people were able to distinguish by eye axes from different sources (Højlund 1981). In Papua New Guinea, in a region to the west of the main quarries in the Mount Hagen area, the Huli people may have no knowledge of the locations of the source sites of non-local axes but they distinguish them on the basis of the direction from which they come, their colour and size. These imported, exotic axes are seen as being very different from the axes produced from local cobbles (Ballard 1994, 136).

So we seem to see a recurring pattern in which axes that circulated over wide areas are visually distinctive. They can also be seen as distinct from axes which can be produced locally from widely available sources. These axes literally carry their place of origin in their colour and appearance. We can suggest that, close to the sources, in the areas where the source sites were visible, a clear connection would be made between the axes and the place of production. As the axes were moved by exchange over greater distances they took on added resonances of exoticism

9.6 A broken porphyritic andesite axe found on the production site on Lambay.

as the human knowledge of the source faded. People may have begun to think of the axes themselves as permanent, something that had always existed (Strathern 1969, 326). In this sense the axe had become part of the social landscape, or as Aubrey Burl put it (1976, 82), 'the symbol of the natural powers'.

ACKNOWLEDGEMENTS

My thanks to my colleagues on the Irish Stone Axe Project, Emmet Byrnes, Stephen Mandal and Finola O'Carroll for their comments on this chapter and to Bob Allen for the Langdale photograph.

CHAPTER TEN

POINTS OF EXCHANGE: THE LATER NEOLITHIC MONUMENTS OF THE MORBIHAN

ANDREW SHERRATT

One of the qualities which Aubrey Burl has brought to the study of megaliths – notoriously mute monuments that they are – is a sense that they were built by real people, with recognisably human motives. His awareness of the fact that their builders incorporated a sensitivity to landscapes and to the cycle of the seasons pervades his descriptions and does not need to be clouded in abstractions. His belief that the ceremonies performed there were ones that addressed everyday concerns, even when couched in formulae and rituals which are incomprehensibly alien to the urban, twentieth-century mind, underlies his whole approach to neolithic times. This brief discussion of some of the world-famous monuments of the Morbihan – perhaps the oldest and most long-lasting concentration of megalith-building activity in the whole of Europe – draws attention to one aspect of neolithic activity which all too often occupies a different chapter in the textbooks: the role of trade and exchange. Taking a clue from their positions in the landscape, and also relative to each other, I hope that this discussion will help to draw together some observations about tombs, ceremonial sites, fortified settlements, and the artefacts that were used or deposited in them and which flowed through them like blood through the veins of a living organism; for this sense of vitality is one which he himself has instilled into their study.

SOUTHERN BRITTANY IN THE NEOLITHIC

The subject of this brief investigation is the later Neolithic of the Morbihan, the 'little sea' which gives its name to the present-day *département* in the centre of the south-facing coast of Brittany.[1] It is an astonishing concentration of megalithic activity, from which some 500 or so monuments survive in recognisable form – though even to isolate them into individual monuments is perhaps an artificial atomisation, since by the end of the megalithic period such highly visible erections (which in the case of menhirs is perhaps a doubly appropriate term) had been accumulating for at least two millennia (Le Rouzic 1965). They might better be considered, therefore, as contributions to a monumental landscape whose sculpting began in the middle of the fifth millennium BC[2] when influences, and probably immigrants, arrived from the Paris Basin to settle among the abundant indigenous populations of the western coastlands of France. The long mounds, initially of earth and timber, to which these early influences gave rise initiated a tradition which was most continuous in the region of its genesis: the zone surrounding the fertile loess-lands of west-central Europe (the Paris Basin and the Rhineland), most closely in touch with the villages of rectilinear timber dwellings and cult-houses of the central European Neolithic and Copper Age. On the Atlantic coastlands, however, and most conspicuously in those areas where indigenous populations had been most dense, new contributions to the megalithic tradition arose: indeed, it was in these areas that stone constructions, and monuments not obviously domestic, developed a life of their own. The effect was to create a continuing typological tension between two models of the organisation of ritual space, one circular and the other elongated or even explicitly trapezoidal, which underlay two thousand years of megalithic elaboration.[3] On the one hand, passage-graves of ever more sophisticated concept and construction grew into the virtuoso essays in stone represented by La Hogue Bie and Gavrinis; on the other, successive generations of long, quadrilateral monuments drew their inspiration from the long-house tradition – first, Carnac mounds, hypertrophied versions of the earliest long barrows; and then a new generation of more explicitly house-like structures which characterised the later Neolithic after 3500 BC: the old taxon of 'gallery graves', including *allées couvertes*, Loire (angevin) dolmens like Essé or Bagneux, lateral entrance graves, and further east the chalk-cut *hypogées* of the SOM culture in the Paris Basin, the *Hessische Steinkisten* or *Totenhäuser* of central Germany and the semi-megalithic graves of the Globular Amphora culture. In smaller compass, the same duality is discernible further west, in Ireland, between the local versions of the passage-grave – which also developed, albeit a generation later, into magnificent monumental complexes like that in the Bend of the Boyne – and the court-cairns of Ulster, which (like most other members of the long-mound family) showed less propensity to individual elaboration. It was the circular concept which was to become dominant in the British Isles as a whole. Ultimately, during the third millennium in Britain and Brittany respectively, both the circular and the quadrilateral traditions evolved beyond the three-dimensionally enclosed spaces of their respective types of tomb, into open forms of ceremonial monument: the stone circles and henges of the British Isles, and the trapezoidal stone alignments of Brittany – each with its world-famous exemplars, Stonehenge and Carnac.

It would be simplistic to take these tombs and ceremonial settings too literally as reflections or echoes respectively of the loess-land long-house and the Atlantic hunter's tent, continued in the round-house; yet this opposition, however subsequently transformed, accurately epitomises the dialectic between centre and west in Europe; and the contrasting houseplans themselves no doubt encapsulate further dimensions of cosmic ordering, whether of calendrical cyclicality or of appropriate orientation and rectitude. It is such ideological continuities, each anchored in a different geographical heartland, which help to explain otherwise incomprehensible re-activations of already age-old symbolism. The Carnac region (Bailloud *et al.* 1995) itself presents perhaps the most spectacular examples of this phenomenon. The earliest monuments of the region had been the long mounds, the *tertres tumulaires* which are by now usually the least conspicuous artificial mounds – frequently it is only their striking *menhirs indicateurs*, like the monoliths of Manio or Kerlescan, which first catch attention (though both forms reached their culmination in spectacular Carnac mounds like Saint-Michel or Er Grah and the grand menhir brisé). Yet it is these mostly modest early long-mounds which provided fixed points for the

The *grand menhir brisé*, Locmariaquer, Morbihan, Brittany, photographed in 1981 before recent excavations of the Table des Marchands passage grave, visible in the background. (Photo: Alex Gibson)

construction of the much later trapezoidal alignments, like those of Kerzerho (Erdeven) or the triple series of Ménec-Kermario-Kerlescan (Carnac). The Manio I long-mound, indeed, lies under the Kermario alignments; and the Kerlescan alignments have their origin (at the broad, i.e. 'entrance' end) in the Kerlescan long barrow with its associated *indicateur* and three-sided enclosure. Such enclosures, and other open settings of stones ('cromlechs' in French usage, and often mistranslated as 'stone circles') arguably stand at the beginning of all the major trapezoidal alignments of the Carnac region, in varying states of preservation (largely intact at Kerlescan, completely gone at Kermario), and it is possible that **all** cromlechs had their origin in enclosures whose open side was originally occupied by a long-mound. While often considered Late Neolithic, such enclosures make sense as part of the Early Neolithic long-mound complex. In any case, the alignments – the latest and most spectacular additions to the megalithic genre – revived the meanings of the earliest long-mounds in two ways: in physically linking their remains, and in consciously echoing their shapes, on a vastly enlarged scale. While such apparent continuity (or conscious revival) over some 2,000 years – sufficient to give rise to these remarkable regularities – is an astonishing conclusion, it is supported by some very specific echoes of detail, such as the use of schist and quartz in opposing rows of stones in the St Just (Ille et Vilaine) alignments, which repeats a motif from the equally early long-mounds (including examples in central Brittany and in eastern Brittany at St Just itself, where the alignments link up earlier long-mounds in the same way that the Carnac ones do).[4]

How is such continuity or revivalism to be conceptualised? It is perhaps unlikely to have been due solely to conservatism at the locations in question. More probably these ideas were periodically re-activated by contacts with areas closer to the continental heartland of the long-

A view looking west of the Late Neolithic stone alignments at Kermario, Carnac, Brittany, photographed in 1981. (Photo: Alex Gibson)

structure tradition, and more specifically in the area between the Paris Basin and Brittany. The two phases of long structures (early long barrows, and alignments or 'gallery graves') in western France corresponded to phases of wider cultural linkage and orientation towards central Europe, separated by a period of southern or Atlantic orientation when passage-graves predominated and Chasséen influences from the south affected the whole of France, perhaps appealing especially to populations of indigenous origin with their circular burial structures. Thus the genesis of long-mounds occurred in the context of the Cerny horizon in the mid-fifth millennium, when Brittany was penetrated by influences coming from the east as a result of the expansion and intermarriage of loess-land groups. The tension between the two models, symbolised respectively in circular chamber-tombs and trapezoid mounds over closed cists, was reflected in the growing scale of both passage-graves and long-mounds, culminating in the dramatic rearrangement of structures associated with the great Carnac long-mounds, and their incorporation in the most elaborate generation of passage-graves, as at Locmariaquer where earlier sculptured menhirs were incorporated in the construction of the Table des Marchands and Gavrinis. This was the apogee of passage-grave building in Brittany. But then a renewed phase of eastward contact took place in the later fourth millennium, with the proliferation of structures of 'gallery-grave' type, over a huge area from Brittany to Poland.

Within Brittany itself, this Late Neolithic period saw a radical alteration in the distribution of megalithic tombs, indicating an expansion of population in previously sparsely settled regions. In particular, the central areas of the Argoat (the wooded interior, as opposed to the coastlands of the Armor, which gave the Celtic region its name) show evidence of sustained occupation for the first time, in the form of *allées couvertes* of the same broad type as those of central France. Loire dolmens are a similar, if more spectacular, version of this same phenomenon further to the south (and with some outliers in eastern Brittany). Other broadly comparable types within the same family of tombs with elongated rectilinear chambers occur at the same time, most commonly on the north coast, in the form of lateral entrance graves which resemble the long *Hunebedden* of the Netherlands and northern Germany (L'Helgouac'h 1966; 1986); and these similarities are confirmed by the occurrence of typical TRB pottery forms like the collared flask – probably a container for a ritual narcotic drink (Huysecom 1986; Sherratt 1991). Although the primary impulses for these new forms of tomb, based on the wooden cult-house, were probably transmitted via the Paris Basin from central Europe (where new features such as ploughs and carts were appearing at this time),[5] there is a generally more international air to this typological variation, with external links both eastwards and northwards. All these new forms of monumental long-mound with a long rectilinear burial chamber occur most commonly in areas outside the older concentrations of megalithic construction. There is, however, at least one example of a lateral entrance grave **within** the Carnac complex; and significantly it is at Kerlescan, immediately to the north of the Early Neolithic long-mound and its enclosure, and the alignments that were subsequently to be constructed.[6]

The chronology of the Neolithic, in an area where large stone monuments are more common than stratified settlements, is insufficiently precise to allow the resolution which is obviously desirable. In broad terms, however, the sequence is relatively clear. A horizon of major changes in the middle of the fourth millennium BC separates the spectacular burst of passage-grave building, represented by monuments like Gavrinis in the older centres of megalithism, from the surge in the building of *allées couvertes* in new areas in the later fourth millennium, and continuing into the third. Some new forms of tomb, heavily influenced by the gallery-grave idea,

The Middle Neolithic passage-grave at Gavrinis during excavation and restoration in 1981. (Photo: Alex Gibson)

came into use in the older-settled areas, though usually in rather marginal positions within them. Gradually, and principally during the third millennium, there began in older-established areas like Carnac the extended construction of quite new forms of open monuments, the trapezoid alignments, perhaps consciously reviving memories of the local long-mound tradition in a new context. (Their specifically trapezoid shape, for instance, would argue for a scaling-up of the original long-mound plan – preserved in examples like the kerbs of the Manio or Kerlescan *tertres tumulaires* – rather than a derivation from the parallel-sided gallery-graves; while the custom of erecting menhirs was itself derived from the long-mound tradition rather than the passage-grave one.) The new context was a time of increased inter-regional contacts, manifested not only in the forms of monuments but also in the greater scale of traffic in objects such as stone axes. Prominent among the latter were the products of the quarries of Plussulien in the interior – one of the newly settled areas where clusters of *allées couvertes* marked the beginning of permanent neolithic occupation.

There is one more form of megalithic chamber-tomb to add to this picture of Late Neolithic complexity. This is the so-called *allée coudée* or angled passage-grave (often right-angled, or *en équerre*), represented by monuments such as les Pierres plates at Locmariaquer. The form presents problems to typologists, but in the context discussed here its significance becomes clearer. It occurs in central southern Brittany, and specifically on the coasts, on the edge of the area of continuous megalithic construction which had seen successive generations of long-mounds and passage-graves. It is itself, technically, a passage-grave, with a chamber approached by a long passage and set within a round or oval mound, usually oriented east–west; but the elongated form of the chamber itself, entered at one end of its long axis, clearly resembles the long, rectilinear cult-house structures whose concept underlay contemporary tomb-types like the *allées couvertes*, Loire dolmens and lateral-entrance graves. Like the last-mentioned type, it is in a sense a hybrid between the passage-grave idea and the gallery-grave idea: a specific, local, syncretic form which continued an expression of the passage-grave exterior with a gallery-like interior. It was also, of course, associated with a new and characteristic form of 'megalithic art', with its instantly recognisable trademark the *poulpe* or 'octopus' (Shee-Twohig 1981). While the specific identification (and now purely denotative terminology) relates to a hyperdiffusionist interpretation of the form as a degenerate version of a well-known Mycenaean motif, its recognition as a symptom of external contacts by sea remains a suggestive insight, as I hope to show. It is hinted at by the very location of les Pierres plates, somewhat offset from the main monumental complex at Locmariaquer, and standing on the seaward side of the Kerpenhir peninsula, overlooking the sea itself. Like its contemporary tomb types, therefore, it also conforms to the generalisation that later neolithic tombs occur in areas outside the earlier concentrations. Even though the sea was then more distant than the nearby strandline of the present day, its aspect is clearly outwards.

In the second generation of Morbihan megalithism, therefore, in the later fourth and earlier third millennia BC, there was a much greater diversity of monuments and a greater range of external connections. The mobility both of goods and ideas was greater in scale and more complex in detail. In the older heartlands, the building of open ceremonial monuments had taken over from the construction of tombs. Elsewhere, tombs were of new forms and had new types of location and function, like the 'expanded village' pattern identified by John Howell (1983, 96–8) and well exemplified in central Brittany (Fig. 10.2). This was complemented by new forms of site, such as defended promontories or fortified 'camps', which appeared for the first time as secular settings for domestic and other activity. These typological changes were set within a different form of cultural patterning. Instead of a few foci of settlement in which alternative concepts and ideologies strove for supremacy, there was a more open ecology of cultures, in which different forms of monument co-existed, while retaining their geographical and structural coherence. It is the logic of this complementary specialisation which provides the subject for the remainder of this chapter.

THE CULTURAL GEOGRAPHY OF THE LATE NEOLITHIC MORBIHAN

(1) Angled passage-graves

The nine examples of this type, certain or probable, known in the Morbihan are listed in Table 10.1.[7] Their distribution is remarkable, for they demonstrate a locational regularity which is immediately striking. While it is tempting to label it as 'coastal', this perception stems in part from the proximity of these sites to the modern coastline: the neolithic coastline was between 2 and 8km further out (depending on slope). A more accurate description would locate these sites on prominent positions overlooking the lower reaches of the major rivers. Between the Blavet and the Vilaine, three inlets (technically rias, or drowned valleys) offer access to the inland: from west to east, the Etel, then (separated from it by the Quiberon peninsula and the long blind beach of Carnac-Plage) the Crac'h, and finally the Rivière d'Auray, opening off the great drowned basin of the Golfe du Morbihan itself, then an enclosed estuary with much enlarged

Table 10.1: Angled passage-graves in the Morbihan

BLAVET AND ETEL RIVERS

Gâvres 1 **Goërem** (Burl: 133)

(On a small peninsula at the mouth of the Blavet, separated by a channel from the town of Port-Louis.)

Angled passage-grave set in an elliptical cairn. The 9m long passage is orientated south-south-west; the 17m long chamber is set at right-angles and to the west of the passage. It is divided by two jambs, one near the entrance and the other midway along the chamber. Two septal slabs set close together form an end chamber, 3m long. Eight decorated stones. Excavated by L'Helgouac'h 1964–7 (L'Helgouac'h 1970). Kerugou ware at low levels; Beaker pottery, four gold mounts with rolled edges (Eluère 1982, 38), barbed and tanged arrowheads and copper awls on top of the paving slabs. Radiocarbon date: 2480± 140BC Gif-1148 on charcoal from primary level, 4th chamber; 2150± 140BC Gif-768 on charcoal from 3rd chamber; 1910± 200BC Gif-329 on charcoal from passage.

Mendon 2 **Le Clef, Mané Bihan.** (Burl: 150f)

Angled passage-grave, south entrance, within the remains of a round tumulus delimited by stonework and some large blocks (diameter 30m). A large quantity of pottery and worked flint (Carnac Museum). Grand-Pressigny point, barbed and tanged arrowhead in yellow flint, fragments of pottery. L'Helgouac'h: SC (1965, 206, Fig. 75)

CRAC'H RIVER

La Trinité-sur-Mer 6 **Mané Roullarde** (Gaillard: Mané Roularde).

(On a hilltop, just north of the village of La Trinité-sur-Mer.)

Ruined angled passage-grave; the passage truncated (though probably with south-east entrance). Now consists of a passage 19m long, orientated north–south, constructed of orthostats and dry walling. Generally classed as an *allée couverte*, but in view of the hilltop situation, the presence of dry walling between the orthostats and the type of art, Shee-Twohig suggests that it is an angled passage-grave (Shee-Twohig 1981, 180). Three orthostats bear engravings. Fragments of pots including Kerugou and Beaker ware, one barbed arrowhead, one callaïs bead, one Grand-Pressigny dagger (Carnac Museum).

Crac'h 11 **Luffang, Tal er Roch** (Lukis: Lufant) (Burl: 192)

(Immediately west of the hamlet of Luffang, on the east bank of the River Crach, just south of the road from the village of Crac'h to the river.)

Ruined angled passage-grave. Circular tumulus, 46m in diameter. A 7.5m long passage orientated south, and a narrow chamber, set at an angle of 130 degrees to the passage. Twenty-five orthostats and dry-stone walling, no capstones survive (Shee-Twohig 1981, 181).Three decorated stones, one transported to Carnac Museum. Two diorite axes, 9 greenstone beads, a rock crystal bead, flint points, 8 barbed and tanged arrowheads, a Grand-Pressigny dagger and miscellaneous pottery including a Kerugou fragment (Carnac Museum). L'Helgouac'h: SC

Carnac 39 **Le Lizo, Er Roch** (Burl: 189a)

(On a hill just east of the village of Le Lizo on the west bank of the River Crach, near Penhoët.)

Ruined passage-grave, entrance south-east, in the remains of a tumulus. In Le Rouzic's plan (1933) the passage-grave appears to consist of an elongated chamber approached by a short passage set at an angle of 159 degrees. It is enclosed in an oval tumulus whose axis lies east–west. Other structures are shown within the mound. Shee-Twohig (1981, 180) notes that Le Rouzic suggests that the decorated stone was found in the mound behind the chamber. Stylistically the decoration belongs to that of the angled passage-graves. She remarks that from Le Rouzic's plan it is clear that the tomb may have been angled, although the angle is markedly obtuse. Furthermore the tumulus is shown as an oval in plan with its long axis east–west which would be normal in an angled passage-grave. Like Gâvres, the mound consisted of an oval cairn covered with a mantle of earth. Finally, although the plan of the tomb is not unambiguous, the juxtaposition of dry walling and orthostats is typical of angled passage-graves (Shee-Twohig 1981). The dolmen contained quantities of pottery including several fragments of Bell beaker, an arrowhead, a serpentine bead and flint flakes (Vannes Museum). L'Helgouac'h: DC 24i

AURAY RIVER

Locmariaquer 20 **Keréré, Mein Plat, Les Pierres Plates** (Burl: 208)

(On the seashore 800m south of Keréré.)

Large angled passage-grave 26m long, with lateral chamber, south entrance (195 degrees), and dry-stone walling. Consists of 38 orthostats and 12 capstones. Twelve orthostats are engraved. L'Helgouac'h: SC (1965, 204, Fig. 74).

Crac'h 19 **Kerentrech**/Point of the empty bottle

Angled passage-grave within the remains of a tumulus.

L'Helgouac'h: DC 26k (three dolmens) SC

Plougoumelen 1 **Le Rocher.** (Lukis: Kernoz; Desdoigts: Le Rocher, Pointe-er-Boursul) (Burl: 211a)
(On the east bank of the Auray River, just south of its confluence with the Bono River, 1km south-west of the village of Bono.)
Complete round mound covering an angled passage-grave. A passage 11m long oriented south-east leads to a chamber 8m long set at an angle of 90 degrees (Le Rouzic 1965). The orthostats are separated by dry-stone walling. Shee-Twohig (1981, 181) describes the cairn as elliptical and its diameter varies from 21 to 28m. All fourteen roofstones are in position. Five decorated stones. Grand-Pressigny point, chloromelanite axe, two axes (Vannes Museum). Pottery, beads, arrowhead, Grand-Pressigny blade, a chloromelanite axe, flint, a bronze ring, and according to Péquart and Le Rouzic (1927, 268) a blackish jade bead, a blue jasper bead and a schist bead (Carnac Museum). Also BM Lukis no. 386. L'Helgouac'h: SC (1965, 202, Fig. 73)

ISLANDS
Groix 12 **Port–Mélite**
(Near and west of Port-Mélite and south of Groix 11.)
Small *allée couverte* apparently angled.

(Sources: Le Rouzic 1965; Shee-Twohig 1981; L'Helgouac'h 1965; L'Helgouac'h 1970; Vannes and Carnac Museums)

---

islands and an extended coastal plain, into which a series of less major rivers debouched. The major concentration of earlier megalithic monuments and later alignments, extending in a broad zone from Erdeven through Carnac to Locmariaquer, is some 3–5km inland from the present coastline and 5–10km from the neolithic one; it lies behind the coastal ridge (followed by the D781), in a series of smaller side-valleys flowing parallel to the coast and draining for the most part into the Crac'h. Although not far from the coast, it is essentially inward-looking. The angled passage-graves, by contrast, occur in close relation to the main rivers: indeed, they occur at prominent points along them, from near the coast to some 15km inland (perhaps the limit of navigation by sea-going canoe?). On the lower Blavet and Etel to the west, just two sites are known, at either extremity: Goërem (Gâvres) is on an eminence overlooking the mouth of the Blavet, and was covered by dunes as the coast came closer. Other examples may be similarly buried, and one might be expected near the small town of Etel, at the mouth of the river from which it takes its name. Further up the River Etel, some 15km inland from the neolithic coastline, is the angled passage-grave of Mané Bihan (Mendon). On the Auray, les Pierres plates overlooks the river-entrance, in the same way as Goërem; 14km upstream from the neolithic coastline two angled passage-graves occur on either side of the river: at Point du vide Bouteille (Kerentrech) and le Rocher (Bono). Both the Etel and Auray rivers continue to their headwaters some 10km upstream (perhaps navigable by coracle, or followable on foot) where they branch into a series of confluent streams at the foot of the Landes de Lanvaux – a granite ridge running parallel to the coast – beyond which lies the basin of the upper Blavet, including the quarries of Plussulien (some 80km inland).

In between the Etel and Auray rivers is the Crac'h, which is much shorter than the others and extends only some 10km inland; but it gives access to the shallow depression north of Carnac, where the densest concentration of neolithic settlement of all periods occurs, and where the greater part of the population may be presumed to have lived. Three angled passage-graves occur along this route, of which two occur within fortified settlements (see Fig. 10.1). The hilltop site of Mane Roullarde (La Trinité-sur-Mer) overlooks its entrance, some 3km from the neolithic coastline; low-lying Luffang (Crac'h) is some 2km further on, on the opposite side of the river; and a further 2km upriver is the monument of Er Roch at Le Lizo (Carnac) on a high point on

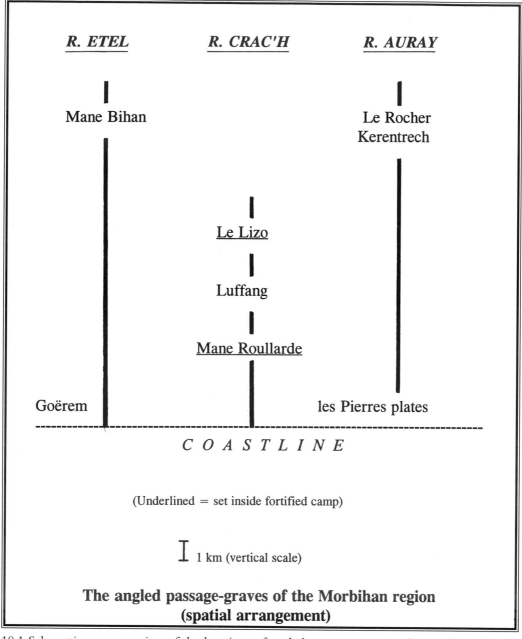

10.1 Schematic representation of the locations of angled passage-graves in the Morbihan, in the region between the Blavet and the Vilaine.

the west bank. There is one more angled monument, at Port-Mélite on the Île de Groix. The locational pattern of these monuments gives a strong impression of being directly related to axes of movement at the interface between sea and land, where the broad estuarine rivers reach deeply inland and give access both to the main area of long-established settlement and the resources and peoples of the interior.

Table 10.2: Fortified camps or promontory sites in the Morbihan

CRAC'H
Carnac 39 **Le Lizo, Er Roch** (Burl: 189a)
(On a hill just east of the village of Le Lizo on the west bank of the river Crach, near Penhoët.)
The enclosure known as the Camp du Lizo measures 200m north to south by 155m east to west and has several embankments overlooking the River Crac'h. Hut floors and cists have been identified towards the southern edge of the enclosure and quantities of neolithic material have been found as well as material of later date (Giot 1960, 84–5). Excavations have produced considerable quantities of pottery, arrowheads, fine flint implements, blades, scrapers, piercers, etc., axes and fragments of polished axes, a copper flat axe, beads of different rocks, fragment of a hammer axe, pounders, saddle-querns and polishers (Carnac Museum). [See Table 1 for megalithic tomb on hilltop.]

La Trinité-sur-Mer 6 **Mané Roullarde** (Gaillard: Mané Roularde)
(On a hilltop, just north of the village of La Trinité-sur-Mer: what appears to be a hillfort, the banks of which are very denuded.) [See entry in Table 1 for megalithic tomb on hilltop.]

QUIBERON
Quiberon 7 **Beg Er Goh Lannec** (Desdoigts: Beg er Goalennec)
Ruined bank, closing a rocky promontory. Flint flakes and the remains of coarse pottery (Vannes Museum); three stone cists. Finds: axe, pottery, beads (Carnac Museum).

Saint-Pierre-Quiberon 11 **Kervihan, Groh Collé**, Croh Collé
(Forming the end of a promontory by the sea, west of the village.)
Bank with upright stones; west of the bank, the foundations of a hut. From hut about 50kg of neolithic pottery, 10 barbed and tanged arrowheads, a quantity of flint flakes, 3 spindle whorls, some carbonised corn, numerous quartz and quartzite pebble implements, saddle-querns and granite pounders (Carnac Museum); 12 pottery vessels, 3 barbed and tanged arrowheads of flint, one axe-pendant and a quantity of flint flakes (Vannes Museum).

ISLANDS
Île de Houat 1 **Er Yoh/**Le Mulon
(Small islet north-east of the port, joined to the island only at low spring tides.)
Finds: from the summit some flint flakes and remains of animal bones. Hut foundations and midden material of shells, animal bones, fish bones and large quantities of coarse neolithic pottery; masses of flint flakes, 13 barbed and tanged arrowheads, 4 polished axes, scrapers, blades and small points, quantity of hammerstones of quartz and quartzite, some grindstones and pounders of granite (Carnac Museum).

Île d'Hoëdic 12 **Coh-Castel**
(Rock escarpment on the north-west point of the island, today forming a peninsula, closed by an embankment.)
Defensive embankment composed of a line of large standing blocks and earth. On the denuded rock of the west part numerous flint flakes and fragments of neolithic pottery were found.

Île d'Hoëdic 13 **Coh-Castel**
Second rock outcrop, some metres north of Île d'Hoëdic 12, filled with midden deposit. Scattered flint flakes, fragments of pottery and a barbed and tanged arrowhead.

Groix 2 **Pen-Men**
(On the headland of Pen-Men to the north-west of the island.)
Ruined mound formed of large round boulders and clay. Appears to be a defensive bank with hut foundations. Hearths with kitchen debris, composed of animal bones, fish bones, shell and bone implements.

(Sources: Le Rouzic 1965, Vannes and Carnac Museums)

(2) Fortified settlements

Two of the three angled passage-graves along the Crac'h occur on conspicuous hilltops within fortified enclosures (Table 10.2). (Indeed, a further example, on the Île de Groix, is situated adjacent to another fortified settlement, mentioned below.) The best known is Le Lizo (Carnac) near Penhoët (Lecerf 1986), where the Crac'h river receives the west-bank tributary stream of Coëtatouz, which drains the broad valley within which the great majority of the tombs to the north of Carnac are set, and which putatively represent a large part of the neolithic population of that area, and a substantial proportion of the Morbihan population as a whole. It therefore controls sea/river access to people, in a way that no site on the Etel or Auray rivers could do. Substantial Late Neolithic occupation of the site is indicated by hut floors, and the defences consist of massive banks and ditches. This site calls to mind the numerous contemporary fortified sites at the mouth of the Loire, and further south the Niortaise and the Charente. The second possible example of an angled passage-grave within fortifications is Mané Roullarde, in a comparably commanding position lower down the river, dominating both the lower reaches of the Crac'h and also (on its western side) an alternative overland route, starting along a small stream in a valley which runs down from Kercado. No excavations of the traces of fortification banks has yet taken place, but they are very eroded by comparison with Iron Age examples, and could well be neolithic. By analogy with the densities of such sites that occur around river-entrances further south, others may remain to be found. These two, however, are strategically situated to control access to the major area of settlement inland.

There are no other hilltops so strongly defended with artificial fortifications, but there are a number of promontory forts on the offshore islands of Houat, Hoëdic and the Île de Groix, and on the Quiberon peninsula (not then joined to the mainland by the coastal sandbar, which accumulated along the present-day coastline). Er Yoh on Houat is at the present time on a small islet, then an isolated hill, on the north of the island. Hut foundations and Late Neolithic occupation debris have been found in excavations. On Hoëdic the promontory fort of Coh-Castel on the north of the island is defended by a bank at its neck, and nearby are abundant Late Neolithic midden traces. On the Île de Groix the headland of Pen-Men on the north of the island has a promontory wall and hut foundations. On the Quiberon peninsula are two sites on the western side (Côte Sauvage): Croh Collé (Saint-Pierre-Quiberon) is again a promontory defended by a bank, with hut foundations and midden deposits; and Beg Er Goh Lannec (Quiberon) is very similar.

The impression given by the distribution of fortified occupation sites reinforces that given by the angled passage-graves: a relationship with patterns of movement by water, within which they occur at nodal points. This pattern, to become so familiar to urban geographers working in later periods, argues for new properties in the locational logic of both tombs and fortifications, different from those of the earlier Neolithic; and it suggests that the multilateral pattern of contacts in the typology of the monuments themselves is symptomatic of a new mobility in transportable materials. Defended settlements on the exposed coasts and islands would have acted as way-stations for canoe traffic working in relays (for the sail was not introduced to this area for another two-and-a-half thousand years, in the first century BC); fortified settlements at crucial bifurcation-points on the river network would have acted as defended centres of exchange with inland population centres; angled passage-graves along the rivers would have marked communities intimately associated with this network of maritime and estuarine or lower-river links. Their direct association symbolises the common identity of the coastal groups engaged in this traffic.

(3) Alignments

What, then, of the most conspicuous Late Neolithic monuments within the long-occupied heartlands of megalith-building populations, in areas such as Carnac itself? I have suggested something of the ideological significance of the form of the trapezoidal arrangements of stone alignments, and imagination may supply something of the ceremonies and processions which may have taken place there. There is no space here to look more closely into their immediate setting in an already old artificial landscape, densely dotted with tombs, into which they were inserted and gradually extended into the complex pattern which they now manifest. There are many levels of significance here, in their positions, orientations and linkages. Instead, I would like to comment on their broader positions within the landscape of the Morbihan *département*, and to include in this some of the smaller, outlying complexes which are less frequently discussed than those of the megalithic theme-park which Carnac has recently become. This pattern will then be compared with other examples in the adjacent *département* of Ille-et-Vilaine, immediately to the east.

The alignments of the communes of Erdeven, Plouharnel, and especially the complex which stretches from the western end of Carnac to La Trinité-sur-Mer, have often been described: they are noted in Table 10.3 along with the more fragmentary remains which may be the traces of others. In almost all cases the classic alignments are associated with, and aligned on, the less impressive remains of *tertres tumulaires*, the long mounds which stand at the very beginning of the monumental tradition in the fifth millennium BC, fifteen hundred or two thousand years earlier than the alignments themselves. They occupy the rim of slightly higher ground that encloses the shallow basin north of Carnac, drained in large part by the Coëtatouz, where the main concentration of earlier passage-graves occurs. From the Etel to the Crac'h, in a cordon arcing round parallel to the coast (and about 5km inland from the neolithic coastline), there follow, from west to east: Kerzerho (Erdeven), Ste Barbe (Plouharnel), Vieux Moulin (Plouharnel), Grand Ménec (Carnac), Kermario (Carnac), Kerlescan (Carnac) and its continuation Petit Ménec (La Trinité-sur-Mer). There may be less recognisable examples among standing stones on the other side of the Crac'h, in St Philibert, Locmariaquer, and the drowned coastlands of the Morbihan. There are certainly others, on a smaller scale but in a precisely comparable position – about 5km from the neolithic coast, in front of a small concentration of megalithic tombs – between the Etel and the Blavet, in the commune of Plouhinec. There are also two examples on the Quiberon insula, at Quiberon itself and St Pierre Quiberon, in the interior of the former island.

Besides these near-coastal examples, there are also at least two others further inland, around 20km from the neolithic coastline. Grand Resto (Languidic) and Forêt de Floranges (Camors) are situated on the upper reaches of rivers which flow into the Etel and Auray rivers respectively, and occupy positions on routes crossing the Landes de Lanvaux to the interior. (Again, they are associated with earlier *tertres* and decorated menhirs of the earliest Neolithic.) These may be compared with the related alignments of the *département* of Ille-et-Vilaine, immediately to the east, of which there are some eight examples including the major megalithic complex at St Just. These, too, make sense in terms of the river network. The mouth of the Vilaine occupies the north-east corner of the Mor Bras ('big sea'), enclosed by the line of granitic islands from Quiberon to Le Croisic above the mouth of the Loire. It offers access inland, via the fan of tributaries which converge at Redon: north-eastwards to the fertile Rennes basin, due north to the Forêt de Paimpont, and north-westwards to the Landes de Lanvaux and the resources of the

Table 10.3: Stone alignments in the Morbihan

NORTH OF CARNAC

Camors 4 **Forêt de Floranges**

Alignments of about sixty fallen menhirs, orientation east-north-east/west-south-west, extending over 100m.

Languidic 1 **Grand-Resto** (Burl: 135a)

(To the east of the village of Le Grand-Resto, north of the road from Languidic to Lambel-Camors.)

Alignments of menhirs, placed in three lines orientated east–west. Axe, flint flakes, arrowhead (Carnac Museum).

CARNAC/LA TRINITE

Carnac 5 **Le Grand Ménec** (Burl: 203b)

Alignments of menhirs, preceded at its western end by a cromlech.

Carnac 7 **Kerderff** (Gaillard: Kerdrew). (Burl: 178)

Two standing menhirs, 5.35m and 3.45m high, possibly outliers of the Grand Ménec complex.

Carnac 14 **Kermario** (Carnac Catalogue: Kerloquet) (Burl: 183b)

Alignments of menhirs, composed of 982 blocks placed standing in 10 lines in a north-east direction.

Carnac 21 **Kerlesca**n (Burl: 180d and 180a)

Alignments of menhirs preceded by a cromlech. This group contains 579 menhirs, of which 39 are placed in a cromlech and 540 are placed in 13 lines ranging in an easterly direction of 95 degrees. Maximum preserved length is 880m with an average width of 139m.

La Trinité-sur-Mer 14 **Kerlescan, Petit Ménec** (Gaillard: le Ménec Vihan). (Burl: 207)

(Near and to the east of the village.)

Alignments of menhirs, perhaps a continuation of the Kerlescan lines (Carnac 21). These alignments are composed of 101 menhirs placed in 7 lines (Gaillard has 8 lines containing 184 menhirs) facing east, forming a bend in a north-east direction at 41 degrees, where there only remain 3 rows (Le Rouzic 1965). Gaillard notes that at their start the lines of stones are oriented east-north-east. Mérimée *Voyage* 1836 p.239 'Quelques personnes âgées de Carnac et d'Auray m'ont assuré qu'elles avaient vu autrefois des alignemens distincts et bien fournis s'étendre à l'Est du Château du Lac jusqu'à la rivière de Crac'h.'

Carnac 68 **Mané Coh Clour** (Desdoigts: Ty-Lann, Mané Coh Clour)

(Near and to the north of Mané Coh Clour. Crossed by the road from Carnac to Auray, north of the junction with the road from Le Moustoir.)

Small fallen menhirs in a line. Several stones from these small alignments were destroyed in the twentieth century.

Carnac 79 **Keriaval** (Burl: 197b)

(About 200m north of the village of Keriaval.)

Three menhirs in a line, and other small menhirs on a north–south alignment.

Carnac 87 **Lann-Granvillanec**

Five fallen menhirs lying on the same line of east–west orientation, apparently the remains of an alignment.

Carnac 106 **Kermabo**

(East of the village and south of the windmill.)

Fallen menhirs placed in a line, which appear to be the remains of an alignment.

ERDEVEN/PLOUHARNEL

Erdeven 2 **Le Narbon, Man Liesse**

(About 450m west-north-west of the windmill on a heath-covered plateau.)

Menhirs, of which five are standing, the remains of an ancient square? Nearby fields contain a quantity of blocks, which appear to belong to cromlechs or alignments.

Erdeven 19 **Kerzerho** (Burl: 187a)

Alignments of menhirs. Comprising 1,100 blocks arranged in 10 lines going in an easterly direction, up to Mané Bras at 88 degrees; then towards the south-east at 125 degrees. These alignments are 2,100m long. The most important part is to the west, near the main road (no. 20) where there is a line of menhirs facing in a northerly direction, of which three are over 6m high.

Plouharnel 13 **Sainte Barbe** (Burl: 213)
Alignments of menhirs, preceded by a cromlech. Thirty-seven menhirs are visible, placed in four lines, orientated east-south-east. Several menhirs have fallen and are buried in the sand.

Plouharnel 14 **Le vieux Moulin**
(South-south-west of the windmill, opposite the railway station.)
Six menhirs standing in a line, orientated north–south; and three other larger menhirs, of which one has fallen, are situated near and to the south-east of the mill about 30m away. Perhaps the termination of the Ste Barbe lines?

PLOUHINEC
Plouhinec 2 **Gueldro**
(Near and to the south-east of the village of Gueldro.)
Remains of menhir alignments.

Plouhinec 6 **Kervelhué** (Burl: 147b)
(Near and to the north-east of the village of Kervilly, exactly to the south of the village of Kervelhué and halfway between the two villages.)
Remains of an alignment of menhirs, three still standing. Le Rouzic counted eight.

Plouhinec 14 **Gueldro** (Lukis: Kerzine) (Burl: 147a)
(Near and north of the mill of Le Gueldro-Hillio.)
Alignments of menhirs placed in eight lines, east–west.

QUIBERON
Saint-Pierre-Quiberon 10 **Keridanvel** (Desdoigts: Keridenvel)
(South of the village.)
Isolated standing menhir in an enclosure 2.25m high, 1.80m wide and 0.30m deep. This menhir forms part of a destroyed alignment of forty stones.

Saint-Pierre-Quiberon 12 **Saint Pierre** (Burl: 204)
Alignments of menhirs preceded by a cromlech. These alignments are composed of 23 blocks arranged in 5 lines, in an east-south-east direction.

(Sources: Le Rouzic 1965 and numerous other publications)

---

upper Blavet. The alignments of Langou, St Just, Carentoir, Guer, Montneuf, and Malestroit, at distances of some 15km from each other upriver, offer stepping-stones along these routes, while Plaudren (on the Arz, in the valley in front of the Landes de Lanvaux) offers a half-way position to the route across the Landes at Camors. In similar fashion to the promontory forts of the islands and defended settlements of the estuaries, these sites give the impression of being relay stations along a network of contacts – in this case, closely related to the rivers. Since trade would have taken place by a whole series of single-step exchanges, such ceremonial sites offered the opportunity to transact under the privileged circumstances of ritual gatherings.

(4) *Allées couvertes* and related types

For the sake of completeness in describing the megalithic environment of the Late Neolithic Morbihan, note should be taken of the tomb types of the interior. Most frequent in the north and centre of Brittany, *allées couvertes* extend as far south as the Landes de Lanvaux, for instance at Plaudren and Trédion – the latter an *arc bouté* type, without capstones, well known further north and west. At Bignan, on the northern side of the Landes where it is crossed by routes from the Morbihan, the *allée couverte* of Kergonfalz has a slightly angled passage with dry-stone walling, linking it to angled passage-graves – even though other features such as the enlarged chamber

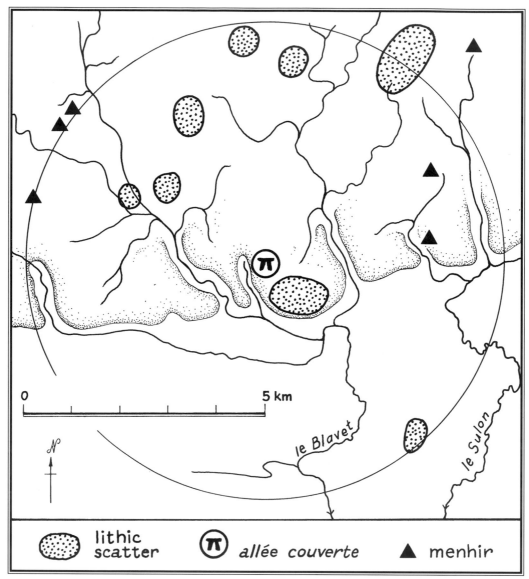

10.2 Results of surface-survey in the region of St Nicholas-du-Pélem in central Brittany, after Le Provost *et al.* (1972). Lithic scatters indicate the existence of a series of hamlets, focused on a central *allée couverte*. Menhirs appear to mark the edges of its territory.

and sloping passage link it to the *hypogées* of the Paris Basin. Such inter-regionalism is understandable in the light of the long-distance links of the period. Similar long-distance links (though here reflected in orthodox expression rather than syncretism) are manifested in the four lateral-entrance graves, two at Carnac (Kerlescan and Kerléarec) and two at St Just (Tréal and Four-Sarrazin), 100km away from their main concentration on the north coast, though linked by an intervening example at Coët Correc (Mur-de-Bretagne).

In eastern Brittany, as in the Loire region, the basic *allée couverte* plan takes the larger and more robust form of the Loire dolmen, such as the Roche aux Fées at Essé (Ille-et-Vilaine). Just over the border into the Morbihan are the examples at La Chapelle and Cournon. For classic *allées couvertes*, the nearest concentration is in central Brittany (actually the south of the *département* of Côte-du-Nord) on the upper Blavet around Mur-de-Bretagne. Here are the three famous tombs at Liscuis, as well as half-a-dozen further examples (as well as the lateral-entrance grave). The surveys of Le Provost, Giot and Onnée (1972) around St Nicholas-du-Pélem have revealed the surface lithic-scatters which provide the complementary domestic sites, corresponding to Howell's 'expanded village' model (1983), initially defined on data from the Paris Basin (Fig. 10.2). The role of Late Neolithic single menhirs as boundary markers, separating communities focused on a central *allée couverte*, is strongly suggested by this high-resolution snapshot of the cultural landscape. Perhaps the best known archaeological feature of this area, however, is the group of dolerite quarries around nearby Sélédin (Plussulien), which may well have been the incentive for this enclave of settlement, and which provide the topic of the next section.

(5) Artefacts and raw-material flows

The Late Neolithic in Brittany saw a greatly enlarged scale of raw material extraction, epitomised in the 10,000m² of quarries and factory debris (in places up to 3m thick) at Plussulien, leaving perhaps some 60,000m³ of waste products (Le Roux 1979, 55). The distinctive epidioritised dolerite, used for axes, is known from as far away as southern England and the lower Rhône valley − a distribution radius of 1000km, comparable to those of contemporary flint products from Grand Pressigny or Krzemionki (Sherratt 1976, Fig. 4). It accounts for about half of the total of stone axes in Brittany, and a third in a surrounding zone including Normandy, the Atlantic coast down to La Rochelle, and the Loire valley as far inland as Angers. Over a further zone, from the Gironde to the lower Seine, it accounts for a tenth of axe finds, with sporadic

Table 10.4: Selected finds of Grand Pressigny flint from sites in the Morbihan
★ indicates monuments listed in other Tables or discussed in the text.

Baden 14 **Le Couëdic**
Bignan 1 **Kergonfals** (L'Helgouac'h: Kergonfalz)★
Carnac 49 **Kergo, Er Rohellec**
Carnac 58 **Le Moustoir, Er Mané** (Burl: 205a)
Carnac 78 **Le Notério, Lannec Rocolan** (Gaillard: En Autérieu, Lannec Rocohan; Desdoigts: Nautério, Lannec Rocolan)
Carnac 91 **Mané Gardreine** (Lukis and Desdoigts: Kergrim)
Carnac 109 **Kerogel, Mané Bras and Mané Bihan** (Davy de Cussé: Grottes de Kerozille, Kerozillé)
Colpo 1 **Larcuste, Colpo I** (Burl: 149)
Crac'h 11 **Luffang, Tal er Roch** (Lukis: Lufant) (Burl: 192)★
Etel 6 **Pont du Sach** (L'Helgouac'h: Moulin du Sach)
Guidel 7 **Lann-Bluenn** (L'Helgouac'h: Lann-Blaen)
Île Aux Moines 1 **Kerno, Ro'h Vraz** (Burl: 139a)
Mendon 1 **Le Clef, Mané er Loh.** (L'Helgouac'h: Mané-er-Hloh, Mané Bras) (Burl: 150e)
Mendon 2 **Le Clef, Mané Bihan.** (Burl: 150f)★
Ploemeur 20 **Beg er Lann**
Plougoumelen 1 **Le Rocher.** (Lukis: Kernoz; Desdoigts: Le Rocher, Pte-er-Boursul) (Burl: 211a)★
Plouharnel 15 **Mané Remor** (Desdoigts: Mané-er-Mor, Mané Remor)
La Trinité-sur-Mer 4 **Kerdro Vihan, Men er Roch** (Lukis: Mein er Roch; Gaillard: Kerdo-Vras)
La Trinité-sur-Mer 6 **Mané Roullarde** (Gaillard: Mané Roularde)★
La Trinité-sur-Mer 12 **Kervilor, Er Rohec** (Lukis: Mané Rouhic)

(Sources: Le Rouzic 1965; Vannes Museum; Carnac Museum: British Museum; and others)

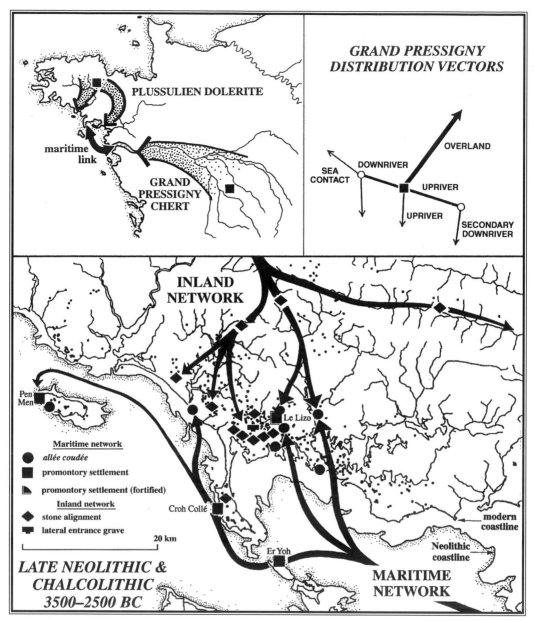

10.3 The Late Neolithic Morbihan (*c*.3500–2500 BC) as the interface between maritime and inland distribution networks.

examples clustering in the middle Seine and Aisne valleys, and in the upper tributaries of the Loire (Le Roux 1979, Fig. 3). It is clear that the Loire valley formed a major artery of distribution, and that Plussulien axes must have reached it by way of the Morbihan and Ille-et-Villaine. Similar observations apply to the hornblendite battle-axes from a source at Pleuvan near Quimper, which are common in the Morbihan and whose distribution extends along the Loire to the middle Seine (Le Roux 1979, Fig. 4).

With gratifying symmetry, products of the Loire catchment occur abundantly in Brittany. The honey-coloured chert of the Grand Pressigny area, on a tributary of the Vienne not far from Poitiers, was also exploited on a vast scale and was used particularly for daggers, made by a neo-levallois technique on the long prepared cores known from their colour as *livres de beurre*. Daggers, gradually becoming the male identity markers of the Late Neolithic and Chalcolithic, had their floruit (in the early Bell-Beaker period) somewhat later than the axes of Plussulien, but nevertheless overlapped for a substantial part of their periods of production. Moreover daggers and other objects of Grand Pressigny chert occur abundantly in Brittany, both in the largely non-megalithic contexts of the Rennes basin, and also in many of the later megaliths of southern Brittany, including several of the monuments already mentioned (Sherratt 1976, Fig. 7). A list of such finds is given in Table 10.4. While it would be simplistic to envisage a trade between central Brittany and the Loire which consisted solely of axes for daggers, the complementarity of these sources was a primary incentive to exchange, and is no doubt symptomatic of a wider range of transactions in less durable materials.

How, then, did these products reach each other's areas? The answer, surely, is via the sites which have just been discussed – step by step, in a series of exchanges, through distribution networks linking the typologically distinctive provinces characterised by different forms of tombs and ceremonial sites. At fortified centres, or at ritual gathering places, materials brought initially by sea and river or overland were exchanged one for another. To move materials from central Brittany to the southern coast, a set of intermediaries would need to be involved, and therefore established centres of population exerted a pull on the movement of materials; but these movements also took place by geographically constrained routes and corridors of contact. One route thus went due south to the Morbihan, over the Landes de Lanvaux to Carnac; the other south-eastwards, along the Oust and via the ceremonial centres of Ille-et-Vilaine to the Vilaine and so to the sea. Other centres like St Just served as intermediaries with the Rennes basin. Along the south coast, from Finistère to the Loire, and down to the Gironde, canoe traffic carried small quantities of cargo both by coastal cabotage and also as riverine traffic, penetrating deeply into western France by way of the major artery of the Loire and its tributaries (cf. Sherratt 1996). In Brittany, such traffic routes did not necessarily follow the rivers directly: it is not the Blavet, but smaller rivers like the Etel and the Auray – closer to the centres of population – which offered an *entrée* into the hinterland of the Morbihan; and much traffic must have proceeded indirectly, through the hands of consumers in the Carnac region itself. Like the braids of a rope, these multiple channels of trade nevertheless made up broadly defined corridors of contact but each individual object went through many human hands along its route (Fig. 10.2).

CONCLUSION: THE CONSTRUCTION OF
NEOLITHIC ETHNICITIES

I have tried to suggest how contemporary diversities were linked in intimate contact through the flows of materials, and yet maintained their distinctiveness; I have also tried to show how aspects of that distinctiveness went back up to two thousand years, and reflected underlying dualities in the cultural heritage of populations in areas such as the Carnac region. These alterities provided a pool of diversity on which to draw in constructing contemporary identities. Even within an area as geographically coherent as the southern Morbihan, Late Neolithic populations apparently espoused at least two identities, corresponding to two networks of contact, one inland and over the hills, the other by sea and beyond the islands. The constructors of alignments seem to have emphasised not only their links to a wider gallery-grave community (along with the builders of *allées couvertes* and related tombs), but also their local roots in a long-mound tradition. That these two concepts were compatible surely relates to their common origin in a tradition oriented towards central Europe. On the other hand, the coastal populations continued to build a form of passage-grave, however transformed under the impact of contemporary ideas. Were they consciously stressing their continuity with a tradition having alternative, Atlantic origins, and roots among a people who were there even before the long-mound builders?

Such contemporaneous variability tempts us to use the term 'ethnicity'. Since ethnicity is situational, no one form of ethnicity is ever like another; and neolithic ethnicity especially was not like the increasingly sharply defined entities that were to result from encounters over increasing distances, and now on an intercontinental (and hence often 'racially' defined) scale. But in so far as contemporary, adjacent and interacting populations accentuated differences in their material culture, not determined by immediate functional differences arising from contrasting environments, and in an apparently conscious way mobilised competing references to earlier monuments and their builders, we are perhaps justified in perceiving a phenomenon which can be labelled 'ethnicity'. Whether this went beyond a dualism expressed in moieties such as 'people of the land' and 'people of the sea' (like the Celtic opposition of Argoat and Armor), or whether these were entities capable of conflict (as fortified sites might suggest), is beyond our perception, but it appropriately summarises the dual personality of the coastlands of western Europe, and the diversity of their megalith-building inhabitants that Aubrey Burl has done so much to illuminate.

NOTES

1. I shall assume some familiarity with the most famous megalithic monuments of western France, as of the British Isles. Readers confronted with an unfamiliar name should consult the obvious sources in English – notably Burl (1985) and Joussaume (1988). The standard account of Breton megalithic tombs is L'Helgouac'h (1965); a recent survey in English is provided by Boujot & Cassen (1993). Additional details from Le Rouzic (1965) and other nineteenth- and twentieth-century sources, including museum catalogues and Lukis manuscripts, are stored on the Oxford Lukis/Le Rouzic database. For the purposes of this essay I have avoided extensive bibliography, and apologise to excavators and others whose work is not acknowledged individually. I have received particular help over the years, in the form of literature and offprints, from Jean L'Helgouac'h, Serge Cassen and Christiane Boujot; though none of these is remotely responsible for my choice of speculative interpretations. This essay had its prototype in one section of the second half of a paper whose first half was published in Sherratt (1990), and which has existed subsequently in a typescript called 'A monumental change: neo-megalithism in later Neolithic Europe'. Some of my earlier essays are reprinted in Sherratt (1997).
2. Calibrated dates are used throughout; though the chronology of megaliths is notoriously imprecise.
3. One could also read other metaphors into the plans and shapes of these monuments: male attributes and axes in the long-mounds and their menhirs, female attributes (and enigmatic representations) in the passage-graves.
4. This is the answer to objections set in print (after a seminar presentation which I gave at Cambridge in 1988) by Chippindale (1993, 30). 'His [i.e. my] scheme happened to have simple box-shaped plans at the beginning and, a couple of millennia later, simple box-shaped plans right at the end. . . . How does one distinguish the conscious revival of a structural type from the chance repeating of a simple shape that would easily arise in any case? Perhaps the distinction could be made, but I do not begin to know how; and I doubt if Sherratt knows either.' Yes he does.
5. This is also the time at which fresh impulses reached north Germany and Scandinavia in the Fuchsberg phase, beginning the TRB MN series of Nordic passage-graves and (I believe) bringing the plough from central Europe.
6. The other is Carnac 28a Kerlearec, Er Velannic (Lukis: Kerlearec; Gaillard: Kerlearec, er Velaneg; Blair and Ronalds: Tas de Pierres) which is about 200m east of Carnac 28, the Early Neolithic long-mound with closed cists at Kerlearec, Mané-Hui.
7. Shee-Twohig's meticulous work on the art, backed up by field evaluation, has significantly increased the numbers since L'Helgouac'h wrote his classic account (1965).

CHAPTER ELEVEN

RADIOCARBON DATES FOR SETTLEMENTS, TOMBS AND CEREMONIAL SITES WITH GROOVED WARE IN SCOTLAND

PATRICK ASHMORE

WITH CONTRIBUTIONS BY ANN MACSWEEN

Aubrey Burl has for many years blessed us with witty, informative texts on stone settings and related monuments (in particular, perhaps, Burl 1976 and 1993). Beyond that, he has helped people to enjoy stone settings in the field (for instance Burl 1995), and he has explored one of the most exciting and controversial topics in British prehistory: the astronomical knowledge of people in Britain before the Roman invasion (in, for instance, Burl 1987a; Thom, Thom & Burl 1980; 1990).

Although the primary purpose of this study is to improve understanding of the dating and in particular the radiocarbon dating of sites with Grooved Ware in Scotland, a subtext is exploration of the *terminus ante quem* for incorporation of ideas about the movements of the sun and the moon in the architecture of major monuments in Scotland. Even with good dating it is difficult to establish what people were trying to do when they set up stones in lines or oriented tomb passages near midwinter sunrise or sunset; but without good dating it is impossible to be sure whether an alignment had a precise or merely a likely general significance.

Quite rightly, a high standard of evidence is required for acceptance or rejection of theories about the intellectual achievements of past peoples (Pedersen 1982, 265ff., 272ff.). However, there is usually insufficient primary data to exclude a large proportion of potentially valid hypotheses about human activities and beliefs in the past, including the period in which stone circles and alignments were built. Indeed, formal proof of particular interpretations is as elusive for most commonly acceptable interpretations as it is for more challenging ideas.

With that encouragement to treat every interpretation here with a large pinch of salt, it seems quite likely that changes in power structures (Renfrew 1979; 1990) took place in the centuries shortly before 3000 BC, when Grooved Ware became common. Some people promulgated vigorous new ideas and created new types of large monuments. It seems quite possible that new religious or magical ideas were used to help consolidate power, and that rituals involving the sun and the moon were part of these. Be that as it may (and the evidence from Newgrange and Maes Howe seems to provide a persuasive argument for accepting that the building of astronomical ideas into the architecture of major structures was quite a widespread phenomenon in the later neolithic period), dating the use of Grooved Ware, and studying the degree of coherence of the pottery styles covered by that term, should provide a more informed base for speculation about the Scottish examples.

DEALING WITH ERRORS

Radiocarbon dates obtained in the 1950s and '60s were so much more useful than traditional ways of estimating the period of structures that their shortcomings were relatively unimportant. They 'brought relative chronological depth to a subject floundering among Ancient Britons and Gauls, all of whom seemed to have no more history than that they were prehistoric' (Daniel 1966, 281). However, some laboratories seem often to have quoted mainly or only the counting error attributable to the random nature of radioactive disintegration of carbon 14. They did not include all of the several other sources of possible error in their measurements. Sometimes all the dates produced by a laboratory may have been consistently too old (or too young) by decades. Other errors may have been random, but larger than allowed for by the laboratory in quoting the date. Archaeologists with adequate resources responded by getting more than one laboratory to provide dates for the same samples, as for instance Pta-1606, SRR-755 and Q-1480 for a burial in pit C at Quanterness (Renfrew 1979).

The accuracy of radiocarbon dating has increased considerably over the past decade, during which period international studies initiated by the Scottish laboratories (International Study Group 1982, 619; Scott et al. 1984, 457; Scott et al. 1988) have helped dating facilities to ensure replicable results. The 1982 study showed that two of the twenty laboratories compared in the study had at that time true errors over four times greater than those quoted, four had true errors over twice those quoted, while eight had errors up to twice those quoted and four had errors less than those quoted. The conclusions of the study group were that errors could vary over time at any given laboratory, and that the errors quoted by liquid scintillation laboratories should be multiplied by between 1.2 and 3.0, depending on what errors had been allowed for in the quoted error (International Study Group 1982, 622, Table 3). Dr M. Stenhouse, then of the Glasgow laboratory (GU numbers), recommended in 1982 that all the errors quoted for GU numbers below GU-1500 should be multiplied by 1.4 and if, after that, they were less than ±110, they should be read as ±110 (Stenhouse, M.J., pers. comm.). Baillie (1990, 366) studied several sets of dates from the early 1980s including a large set obtained at the GU laboratory. He concluded that the errors quoted for these dates should be multiplied by 2.6. In fact the GU dates had been obtained by a research student using machinery other than that used for standard dates at the time, and Baillie's conclusions do not apply to dates supplied to archaeological customers in the early 1980s. They do, probably, give a good impression of the errors which should be applied to dates obtained a few years earlier; frustratingly, it is not possible to say to which dates this larger error factor of 2.6 should be applied.

There is no published basis for attaching any particular correction factor to any particular dates

Table 11.1: Some Scottish sites with dated contexts containing Grooved Ware.

Site	Council Area	NGR	Dates used	Citation
Balfarg	Fife	NO281032	GU-1160, GU-1161	Mercer 1981
Balfarg Riding School	Fife	NO285031	GU-1670, GU-1904, GU-1907, GU-1905, GU-1902, GU-1906	Barclay and Russell-White 1993
Barnhouse, Stenness	Orkney	HY308126	OxA-3498, OxA-3499, OxA-2734, OxA-3765, OxA-2735, OxA-3501, OxA-3500, OxA-3766, OxA-2737, OxA-3764, OxA-2736, OxA-3763	Richards C. 1995
Beckton Farm, Lockerbie	Dumfries and Galloway	NY130824	GU-3534, AA-12587	Pollard A. pers. comm.
Links of Noltland, Westray	Orkney	HY429290	GU-1697, GU-1691, GU-1696, GU-1429, GU-1428, GU-1694, GU-1693, GU-1431, GU-1430, GU-1692, GU-1433	Clarke et al. 1985
Machrie Moor, Arran	N. Ayrshire	NR912324	GU-2316, GU-2325	Haggarty A. 1991
Quanterness	Orkney	HY417129	GU-1363, SRR-754, Pta-1626, Q-1479, Pta-1606, Q-1451, Q-1480, SRR-755	Renfrew 1976; 1979
Quoyness, Sanday	Orkney	HY676378	SRR-753, SRR-752	Renfrew C. 1976; 1979
Skara Brae Period 1	Orkney	HY231197	Birm-637, Birm-638, Birm-639, Birm-636, Birm-480, Birm-789, Birm-791, Birm-794, Birm-795, Birm-790	Clarke 1976; Buck et al. 1991
Skara Brae Period 2	Orkney	HY231197	Birm-788, Birm-786, Birm-787, Birm-436, Birm-434, Birm-435, Birm-433	
Skara Brae Wet Midden	Orkney	HY231197	Birm-793, Birm-438, Birm-477, Birm-792, Birm-478, Birm-437	
Stones of Stenness, Stenness	Orkney	HY306126	SRR-350, SRR-351	Ritchie J.N.G. 1976

listed here (apart from those GU dates covered by Dr Stenhouse's advice). However, it seems very likely indeed that the errors attached to the dates produced by many (but not all) laboratories before about 1982 should be increased substantially if they are to be comparable with errors quoted today. In what follows I have increased the errors attached to dates obtained before 1982 by multiplying them by 1.4 and then making them at least ±110. Although there is no scientific basis for this procedure except for GU dates, it would be incautious to use only the published errors.

THE DATES USED HERE

Two of the sites discussed here have major periods of use before the phase in which Grooved Ware occurs. Plain neolithic pottery, in contexts with appropriate dates, has been obtained at Machrie Moor (GU-2320, GU-2315, GU-2321; Haggarty, 1991) and at Balfarg Riding School (GU-1903, GU-2604, GU-2605, GU-2606, UtC-1302; Barclay & Russell-White 1993).

Not all dates from contexts with Grooved Ware are discussed here. GU-1163 and GU-1162 from Balfarg are from oak, and the alder dates in Table 11.1 are preferred. Q1294 (4590 ±75) from organic soil in the chamber of the tomb at Quanterness can be ignored for the purposes of this study since the average age of the material dated relative to human activity at the tomb may be measurable in decades or centuries. None of the dates from Raigmore, Beech Hill House and Pierowall has been included. It is difficult to interpret the dates from the former two sites, and those from the latter all seem to belong to later contexts. Several dates from the sites in Table 11.1 have been omitted because they are from later periods of activity.

INTERPRETING THE DATES

There is a complication in assessing the calendar date for the first Scottish Grooved Ware. Fig. 11.1 shows the results of exploring hypothetical radiocarbon dating of grain from 3000, 3100, 3200, 3300 and 3400 BC. I have allowed the hypothetical radiocarbon dates to 'come out accurately' and have expressed them ±70 years (if these grains had been dated in real life, usually only three of the five resulting dates would lie within 70 years of their 'true' radiocarbon date).

The grain of 3000 BC appears to be dated to between 3100 and 2900 cal BC. The grain of 3400 BC appears to be dated to between 3500 and 3300 BC. Both of these results are very satisfactory. However, nothing more precise can be said about the grains with true dates of 3100 BC, 3200 BC and 3300 BC and accurate radiocarbon dates, than that they came from somewhere in the period 3400 to 3000 (or even 2900) cal BC.

Fig. 11.2 shows site by site probability distributions of the dates for the material assayed in contexts with Grooved Ware and related contexts. At first glance it suggests that there is a high probability that some contexts date to well before 3200 cal BC. However, because of the calibration ambiguity described above, Fig. 11.2 requires considerable interpretation. It must be stressed that the curves represent relative probabilities that the dates really belong to particular periods, and do not represent continuities in use or occupation. Take, for instance, the curve for Quoyness, which has two radiocarbon dates. The curve suggests that both dates fall between 3000 and 2500 cal BC. However, for all we know from those two dates, the tomb was used for a short time around 3000 cal BC and then again around 2500 BC and not at all in between.

Dates from the two main phases at Skara Brae have been analysed by Buck *et al.* (1991). They used the quoted errors, rather than applying a scaling factor of 1.4 or more, and their conclusions were slightly different from those reached here. They treated residuality in a slightly cavalier fashion, given that the people who lived at Skara Brae do seem to have disturbed earlier layers in constructing later buildings. Their method required that they treat dates for bones as dates for the contexts in which the bones were found and that, technically, invalidates their analysis; but pragmatically their results were probably sound enough.

Their conclusions were that occupation started at the earliest at 3360 and at the latest at 2920 cal BC (*ibid*, Table 3), and most likely about 3100 and 3000 cal BC (*ibid*, Table 4). Figs 11.1 and 11.2 above seem to me to support this interpretation, despite use here of a scaling factor of 1.4

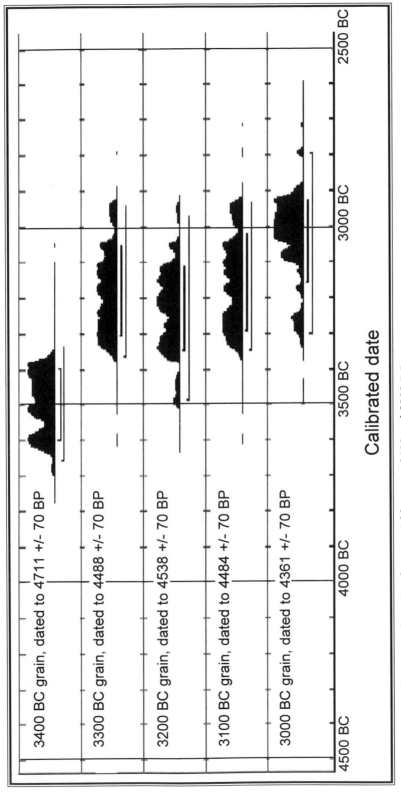

11.1 Exploring calibration ambiguities for material between 3600 and 2900 BC.

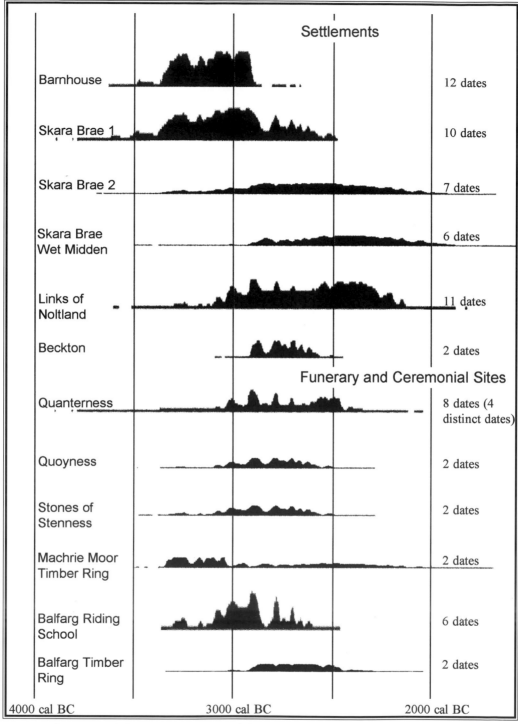

11.2 Site by site probability distributions of the dates for the material assayed in contexts with Grooved Ware and related contexts.

times the quoted errors. In other words, the bulk of the probability curve between 3400 and 3100 cal BC is probably caused by the ambiguities of the calibration curve (Fig. 11.1), rather than the true date of any of the samples falling in that period.

An analysis of the kind carried out for Skara Brae is impossible for Barnhouse, since its direct stratigraphic relationships are few. The earliest four radiocarbon dates from Barnhouse are earlier than those from Skara Brae. Reference to Fig. 11.1 above shows that calendrically earlier material can give a later radiocarbon date and *vice versa*. The similarity of the two probability curves is probably illusory, given that the errors attached to the Barnhouse dates are on average less than half the (scaled by 1.4) errors attached to the Skara Brae dates. In other words it is quite likely that Barnhouse was occupied earlier than Skara Brae 1. However, all that can be said rigorously is that Barnhouse was settled some time between 3400 and 2900 cal BC and abandoned some time in the same period.

Judging by Fig. 11.2 and the conclusion of Buck *et al.* that Phase 2 at Skara Brae did indeed start after the end of Phase 1 (*ibid.* 819), Skara Brac 2 was probably occupied from about 2900 cal BC onward. The settlement at Links of Noltland on Westray probably started about the same time or a little earlier (but not before 3000 BC) and continued in use until after 2500 (perhaps as late as 2400) cal BC.

The probability curve for Quanterness seems more like that for the earlier part of the period of settlement at Skara Brae 2 and Links of Noltland than those for Barnhouse or Skara Brae 1. (An early date for one burial at Quanterness has a large error attached to it.) The numbers of dated contexts at Stenness and Quoyness are too small for any confidence that they represent the full span of use of those sites; but for what they are worth they suggest the same.

DATES FOR GROOVED WARE

One might tentatively suggest from the very limited evidence available so far that Barnhouse and Skara Brae 1 were roughly contemporary and were settled from possibly as early as 3400 cal BC but somewhat more likely from after 3100 BC. Barnhouse has three main types of decoration – incised lines and chevrons; opposing sets of incised wavy lines (70–80 per cent of the assemblage); and pinched-up cordons with stabs on either side, giving the impression of a wavy line (Colin Richards, pers. comm.). In the Skara Brae 1 assemblage the predominant form of decoration is applied parallel cordons – one, two or three below the rim. Other forms of decoration are much less common but include applied lattices/trellises, scalloped rims and applied bosses (Ann MacSween, pers. comm.).

All the other radiocarbon-dated Orkney sites, including Skara Brae 2, were probably in use mainly after 3000 cal BC. There is little obvious difference between the pottery from Skara Brae 2 and that from earlier in the sequence. Within the assemblage from Links of Noltland there is a wide variety of decoration on the pottery, including applied horizontal cordons (single and multiple), wavy cordons, lozenges, fish-scale decoration and trellises, applied studs and scalloped rims as well as parallel horizontal incised lines and incised chevrons (Alison Sheridan, pers. comm.). The pottery from Quanterness is decorated mainly with incised chevrons and horizontal lines. One vessel has a zigzagging cordon, itself decorated with incised lines (Henshall 1979). The pottery from Quoyness is less distinctive – there are nine sherds, one of which has a cordon or carination below the rim.

Turning to sites south of Inverness, only the Machrie Moor timber circle may be comparable in date to Barnhouse and Skara Brae 1. Since the timbers there were quite large it may be wise to assume the charcoal used for dating was from tree rings a century or so old when the tree from which they came was cut down. It may date to 3000 BC or later. Machrie Moor has a small assemblage of seven or eight pots. The decoration is by grooved lines, combined in two cases with impressions. The only applied decoration is in the form of two small knobs decorating the rim of one of the vessels (Haggarty 1991).

The ritual structures at Balfarg Riding School probably dated to around 3000 BC, possibly with reuse at about the same time that the Grooved Ware was in use at the nearby Balfarg henge monument. In the assemblage from Balfarg Riding School, applied cordons are more common than incised lines. Some are impressed cordons, often forming lozenges which cover the whole vessel. Wavy lines formed by stabbing at alternate sides of a cordon are common (Henshall 1993). At the adjacent site of Balfarg Henge, the decoration is much more limited than on the Balfarg Riding School assemblage. However, there is only one example of the wavy lines in relief which were used so extensively at the Henge (Henshall & Mercer 1981). The settlement at Beckton in southern Scotland was probably in use during the duration of Noltland and Skara Brae 2. Its assemblage includes decorated cordons, some perhaps forming chevron decoration, and incised, infilled chevrons (Tony Pollard, pers. comm.). Note that, given the small number of dates from Balfarg and Beckton, it is not possible to say that they were contemporary with each other.

There is thus nothing to suggest that a single sub-style of Grooved Ware was in use throughout Scotland at any period, even at the time the style first appears in the archaeological record. The two (or possibly three) assemblages identified as 'early' from their radiocarbon dates (Barnhouse, Skara Brae I and possibly Machrie Moor) are very different in their composition. Again, there is nothing in the composition of the 'later' group of sites (including Quanterness, Links of Noltland, Skara Brae II, Balfarg Riding School, Balfarg Henge and Beckton) to identify them as a distinct group. Further, in looking only at these radiocarbon-dated assemblages, there is nothing to suggest an earlier and a later group typologically.

MacSween (1995), in her review of the taxonomy of the available assemblages of Grooved Ware from Scotland, was unable to identify any clear regional groups, although possible indications of regional preference for certain decorative styles were noted. The study suggested a common tradition, indicated by the presence of pottery with chevron-based incised decoration and all-over applied lozenges throughout Scotland, while the wide variation in motifs and their arrangement probably indicated that there was scope for individual expression within the limits of what was socially acceptable. As more well-dated assemblages are recovered, stronger regional chronological and typological patterns may begin to emerge. In Orkney, for example, where incised-decorated and applied-decorated Grooved Ware have been found stratified on the same site, for example at Pool (Hunter & MacSween 1991), the incised-decorated pottery is earlier, although from the radiocarbon dating evidence it would appear that both variants were in use for at least some time. The number of well-dated assemblages is too small at present to allow more detailed questions to be addressed.

A general implication of the dating evidence available now is that calculations of the significance of any potential astronomical orientations of Grooved Ware sites will have to take a wide range of possible dates into account, making the inherent probability of any particular date in this period less than if it had fallen into a shorter overall range of possibilities. For instance, Maes Howe was most likely built during the floruit of either Barnhouse (which is not far away) or Quanterness, Quoyness and Skara Brae 2, which has graffiti similar to those in Maes Howe

(Ashmore 1986). Therefore hypotheses, including theories about the significance of the position at which the sun set, must be tested against possible dates ranging from 3400 cal BC to after 2400 cal BC, with a concentration on dates between 3100 and 2400 BC.

The typological evidence does not prove that there will be variations in local expressions of the powerful ideas underlying the creation of major ceremonial and ritual monuments; but it is suggestive. Perhaps the variation was indeed within a coherent tradition which allowed variation within socially acceptable norms; but possibly the new practices took on local flavours, sowing the seeds for considerable subsequent variability. In either case, if Grooved Ware is at all a suitable proxy for early astronomical activities, we should probably not expect Scotland-wide studies to show up statistically acceptable precise and consistent patterns in alignments and geometries. At the other extreme, worries about the significance of apparent alignments must remain for all but the most unambiguously oriented of sites. Instead the most sensible approach is probably that of those who have, with an eye on the wider picture, concentrated their attention on the possibility of patterns within fairly small regions (for instance, among many others, Burl 1976; Ruggles 1984; Thom et al. 1980; 1990).

CHAPTER TWELVE

THE WELSH 'JET SET' IN PREHISTORY: A CASE OF KEEPING UP WITH THE JONESES?

ALISON SHERIDAN & MARY DAVIS

INTRODUCTION

A decade ago, upon joining the National Museums of Scotland in Edinburgh, one of us (AS) was given a piece of invaluable advice by Aubrey Burl 'not to try and drink yourself along Rose Street' – a traditional pastime favoured by some visitors and natives alike. This contribution, offered with our best wishes, is the direct outcome of heeding Aubrey's wise counsel.

The subject matter – jet and jet-like objects from pre-Iron Age Wales – has been chosen because it fits with two of Aubrey's interests: the archaeology of the so-called 'Celtic fringe' countries, and the archaeology of belief, ritual and magic. Jet from Britain's only major source, around Whitby in Yorkshire, has been used as a precious and prestigious material for over five and a half millennia. The reasons for using it – in addition to its aesthetic appeal and rarity value – are likely to have included a belief (probably inspired by its electrostatic properties) that it possessed special powers: its use for amulets, and references to its alleged magical and healing properties, are documented from Roman times until the recent past (Allason-Jones 1996; Wilson 1851).

The research described here is part of an on-going, long-term project designed to investigate the use of jet and similar-looking materials in pre-Iron Age Scotland and Wales. The project's geographical scope was originally limited to Scotland but, when invited by Frances Lynch to examine the small but interesting set of material from Wales, the authors ventured gladly into this territory. There is no intention to tackle English finds – for purely practical reasons, and because some work has already been done on these (Bussell 1976; Bussell et al. 1982; Pollard et al. 1981) and is continuing (Watts et al. 1997). The results presented here represent work in progress: a few of the Welsh objects remain to be examined, and further research is required on potential sources of non-jet raw materials in Wales. However, the results so far present an intriguing picture of strategies used to signify status and – as the title implies – to 'keep up with the Joneses' in prehistoric Wales.

12.1 The Caergwrle boat-shaped bowl. (Photo reproduced courtesy of the National Museums & Galleries of Wales)

JET AND JET-LIKE ARTEFACTS IN PRE-IRON AGE WALES

Ironically, the best-known object in this category is also the most enigmatic: the unique, boat-shaped bowl with applied gold foil and inlaid gold-covered tin of probable Middle Bronze Age date from Caergwrle, Flintshire (Fig. 12.1; Table 12.1, 23). Research undertaken for Stephen Aldhouse-Green concluded that the black material used for its manufacture was oil shale from Kimmeridge in Dorset, some 320km to the south; a Cornish source for the tin, and west Welsh or Irish source for the gold was suspected (Aldhouse-Green 1996; Smith & Owens 1983). A date for this object of around 1200–1000 BC was estimated on the basis of the gold's composition.

If one leaves aside the intriguing mesolithic find of nearly 700 finished and partly worked beads of local blue-grey shale from the Nab Head, Pembrokeshire (David 1997), then the remainder of the Welsh corpus of material

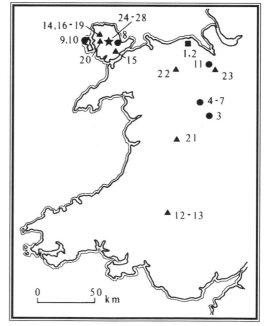

12.2 Distribution of Neolithic and Bronze Age jet/jet-like artefacts. Numbers correspond to Table 1. Key: square – Neolithic; circle – Early Bronze Age I; triangle – Early Bronze Age II and Middle Bronze Age; star – Late Bronze Age.

Table 12.1. Artefacts of jet and similar-looking materials from Neolithic and Bronze Age Wales

No.	Findspot	NGR	Site type	Object/s	Location	Associations	References
Neolithic							
1, 2	Gop Cave, Flintshire	SJ 087802	Communal stone-built grave inside cave	Two 'belt sliders'	Unknown; not Manchester or Buxton Museums	Found near ground flint flake, which was adjacent to flexed leg bones. Remains of fourteen crouched inhums. (M+F, various ages) in and near chamber; Mortlake bowl fragments and quartz pebbles in chamber.	Boyd Dawkins 1901; McInnes 1968
Early Bronze Age I							
3	Four Crosses (site 5), Powys	SJ 27531920	Grave pit within ring ditch – Phase 2 of 3-phase monument	V-perf. button	CPAT	Traces of extended adult inhum.; traces of wooden coffin. Button close to chest.	Warrilow *et al.* 1986
4–7	Ysgwennant (grave pit 2), Powys	SJ 189305	Grave pit under ditched oval barrow	Two V-perf. buttons, two 'pulley rings'	NMGW 64.53/2–5	In north part of pit: circular patch of hardpan with flint knife and iron pyrites; two 'sponge finger stones', crem. bones, charcoal; in south part, beaker (S2(W)/step 6), flint flake knife, charcoal. Pit large enough to take inhum., but none found.	Day & Savory 1972; Savory 1980
8	Merddyn Gwyn, Anglesey	SH 521792	Grave pit under approximate centre of oval cairn	V-perf. button	Bangor 4088–01	Crouched adult inhum., beaker (FN/step 7), copper alloy knife-dagger, fragment flaked chert	Hughes 1908; Lynch 1991
9, 10	Pen y Bonc, Anglesey	SH 219815	Rock-cut cist grave under round barrow	Spacer plate necklace, V-perf. button	BM 1870 11–26 1	Presumably crouched inhum. but no bones found; allegedly two 'urns' and two bronze armlets. Finder's claim for presence of coin discounted. Necklace in corner; Way (1867) suggests missing beads dispersed on discovery in 1828.	Way 1867; Stanley 1868; Lynch 1991
11	Llong, Flintshire	SJ 258625	In round (primary) cairn over grave	Five-strand disc-and-fusiform bead necklace	Clwyd Museum Service, Mold	Found among lower stones of cairn, above (but contemporary with) primary grave with crouched inhum., probably female. Also present in cairn: one fragment of unburnt cranium, parcels of crem. bones (two infants, one adult, burnt animal bone, charcoal, flint implements.	Lynch 1984

Early Bronze Age II and Middle Bronze Age

No.	Site	Grid ref.	Context	Object	Museum/accession	Details	References
12–13	Mynydd Epynt (Llanfihangel Nant Brân), Powys	SN 920383	Secondary grave pit under round turf and stone kerbed cairn	One intact biconical bead; another in fragments	NMGW 42.54/41 (just one fragment)	Crem. young adult; charcoal; accessory vessel; flint knife; squat fusiform bead; ceramic woven material. Artefacts 'appear to have been placed on the burnt bones soon after they were gathered from the funeral pyre'.	Dunning 1943
14	Bedd Branwen (grave C), Anglesey	SH 362849	Pit: one of five primary graves under complex cemetery barrow	Fusiform bead	Bangor BB/C	Collared urn; crem; two tiny unburnt flint flakes.	Lynch 1971; 1986b; 1991
15	Capel Eithin (urn C2), Anglesey	SH 490727	Pit paired with grave pit in 'urnfield'	Ribbed bead	Bangor CLE 80 [251] (41)	Collared urn used as accessory vessel (i.e. without crem.); assoc. pit C3 had collared urn with crem.	Lynch 1991
16–19	Bedd Branwen (grave H), Anglesey	SH 362849	Polygonal cist: one of five primary graves under complex cemetery barrow	Four grooved biconical beads	Bangor BB/H/f-i	Large collared urn; crem. adult male; six unburnt amber beads, and specks; burnt bone bead; burnt bone knife pommel. Beads (as necklace) deposited on top of bones.	Lynch 1971; 1986b; 1991
20	Treiorwerth, Anglesey	SH 354806	Disturbed burial in round clay-capped cemetery cairn	Grooved biconical bead	Lost	Unclear, but probably collared urn; crems in collared, Enlarged Food Vessel and atypical cordoned urns present in cemetery.	*Arch Camb.* I (1870), 365; Barnwell 1873; Stanley 1875; Lynch 1971; 1991
21	Carneddau (site 6506), Powys	SN 99339985	Rock-cut pit partly underlying ?recent stone ring bank	Flat bead	Powysland Museum, Welshpool	Dark sticky silt; charcoal; small stones.	Gibson 1993
22	Brenig (site 45), Denbighshire	SH 98305731	Walled barrow: on top of turf mound beneath clay capping	Lump, partly worked	NMGW 91.80H/1270	One of numerous finds from mound including c. 200 artefacts of flint and chert of various prehistoric dates.	Lynch 1993; and see text for discussion of date
23	Caergwrle, Flintshire	?SJ 311570	In bog, formerly lake	Bowl	NMGW 12.128	None; presumed to be votive deposit	Aldhouse-Green 1996; Green 1985 (with refs)

Late Bronze Age

No.	Site	Grid ref.	Context	Object	Museum/accession	Details	References
24–8	Llangwyllog, Anglesey	SH 430797	Hoard, from stream bank	Two ?beads with lateral transverse perforations; three beads	BM 1865 10–13, 23–4, 27–9	Sixteen amber beads; copper alloy; razor; tweezers; wire bracelet; five harness studs; nine rings (?strap links); two small rings; one broken double link; ?mount.	Lynch 1991; Stanley 1865; Way 1866

Key: NMGW = National Museums & Galleries of Wales; CPAT = Clwyd-Powys Archaeology Trust; BM = British Museum. Beaker classifications from Clarke 1970 and Lanting and van der Waals 1972

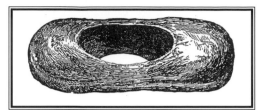

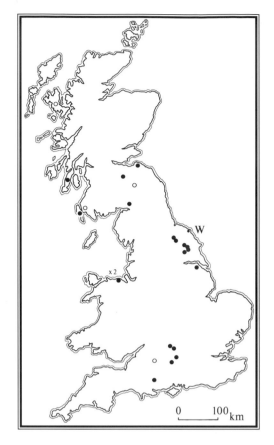

12.3 Neolithic belt sliders. Above: example from Gop Cave (from Boyd Dawkins 1901), length 70mm; right: overall distribution (after McInnes 1968, with additions). Open circles: exact findspot unknown; W=Whitby.

consists of twenty-eight objects (one lost, three missing) from fourteen findspots, all but three lying in the northern counties of the former Clwyd, Gwynedd and Anglesey (Fig. 12.2), and all but three coming from definite or presumptive funerary contexts. (See Table 12.1 for contextual information and references.) With the exception of the partly worked lump of material found among barrow material at site 45, Brenig, Denbighshire (Lynch 1993), all the objects are jewellery or dress accessories, of general types well known from elsewhere in Britain.

The earliest specimens are two neolithic belt sliders found in a communal grave structure inside Gop Cave, Flintshire, in 1886/7 (Fig. 12.3; Table 12.1, 1–2). The overall distribution of such objects in Britain is sparse, with only twenty-three examples known (Fig. 12.3), but a clear contextual pattern is evident. Non-stray finds have come from funerary contexts, particularly (but not exclusively) from individual inhumations of high-status males such as at Handley Down 26, Dorset, and from river and other wetland contexts (McInnes 1968). Possible river burial and votive deposition seem the most plausible explanations for the latter, which tend to occur – as Ian Kinnes has recently observed – at some distance from the principal concentration of dryland graves in Yorkshire/Lincolnshire (the area closest to the Whitby jet sources). A late fourth/early third millennium BC date has been established for the example from the single burial at Whitegrounds, Yorkshire (from the associated human bone: 4520±90 BP, *c.*3500–2900 cal BC at 2σ, HAR-5587; Brewster 1984); later dates recently obtained from a double grave under an oval barrow at Barrow Hills, Radley, Berkshire, were regarded by the excavator as unreliable, given the condition of the dated skeletal material (Bradley 1992). So far, to the authors' knowledge, no examples of the other neolithic type of jet/jet-like artefact – the large bead (cf 'Ardiffery', Aberdeenshire: Kenworthy 1977) – have been found in Wales, although examples are known from Cotswold-Severn tombs at Eyford and Notgrove, Gloucestershire (Clarke *et al.* 1985).

Artefacts dating to the late third and second millennia BC (in calendar years) are more numerous, in keeping with wider British trends, but are nevertheless sparse. Needless to say,

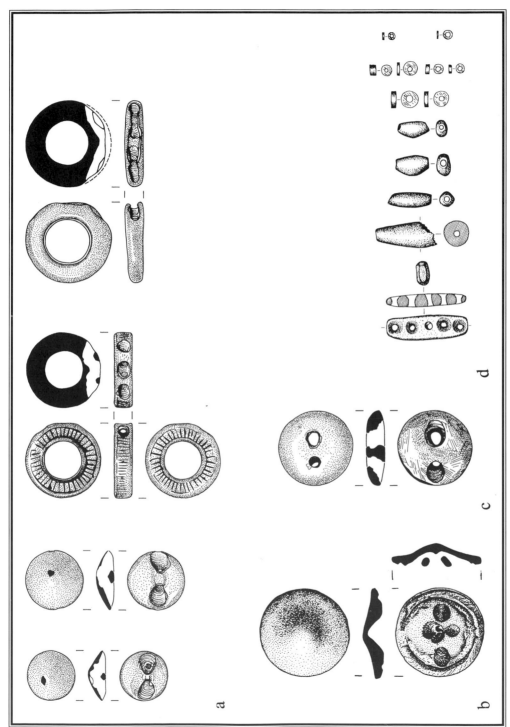

12.4 Early Bronze Age I artefacts. a: Ysgwennant (left to right catalogue nos 4–7); b: Four Crosses (after Warrilow *et al.* 1986); c: Merddyn Gwyn; d: Llong (from Lynch 1984). Scale 2:3. (Illustrations a and c by Helen Jackson)

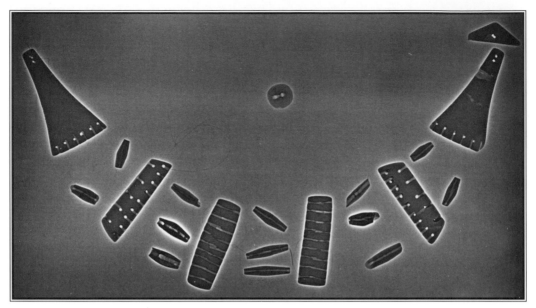

12.5 Xero-radiograph of the Pen y Bonc necklace and button. Definite jet items are the button and the fourth bead from the left on the top strand; the lignite or low-grade jet bead is on the bottom strand, far left. Fine lines extending from some of the pieces are modern nylon thread. (Reproduced by courtesy of the Trustees of the British Museum)

the absolute dating of individual items is fraught with difficulties, but for descriptive purposes the Early Bronze Age material can be divided into two broad groups: that associated with Beaker pottery and/or with inhumation as a funerary rite, and that associated with urned and un-urned cremations. Although these will be described as 'Early Bronze Age I' and 'Early Bronze Age II' respectively, some chronological overlap (as yet indeterminable) might have been involved.

The 'Early Bronze Age I' finds comprise the V-perforated button from Four Crosses, Powys (Fig. 12.4b; Table 12.1, 3); the two V-perforated buttons and two pulley rings associated with a possible pouch from Ysgwennant, Powys (Fig. 12.4a; Table 12.1, 4–7); the V-perforated button from Merddyn Gwyn, Anglesey (Fig. 12.4c; Table 12.1, 8); a spacer plate necklace and V-perforated button from Pen y Bonc, Anglesey (Fig. 12.5; Table 12.1, 9–10); and a multi-strand disc-and-fusiform bead necklace from Llong, Flintshire, (Fig. 12.4d; Table 12.1, 11). A further item which has been claimed to be of Early Bronze Age date can be discounted: what was published as a 'Worn fragment of a V-perforated button made of shale or cannel coal' (Savory 1980, no. 346) from Merthyr Mawr Warren, Mid-Glamorgan, is in fact part of a dome-headed, iron-shanked pin of Roman Iron Age type (cf examples from Traprain Law, E. Lothian and Crichie, Aberdeenshire: Stevenson 1955).

While the buttons and pulley rings do not differ significantly from their counterparts elsewhere in Britain, the necklaces are unusual: the Pen y Bonc example has curving terminal plates, narrow spacer plates, long slender beads and narrow perforations; the Llong example is

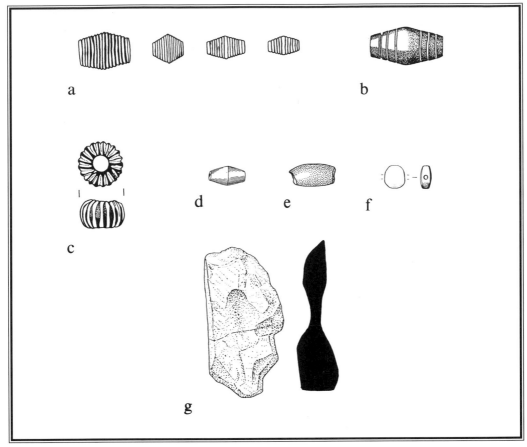

12.6 Early Bronze Age II and Middle Bronze Age artefacts. a: Bedd Branwen grave H (left to right catalogue nos 16–19); b: Treiorwerth (from Lynch 1971); c: Capel Eithin; d: Llanfihangel Nant Brân (from Dunning 1943); e: Bedd Branwen grave C; f: Carneddau (from Gibson 1993); g: Brenig (from Lynch 1993). Scale 2:3. (Illustrations a, c and e by Helen Jackson)

multi-stranded, with a narrow spacer plate (not dissimilar to the Pen y Bonc ones, although perforated through its broadest face) and a large number of beads (958). Despite these local idiosyncrasies, all these items are recognisable as part of an Early Bronze Age tradition of prestige jewellery and accessories, which is particularly well represented in northern Britain. (See, for example, Shepherd 1973 on V-perforated buttons.)

Notwithstanding the difficulties of establishing a date range for this material (cf. Kinnes *et al.* 1991 on dating Beaker pottery), an upper limit of *c.* 2300 BC can be proposed, on the basis of Stuart Needham's periodisation of the British Bronze Age (Needham, in prep.) and on the date of 2204–1866 cal BC (at 2σ; 3655 ±75 BP, OxA-4659) recently obtained for the hoard from Migdale, Sutherland, whose V-perforated buttons appear, by their associations, to be among the earliest British examples of this artefact type (Sheridan *et al.* 1995). A lower limit is harder to establish, because buttons and disc and fusiform beads continued to be used in various forms in Britain until at least the mid-second millennium BC. However, their association with <u>inhumation</u> burials does not seem to extend beyond the time when funerary fashions were changing in Wessex (the so-called 'Wessex I–Wessex II' transition – see below for dating). It is likely that the Pen y Bonc and Llong necklaces, with their associations with presumed and definite crouched inhumations respectively, are earlier than this.

While most of the comparanda for the Early Bronze Age I materials are to be found in northern Britain, a distinct shift of emphasis towards Wessex can be identified among the Early Bronze Age II items. The four grooved biconical beads from Bedd Branwen grave H (Fig. 12.6a; Table 12.1, 16–19), and the similar bead (now lost) from Treiorwerth (Fig. 12.6b; Table 12.1, 20), both in Anglesey, are strongly reminiscent of the biconical shale bead with bands of inlaid gold wire from the 'Manton' barrow, Preshute, and of the grooved gold-covered biconical bead of ?lignite from Wilsford G7, both in Wiltshire (Annable & Simpson 1964 – henceforth 'A&S' – nos 196, 157; Bussell *et al.* 1982). Indeed, the Preshute gold bands are echoed in the 'white substance' reportedly present in the grooves of the Treiorwerth bead. Other grooved biconical beads are known from rich Wessex graves, in 'stone' (Wilsford G46: A&S no. 338) and amber (Wilsford G16: A&S no. 310); further afield, examples in faience are known from Boscregan, Cornwall (Briard 1984). A further Wessex connection for the Bedd Branwen material is the polished bone bead: a similar bead was found with three plain biconical jet beads at Upton Lovell G2(a) (A&S no. 253; Bussell *et al.* 1982).

The ribbed bead from Capel Eithin (Fig. 12.6c; Table 12.1, 15) also has close Wessex parallels (e.g. the 'Manton' barrow and Wilsford barrows G7 and G16: A&S nos 197; 147, 154; 308–9). And yet another Wessex link is provided by the plain, gently angled biconical beads from the accessory vessel cremation grave at Mynydd Epynt (Fig. 12.6d; Table 12.1,12–13; cf. the aforementioned beads from Upton Lovell G2(a), A&S nos 250–2). Indeed, the assemblage from the cremation grave under barrow XI at Aldbourne, Wiltshire (Kinnes & Longworth 1985, no. 285) offers several points of comparison with Mynydd Epynt, with its accessory vessel, its biconical/fusiform bead of ?shale, and its squat fusiform beads of bone (the latter echoing the clay bead from Mynydd Epynt).

However, the use of plain biconical beads is not restricted to Wessex; for example, a similar example in 'jet' is known from Stockbridge in Hampshire (Longworth 1984, no. 638), and at North Molton, Devon, two examples in faience were found (Fox 1964, pl. 35). Similarly, the simple fusiform bead found inside the collared urn at Bedd Branwen grave C (Fig. 12.6e, Table 12.1, 14) has parallels which are not restricted to Wessex. Examples have been found, for instance, at Balneaves, Angus (Russell-White *et al.* 1992) and Westbourne, Sussex (here in bone: Longworth 1984, no. 1577).

Dating of this Early Bronze Age II material is once more problematic. There is a difference of opinion over the date of the best Wessex parallels for the grooved biconical and ribbed beads (i.e. the 'Manton' and Wilsford G7 barrows); and although both bead types occur together in these barrows, the radiocarbon dates for the Welsh examples suggest a statistically significant difference between the Capel Eithin ribbed bead and the Bedd Branwen biconical beads (Lynch 1991). The 'Manton' and Wilsford G7 barrows belong to Sabine Gerloff's 'Wilsford' series of rich female graves (Gerloff 1975; 1993), which are believed to belong to the late Wessex I–Wessex I/II transition period. Gerloff dates this, on analogy with dendro-dated finds from central Europe, to the late seventeenth–sixteenth century BC (Gerloff 1993), and this date accords with that of 1690–1321 cal BC (at 2σ, BM-453) obtained for an urn contemporary with grave H at Bedd

Branwen. However, others have put the date of the Wessex I/II transition earlier, around 1700 BC (Burgess 1986), and this is supported by a date of 1760–1675 cal BC (at 1σ, BM-2909) for a 'transitional' grave assemblage from Norton Bavant, Wiltshire (Needham pers. comm.). The date of 2192–1771 cal BC (at 2σ, CAR-448) for the Capel Eithin ribbed bead places it within a period when the use of ornaments – especially those of prestigious materials – proliferated in Britain (Needham in prep.).

As for fusiform beads, a currency extending into the Wessex II period (1700–1500 BC, according to Needham and Burgess) is clear, and the aforementioned Bedd Branwen date of 1690–1321 cal BC, believed to be contemporary with grave C as well as with grave H, accords with this.

The remainder of the second millennium material comprises miscellaneous items: the flat bead from Carneddau (Fig. 12.6f; Table 12.1, 21); the partly worked lump of raw material from Brenig site 45 (Fig. 12.6g; Table 12.1, 22); and the aforementioned Middle Bronze Age boat-shaped bowl from Caergwrle (Fig. 12.1; Table 12.1, 23). The last is discussed fully in other publications (Green 1985). As for the flat, pill-shaped bead from Carneddau, dated to 1740–1528 cal BC (at 1σ), this has no obvious parallels. As indicated above, the Eyford and Notgrove comparanda tentatively proffered by Gibson (1993) are more likely to be Neolithic than Bronze Age. The fact that this item had not passed through the funerary pyre with the corpse suggests that it is more likely to have been a bead than a toggle: the variously shaped bone toggles found with Bronze Age urned cremations are almost invariably burnt (Piggott 1958). As for the partly worked lump of raw material from Brenig, all that can be said is that it appears to have been present in the turves which were brought to the site to form the primary barrow around 2070–1780 cal BC (Lynch 1993). The 200 or so pieces of flint and chert which were also present in the barrow include artefacts of Bronze Age, Neolithic and Mesolithic date; the raw material lump has no diagnostic features allowing it to be ascribed to a particular period, so its inclusion here among 'Early Bronze Age II' objects should not be taken as a firm indicator of its date.

A firmer date, of c. 950–800 BC, can be suggested for the hoard from Llangwyllog, Anglesey, on the basis of its Ewart Park phase metal items (Fig. 12.7; Table 12.1, 24–8; pace Lynch 1991). This hoard contains several items which link it to Ireland – not least the amber necklace, which is more likely to have been obtained from Ireland than from its ultimate source in Scandinavia (Eogan 1994). The function of some of the black-material items is uncertain: while the three simple beads (Table 12.1, 26–8) can be understood as likely components of the necklace, the two items with additional transverse perforations (Table 12.1, 24–5) are more problematic. Bronze rings with transverse perforations are known from several Irish hoards (and indeed at Llangwyllog), and at Ballytegan, Co. Laois, one was found as an integral part of a wire armlet (Eogan 1983b, no. 94; see Raftery 1971 for comparisons). A wire armlet was present at Llangwyllog, but this does not seem to have required a transverse perforated ring to help its fastening. One other possible function is as a spacer bead for a multiple-strand necklace: examples in amber, albeit without such concave edges, are known (e.g. Meenalaban, Co. Donegal: Ó Ríordáin 1935). This use seems plausible for the Llangwyllog examples, although it does not account for the small hollows around the central perforation of one of the specimens (Table 12.1, 24). Unfortunately, the Scottish comparanda for transverse-perforated annular objects in jet-like materials – from Green Castle, Portknockie, Banff (Ralston 1980, fig. 2.12), and from Luce Sands, Wigtownshire (Hunter, pers. comm.) – shed no additional light on the matter, other than confirming suspicions that such objects are more likely to be items of human jewellery than pieces associated with, say, horse harness.

INVESTIGATIVE AND ANALYTICAL TECHNIQUES

Previous experience, and that of other workers (Bussell *et al.* 1982; Hunter *et al.* 1993; Watts *et al.* 1997), has demonstrated that the simplest form of non–destructive analysis is X–ray fluorescence spectrometry (XRF), used in combination with macro- and microscopic examination and X–ray imaging (Davis 1993, and see Figs 12.5 & 12.7). Compositional analysis using XRF is effective in differentiating between jet and lignite on the one hand, and cannel coal and shale on the other; further differentiation, between lignite and jet, and between some cannel coals and shales, has been reasonably successful. The pinpointing of raw material sources by XRF is more problematic, since cannel coals and shales are widely distributed, and can have highly variable compositions within as well as between deposits. Furthermore, jet sourcing may not be as straightforward as previously assumed, since recent work by Watts *et al.* (1997) has demonstrated the existence of a deposit of true jet at Kimmeridge, which early and limited analysis by XRF suggests is difficult to distinguish from Whitby jet. However, the actual exploitation of the Kimmeridge jet source has not yet been demonstrated, and the size of the deposit remains to be documented fully. Furthermore, notwithstanding the presence of several jet objects in Devizes Museum, there does not appear to be a concentration of jet artefacts around the Dorset source, as seems to be the case with the Whitby source.

Operational factors dictated that some of the XRF analyses would have to be done in the National Museums of Scotland's Conservation and Analytical Research laboratory, and some at the British Museum's Department of Scientific Research. The same reference samples of raw materials were used, and the machines are very similar to each other, but the results are not directly comparable in their existing form. All results obtained are semi-quantitative, because of the need to avoid destructive surface preparation and due to the difficulty of calibrating the data for the range of material being investigated.

The range of reference materials was restricted to samples of Whitby jet and Kimmeridge oil-shale and of cannel coals, shales and lignites from Scottish sources; expansion of the reference material to encompass Welsh materials such as anthracite is thus a priority. As indicated in the Introduction, the results of the analyses must, therefore, be regarded as preliminary statements as to material type – although identification of Whitby jet is (with the above minor caveat) reasonably secure.

RESULTS

As expected, a variety of materials were found to have been used; the results for all the analysed artefacts are summarised in Table 12.2. Only a few items were found to be of true jet: the Ysgwennant 'pulley rings' and buttons; the button and one of the beads in the Pen y Bonc necklace; and the biconical bead from Llangwyllog. Among the Ysgwennant material, the two buttons are so similar that they could have been made from the same parent lump of material. The fusiform bead from Bedd Branwen grave C, and one of the Pen y Bonc beads, though jet-like in appearance, have a composition which does not match 'classic' Whitby jet. They may be of low-grade jet or lignite.

Although it was not possible to identify all of the other raw materials precisely, it was clear that most of the Pen y Bonc necklace had been made of a single, compact material, high in iron, black in colour, and with a tinge of dark grey (Fig. 12.8); and that the grooved biconical beads from Bedd Branwen and the ribbed bead from Capel Eithin had been made from another homogeneous compact material, relatively soft, and with a blue-grey tinge. Further work on raw material sources from Wales and elsewhere should identify whether these distinctive materials were local to Anglesey.

Cannel coal and similar substances with a relatively high iron content were identified for several items,

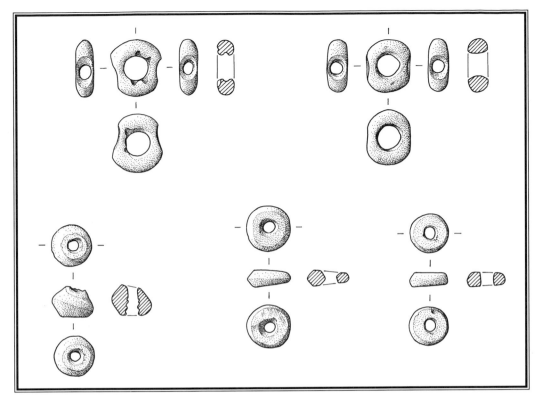

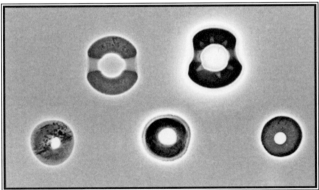

12.7 Transverse-perforated objects and simple beads from the Llangwyllog hoard. Line illustrations: top line – catalogue nos 24–5, lower line – catalogue nos 26–8. Scale 2:3. Xero-radiograph: Numbers as above except 24 and 25 transposed. (Illustrations by Nick Griffiths, xero-radiograph reproduced by courtesy of the Trustees of the British Museum)

such as the Merddyn Gwyn button, the Brenig lump and most of the Llangwyllog items. Cannel coal is relatively abundant in Wales; in order to demonstrate whether or not local supplies had been used, some form of destructive analysis would be necessary. That this could be fruitful is indicated by the results of Lindsay Allason-Jones's collaborative project on sourcing artefacts of cannel and detrital coals in north-east England (Allason-Jones and Jones 1994). This involved drilling a 2mm wide, 2–3mm deep sample from each object and examining it, in oil, in reflected light at ×600, and comparing the results against a reference collection. There may be scope for developing the Welsh project along similar lines.

Finally, as for the Mynydd Epynt biconical beads, unfortunately all that can be found of the 'intact bead plus fragments of a second' is a single fragment. The original excavation report stated that Dr F.J. North (then Keeper of Geology, National Museum of Wales) had identified the beads' material as anthracite, probably from nearby Carmarthen. The method of identification was not specified, but visual assessment rather than elemental analysis is likely to have been involved (Chambers, pers. comm.). Our own analysis does not support the anthracite identification, but instead indicates a material with a very high iron content, probably shale.

DISCUSSION AND CONCLUSIONS

If the degree of wear as well as the type of raw material is taken into account, an intriguing picture emerges. All of the objects made of jet show signs of wear, indicating that they had been used for some time before deposition and suggesting that they had been treasured possessions. The undecorated 'pulley ring' from Ysgwennant (Table 12.1, 7) shows the most extreme wear: the complex double-V perforation on its narrow edge had been worn through, rendering this means

Table 12.2: Results of XRF analyses (numbers as per Table 12.1)

No.	Findspot	Object	Composition/material
4–7	Ysgwennant	Two V-perforated buttons, two 'pulley rings'	All jet
8	Merddyn Gwyn	V-perforated button	Cannel coal
9, 10	Pen y Bonc	V-perforated button, spacer plate necklace	Button and one of the beads: jet. One further bead may be of lignite or low-grade jet with uncharacteristically high iron content. Remaining beads and plates: distinctive non-jet, iron-rich material – compact, black with greyish tinge
13	Mynydd Epynt	Fragmentary biconical bead	Not jet. Very high iron; mixture of other impurities, indicative of shale
14	Bedd Branwen grave C	Fusiform bead	Either jet (possibly low grade) or lignite; not classic Whitby jet composition
15	Capel Eithin	Ribbed bead	Not jet; compositionally similar to cannel coal, softish material, black with a blue-grey tinge
16–19	Bedd Branwen grave H	Four ribbed biconical beads	Visually and compositionally very similar to Capel Eithin
21	Carneddau	Flat bead	Not jet; high iron, very little else
22	Brenig 45	Partly-worked raw material lump	Not jet; probably cannel coal
24–8	Llangwyllog	Two ?beads with lateral transverse perf.; three beads	24: shale/canneloid shale; 25: not jet/lignite, unusual composition – ?kind of bitumen; 26: jet; 27–8: cannel coal

Note: the following items, whose current location is known, have not yet been analysed:
| 3 | Four Crosses | V-perforated button |
| 11 | Llong | Disc-and-fusiform bead necklace |

The Treiorwerth bead (no. 20) is lost, the two belt sliders from Gop Cave (nos 1, 2), and the intact biconical bead from Mynydd Epynt (no. 12) cannot be located, and the Caergwrle bowl (no. 23) has already been dealt with by Stephen Aldhouse-Green.

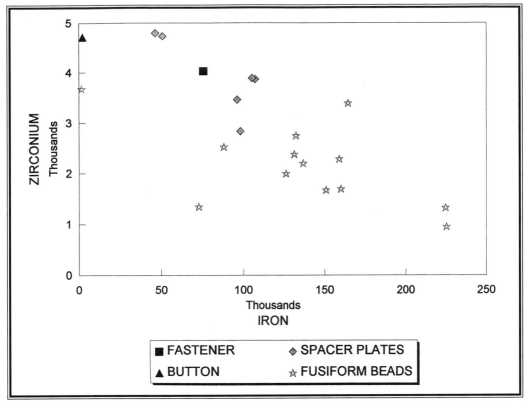

12.8 Scattergram showing the zirconium and iron content of the Pen y Bonc button and necklace components. True jet is characterised by a high zirconium, low iron content.

of attachment unusable. The recycling of jet fusiform beads from old necklaces is suggested at Pen y Bonc and Bedd Branwen grave C (although see above for comments on the latter's material). And although the Llong necklace has not yet been analysed, the heavily worn fusiform beads and spacer plate suggest that a similar recycling of material has taken place: the necklace may have been 'rejuvenated' by the addition of large numbers of (definitely non-jet) disc beads.

In contrast, some of the non-jet items show few signs of wear. Despite the dilapidated appearance of its upper surface, the cannel coal V-perforated button from Merddyn Gwyn still has discernible file and borehole marks from its manufacture, suggesting that it had not seen heavy use. The relatively unworn boreholes and still-crisp carving on the 'fancy' beads from Bedd Branwen grave H and from Capel Eithin suggest that these, too, were not very old when buried. The same applies to the Carneddau bead. And the non-jet components of the Pen y Bonc necklace do not show signs of heavy wear, although some string wear and bead-end abrasion is visible on some of the plates. (Whether the absence of most of this necklace's beads is due to its burial in an incomplete state, or to the former presence of organic beads, or – as Way suggested (1867) – to the probable dispersal of beads upon discovery in 1828, cannot be determined.)

What does this tell us about the patterns of procurement, use and deposition of prestigious materials in prehistoric Wales? Firstly, we would argue that it confirms that the inhabitants of North Wales were indeed 'plugged into' a network of contacts allowing them access to Whitby jet, and to the fashions in jet jewellery. We would contend that the distributional evidence for items such as V-perforated buttons and 'pulley rings' is consistent with an origin for the jet in Whitby, and not in Dorset (where most of the buttons are of non-jet materials). The idiosyncratic rendering of a north British jewellery item – the 'jet' spacer plate necklace – at Pen y Bonc suggests to us that it is likely to have been manufactured from locally available material (incorporating one piece of recycled jet and one piece of lignite or low-grade jet as well). Its burial in a not heavily worn condition is characteristic of other necklaces which have been made from locally available materials in Scotland (e.g. Burgie Lodge Farm, Moray; 'Yirdies', Lanarkshire). Furthermore, like these Scottish examples, its maker has 'gilded the lily' of the spacer plate necklace design by incorporating a larger-than-normal number of bead strands. The importance of the individual with whom this necklace was buried is underlined by the fact that the grave had been rock cut, and that a pair of metal armlets is alleged to have accompanied the necklace. This makes Pen y Bonc one of the richest graves in Anglesey, and invites comparisons with the necklace-plus-armlets graves from Melfort and Masterton in Scotland.

We do not know whether this membership of the north British 'fashion scene' occurred as early as the Neolithic, since the Gop belt sliders cannot be located. However, most other sliders which have been analysed or examined macroscopically appear to be of jet, so an origin in Yorkshire is a possibility. The relatively unworn condition noted by Boyd Dawkins suggests, however, that these had not been worn for long before burial; the apparent absence of wear appears to be a feature of many sliders (McInnes 1968).

Our second main conclusion is that a shift in the pattern of contacts/emulation did indeed occur during the 'Early Bronze Age II', as Frances Lynch has previously suggested (1991) and as other Welsh material indicates (e.g. Breach Farm, Glamorgan: Grimes 1938). We do not yet know whether the 'fancy' beads from Bedd Branwen and Capel Eithin were actual imports, and it is regrettable that the Treiorwerth bead is lost, but the cultural references of these items are clear. That material was indeed imported from southern England at some stage during the second millennium is indicated by the Caergwrle bowl. However, the Mynydd Epynt biconical beads, and probably also the Carneddau bead, remind us that local manufacture of some items was probably taking place (with the latter possibly reflecting purely local tastes).

Finally, the hoard from Llangwyllog confirms the complex pattern of contacts maintained during the Late Bronze Age, with the jet bead possibly being obtained from northern Britain, and the amber beads and some other elements (including, possibly, the design idea for the transverse-perforated items) coming from Ireland. The presence in the hoard of a mount made of tin, presumably from Cornwall (Lynch, pers. comm.), confirms once more contacts with south-west England (cf. the Caergwrle boat tin components).

ACKNOWLEDGEMENTS

Special thanks are offered to Alex Gibson, for his forbearance and for obtaining the Clwyd-Powys Archaeological Trust's permission to reproduce the illustration of the Carneddau bead, and to Frances Lynch for having inspired us to embark on the Welsh work, and for invaluable assistance thereafter. The following are also (alphabetically!) thanked for their advice and help: Stephen Aldhouse-Green, Pat Benneyworth, Sheridan Bowman, Mike Cowell, Nick Griffiths, Dorothy Harding, Fraser Hunter, David Jenkins, Janet Lang, Stuart Needham, Brendan O'Connor, John Prag, Niall Sharples, Elizabeth Walker, John Williams and Paul Wilthew.

CHAPTER THIRTEEN

WOOD SPECIES FOR WOODEN FIGURES: A GLIMPSE OF A PATTERN

BRYONY COLES

INTRODUCTION

At the beginning of *Stone Circles of the British Isles* (1976), Aubrey Burl gave a quotation from John Aubrey which includes the phrase 'from an utter darkness to a thin mist'. While this is apt for the light which Burl has brought to bear on the study of stone circles and other aspects of prehistoric ritual, it would be overstating the case for the pages that follow. The anthropomorphic wooden figures from Britain and Ireland are far fewer in number than the stone circles, and they mostly lack context and associations. But the evidence which they themselves contain, aided by reference to oral tradition, may allow the occasional glimpse through the thick swirling fog of ignorance, enough to suggest that the carvings stem from a coherent and complex prehistoric world view. Their various attributes and properties are not accidental, nor the whim of the carver, but consonant with the beliefs and rituals of the society that produced them.

There are a number of prehistoric wooden figures from Europe, recently surveyed by Capelle (1995). This chapter is concerned only with those from Britain and Ireland, which can be considered in three categories: those that survive and are known to be of prehistoric date; those that survive but have yet to be dated; and those that are known only from a written record ('paper figures' to borrow a useful term from bog-body archaeologists). Figures from the second and third categories may or may not belong to the same tradition as the first.

The dated figures range chronologically from the Neolithic to the Iron Age, they vary in size and in style, and there are only seven isolated finds and one small collection of carvings to consider. In chronological order, they come from the Somerset Levels, Dagenham on the Thames estuary, Lagore and Ralaghan in eastern Ireland, Ballachulish in north-western Scotland, Roos Carr in north-eastern England, Kingsteignton in south-western England, and Corlea in central Ireland (Figs 13.1 and 13.2; Table 13.1). The first seven of these finds are discussed in Coles (1990); Corlea, the most recent find (Raftery 1996), is now included in the group since, for reasons that will become apparent, it is likely that it was a deliberate if stylised representation of an anthropomorphic being.

There are four undated figures, two extant and two known only from the paper record (Coles 1993). Two or perhaps three of the four may belong to the same tradition as the dated figures,

Table 13.1: Wood Species, Sizes and Dates for Wooden Figures

Figure	Wood species	Height (mm)	Date
Lagore	Oak	470	OXA 1720; 2135–1944 cal BC
Kingsteignton	Oak	340	OXA 1717; 426–352 cal BC
Somerset Levels	Ash	160	Date of Bell trackway: 2700–2400 cal BC
Corlea	Ash	Head 160mm (total pole 5m)	Dendrochronological date of Corlea 1 trackway 148 BC
Dagenham	Pine	495	OXA 1721; 2351–2139 cal BC
Ralaghan	Yew	1135	OXA 1719; 1096–906 cal BC
Roos Carr assemblage	Yew	350–400	OXA 1718; 606–509 cal BC
Ballachulish	Alder	1480	HAR-6329; 728–524 cal BC

but the evidence is slight, or yet to be examined in detail, and these figures will not be discussed further in the present context.

In earlier discussion of dated figures, the possibility was raised of links with Scandinavian rock art, with the north-western European bog-bodies, and with the god Odin of northern mythology (Coles 1990, 330–2). These other spheres of activity all have a ritual aspect, and although they do not necessarily have anything directly in common with each other, it may be that they and the wooden figures reflect different facets of the same widespread prehistoric system of beliefs. As such, they may be concerned with ritual in its widest sense, festive as well as funereal, celebratory as well as surreptitious, mundane as well as awesome.

The wooden figures have been found in wetland contexts, the only likely context for the preservation of prehistoric wood given the climate and general environment of Britain and Ireland. It is therefore uncertain whether the wetland context is fortuitous or obligatory: were carved figures used, displayed and deposited in many different situations, to survive only in the wet, or was the watery ambience a necessary element in the ritual? There is abundant evidence to demonstrate the significance of wet contexts for prehistoric activities of a ritual character (Bradley 1990; Coles & Coles 1996; Van der Sanden 1996) and it may be reasonable to suggest that the wooden figures were deliberately put in watery places, not accidentally lost. It then becomes relevant to recognise a distinction between wetland sites that were ritual in primary intent, such as the lakes of Llyn Cerrig Bach and Nydam, and wetland sites with some other primary purpose where ritual was associated with dangerous or eventful aspects of the site, for example trackways across a dangerous stretch of bog as in Lower Saxony (Hayen 1987). In one or two cases, it may be possible to make this sort of distinction for the sites where wooden figurines have been found.

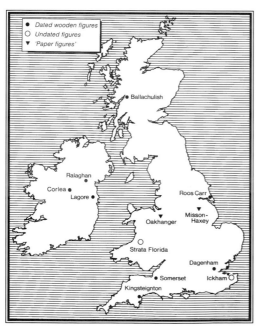

13.1 Location map of wooden figures from Britain and Ireland.

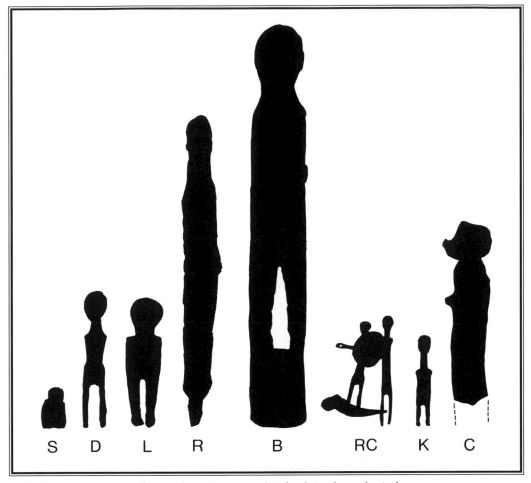

13.2 The dated wooden figures from Britain and Ireland, in chronological sequence.

A PATTERN IN THE WOOD?

During recent conservation work on several of the wooden figures, two of the early identifications of wood species have been checked and found to be wrong. The Ballachulish figure was carved from an alder tree, not oak, and the Roos Carr group from yew, not pine. Amending the previously published list (Table 1 in Coles 1990), a pattern emerges which suggests that the wood species for carving a figure was not selected at random but according to the character and attributes of the anthropomorph to be represented. The two oak figures, Lagore and Kingsteignton, are the two which are unambiguously male (Fig. 13.3). The figures carved from evergreen conifers, yew or pine, are those which have a pubic hole and which might be male or female – Dagenham, Ralaghan and the Roos Carr group. The one alder-wood figure is the one unambiguous female, from Ballachulish. The two ash-wood figures, from the Somerset Levels and from Corlea, are more crudely carved than the others, and both come from a trackway context. The carvings grouped by species are illustrated in Figs 13.3–13.6.

When the carvings are grouped in this way, further details of a possible pattern can be glimpsed. The yew and pine figures (Fig. 13.4), carved from evergreen trees, have a left eye socket which is less deeply cut than the right eye socket. They have probable or certain damage to the left side of the face in antiquity, although Ralaghan is not quite as clear as Dagenham and the Roos Carr figure in this respect. The Roos Carr carving which is illustrated is one of five surviving figures and a boat, and it is the only one with a shallow left eye socket and damaged left face; in previous discussions, it is the one identified as Fig. 3 or Image 3 of the Roos Carr group. In 1993, when the figures were being removed from the boat-base for conservation, they could be seen to divide into two crews, and it was suggested that Image 3 belonged to a crew of three that fitted the boat, and that its legs were shaped to fit the holes nearest to the animal-headed prow (Coles 1993, 21–2). In 1997 it was possible to examine the figures again in the Town Docks Museum in Hull. The long process of dis-assembly and conservation had been completed and the division into two crews could be confirmed. However, Image 3 showed further slight differences (in addition to the treatment of the left eye and damage to the left side of the face), setting it apart from its two companions. Its face is slightly more worn than the others, it has a slightly rounded rather than very flat chest, its pubic hole encroaches on the pubic bump rather than sitting immediately above it, it has no spinal groove up the back beyond the buttocks, and the surviving arm-hole opening is relatively square rather than round. We know that there were originally more than five Roos Carr figures, and so it is impossible to say to what extent Image 3 was distinguished from all its fellows. For the present, we should note that there are four yew-wood figures from Roos Carr which have pubic holes but do not have shallow or damaged left eyes; there is one distinctive figure, illustrated here, which is easily singled out in this respect.

Of the remaining dated figures, the only female is the only alder-wood carving. The two ash carvings, both of them fairly crudely executed compared to the remainder, were both found within the sub-structure of a trackway, and none of the other carvings is thought to come from a trackway context.

Small though it is, the sample of British and Irish anthropomorphic wooden figures seems to show some patterning, with a link between species of wood used for the carving and the attributes of the figure carved. In sorting the sample by wood species, the different types of figure have become easier to distinguish. This suggests that choice of wood was significant, and it is here that northern mythology may contribute some glimmerings of an understanding of what lay behind the choices made.

WOOD SPECIES AND WOOD MAGIC IN NORTHERN MYTHOLOGY

The oral traditions of northern mythology were first caught in the written word several centuries after the most recent of the wooden figures under discussion was carved. The traditions have been preserved for us largely from regions outside Britain and Ireland, although from a time when there was much contact among the countries bordering the North Sea basin and the north-western Atlantic. They must, therefore, be handled with care by the prehistorian. They represent, at best, developed versions of the world views and belief systems prevalent when the figures were carved, and with the carving spanning two millennia there will have been change within that time as well as subsequently. Indeed, the personages of Norse mythology and their attributes and activities can be seen to evolve from the earlier to the later records. Some gods are

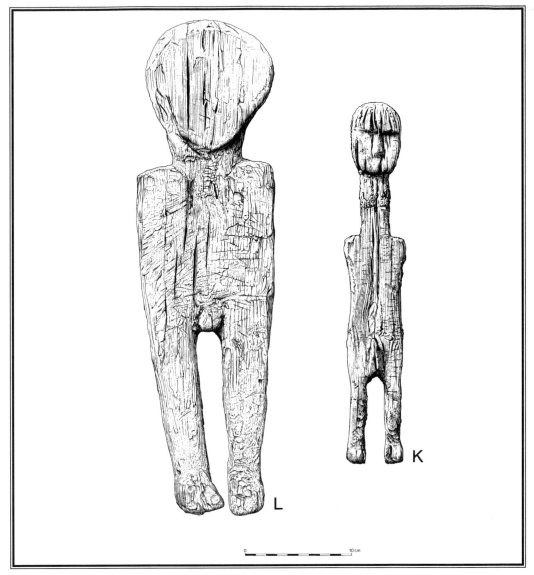

13.3 The dated wooden figures from Britain and Ireland, grouped by tree species: oak. L: Lagore (drawn by S. Goddard); K: Kingsteignton (drawn by M. Rouillard)

barely known, others wax or wane in popularity, the attributes of one become confused or conflated with those of another (e.g. Turville-Petre 1964, ch. 8).

It may, however, be possible to use the written records (or rather several of the scholarly surveys and analyses published over this century) to provide a general background to understanding the ritual world of prehistoric northern Europe, and to suggest an occasional link with a particular character or attribute. This will be done first for wood species, and then for wood magic, sorcery and shamanism.

NOTES ON WOOD SPECIES

Oak

The oak tree is said to be associated with the god Thor (Ellis-Davidson 1969). Simek (1993) and others note that when Boniface, the English missionary, was undertaking the conversion of the Germans in the early eighth century AD, he caused *rubor jovis* or 'Jupiter's Oak' in Giesmar to be felled. Jupiter being the Latin version of Thor, this would seem to be a clear and fairly early record of the link between oak and Thor. There is, however, little other reference to oak trees or oak wood, and the species perhaps carried a greater wealth or variety of meaning in western Europe than in the north.

Ash

Ash plays a role in the creation myths of the north: Odin, and his brothers Vili and Vé, found two logs on the seashore. They brought them to life as the first man, *Askr*, and the first woman, *Embla*. Askr is 'ash tree', Embla less certain but possibly 'elm' (Simek 1993, 74); or 'creeper' or 'vine' (Simek 1993, 74; Dumézil 1973, 101; Turville-Petre 1964, 276). An ash tree enabled Thor to save himself from drowning (Simek 1993, 20).

   Yggdrasil, the World Tree of northern mythology, is often said to be an ash tree, but it was also evergreen and possibly yew, and its significance in the present context is explored under the latter species.

Yew

One of the little-known gods of whom Turville-Petre said 'Their cult was so old as to be obscured by the time our records took shape' (1964, 180) was the god Ull, who lived in Yewdales. Ull, among his other attributes, was a skilled skier, archer and hunter, and there may be a link here between living where yew trees grow and using a bow, although prehistoric bows were not exclusively made of yew. At one point, Ull replaced Odin when the latter was banished for ten years by his fellow gods for having disguised himself as a woman (Turville-Petre 1964, 180, 182–3). Strutynski suggests Ull as a variant of Thor (Introduction, Dumézil 1973, *xxv*), but it is perhaps more likely that he was Odin in another guise, or rather that Odin was a later manifestation of the ancient god Ull.

   Yew has another possible association which, if it is valid, is of great significance. Central to the mythical world was the tree *Yggdrasil*, which provided a framework or scaffold for the cosmos and a ladder between sky, earth and underworld. Odin hung himself on *Yggdrasil* for nine nights, when he sacrificed himself to himself to acquire knowledge of runes. He also sacrificed one of his eyes, to gain wisdom and understanding from one of the three springs or wells beneath *Yggdrasil* (Turville-Petre 1964, 42ff.; Simek, 1993, 240ff.). *Yggdrasil* is described as evergreen, yet is identified in the sources as an ash tree, the sort of puzzling contradiction that might be appropriate to a magical tree:

> An ash stands, I know; its name Yggdrasil,
> A lofty tree sprinkled with bright water.
> Thence come the dews that fall on the dales.
> Evergreen it towers over the well of Urd.
> (*Völuspá* trans. Page 1995, 206)

Simek, however, notes that *Yggdrasil* has also been identified as a yew tree, though by recent scholars rather than in the sources. The name would then mean 'yew pillar', appropriate for the evergreen support of the world. Alternatively, *Yggdrasil* may be identified simply as a conifer, and not to species (Simek 1993, 375–6).

Another evergreen was described by Adam of Bremen in the later eleventh century AD, this time an actual tree growing near the pagan temple at Old Uppsala in Sweden:

> Near this temple is a huge tree, its branches spreading
> far and wide. It is always green, winter and summer alike.
> Nobody knows what species it is. There is also a well there
> where they have the practice of holding pagan sacrifices.
> A living man is plunged into it. If he does not surface again,
> the people's desire will be fulfilled.
> (Adam of Bremen, trans. Page 1993, 221)

Growing just short of the northern limit for yew (Godwin 1975, 115ff.) the Uppsala tree might have been of that species and perceived as both special and un-named because rare. But ash, though more prolific, had a similar distribution, and no distinction can be made between the two species in this respect. However, the Uppsala tree was a living rather than a mythological evergreen, and as such more likely to be yew, or at least a conifer, rather than ash. The references to a well at its foot and to human sacrifice provide reminders of Odin and perhaps reinforce a 'Yew–sacred tree–Odin' connection.

NOTES ON WOOD MAGIC, SORCERY AND SHAMANISM

We have seen above that in one northern creation myth the first man and first woman were created from two logs: the ancestors were fashioned from wood. Alongside this benign activity practised on or through wood in human shape, there was another aspect which Simek links with sorcery and shamanistic activity. Termed *treniđ* (wooden derision) or *niđstong* (derision pole), this involved setting up wooden poles carved with a human head, or perhaps with a horse's skull on top, to curse, deride or deter particular people (Simek 1993, 200). Anisimov, recounting the preparation of a shaman's tent by the Evenk in Siberia, in the 1920s or '30s, describes the many wooden figures set in prescribed positions around the tent, including anthropomorphic wooden figures which are shamanistic spirits guarding the road to the upper world. The shaman addresses them as 'grandmothers, grandfathers, ancestors, forefathers, guardians of the clan' (Anisimov 1963, 88 and Fig. 2a). Here, perhaps, is a context where the two notions of log or pole-like anthropomorphic wooden figures, as ancestors and as images or beings imbued with a degree of power, come together. The same conjunction may have been present in prehistoric contexts.

The god Odin was a sorcerer or shaman, who practised *seiđ* or *seiđr*, the wood magic being one relatively minor aspect of this. *Seiđ* was a female activity (Steinsland 1992) which Odin taught to himself, probably when he hung on *Yggdrasil* as well as when he sacrificed his eye to the spring or well at the foot of that tree. As a shaman, Odin was perceived as sexually ambiguous. For this, he was accused of perversion by his fellow gods by the time the myths were written down, for effeminacy was 'a quality the Vikings abhorred' (Page 1995, 203). Anisimov notes that the Evenks of Siberia believed the first shamans to have been women, and that their present shamans wore clothing which in style and ornament resembled women's dress. An association of shamanism with female attributes is found elsewhere in the world (Orme 1981, 239), and the shaman-god of pre-Viking times might be more properly described as able to be either male or female, rather than as an effeminate male. Stuart Piggott (1962) discussed briefly the possibility of Bronze Age shamans in Britain, in relation to the interpretation of one of the Wessex burials, a possibility that was further examined by Hemming (1991). A god with shamanistic attributes would not be out of place in a society where practising shamans were afforded elaborate burials, and Burl has emphasised that shamans are more likely than astronomer-priests as performers of ritual associated with stone circles (Burl 1976, 87; 1979, 202).

By the first millennium AD, Odin's popularity would appear to have been on the wane, as Thor became more prominent in people's lives (Ellis-Davidson 1969). Thor was definitely not a shaman, and his replacement of Odin may signify a move away from shamanism, possibly but not necessarily influenced by the spread of Christianity. It may have been at this time that the blinded eyes of the yew-wood carvings were slighted.

DISCUSSION

Bringing together wood species, the attributes of the carvings, and the beliefs about wood and trees outlined above, it can be argued that the choice of wood used for an anthropomorphic carving was deliberate, and that it is indicative of the character and powers of the being which is represented. Similar relationships between subject and wood species are known elsewhere in the world, for example as recently discussed by Saunders and Gray (1996) in a Jamaican context.

If oak is to be associated with Thor, it seems likely that it was a deliberate choice to use oak wood to carve the two definitely-male wooden figures, from Lagore and from Kingsteignton. These figures are likely to represent or belong to Thor in some sense, or to a predecessor of Thor.

The group of figures previously linked with Odin, through their attributes of sexual ambiguity and loss of an eye (Coles 1990, 332), are now seen to be carved from yew in the case of Ralaghan and the Roos Carr assemblage, or from another evergreen conifer, pine, in the case of Dagenham. It is likely that these were also deliberate choices, given the possible associations between yew-wood (or another evergreen), *Yggdrasil*, Odin and magic or sorcery. If so, the pubic hole of these carvings may be placed in its rather odd anatomical position (Fig.13.4) so that they look plausibly female when displayed without a penis and plausibly male if one is added. In female form, these carvings would be associated with Odin the shaman, and in male form with Odin leader of the gods.

The two ash-wood carvings, from the Somerset Levels and from Corlea, should perhaps be associated with ancestor-figures since ash was the first man, *Askr*, created by Odin and his brothers. Both these carvings were found buried within a wooden trackway crossing a wetland, and it may be that as ancestor-figures they were put there as guardians of the route, to protect those who walked along it. If their quality was more that of *treniđ* or *niđstong*, perhaps their function was to prevent the passage of unwanted persons or evil spirits. Their context, hidden in the body of the tracks, suggest the latter role. The oak-wood figures found beside a dangerous stretch of one of the Iron Age trackways in Lower Saxony could also be ancestor-figures, acting

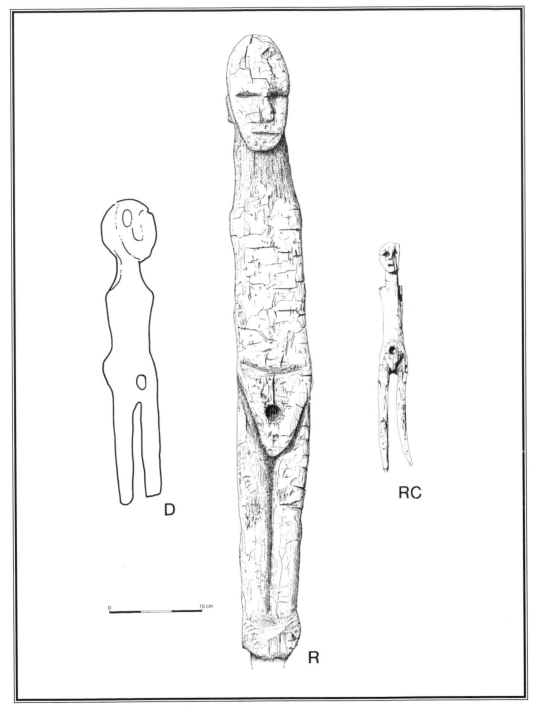

13.4 The dated wooden figures from Britain and Ireland, grouped by tree species: yew and pine. R: Ralaghan (drawn by S. Goddard), RC: Roos Carr (drawn by M. Rouillard), D: Dagenham (outline based on photograph).

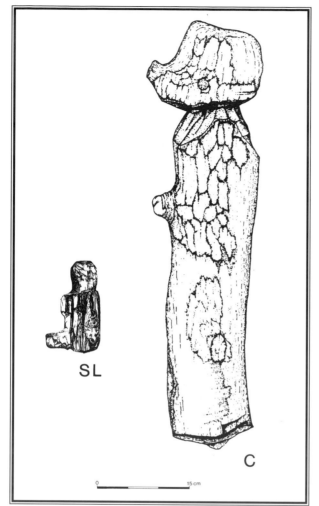

13.5 The dated wooden figures from Britain and Ireland, grouped by tree species: ash. SL: Somerset Levels (drawing Somerset Levels Project), C: Corlea (drawing Irish Archaeological Wetland Unit)

13.6 The dated wooden figures from Britain and Ireland, grouped by tree species: alder: B: Ballachulish. (Photo taken at time of discovery, courtesy of Royal Museum of Scotland)

as guardians and protectors of the traveller (Hayen 1987); made of oak, they do not conform to the pattern discerned here for Britain and Ireland, and they serve as a reminder of the holes and imperfections which must be present in this outline, based as it is on so few glimpses through the obscuring mists of time.

For the moment, the alder-wood female from Ballachulish remains apart, with nothing to suggest a choice of wood species influenced by the belief-systems of the carvers. It would be fitting if *Embla*, the first woman, were alder, but unfortunately there is not the slightest suggestion of such a link in the literature. Recent work on Ballachulish Moss (Clarke 1996) has reinforced an earlier suggestion that the area was used for ritual deposition over a long period, and it remains likely that the figure had considerable ritual significance, perhaps linked to the same beliefs as the human bog bodies of later prehistory.

The purpose of this chapter has been to make suggestions rather than to come to firm conclusions, and to explore the ways in which northern mythology can assist in the interpretation of a particular series of prehistoric artefacts, to demonstrate that they have strong ritual associations and to explore the character of the belief-system that produced them. Whether or not there is any validity in the suggestions made here concerning the identity of the figures, it seems very likely that choice of wood species was deliberate, and significant for ritual rather than for functional reasons.

ACKNOWLEDGEMENTS

My thanks to Sue Rouillard for preparation of the illustrations, to Jennifer Warren for typing the text, to Michael Swanton for guidance amongst the scholars of northern mythology, to Barry Raftery for Corlea information and illustration and to Erica Hemming for drawing my attention to Piggott's shaman and to Anisimov's work.

PART THREE

THEORY AND PRACTICE

CHAPTER FOURTEEN

TYREBAGGER RECUMBENT STONE CIRCLE, ABERDEENSHIRE: A NOTE ON RECORDING

GRAHAM RITCHIE

The recumbent stone circles of north-east Scotland have long attracted archaeological comment, and the recording of them is an important part of Scottish antiquarian tradition. Among the most attractive and accurate representations are those of James Skene of Rubislaw in the 1820s and '30s, and his drawing of Cothiemuir Wood is given as an example of the genre (Fig. 14.1). Part evocation, part scientific illustration, with the sizes of two of the stones given as well as the date of execution (2 May 1827), such a record was made for personal satisfaction rather than with publication in mind. The notebook from which the drawing comes is in the Society of Antiquaries of Scotland collection in the National Monuments Record of Scotland. Systematic measured survey was not undertaken until the work of Fred R. Coles, and photographic survey began with James Ritchie. It is the intention of this short chapter to explore the contribution of these two early archaeologists to the background information distilled into the comprehensive studies made by Aubrey Burl of all the circles of Britain and indeed beyond. An historical approach to the illustration of stone circles may seem all too similar to that adopted in a contribution to the celebration of another pioneer of megalithic studies, Alexander Thom (Ritchie 1988), but it has been a vital part of Aubrey Burl's own exploration of megaliths in the landscape today. Another historical excursus into a single site was prepared by Mercer in 1978 in which the various plans of Castle Fraser (Balgorkar) were critically examined. An understanding of past recording is an important part of how we prepare present records. Seldom in the past is what we would now call the specification clear (see chapter 18). Here the illustration of one particular site, Tyrebagger, in the City of Aberdeen, will be used to demonstrate the methods of Fred R. Coles and James Ritchie.

Coles's paper in the *Proceedings of the Society of Antiquaries of Scotland* in the 1899–1900 session (Coles 1900) was the first of a series of studies that provided plans and descriptions of stone circles in Scotland funded through a gift to the Society by Dr R.H. Gunning in 1887 to commemorate Queen Victoria's Jubilee. Coles was the Assistant Keeper in the National Museum

14.1 Cothiemuir Wood, Aberdeenshire, by James Skene, 1827. (By permission of RCAHMS, Crown copyright reserved)

14.2 Rothiemay, Aberdeenshire, cup-marked recumbent stone, photographed by James Ritchie, 1905. (By permission of RCAHMS, Crown copyright reserved)

14.3 Cothiemuir Wood, Aberdeenshire, recumbent stone circle, photographed by James Ritchie, 1910. (By permission of RCAHMS, Crown copyright reserved)

of Antiquities of Scotland, under the redoubtable Joseph Anderson, and the survey was part of a range of research projects undertaken by the Society in the period between 1891 and 1913 (Stevenson 1981, 173–9). Coles's paper is now more usually quarried for information about individual sites and information about the state of a monument a hundred years ago, but his introduction with a statement of his method is particularly relevant.

In submitting his report he makes mention of the measured plans and drawings, and a footnote explains that the plans are all reduced to a uniform scale of 20 ft to 1 in.

Almost throughout this survey, I enjoyed the willing, and indeed indispensable, assistance of my two eldest children, several of the sites examined, in Kincardineshire especially, being now so densely crowded with larches and Scotch firs in addition to luxurious undergrowth, that single-handed commensuration would be absolutely impracticable.

He also outlined the survey methodology.

After a general look around the area to be surveyed, we began by laying off an oblong which included the Recumbent Stone and its two pillars in those circles where this characteristic feature still exists. Then having chosen the western angle of the west pillar as a starting point, measurements were made by triangulating from this to two other points marked by pins, and so on, round the entire space, taking, of course, cross-check lines where the area was clear enough to admit of this. In a few instances we ran out diagonals from each stone throughout the whole group, by using a stout cord and measuring with short lengths of tape, my first endeavour always being to treat the circles purely from a surveyor's point of view, that is, merely as mathematical points, and paying no attention to anything but the number of feet between the fixed points at the bases of the stones. Afterwards we took the correct measurements, first of the bases, and next of the heights, of each Standing Stone, further noting whether it was vertical or out of plumb, and the direction of its leaning, also any peculiarity of shape at its summit, and of its mineralogical composition. When all the measurements were finished, the orientation was ascertained as carefully as possible. I then made drawings of such important features as lent themselves to such treatment. (Coles 1900, 139–41).

14.4 Sunhoney, Aberdeenshire, recumbent stone circle, photographed by James Ritchie, 1902. (By permission of RCAHMS, Crown copyright reserved)

Although the method of survey would be different today, the systematic approach to recording, measuring and describing will strike a chord with many a fieldworker; indeed an on-going survey of chambered cairns, continuing a tradition from a pre-metric age, uses a scale of 1in to 10ft to great effect. It is interesting to note that Coles does not appear to consider photography as a component of survey, for the other contemporary cataloguing project of the Society of Antiquaries of Scotland, the recording of early Christian sculptured stones, was intended to make particular use of the medium. His own skills as an illustrator have certainly enabled a more consistent record to be published. Stone circles are often difficult to photograph, particularly where the vegetation is dense. His apparent reserve about photography may indeed have resulted from the difficulties that the Antiquaries were experiencing with the preparation of the volume on early Christian sculpture, for Coles himself was to undertake the tracing of outline drawings from rubbings, as photographs were found not to be suitable for publication (Allen & Anderson 1903, vi–vii). Thus for stone circles and for single standing stones reputed to be the remnants of circles in Aberdeenshire and Perthshire we have an incomparable and consistent record on which to build.

Tyrebagger is a good example of the published results in survey and illustration. It is situated 3.3km west of Dyce and is today approached by a series of farm and forestry tracks. The airport for Aberdeen is now situated on the flat ground below the circle to the south and the circle is one of the few sites from which the landing instructions of an airport control tower can audibly be made out, a potent reminder of how rapidly use of the landscape changes, and thus the

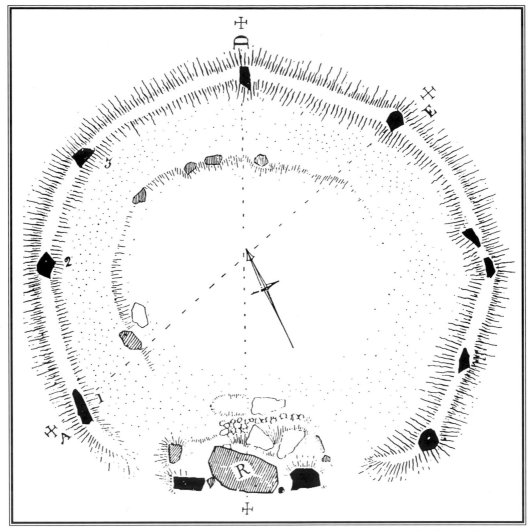

14.5 Tyrebagger, City of Aberdeen, plan by Fred Coles. (By permission of RCAHMS, Crown copyright reserved)

importance of recording antiquities. The recumbent is a large slab leaning to the inside of the circle and is shown hatched (Fig. 14.5). The remaining stones are upright and are shown black. A confusing feature of the site today is the low wall or bank that appears to link the stones, but Coles makes use of an earlier account by Logan to explain that the circle had been formed into a cattle-pound. Coles's plan and the accompanying sections and drawings successfully record the site as an element in a consistent inventory. His drawing of the recumbent and flankers successfully conveys the scale of the slabs (Fig. 14.6). That he continued to keep his own records up-to-date is known in a rather unusual way, for the Library of the National Monuments Record of Scotland has part of Coles's personal set of the Society's *Proceedings* on its public shelves. Page 141 is annotated 'The polar North is 18° East of the compass bearings here given. FRC'.

14.6 Tyrebagger, City of Aberdeen, view from inside showing the recumbent, by Fred Coles. (By permission of RCAHMS, Crown copyright reserved)

The surveys by Fred Coles were part of the major effort by the Society of Antiquaries and others to bring knowledge of Scottish antiquities to as well organised a state as possible. But considerable work was also being done by what would now be called the voluntary sector. The photographic work of James Ritchie (1850–1925) and his various papers to the Society of Antiquaries of Scotland are examples of such endeavour. Ritchie was a schoolmaster at Port Elphinstone near Inverurie, and we know about him because his son and grandson have passed down information about his approach to the recording of antiquities. Ritchie's papers were intended to supplement the work of Coles with additional information and to illustrate this with photographs (1919; 1920a). James Ritchie's grandson Dr A.E. Ritchie CBE FRSE, recalls the camera he used: 'It was a full-plate [8½ by 8½ in], made of mahogany and brass with all the conceivable tilts and adjustments that could be needed. The leather bellows were very long to allow of different focal length of lenses; there was no shutter and exposures were made by taking off and putting on a lens cap.' His son, also James, recorded that 'Often he would walk a score of miles day after day, burdened with a heavy camera after the objects of his investigation, and I have known him spend the night with his camera at remote sculptured stones, if he knew that the ancient carving was thrown into the best relief by the rays of the early morning sun (Ritchie 1927). His methods were successful in the recording of cupmarks (Figs 14.2, 3 and 4).

An unusual feature of Ritchie's systematic gathering of material was his incorporation of a hand-written caption along the edge of the glass-plate negative; the title and date mean that the photograph can be used to record a precise moment. Ritchie's Tyrebagger view cannot edit out

14.7 Tyrebagger, City of Aberdeen, view by James Ritchie, 1902. (By permission of RCAHMS, Crown copyright reserved)

the surrounding trees as Coles's illustration does, but the overall impression is very similar (Fig. 14.7).

The importance of the twin methods of recording, drawn record and photography, has been part of the impetus of the preparation of this contribution. Aubrey Burl's unique approach has been to create an impression of a site in words that conjure up the stones within a recognisable landscape, and to take many atmospheric photographs that also help to set the scene.

CHAPTER FIFTEEN

FROM RITUAL TO ROMANCE: A NEW WESTERN

IAN KINNES

From Archaeology
One moral, at least, may be drawn.

By standing stones the blind can feel their way,
And even madmen manage to convey
Unwelcome truths in lonely gibberish.

W.H. Auden, 'Archaeology, The Useful'

For time is inches

W.H. Auden, 'This Lunar Beauty'

In the late stages of Coppola's film *Apocalypse Now* the compelling figure of Colonel Kurtz (Marlon Brando) has created a new and psychopathic society in the heart of darkness, fuelled by the alienness of Vietnam and the Vietnamese insurgence and maintained by a strict ritualisation based on a handful of bedside paperbacks, notably Jesse Weston's *Golden Bough*-derived *aperçu From Ritual to Romance*. In the unsurpassable Western *œuvre* of John Ford there are two more than usually exceptional scenes, both communal dances: in *Fort Apache* (1948) a strict military measure brings Old World convention to a new empire as aboriginal gives way to second-hand Victoriana; in *My Darling Clementine* (1946) there is an unforgettable celebration as farming pioneers, multi-cultural immigrants, raise their first church building in a new (to them) world. Apart from an attempt to engage Aubrey's interest in this chapter, what is the point of these references?

The point is that ritual is embedded in being human and is therefore conscious. But conscious of what? Is ritual necessary or occasional? Can ritual be improvised or invented to meet a transient need? How does ritual work? What is it for? It does seem to be invariable to all known human societies. At base it appears as a way of reconciling everyday experience with the unknown or unexpected. It therefore runs the gamut from the personal or individual (since Freud, ritual behaviour is commonly regarded as an obsessional or pathological condition) to the communal, condoned and approved by a larger society or regime. At both extremes it is expressed by rules of behaviour and action; belief in a supernatural component is not mandatory. It is a binding social mechanism, which may explain why it is persistently integral to all societies, and hence a very useful means of control by whatever hierarchy.

The outstanding British topographic tradition, ranging from Aubrey (not Burl!) to the ultimate barminess of Stukeley (Piggott 1989; Burl *passim*), apart from British, Roman and Danish camps, could only see the most resilient and obvious survivals of the past as ritual – stone settings, dolmens, barrows; from what passed for the ancient literature sacred groves could be extrapolated and Druids interpolated. In recent years there has been a major growth and embedding of the blindingly obvious: that ritual – in whatever sense (non-rational, invocatory, evocatory, formalised, repetitive, structured, occasional, millennial, reactive, etc.) – permeates human thought and action (*see* Thomas, Tilley, etc. *passim*). Only the unaware could be led by academic paths alone to what is a natural awareness for others. When this reaches the dizzy heights of claims that in the insular neolithic cereals were grown only for ritual use, or even that they were not grown locally but were instead imported for the purpose on the Dover–Calais run of the good ship *Potemkin*, or that flint was ritually mined, ritually worked, ritually unused and ritually discarded, we are living in strange times. This misses the basic point that ritual is integral to daily experience enacted through the standard activities of daily life. Barrett's (1994) aware and closely argued experience is a welcome retaliation to the unread (in archaeology at least) core and wilder periphery.

In this chapter I shall look at the concept of ritual landscapes, a recurrent theme in the literature of the last twenty years, where monuments 'lie in close proximity though the degree of association between them, if any, is unknown', where 'sites were constructed with their neighbours in mind' (Harding & Lee 1987: the least cluttered definition). Most are cumulative in form and chronology, a point to which I shall return; even where, as in the Milfield Basin, there is general uniformity of style, there are variations of form, size or detail. Are these variations chronological or, for what the term's worth, functional? Do cosmography or choreography compel these variations? Is it, as Harding says, polytheism, the multiple aspects of a single cult, cyclical usage? We do, of course, assume usage and sometimes excavated results indicate this. Available chronology gets us within 200 years of any event or process in the Neolithic: it is still a long time.

Apart from those areas where topography and/or economic activities assisted monument survival, and with rare exceptions most seem to define ritual landscapes by monument clusters, the impact of aerial photography over the last fifty years has been dramatic. Three forms of monument illustrate this, comparing numbers of known and probable sites in 1950 and now:

Monument type	1950	Present
Causewayed enclosures	13	*c.* 70
Cursus monuments	8	at least 60
Henges	30	at least 100

The other familiar components of these landscapes, ring-ditches of varying size and complexity, are more or less ubiquitous. Fifty years ago notable clusters of more or less relatable monuments were few and dependent primarily on upstanding survival, the Stonehenge complex being the classic example to the point where the rarity of other concentrations and their smaller scale enhanced the perception of Stonehenge itself as the focal antiquity for Ancient Britons (or indeed, Ancient Bretons – Burl 1997), a view now easily seen as deluded. Interestingly, even in zones of good survival, aerial survey can still enhance and complicate monumental presence and potential sequence. Long Meg and her Daughters is a good example of this (Soffe & Clare 1988).

While there is no question that such information has transformed the perception of neolithic achievement, or at least should have done, its application does have limitations with a reluctance to move far from the familiar in seeking causation or explanation – the Avebury region may well be a laboratory or lyceum of prehistory but the benches are somewhat crowded (*inter alia* Thomas 1991; Barrett 1994).

On this theme one of the more interesting implications for those of us prehistorians who have lived through more than two or three generations of fashion in thought or perception (a generation here is more or less ten years, unless flawed by New World chronology in the shorter term or *la longue durée* for those more philosophically inclined) is how this information has been assimilated to a new, or more so, world picture. Were the riches of the Milfield or Walton Basins to be predicted as loss-leaders in the consumer market of what was available to us from the burgeoning Neolithic? I think not. It now seems that land uptake and its apportionment to the 'non-functional' was extensive, particularly in locations which would seem to favour the agricultural but were increasingly set aside to the monumental. Pryor (1988) had already suggested that the apparent marginality of causewayed enclosure location was as much to do with relative land use as tax-free zones for negotiation and exchange of whatever commodities for whatever purpose. Much depends on two quintessential components of real archaeology – absolute or relative chronology (what monuments in what sequence) and environmental reconstruction (where and in what circumstances). The situation is complex; perhaps the clearance for cultivation and by or for herds was early and cumulative, or maybe the open landscape familiar since the Enclosure Acts coincided with the adolescence of the English archaeo-topographic tradition to guide many, but not all, perceptions. I have previously expressed doubts over the critical values of local charcoal and more distant pollen analysis (Kinnes 1988) and remain unconvinced that such expensive techniques have yet to offer more than an assessment of sampling methodology. On the other hand, field archaeology *sensu stricto* can offer some comfort. The extraordinary circumstance of four intersecting cursus monuments at Rudston, proven – if only in one cutting – not to be sequential (Kinnes forthcoming), would seem to make sense only topographically. They are focused on a bend in the river (or at least the Gypsey Race – seasonally variable but none the less the only permanent water source in the Wolds), the nexus being the Rudston monolith. The interesting component is that where the terminals are known (and aerial photography can only do so much) all end precisely at the contour point of intervisibility but only in an essentially treeless landscape; topography dictates length and layout, the monolith on its dominant spur (where the church is now) precedes or celebrates. Interestingly, despite earlier reservations on the unavowed limitations of environmental science, some recent work suggests (without explaining the apparent local variation from the norm) that the Great Wold Valley had essentially been open country since the last glaciation. There is another component of interest for alluvial valleys or basins elsewhere: these are usually fertile and often the best land for their catchment; this is why, to return to an earlier point, monuments are now largely recognised from the air after plough destruction; farmland in this valley still brings the best auction prices in the East Yorkshire granary.

Concentration, either through visibility, building on opportunistic observation or through an unspoken desire to embellish, has very much intensified the aerial photographic record for

Silbury Hill. (Photo: Alex Gibson)

designated areas – this may be a shade unfair, but the temptation throughout the spectrum of paying, paid-for and consumer-led archaeology is obvious.

To return to ritual landscapes. On the chalklands we find a gradual and historically accrued circumstance: Stonehenge itself, one or two (now two) cursuses, the avenue, barrows (by 1820), more or less distant, some other henges, pits and flint scatters (Richards 1990; Cleal *et al.* 1995); Avebury – the site, avenues, the Sanctuary, Silbury Hill, barrows – more by accruement but mainly the West Kennet enclosure complex (Smith 1965; Whittle 1991). The fervour of Rescue in the 1960s, leading ineluctably into the market-led denial of research designs by PPG 16, created information without explanation, apart from some brief state-led optimism which created in the mid-1980s corpora, surveys and structures. Since then, a combination of happenstance and individual devotion, neither particularly funded (innovator Miket in Milfield Basin, now Gibson in Walton), have tried to make the best of an accrued but underused data-base. That is probably enough in terms of the message for this chapter, but I do believe that it is an important one: the visible past, by whatever medium, runs through the life-work of Aubrey Burl and we should all be conscious of it.

So, to return to 'ritual landscapes'. We should look at their nature and how they may, or may not, work. There are two immediate aspects: the landscape itself and the landscape's history, mainly anthropogenic. The landscape proper, from any level of recognition, from a particular oak-tree to a particular tor (Williams 1989; Tilley 1994) clearly dictates, or at least informs; landscape history produces a 'sequence of changes . . . to suggest that over a period of some hundreds of years a number of different spatial orders were imposed on a given space, each one transforming the way in which previous configurations could be read' (Thomas 1991, 41, on the Bradley & Chambers 1988 reworking of the Dorchester complex), and, more tellingly, 'landscape, its form constructed from natural and artificial features, became a culturally meaningful resource through its routine occupancy' (Barrett 1991, 8); at last we have a script, if not necessarily any actors. So, where is the cast ? We can variously quantify the hours, months, years of construction (Startin & Bradley 1981) for the builders and set this against their presumptive calendar and we might assume that some or all of these then used the created spaces; who, in what number and how is less easy. The excavated evidence is, unsurprisingly, small; the material songlines tell of approach, often diverted or screened, congregation and separation (assumed from plan), fire (universal and often undated), specific deposition (sometimes), rarity of ritual paraphernalia. Apart from the formats, which appear not to define pig-wallows or parks, we are at a loss but seemingly can say 'these are areas where virtually all the activity is non-domestic and related to the gods . . . a special area set apart and perhaps holy' (Clarke *et al.* 1985). Well, *perhaps*. But what else do these spaces do?

The *quincaillerie*, not *bricolage*, of archaeological technique provides dominant locales, frequently visited, binding space and time (Thomas 1993), storing 'authoritative and allocative resources' (Giddens 1981), a resource to be drawn on, re-used, referenced to create tradition and evoke continuity (Hobsbawm 1983); history is turned into nature (Edmonds 1993), reading this in any number of ways accords with personal or group experience (Moore 1986), spatial metaphors for the enduring qualities of society and its specific hierarchy of relationships (Harding 1995). So monuments are texts to be read at will and as you will; any aerial photograph or map is a field of discourse.

Apart from those previously mentioned – essentially those of the topographers – the first discovery, really, is Dorchester: recognised by a tyro, dug by a tyro (and finally published by a different generation: Whittle *et al.* 1992). Post-war perception or practicality led gently into set-piece or almost random excavations. Somewhere down the line the combination of the unrivalled British topographic tradition, sheer optimism, salvage and research as rescue created a platform for a larger and younger archaeological community. Dealing with their own perception of this record (good and formative example: Bradley & Gardiner 1984), the concept of ritual landscapes began to emerge.

So, the combination of a largely unacknowledged native tradition and accumulated record was being slowly recognised at the same time as explanation could only be sought externally (classically the defunct Chapman, Kinnes & Randsborg 1981; Kinnes 1992) and internal information quietly accrued. To be more positive, we should recognise that Neolithic to Early Bronze Age sites burgeon throughout the terrain, that their scale and variety grows, but where does that leave us with ritual landscapes? We should return to the first, even before Avebury entered the canon as cathedral to exceed the parish church – Stonehenge. Intervisible and remnant in sheep pasture, barrows long and round span as much as two millennia or so; three henges more or less distant were used, if not in the same way, at about the same late neolithic time; placed deposits in randomly discovered pits (the unacknowledged arbiters of practice?) span a few centuries; two cursus monuments are adjacent and unclear in location or function (RCHM 1979). Stonehenge itself perhaps has at some point a focal role; from middle neolithic enclosure through timber to stone, for whatever reason reactivated over several millennia to produce an icon but not necessarily a spirit-guide (documented now in Cleal *et al.* 1995, anticipated by Burl 1987), absurdly but inevitably now, a henge. So, turn to the cathedral. Avebury too has its barrows and a causewayed enclosure; no cursus but stone-lined avenues, one of which at least connects to circles which should be contemporary (Pollard 1992); the largest artificial mound in Europe; an extraordinary palisade enclosure and alignment complex in the stream valley; some odd pits. Avebury, the Sanctuary and Silbury Hill were at least built, to the best of our knowledge, by users of the same Grooved Ware pottery, somewhat like the fluorescence of the broader Stonehenge territory. What else of the traditional?

The Dorset cursus is clearly a law unto itself, the longest 'non-functional' construction ever, although it has been assigned a regional role by majority over adjacent minority to justify its presence (Barrett *et al.* 1991). Or again, preserved henges and barrows at Knowlton (now enhanced through aerial photography) still await resolution, but are seductively close to Cranborne Chase on the right scale of map. The Cumbrian enclave of King Arthur's Round Table, Little Round Table and Mayburgh seemed once a northern rustic outpost of Wessex, though sufficient to attract the intellectual likes of Collingwood and Bersu (Bradley 1994), but could perhaps now be seen as the recognised precursor of river-catchment concentrations of diverse but conceptually allied monuments. Of course the take-off point came with aerial photographs and the epochal recognition and area excavation at Dorchester. The growing intensity of aerial survey has identified many concentrations of plausible-looking monuments under the plough, mostly untested by excavation, as state parsimony and developer-led finance dictate. The interpreted record, however grateful to the sop of NMR or SMR, or the crumbs from desktop assessment, suffers inevitably. Some of us recall the Mucking henge – now a Late Bronze Age ring-fort, or attempts to classify morphology from the air as a means of financial (or rather strategic or pragmatic) prioritising as formative to this record. If the record assumes its own reality it can at least, unlike the sites, be copied infinitely and virtually realised forever.

It really is time to return to the topic, although I would hope that some might think it had never been forsaken. Essentially we are looking at clusters, of whatever scale, of perceived monuments, rather than dispersed distribution. We might begin with the basics. By and large the recorded format is linear or circular, but there are inevitably variations and cross-overs. Once, linear was mainly early and circular later, a differentiation based largely on barrow forms (after Thurnam 1869; 1872); recognition of 'precocious' round barrow forms (Kinnes 1979 and forthcoming) altered this security. Setting this aside, why the distinction: linear especially façaded at the front, dominates, side on, and the longer it is, the more it presumes, to dictate more than the immediate locale; round is inevitably uniform in appreciation from all directions but access is special, which is presumably why screening and separating arrangements are often noted at entrances. The historic record says round for audience to central event, as at the Coliseum or whatever, and linear for progression or marching – particularly in the avenues of the replanned capitals of the nation states of early modern times. Precise format, even when archaeologically contemporary, can vary within a short walk – Avebury is a good example; banks or palisades can of course exclude or include; were spaced stone settings free for multi-access or did now-lost wooden panelling complete the barrier? Much depends on the political upbringing or attitude of the reporter.

Next chronology, an inexact science. If we are to see cumulative landscapes, of what timespan and of what duration? If we assemble the full cast then it is the entire Neolithic and some part of the Bronze Age, something like two thousand years. Clearly over this time the perception of sites would be redefined, a recognition sometimes emphasised by structural alteration or addition – a long mound is crowned by a round barrow or incorporated into a cursus or causewayed enclosure (Kinnes 1992, 116); a cursus slices through a causewayed enclosure (at Fornham All Saints) or its through-route is blocked by a henge (at Thornborough); many monuments increase in scale or complexity. There can be no certainty that original function was appreciated much beyond the first context of its creation but the earth had been visibly altered (Williams 1989; Bradley 1993). As Bradley says, there are changing needs, memory is unstable, monuments orchestrate human experience in a language of size (and, surely, of shape); what is really new for the Neolithic is the decision to build, an idea, a project. The other aspect of this cumulative manipulation is at what point were monuments desecrated or destroyed? Beaker ploughing against, but not over, the South Street long barrow is early but otherwise where does neglect begin? The benign version of the English landscape — plough, pasture, woodland reserves, thatched cottages in hamlets — seems to emerge in the Middle Bronze Age when there appear to be no monuments and even the Itford cemetery yields little more experience than the token ritual at a modern ring-road crematorium. Swords in rivers, post alignments and ring-forts restore some sense of place in the later Bronze Age but into the end of the millennium, Early Iron Age settlements, whatever their own internal ritual (Hill 1995), commonly sat on, not incorporated into, the monuments. In more recent times, the common combination of Christianity, prejudice and greed has, of course, horribly flawed the preserved past. As I may have indicated, the 'Age of Extremes' (Hobsbawm 1994) has done its best to complete the process: like the good dog William walking upon his hinder legs, you are surprised, given all this, to find the archaeology of monuments and ritual done at all, but it has, and can be (Burl *passim*).

And finally, Aubrey — 'Any severely mechanist account of inexorable change beyond the consciousness and control of social actors, whether told in a structuralist or Marxist manner, cannot square with our understanding of social actors' (Johnson 1993).

CHAPTER SIXTEEN

THE TIME LORDS: RITUAL CALENDARS, DRUIDS AND THE SACRED YEAR

MIRANDA J. GREEN

Time is the conscious experiential product of the processes that allow the [human] organism to adaptively organize itself so that its behavior remains tuned to the sequential (i.e. order) relations in its environment.

(Michon 1985, 20)

The concept of time as a powerful, often sacred, force has long been recognised by archaeologists and anthropologists. Scientists researching psychological time have constructed models of temporal cognition, one of which – time as succession – is concerned with 'the sequential occurrence of events (i.e. changes), from which an organism may perceive successiveness and temporal order' (Block 1990, 1–35). Clearly, the observation by pre-urban communities of the cyclical behaviour of the sun, moon and seasons falls within this cognitive model of time-perception. The association between ancient ceremonial monuments and phenomenonological change (i.e. observed successive changes in weather and in astral bodies) is well illustrated by Aubrey Burl's work on megaliths, and so it is appropriate that a chapter on the archaeology of time and ritual be included in this volume of essays in his honour.

This chapter examines the evidence for the ritual control and measurement of time in western Europe during the later first millennium BC and the early first millennium AD. Much of the evidence is archaeological but, from the first century BC, literature provides some information on the construction of sacred calendars, and the existence of individuals whose apparent ability to manipulate time for religious purposes endowed them with considerable power. Julius Caesar – and other Classical writers describing the customs of the Gauls and Britons during the first century BC/AD – associates temporal measurement, the maintenance of calendars, the prediction of future phenomena and events and the keeping of an oral tradition with a priestly class called Druids. In a sense, the Druids were the keepers of time: past, present and future.

The association of time with ritual probably began in early human prehistory. According to Clark (1994, 39–59), perceptions of time were associated with the ability of early communities to conceptualise death, and with a correlated awareness of a past inhabited by ancestors, a perception that would have given rise to myths explaining origins and identity. Additionally, both prehistoric peoples and members of modern traditional societies would need to take cognisance of seasonality and its effect upon food resources. The Micmac Indians of eastern Canada are a good example of a people whose seasonal division of their calendar is associated with the condition of faunal and vegetal resources (Wallis & Wallis 1955; Clark 1994, 46). The pre-modern traditional communities of Simbo (Solomon Islands) link their calendar to the growing and harvesting of two strains of a special nut which are important not as a direct food resource but for exchange for desired commodities only available from the neighbouring island of Rembo. The power of the *bangara* (The 'Big Man' and calendar-keeper) is connected with his ability to predict seasonal change, and he has been described as controlling time itself (Burman 1981, 251–67; Gell 1992, 306–13).

This preoccupation with seasonal change involves concern with the future, and the ability of communities to predict, plan and anticipate weather patterns. Indeed, the building of large, durable structures, such as megalithic monuments, testifies to a conceptualisation of a long future time-perspective.

16.1. Bronze Age cult wagon mounted with gilded sun-disc, *c.* 1200 BC; from Trundholm, Denmark. Length *c.* 600mm. (By permission of the Nationalmuseet, Copenhagen)

16.2. Gold bowl, decorated with animals, including deer, crescents and circles, sixth-century BC; from Altstetten, Zürich, Switzerland. Diameter 250mm. (By permission of the Schweizerisches Landesmuseum, Zürich)

SYMBOLS OF TIME: AN ARCHAEOLOGICAL PERSPECTIVE

Since temporal cognition is concerned with conceptual processes, the material culture (or archaeology) of time in later prehistoric Europe may be difficult to identify and interpret, particularly in the absence of recognisable chronometers. It is even more problematical to demonstrate – archaeologically – a link between the control of time and the possession of power, whether sacred or secular. However, there are certain indicators that temporal cycles, diurnal, monthly or annual, were acknowledged and symbolised. For the immediately pre-Roman Iron Age, the evidence of material culture serves to complement and support contemporary literature.

Certain depictions of celestial symbols are probably indicative of the recognition of successive time-phases. Where such imagery consists of more than one motif and where these show differentiation one from another, juxtaposition of the symbols constitutes an illustration of time as succession. The Bronze Age model horse-drawn wagon from Trundholm (Denmark) (Fig. 16.1) is an outstanding example of an early depiction of the sun in two phases: one surface of the bronze sun-disc is gilded and has been interpreted as representative of the bright morning sun, while the other side is plain bronze, perhaps representing sunset (Briard 1987, 50; Sandars 1968, 283–5; Glob 1974, 99–125; Green 1991, 114–15 & Fig. 45). If the Trundholm cart is a cult-wagon and the disc a solar motif, the perception of the sun's diurnal journey across the sky is reflected in its carriage on a moving platform. This idea is widespread among ancient Indo-

European communities, from India and Persia to Greece, Italy and northern Europe (Green 1991, 112–13; Cook 1914, 198–253; Frazer 1926, 443–60; Halsberghe 1972, 26–9; Gelling & Davidson 1969, 9–27); and both in Bronze Age Scandinavian rock-art (Fredsjö *et al.* 1975, nos. 317, 320; Gelling & Davidson 1969, 49–52) and in Egyptian imagery (Lurker 1974, 113; Hawkes 1962, 91–2), the sun is sometimes depicted as travelling by ship. Both vehicles evoke the image of motion through space and time.

Certain motifs – particularly lunar symbols – on Iron Age European metalwork and on some Gallo-Roman tombstones reflect changes in astral bodies over time. The gold bowl from Altstetten, Zürich (Fig. 16.2) dates to the sixth century BC (Megaw 1970, no. 4; Nagy 1992, 101–16). Its decoration includes an antlered stag and other animals beneath a frieze of alternating crescents and circles. These have been interpreted in the past (e.g. Megaw 1970; Green 1991, 69) as solar and lunar symbols, but probably new and full moons are represented (Fitzpatrick 1996, 385), thus reflecting temporal change over the 28-day lunar cycle. If one of the beasts depicted on the bowl is a hare, then the nocturnal habits of that animal may form a link with the depiction of the moon.

In a recent paper, Fitzpatrick (1996, 373–98) has drawn attention to a significant group of anthropomorphic-hilted short iron swords bearing distinctive engraved or stamped signs, inlaid with gold or other contrasting metals which appear to take the form of astral motifs (Figs. 16.3, 16.4). Such designs, and other symbols, have also been noted on long Middle Iron Age swords (Drack 1954–5, 193–235) while the short swords range from about 300 to the early first century BC. The motifs are fairly standard-

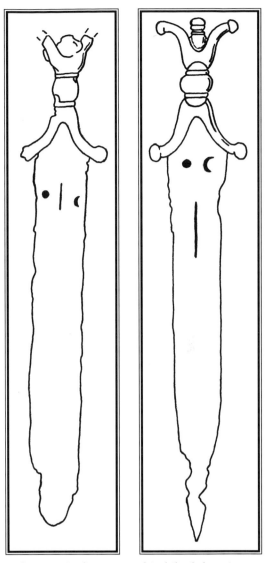

Left: 16.3. Anthropomorphic-hilted short iron sword, with lunar motifs, third/second century BC; from Lysice, Czech Republic. Length 364mm. (After Fitpatrick 1996, fig. 19)
Right: 16.4. Anthropomorphic-hilted short iron sword, with gold-inlaid lunar motifs, third century BC; from the River Rhine at Mainz. Length 450mm. (After Fitzpatrick 1996, fig. 16)

ised, most consisting of a vertical median line with a circle to the left and a right-facing crescent to the right: the weapon found at Lysice in Moravia (Fig. 16.3) is an example (Čižmař 1989, 69–72). Significantly, the so-called astral signs are the only motifs adorning the short-hilted

16.5. Gold wheel-pendant, with applied motifs in the form of a perforated circle and crescent, second century AD; from La Guillotière, Lyon. Diameter of wheel *c.* 20mm. (By permission of the Trustees of the British Museum)

swords. The symbols have been identified as the full and new moon respectively, and thus represent phases of the lunar month, with the vertical line corresponding to the division of its halves (the 'bright' waxing half and the 'dark' or waning half (Fitzpatrick 1996, 386–7)).

It is possible that the swords belonged to individuals responsible for recording and keeping calendrical time, perhaps for religious purposes. Given the rarity with which human figures were portrayed in Iron Age art (Green 1996, 142–3), Fitzpatrick's suggestion that the anthropomorphic hilts of these swords are indicative of terrestrial power or of divinity has plausibility. Thus the owners of the engraved swords may have been people of rank, possibly priests, maybe even Druids, who expressed their cosmological powers by the possession and display of objects marked with lunar symbols. In the

16.6. Gold wheel-pendant, with applied crescent and double-axe symbols, Roman period; from Balèsmes (Haute-Marne), France. Diameter of wheel *c.* 20mm. (Illustrator Paul Jenkins, after Déchelette)

context of the identification of lunar imagery in the later Iron Age, it is significant that both Caesar (*de Bello Gallico* VI, 18) and Pliny (*Natural History* XVI, 95) comment on the Gaulish practice of counting time by nights rather than days. The literary evidence for the link between sacral rulers and the control of time is discussed below.

It is worth considering whether there is other, roughly coeval, archaeological evidence for the representation of time as succession. A particular group of objects, dating to the Roman period, consists of gold and silver jewellery, comprising chain necklaces with attached pendants in the form of miniature wheels accompanied by crescents (Fig. 16.5); gold chain necklaces with wheel-shaped pendants have a widespread distribution within the Roman empire (Galliou 1974, 259–83) but the rarer combination of wheel and crescent is exemplified by finds from Dolaucothi (western Wales), Backworth (northern England) and Newstead (southern Scotland) (Nash-Williams 1950–2, 78–84;

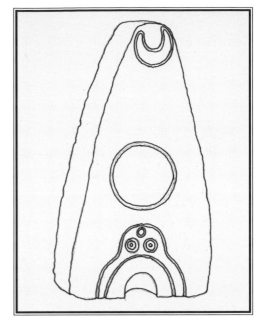

16.7. House-shaped tombstone, decorated with circle, crescent and concentric circles, first/second century AD; from the Forêt de Walscheid, near Saverne, Alsace. Height 92cm. (Illustrator E.R. Aldhouse)

16.8. Detail of the gable at the top of a house-shaped tombstone, decorated with crescent flanked by two circles, first/second century AD; from the Forêt de Walscheid, Alsace. 'Diameter' of crescent *c.* 120mm. (Photo: author)

Romilly-Allen 1901, 32; Charlesworth 1961, 34; Curle 1911, no. 34, pl. 87). In France, a miniature gold wheel-pendant from Balèsmes (Haute-Marne) (Fig. 16.6) has motifs of a double-axe and crescent soldered to the spokes (Déchelette 1913, 260ff). Wheel-motifs in later prehistoric and Romano-Celtic Europe (Green 1984; 1991) have been interpreted as solar motifs; if correct, the presence of juxtaposed sun and moon symbols may represent day and night or another level of time-succession, such as summer and winter. The double-axe on the Balèsmes pendant presents an enigma, but one interpretation of double-axes in Mediterranean antiquity is as symbols of regeneration (Dietrich 1988, 12–25), appropriate in cyclical imagery.

A series of Gallo-Roman stone monuments (c. AD 100–250) displays imagery closely resembling that of the swords and pendants. These monuments consist of tombstones, marking cremation-burials, occurring with particular frequency in the territory of the Mediomatrici, in the Vosges region near Strasbourg. The tombstones are idiosyncratic in design, and are termed 'stèles-maisons', on account of their characteristic shape – single or multiple triangular-faced gables or houses (Linckenheld 1927). Many bear astral symbols: rosettes, spoked wheels, crescents, and single and concentric circles; the stele from Wasserwald (Bas-Rhin), in the vicinity of Saverne is a prime example (Espérandieu 5684; Forrer 1909–12, 28–34, Taf. II, Fig. 1). Occasionally a pattern of symbol association depicting the succession of time may be discerned. A 'stèle-maison' from the Forêt de Walscheid (Vosges) (Fig. 16.7) bears a crescentric motif at the apex of the gable, a circle in the centre and three possible stars beneath (Espérandieu 4549; Green 1984, B44, Pl. XIV, Fig. 31; Linckenheld 1927, 90); and stones from La Horgne au Sablon near Metz (Espérandieu 5716) and Walscheid (Fig. 16.8) (Espérandieu 5710) each bear two circles flanking a crescent. If the identification of these motifs as astral symbols is correct, then the three stones appear to depict the passage of time, with full and new moons thus representing a complete lunar month.

Linckenheld (1927, 74–103) has argued that these designs are indigenous to Gaul, emphasising the rarity of celestial motifs on Roman tombstones. A new, detailed study of Romano-British tombstones (Raybould 1997) has revealed very few with astral symbols similar to the Vosges examples, although two from Chester (RIB 487, 529) display crescents with flanking circles or rosettes. In terms of sepulchral symbolism, the passing of time – as marked on the Alsace monuments – may have a dual function: at one and the same time, new and full moon motifs may reflect apotropaic (or talismanic) symbolism, both indicating a perceived desire to protect the dead in the journey to the afterlife and acknowledging a pattern of death and rebirth as inevitable as the lunar cycle. Moreover, the presence of astral motifs may reflect cosmological perceptions perhaps associated with a belief in cremation as a means of reaching an Other-world situated in the upper air.

Different, perhaps more speculative, evidence may be found through scrutiny of the axis and orientation of constructed space, whether in houses, shrines or graves. Parker Pearson has suggested (1996, 117 32) that British later Bronze and Iron Age round houses 'acted as a microcosm of the Universe, with the passing of time measured around the walls of the house' and that the common occurrence of east-facing entrances could be related to the sunrise and the endlessly repeated cycle of light and dark revolving around the house. Oswald (1991) has demonstrated that most round houses face due east or south-east, towards the equinoctial sunrise and mid-winter solstice respectively, a trend which appears to have first developed in the later Bronze Age. Similar patterns have been recognised in settlement enclosures, like the one at Longbridge Deverill Cow Down in Wiltshire (Guilbert 1982, 67–86), in Irish raths (Piccini 1992), and in hillfort entrances in Wessex (Hill 1996, 95–116, Figs. 8.8, 8.10).

Iron Age shrine- and burial-orientations also show a predilection for east-facing entrances and for axial symmetry between the entrance and the rear (Wait 1985, 177; Webster 1995, 459–60). Tombs which display a desire for the dead to face the rising sun have a wide distribution in Britain and Europe: excavations outside the defences of the Iron Age *oppidum* of Bibracte in Burgundy have revealed a first century BC cemetery consisting of square-ditched enclosures with east-facing entrances and containing mainly cremation-burials. This accords with orientation-practice noted elsewhere in Gaul and in areas of Iron Age Britain (Wait 1995, 496, 500).

SACRED CALENDARS

Winter, spring, summer have a meaning and name; of autumn the name alike and bounties are unknown
(Tacitus *Germania* 26)

your new moons and your appointed feasts my soul hateth: they are a trouble unto me; I am weary to bear them
(*Isaiah* 1, 14)

Humans recognise several different but related elements of cyclical time which are in tune with the annual, seasonal cycle: day and night, the lunar month, the seasons, and the human life cycle. In various past societies calendars have been constructed both as a secular means of measuring time and to maintain the natural cycle of diurnal succession in accordance with particular sacred events. Calendars may have early origins (Renfrew & Bahn 1991, 350; Marshack 1972, 445–77): an upper palaeolithic ivory plaque from Mal'ta in Siberia, engraved with a complex series of pits arranged in spirals, has been interpreted (by analogy with some modern Siberian tribal practices) as a calendrical device (Frolov 1977/8, 142–66; 1978/9, 61–113). The Old Icelandic calendar was marked by seasonal blood-sacrifices: in mid-October for a good year; in mid-winter for a good crop; and in mid-April for victory in battle (Lyle 1990, 75–85). The best-documented – and extremely sophisticated – calendrical system in the New World is that of the Classic Maya (AD 300–900) (Renfrew & Bahn 1991, 114–15; Coe 1987).

In ancient Greece, a major purpose of the Athenian calendar was to regulate the days of the month in step with the lunar cycle, ensuring the correct timing of festivals (Pritchett 1963, 345). According to Mikalson (1975, ix) calendars in Greek religion were to 'systematize and regularize the celebration of religious festivals within the city-state'. In Greek religion, the sacred calendar was closely linked to the lunar cycle; all communities regarded the first day of the month, the *Noumenia* (New Moon Day) as extremely holy; and in Athens, the main monthly festivals clustered in the first half of the month, the fortnight when the moon waxed towards full strength (Mikalson 1975, 13–14, 24).

The Roman calendars, *Fasti*, had a similar function. Until 304 BC, access to calendrical information – dates of festivals

16.9. Detail of Gaulish bronze calendar, showing the words SAMON and ATENOVX, first/second century AD; from Coligny (Ain), France. (Photo Simon James. By permission of Thames and Hudson Ltd)

and sacrifices, days on which no business could take place, and astrological phenomena – was strictly the province of priests and higher magistrates (Salzman 1990, 6). But thereafter, responding to popular demands, calendars were made public and posted in the Forum. The first recorded Roman calendar of named holidays was probably made of wood, and dates to 450 BC. Most calendars inscribed on stone belong to the earlier first century AD but one from Antium (the *Fasti Antiates Maiores*), which was painted in red and black letters on plaster, was drawn up between 84 and 46 BC (Scullard 1981, 46–9, Fig. on p. 49). Calendar production continued into late Roman antiquity: the illustrated Codex Calendar, naming pagan festivals, anniversaries and astral events in Rome during a single year, was presented as a gift to a Christian in AD 354 (Salzman 1990, 3).

It is within the context of the great bronze calendar discovered at Coligny (Ain), France in 1897 (Kruta 1991, 494–5; Duval & Pinault 1986) that the calendrical systems of Greece and Italy are of especial interest, because of similarities in both calculation and apparent function. This calendar (Fig. 16.9), together with a few fragments of what appears to be a similar inscription from Villards d'Héria (Jura) (Duval & Pinault 1986, 275–62), has been variously dated to between the second century BC and the second or third century AD. The Coligny calendar is inscribed in Gaulish or Gallo-Latin but using Roman script. Its essentially indigenous origins are confirmed by its divergence from the Julian calendar used by Rome and, if it does belong to a period later than the Roman conquest of Gaul (mid-first century BC), it is probably the result of codification of earlier 'free Gaulish' custom (Fitzpatrick 1996, 386), perhaps a post-conquest attempt at Gaulish self-determination and reassertion similar to that suggested for the genesis of Gaulish and British iconography under Roman rule (Green 1998, in press). The lengthy Coligny calendar consists of sixteen columns of sixty-two consecutive months covering a five-year period. The name of each day is accompanied by a small peg-hole which enabled detailed calendrical calculations and cyclical revisions to be made. The names of the months are accompanied by the abbreviations MAT(U) or ANM(ATU), which stand for 'good/complete' and 'bad/incomplete' respectively, and refer to whether the month in question had thirty or twenty-nine days; in this respect, the Coligny and Athenian calendars are in accord. Moreover, like the Athenian month, the Gaulish month was based on the lunar cycle and was divided into halves, the first fifteen days commencing with the new moon being divided from the remaining fortnight by the word ATENOVX ('returning night'). Thus the first half of the Gaulish month was perceived as the 'bright' half (i.e. leading up to the full moon) and the second the 'dark' half (when the moon waned). The year began with the month of SAMON (meaning 'the end of summer') and the second six months were introduced by GIAMONI ('the end of winter'). The Coligny inscription was a sophisticated piece of calendrical calculation, which included the insertion of intercalary months to allow the correlation between lunar and solar years (Fitzpatrick 1996, 386–7; Kruta 1991, 495).

The Coligny calendar (and presumably also the fragments from Villards d'Héria) was probably designed to be placed in a temple, and must have been maintained by the priestly class in Gaulish society. It had been deliberately broken before its disposal, possibly as a ritual act or for secrecy. That such a calendrical system belonged to a wider than tribal context is demonstrated by the provenance of the two calendars: Coligny in the territory of the Ambarri, Villards d'Héria in that of the Sequani. It is interesting to speculate on the distribution of such calendrical knowledge within the population. As we have seen, the Roman calendar was jealously guarded until this position became untenable. Did the priests and senior Gaulish political figures alone have access to calendrical information and, if not, what were the mechanisms for its dissemination throughout rural areas? Are we to assume the one-time presence of wooden versions of calendars which were available for local consultation? It has been suggested (Pritchett 1963, 347) that heralds communicated the progression of days within sacred cycles to ancient Greek communities, and thus announced ceremonies and festivals. But knowledge is power and it may well be that the Gaulish calendar remained the sole province of sacro-political leaders.

KNOWLEDGE AND POWER: THE KEEPERS OF SACRED TIME

They [the Druids] hold long discussions about the heavenly bodies and their movements, about the size of the universe and the earth, and about the nature of the physical world.

(Caesar *De Bello Gallico* VI, 14)

The foregoing has presented evidence illustrating that, by the later Iron Age, there existed a 'considerable body of astronomical knowledge' involving calendrical counting by nights (Fitzpatrick 1996, 386–7) and arguably maintained by powerful individuals. This model is endorsed by Classical commentators who describe an influential elite whose functions embraced both the religious and political arenas, one of their spheres of responsibility being astronomy and the recording and prediction of time-succession: these were the Druids (Chadwick 1966; Piggott 1968; Green 1997). It is all the more significant that Caesar and other authors note the doctrine of the Gaulish Druids which included calendrical calculation by nights; Caesar explains this practice: 'The Gauls all assert their descent from Dis Pater and say that it is the Druidic belief. For this reason they reckon periods of time not in days but in nights' (Caesar *De Bello Gallico* VI, 18).

Dis Pater was a Roman god of the dead (Ferguson 1980, 54). His veneration by the Gauls as early as the mid-first century BC is unlikely but Caesar may have identified a local god of the underworld with a divinity more familiar to his Roman peers. It is equally likely that Caesar noted the Gaulish practice of lunar calendrical calculation, illustrated by such objects as the Coligny calendar, and sought to explain such a custom with reference to a god associated with night, darkness and death. Pliny, writing in the first century AD, also observed the importance of the moon for the Gauls:

For it is by the moon that they measure their months and years and also their cycle [*saeculum*] of thirty years which was fixed in the sixth moon, when the moon had enough strength without being at its height.

and in the same passage:

Mistletoe . . . is gathered with great ceremony, and particularly on the sixth day of the moon. . . . Hailing the moon in a native word that means 'healing all things' they [the Druids] prepare a ritual sacrifice. (Pliny *Natural History* XVI, 95)

Other ancient writers associate the Druids with a knowledge of natural science and of the way the world worked. The first century AD poet Lucan (*Pharsalia* I, 447–62) alludes to their claim to understand astrology; and Pomponius Mela – a broad contemporary of Lucan – says that they proclaimed their knowledge of the universe:

their Druids, teachers of wisdom, who profess to know the greatness and shape of the earth and the universe and the motion of the heavens and of the stars (*De Chorographia* III, 2).

Cicero records the skill of a Druid known personally to him, a pro-Roman leader of the Burgundian tribe known as the Aedui, who supported Caesar in his Gaulish campaigns:

I know one [a Druid] of them myself, Divitiacus, the Aeduan. He claimed to have that knowledge of nature which the Greeks call *physiologia*, and he used to make predictions, sometimes by means of augury and sometimes by means of conjecture. (*De Divinatione* I, 90)

Apart from the averral by Classical writers that the Druids were concerned with the behaviour of celestial bodies, particularly the moon, there is also specific written testimony about calendrical calculation, notably from Hippolytus (*c.* AD 170–236), a Christian writing in Greek and living in Rome (Chadwick 1966, xvii):

And the Celts believe in their Druids as seers and prophets because they can foretell certain events by the Pythagorean reckoning and calculations. (*Philosophumena* I, 22)

A notable function of the Druids was divination, the ability to predict the future by magical means, whether in the form of changes in the weather or the seasons, celestial occurrences, the outcome of battles or the identity of a new ruler (Green 1997, 89–90). Some divination was by sacrifice (human or animal), some by augury (observation of birds in flight). Experiences encountered in dreams or visions, perhaps induced by hallucinogens (Creighton 1995, 285–301) or by natural means, such as hyperventilation, meditation or dance, were also used by the Druids in their search for divinatory inspiration. Calendrical knowledge would have enhanced their reputation as seers and prophets, particularly if such knowledge were kept secret. In this respect both the deliberate destruction of the Coligny calendar and Caesar's comment (VI, 14) that the Druids did not entrust their studies to writing are significant; in the same passage, Caesar states that, during their long training, the Druids committed a great deal to memory. Although, at first glance, the presence of the Coligny calendar and Caesar's remark are mutually contradictory, this in itself can, perhaps, be explained if the written calendars were later in date than the mid-first century BC when secrecy may not have been so vital. If Druidic skill at calendrical calculation was guarded as their private preserve (as in the earliest calendrical constructions of Greece and Rome), then the prediction of events, the taking of omens and the interpretation of portents (some of which would have been enabled by consultation of the calendar) would have considerably increased the awe and esteem in which the Druids were held. Moreover, scrutiny of the calendar made it possible to plan ahead and to fix the dates of sacred and political occasions. Caesar describes the precise plotting of one such event by the Druids: 'On a fixed date each year they assemble in a consecrated place in the territory of the Carnutes' (*De Bello Gallico* VI, 13).

Classical writers agree on the concentration of power in the hands of the Druids by the first century BC, although by then their influence may have already been in decline. They were heavily involved in political decision-making and some, like Divitiacus, were themselves rulers. They acted as judges and arbiters, and their scientific knowledge endowed them with great prestige. Their committal of tribal knowledge to memory, their high political profile and their ability to predict the future – whether by calendrical or divinatory means – gave them a very real control of all aspects of time: past, present and future.

SACRED SEASONS: PAGAN FESTIVALS IN EARLY IRELAND

Ireland was never subjugated by the Romans and, although there is some archaeological evidence for Roman activity, cultural influences from the Mediterranean world took no real or lasting hold there. The earliest Irish historical and mythic documents which were written, for the most part, between the sixth and twelfth centuries AD, contain material relating to the pre-Christian period, including some interesting references to calendrical events.

The early Irish literature makes frequent allusions to *óenachs* – assemblies held in both pagan and early Christian Ireland. It was the king's duty to convene such gatherings regularly, and the sources imply that these took place on sacred land (Raftery 1994, 81–2). Some of these assemblies were held at the time of the great pagan seasonal festivals, and were thus themselves imbued with sanctity. Both *óenachs* and sacred festivals were scheduled for specific dates within the year, requiring fairly precise calendrical knowledge.

The Irish myths, notably the *Leabhar Gabhála* (*Book of Invasions*) and the *Dinnshenchas* (*History of Places*), the earliest extant versions (or recensions) of which date to the twelfth century (O'Rahilly 1946), describe an Irish ritual year whose four quarters were each demarcated by a holy festival celebrating seasonal change. All were associated with the Druids and were based on the cycle of the farming calendar. Their purpose was partly as *foci* for markets and fairs, partly as excuses for jollification after episodes of intense work on the land, but a more important function was to provide a formal context for propitiating the gods so that livestock and crops would be healthy and fruitful (Green 1997, 34–7). The spring festival of Imbolc (1/2 February) was a purification festival associated with lambing (Vendryes 1924, 241–4) and is noteworthy as originally belonging to the pagan goddess Brigit. It was retained as a holy festival for the transmuted Christian saint (Bray 1987, 209–15; O Catháin 1995). Beltane welcomed the summer, a celebration of returning warmth and the movement of livestock on to summer pasture; it was a fire-festival, a magical wooing of the sun, and the ninth-century commentator Cormac refers to the lighting of two great ritual bonfires by the Druids, through which cattle were driven to protect them symbolically against disease. The chief assembly at the royal site of Tara (Co. Meath) was at Beltane (Binchy 1958, 113–38; Rhŷs 1901, 308–10). The *Book of Invasions* contains an account of the first Beltane fire to be lit, by a Druid called Mide (Minahane 1993). Lughnasa was a harvest festival marking the beginning of autumn, and the main festival day was traditionally on 1 August, although celebrations went on for a month, from 15 July to 15 August. The festival was named after the god/hero Lugh, a supernatural warrior and god of light (very possibly a solar deity), and it was celebrated at a number of royal centres in Ireland, including Tara (Connacht) and Emhain Macha (Ulster). The *Dinnshenchas* describes Lughnasa as a festival of assembly, where political and legal matters were discussed, and where ritual activities were carried out in juxtaposition with games and feasting (MacNeill 1962; van Tassell Graves 1965, 167–71).

Samhain (31 October/1 November) is the ancestor of Hallowe'en and All Souls' Day. It marked the end of the old year and of warm weather. It is of greatest interest here because it may probably be identified with SAMON, the month beginning the winter half of the year and whose name is inscribed on the Coligny calendar. A great political assembly took place at Tara during Samhain, thus indicating a close link between civic and ritual events in pre-Christian Ireland. Samhain also had pastoral origins, associated with rounding up livestock for selective culling or retention over the winter for breeding (Macalister 1931; Le Roux 1961, 485–506; Green 1992, 185–6). Early descriptions of Samhain contain significant information about the symbolism of this particular time of year, which was regarded as especially perilous because the barriers between the earthly and spirit worlds were temporarily dissolved, and other-worldly beings had free access to the human domain. But perhaps more important to the present study are the literary references to Samhain as an occasion when time itself was in abeyance, and was irrelevant for the duration of the festival. This suspension of time, or 'time of no being', could be perceived as even more dangerous, in that time meant power, order, control (by Druids or kings), and its absence signalled chaos, lawlessness and the triumph of untamed, anarchic forces over rationality and the rule of law. Fear of such a state may be paralleled by the tension and opposition between *nomos* (law and order) and *physis* (wild nature) in ancient Greek society and so vividly illustrated in Euripides' powerful play *The Bacchae*.

CONCLUSION

The symbolic acknowledgement of time as cyclical succession manifests itself in material culture in later prehistoric and Romano-Celtic Europe. Astral imagery on swords, personal regalia and tombstones depicts the passage of time either in terms of day and night (sun and moon) or of successive weeks in the lunar month (full moon and new moon). In view of the astronomical and cosmological knowledge attested for earlier phases of prehistory, clearly represented by megalithic monuments, it is no surprise to be able to identify such calendrical perceptions during the later Iron Age.

Weapons and pendants bearing what have been interpreted as symbols of the new and full moons may have belonged to high-ranking individuals, and perhaps were used as status-indicators and specialist ritual implements, for sacrifice or ceremony. Their prestige-value may have lain in their acknowledged possession by sacro-political figures responsible for temporal control and prediction. Additionally, the symbolism of time as a regenerative force is suggested by the Roman-period tombstones from Alsace, carved with differential lunar motifs. These Romano-Celtic monuments may have expressed perceptions which were essentially similar to those of much earlier megalithic tombs, such as Newgrange, which were orientated towards specific annual solar or lunar events.

Literary observations in the first centuries BC and AD indicate the presence of powerful figures, Druids, with combined sacred and political rôles, one of which was responsibility for the management of time. The physical remains of calendrical devices, like the bronze plate from Coligny, demonstrate mastery over the complexities of solar and lunar duration and the calibrations between one and the other, coupled with a consequent ability to plot calendrical events over a long timespan. It is argued here that at least part of the Druids' power lay in their skill at controlling and predicting both natural and humanly-constructed occurrences: using complex calendars, they could anticipate seasonal change, the solstices and equinoxes and, with that knowledge, they could plan cyclical ceremonies. The evidence from early Irish documents displays the necessity of plotting the correct days for the major seasonal celebrations. With their additional rôle as keepers of oral tradition, the Druids' temporal knowledge embraced the past, present and future, and made it possible to predict auspicious or inauspicious days for important occasions; it is likely that such wisdom endowed its possessors with immense authority, based upon a scholarship that was retained as their exclusive and arcane preserve.

Abbreviation

RIB: Collingwood, R.G. & Wright, R.P. 1965. *The Roman Inscriptions of Britain*, vol. I: Inscriptions on Stone. Oxford, Oxford University Press.

CHAPTER SEVENTEEN

RITUAL ASTRONOMY IN THE NEOLITHIC AND BRONZE AGE BRITISH ISLES: PATTERNS OF CONTINUITY AND CHANGE

CLIVE RUGGLES

INTRODUCTION

We have progressed far since the days when archaeologists argued, sometimes vituperatively, against astronomers and engineers about astronomical computers and megalithic observatories. Aubrey Burl played a prominent role in this reconciliation. His seminal article on 'Science or symbolism' (Burl 1980) led the way to a discussion that placed astronomy firmly in the context of prehistoric ritual and ideology (for a commentary *see* Ruggles 1998, ch. 4). Nowadays most archaeologists interpret architectural alignments upon astronomical phenomena in relation to wider questions of cognition and world-view. As Richard Bradley has said of the Dorset cursus, 'By incorporating into its structure an important astronomical alignment, those who built it made those developments appear to be part of the functioning of nature' (Bradley in Barrett *et al*. 1991, 58). Another area in which Burl's influence was seminal was in stressing the importance of repeated trends in regional groups of similar monuments. This has strongly influenced developments in archaeoastronomy since the early 1980s, and even in these days when the importance of the particular and the contextual has rightly been recognised and emphasised within interpretative archaeology, regional studies may reveal common elements of ritual tradition (and hence world-view) that can be identified with some confidence as something that was intentional and meaningful. This has an important role in ensuring that we continue to consider the extent to which theoretical ideas are actually supported by direct evidence visible in the archaeological record (for further discussion *see* Ruggles 1998, ch. 10).

Yet a communications problem evidently remains. On the one hand, the year 1996 saw the appearance of a book by a prominent historian of science in which a variety of Wessex monuments from the Early Neolithic onwards (including, inevitably, Stonehenge) are each interpreted in terms of stellar, solar or lunar alignments within a broad theme of astronomical development (North 1996). On the other hand, many archaeologists continue to be completely dismissive of astronomy: for Chippindale (1994, 230) the very use of the term carries the inevitable overtone of Western analytical science, while for Wainwright 'the answer to the mysteries of Stonehenge lies in [understanding its role as a symbol of power and a device for legitimising existing power structures], not in the patterns of the heavens' (Wainwright 1996). Fortunately, this polarisation of views is no longer typical; there is a consensus which seeks to identify possible astronomical symbolism in a wider interpretative context. None the less, there is still a major difference of approach between those who – mainly in the mainstream literature – use particular astronomical alignments as part of wider interpretations of prehistoric monuments and landscapes, and the studies of groups which continue as the norm within archaeoastronomy itself.

In the first of these two categories, the majority of architectural alignments that have found tacit acceptance are towards sunrise or sunset at one of the solstices. Examples include the Dorset and Dorchester cursuses (Bradley in Barrett *et al.* 1991, 56; Bradley & Chambers 1988, 286); the Newgrange roofbox (O'Kelly 1982, 123–4); Maes Howe (Ritchie 1985, 127) and a large building in the nearby settlement at Barnhouse (C. Richards 1990, 312–13); Stonehenge 3, Woodhenge and Coneybury (J. Richards 1991, 89–96, 98); and the passage tombs at Balnuaran of Clava (Bradley 1996; 1997). Claims of equinoctial alignments are encountered at the Stonehenge cursus (Bradley & Chambers 1988, 286; Bradley 1993, 62; Darvill 1996, 254; but *see* Burl 1987, 44), Knowth (Eogan 1986, 178), and elsewhere (Parker Pearson 1993, 62; Gibson 1994, 207). There are also a number of instances of orientation upon sunrise or sunset at mid-quarter days, halfway in time between the solstices and equinoxes, and particularly on 1 May: the oldest of these is the axis of symmetry of the early neolithic timber setting at Godmanchester, Cambridgeshire (Parker Pearson 1993, 62); later neolithic examples include Bryn Celli Ddu (Green 1991, 11) and Druid's Circle, Gwynedd (Burl 1995, 177).

The reason for listing this diverse catalogue is that this sort of evidence is used by some to support the claim that, even surprisingly early in the Neolithic, a seasonal calendar was in use in which the year was divided into eight roughly equal parts, extending by continuity of tradition right through to Celtic times (Krupp 1994, *xi*). In the author's view this is insupportable, for a number of reasons. First, the statistical evidence for Alexander Thom's eight- or sixteen-part 'megalithic calendar', which is usually invoked in support of the argument, did not survive reassessments in the early 1980s (for a detailed discussion *see* Ruggles 1998, ch. 2). Secondly, the much-quoted idea of a (single) 'Celtic calendar', with its seasonal festivals dividing the solar year into eight exactly equal parts (e.g. MacCana 1970), stands on much weaker foundations than is generally assumed (Hutton 1996, 408–11 and references therein; Ruggles 1998, ch. 8). Thirdly, the assumption that the equinoxes and mid-quarter days were likely to have been of any significance whatsoever in prehistoric seasonal calendars falls into the trap of imposing Western concepts, including that of the equinox itself, onto non-Western world-views (Ruggles 1997; 1998, ch. 9; 1999). With the possible exception of the group of oval stone rings in North Wales – the orientations of the long axes of which are, according to Burl (1985b, 81–2), clustered around sunset in early May – the idea of deliberate alignments upon the equinoxes and mid-quarter days rests only upon diverse instances; it finds no support in any systematic studies of the evidence from regional groups of monuments (Ruggles 1998, ch. 8).

These systematic studies do, however, reveal some strong regional trends that indicate patterns of continuity in ritual practice, even in times of considerable social change (cf. Bradley 1991a,

217–18). A brief overview of the evidence follows; a more detailed account is given elsewhere (Ruggles 1998, ch. 8).

PATTERNS OF CONTINUITY AND CHANGE

Even though the available orientation evidence is generally accurate only to the nearest one-sixteenth division of the compass (i.e. to within an azimuth band of width 22.5°), it is quite clear that orientation was of great symbolic importance even in the Early Neolithic. Strong and similar general patterns are evident among a number of regional groups of earthen long barrows and long houses in northern Europe, with the spread of orientations generally being centred upon the east or south-east (Hodder 1992, 54–5; on the earthen long barrows of southern England see Ashbee 1984, 21–4 and Figs. 19–22). Even at this level of precision such consistency over wide areas could only have been achieved by reference to the daily motions of the heavenly bodies. But on such evidence it is impossible to be more specific.

Aubrey Burl's systematic regional survey of sixty-five long barrows on Salisbury Plain (Burl 1987b, 27–9), determining their orientations to within ±2°, allows us to say more about Early Neolithic Wessex. But the evidence is not conclusive. All but thirteen barrow orientations fall inside the solar arc; all but six fall inside the wider lunar arc. This in itself gives no strong backing for choosing between solar and lunar hypotheses (see, for example, Ruggles 1997; 1998, ch. 8), even though the assumption that the distribution is related to the moon provides one of the main supports for the idea that predominantly solar symbolism in the Late Neolithic replaced earlier, predominantly lunar, symbolism, an idea that has permeated the literature (e.g. Bradley in Barrett et al. 1991, 56–7; Tilley 1994, 196–7). More significant, perhaps, is the fact that the bulk of the outlying orientations are to the south rather than to the north of the solar and lunar arcs. This suggests that it might have been important to orient the entrance upon a direction where the rising sun or moon would sometimes be seen to pass, possibly as it was climbing in the sky rather than necessarily at its actual point of rising (cf. Hoskin et al. 1995 on Andalusian tombs).

Turning to neolithic chambered tombs, systematic studies of astronomical potential among regional groups were once again pioneered by Burl (1981b; 1983, ch. 5). Some general patterns of orientation were already well known: the forecourts of Clyde-Solway tombs cluster around north-east, Camster tombs face around due east, Shetland heel-shaped cairns are oriented close to south-east, and so on (Burl loc. cit.). But while the orientations of the stone-lined passages of chambered tombs are generally easier to determine than those of earthen barrows, careful studies of groups of orientations, working at a suitable level of precision and taking into account horizon altitudes so as to calculate declinations and hence determine specific astronomical associations, were virtually non-existent. Not all local groups of chambered tombs show distinct orientation trends and, even where they do, the simplest explanation may not always be an astronomical one. But Burl's evidence from the Clava cairns of Aberdeenshire – anomalous because of their predominantly south-westerly orientation – is important because it shows that, with the exception of the main site at Balnuaran of Clava itself, their orientations coincide closely with the major and minor standstill limits of the moon, implying an awareness of the changes in the setting position of the midsummer full moon over a cycle of nearly nineteen years (Burl 1981b, 257–65).

Low-precision astronomical alignments found repeatedly among henges and stone and timber rings give numerous hints that astronomy was very much a part of ceremonial tradition and

Callanish. (Photo: Alex Gibson)

practice in the Late Neolithic, at least in certain places at certain times. So also do apparent alignments upon prominent natural features in the landscape (Ruggles 1998, ch. 8). But there is no simple overall picture, and systematic studies of regional monument groups are still few and far between. One exception is the large stone circles of Cumbria and south-west Scotland, which may have been designed to encapsulate two alignments, one to a cardinal point and one to sunrise or sunset at an important time of year (Burl 1988b). Apart from the stone circles at Callanish, which, it has been suggested, formed part of a 'complex' of monuments located so as to frame ranges of sacred hills in relation to the rising and setting moon (Curtis & Curtis 1994), relatively few systematic associations have been claimed in recent years between groups of stone circles and the moon. Even at Stonehenge, the evidence to support claims of lunar symbolism in the early phases is equivocal, and the only reasonably uncontroversial interpretation is that the change of axis to incorporate a solstitial alignment around the time of the arrival of the bluestones in *c.* 2550 BC was simply part of the process of adding considerably to the symbolic power of the monument (Ruggles 1997; 1998, ch. 8).

It is in the Early Bronze Age that systematic studies of the location and design of ceremonial monuments in relation to the surrounding landscape and to celestial events have been most fruitful. Traditions of astronomical symbolism are most evident where we find many small monuments that appear to have been the ceremonial foci serving relatively small groups of people: these include the recumbent stone circles (RSCs) of north-east Scotland; the short stone rows of Argyll and the Hebrides, Ulster, and south-west Ireland; and the axial stone circles (ASCs) of Counties Cork and Kerry. Perhaps neolithic practices of public monument

Dervaig North stone row, Mull.

construction and use were being perpetuated, although on a much smaller scale. The large numbers of simple monuments facilitates the study of repeated trends and helps us gain reliable insights into elements of common practice that were both deliberate and meaningful.

Work on these groups has begun to reveal a surprising wealth of detail. The Scottish RSCs, apparently perpetuating an earlier tradition in the Clava cairns, are predominantly oriented to the south-south-west, and the majority appear to be related to the southerly limit of the rising or setting moon as well as to terrestrial features such as prominent hilltops (Ruggles & Burl 1985). The Scottish and south-west Irish rows generally conform to patterns of location and orientation related to prominent landscape features and the moon, although in different ways in the two regions (Ruggles 1998, ch. 6). On the other hand the Irish ASCs, while mimicking the Scottish RSCs both architecturally and in their predominantly south-westerly orientation, show very little consistency as regards astronomical potential or in their locations in the landscape, giving rise to the suggestion that the ASC tradition may derive from the RSC tradition, retaining some elements of that tradition while having lost various subtleties of symbolic association (Ruggles 1998, ch. 5; Burl 1982, 159–60). In order to explore wider sets of ideas concerning symbolism of place we need to integrate archaeoastronomical field techniques with more conventional methodologies of landscape survey. A project of this type has already been attempted in north Mull, and has indicated complex relationships between site locations, astronomical events, and prominent features in the landscape (Martlew & Ruggles 1996; Ruggles 1998, ch. 7).

CONCLUSIONS: CULT AND COSMOLOGY

Hutton (1996, 4–5), in attempting to sum up the evidence on astronomy in the prehistoric British Isles, concludes that 'the vast majority [of monument orientations] do not relate to any of [the astronomical bodies]' and that 'no overall or enduring pattern of cult may be detected'. Certainly, the evidence is very patchy and no clear picture emerges of overall astronomical development, but then this is scarcely surprising over a period characterised by huge transformations in subsistence methods and economy, together with continual social change and upheaval, and often considerable variation from one geographical region to another; it would be surprising indeed to discover any simple, overall pattern of developments in cognition, concerning celestial phenomena or anything else. In fact, Hutton considers only solstitial and supposed equinoctial alignments, a constraint that is both unnecessary and misleading, since we should not prejudge what constitutes significant targets, and certainly not according to Western criteria. Examining groups of monuments with an open mind, an approach which Burl has championed for many years, suggests a variety of other ways in which astronomical alignments could have been encapsulated within them so as to convey symbolic meaning, not constrained to alignments upon actual rising and setting, to particular stations of the sun, or indeed to the sun as opposed to the moon or other astronomical bodies. A deconstruction of some of the Western astronomical concepts and assumptions inherent in archaeoastronomy (Ruggles 1997; 1998, ch. 9) helps us to consider a broader set of ideas.

Monuments played a fundamental role in the organisation of the prehistoric landscape, helping to mark and characterise important places in the perceived scheme of things. They were key elements in 'sacred geographies': landscapes charged with meaning. By understanding symbolic associations between monuments and the natural landscape around them we may hope to gain insights into the prevailing world-view. But non–Western world-views do not separate the land and the sky; astronomy is an integral part of every indigenous cosmology, and this means that we are unwise to study sacred landscapes in isolation from the sky.

Perhaps astronomical alignments simply helped to affirm a monument's place at 'the centre of the world' (Renfrew 1984, 178–80); perhaps they had more to do with making its power unchallengeable and thereby affirming ideological structures and political control (Bradley in Barrett et al. 1991, 56). Perhaps they were framed from a straightforward concern to harmonise the monument, or the place where it was located, with the cosmos. Whatever the precise motives,

this may have been what a stone circle was to its people, a place where axes and gifts were exchanged, a place where annual gatherings were held, a place to which the bodies of the dead were brought before burial, but, above all, a place that was the symbol of the cosmos, the living world made everlasting in stone, its circle the shape of the skyline, its North point the token of the unchangingness of life, a microcosm of the world in stone, the most sacred of places to its men and women.

(Burl 1988b, 202)

CHAPTER EIGHTEEN

RECORDING ORTHOSTATIC SETTINGS

ROGER J. MERCER

It gives me the very greatest pleasure to have been invited to contribute to this volume celebrating Aubrey Burl's achievement in a lifetime spent observing, recording, excavating and interpreting the orthostatic monuments that form such an unusual and ubiquitous feature of the earlier prehistoric archaeology of the British Isles and north-west France. In doing so he has deployed his immense knowledge, hard won on many a rain-sodden moor (as well, of course, as that vital component of fieldwork support, teasing out gems of local knowledge in warmer and more lubricative circumstances), to bring together scholars from widely different backgrounds and interests to arrive at a proper understanding of one another's work and achievements. Mediators undertake work that is often frustrating, usually unsung, and sometimes risky, and it is a tribute to Aubrey's gentle modesty, infectious enthusiasm and unrivalled dedication that he has been so successful in convincing field archaeologists of the validity and value of much astronomical interpretation of the monuments, often undertaken by non-archaeologists, as well as convincing workers in this latter specialised sphere of the proper concerns of the archaeologists themselves. The rewarding counterpoint established between the two disciplines, especially in Britain, is, I believe, very largely due to Aubrey Burl's unobtrusive, persuasive yet persistent efforts.

This chapter began life as a footnote-study to examine one small group of orthostatic monuments from the point of view of the available record (which was historical as well as recent – with intermediate phases), with several objectives in mind: first, to establish the evidence (or not) of the deterioration of the monuments concerned, secondly, to assess the changing view of the landscape around them, and lastly, to assess the changing attitudes towards their survey.

Straightforward as these objectives, by and large, were, I found that the material available both in archive form (as held in the NMRS), and in published form was quite inadequate to the task. There has been no standard of recording, and frequently whatever standards there were have been engulfed by the tide of interpretation that has so often been its prime mover.

In preparing this chapter, it struck me that *festschriften* are not about the past but about the future – and my objective at once became clear: to set down a draft standard for orthostatic setting recording that would at least resolve my perceived problems and those I had understood from the work of others. This notion coincided with the needs of staff of the RCAHMS about to embark upon a major recording exercise in this area.

Researchers at Glassel stone circle. (Photo: Alex Gibson)

But such a standard cannot be set unilaterally, nor should it be, even if a start needs to be made. What follows, therefore is an organised statement of intent. Inevitably there are weaknesses and I will welcome comment that will lead to its refinement, reorganisation or re-casting. This 'draft standard' is set out under headings (1, 2 and 3) that define the type of survey required and then explores (under headings 4.1 to 4.6) the objectives of that survey and their proper attainment. Under heading 5 the problems of publication are briefly explored and then expanded on in tabular form.

TYPES OF SURVEY REQUIRED

1. Scale of Survey

Because orthostatic monuments vary so widely in size (from a few metres to kilometres in extent) there can be no question of a standard scale of recording. A scale should be chosen that with reasonable reduction (3 or 4 times) (and never expansion) enables the drawing to be reproduced on a standard format page. In special cases 'pull-out' sheets may be visualised as a publication medium, but these are becoming increasingly impractical.

Scales should always be 'metric': 1:10, 1:20, 1:50, 1:100, 1:250, 1:500, 1:1000, 1:1250 or, 1:2500.

2. Limits and Constraints of Survey

These should always be indicated on the archive drawing. Outliers may be indicated by a directional indication, and precise distance with a correctly oriented on-plan ground-section.

Areas within the survey area where special constraints to the visibility of orthostatic, earthwork or other features apply (for example waterlogged areas, forestry plantation, stone clitter, dense undergrowth, etc.) should be indicated.

The method of survey should be clearly described in detail on the archive drawing and in text in the publication (including information about the instruments used, specified limits of error, frequency of measurement, method of orientation, method of checking).

3. Method of Survey

Only the highest standards of accuracy can be permitted in an area where precise alignments or relationships may form the basis of derived hypothesisation. Adequately accurate survey may be achieved by any of the commonly available survey methods: plane-table and self-reducing aledade (for structures up to 100m in overall size); theodolite and tape (not tacheometry) up to 100m. For all distances, however, electronic impulse emitting survey equipment is now the only real answer to the problems posed by the need for accuracy where precision to within millimetres can be relatively easily attained over distances up to 500m. This advanced equipment is expensive but the loan of equipment may be possible from a variety of organisations, provided that it is adequately insured. The value of this approach is massively enhanced by the possibility of add-on appliances that will enable the inspection of a produced plan 'in the field' (through software such as PENMAP) and which, through the intermediary of AUTOCAD or a Geographical Information System, will allow, in conjunction with the availability of digital OS mapping, the production of models of terrain, situation and intervisibility that will automate, and enhance the accuracy of, the wider terrestrial and celestial concerns that form one focus of current research. For let there be no doubt about the objective of the survey of earlier prehistoric orthostatic structures: the search is for methods of totally accurate survey that will also allow accurate interlocation within the immediate, and indeed distant, landscape. Before the survey is completed check measurements, randomly selected, should be made by tape between clearly identifiable points and cross-checked against the scaled measurements on the produced plan.

4. Aims and Objectives of Survey

4.1. Objective 1. An accurate ground plan survey of the stone setting.

This requires the ground section plan of all orthostats on the site and this means exactly what it says – points accurately taken at ground level (whatever that level, which will vary over the site) to achieve a ground plan. This is the surveyors' and archaeologists' document – the product of the age of mapping and enlightenment of the seventeenth century and later, but not a view that would communicate anything necessarily to a prehistoric mind. Furthermore a ground section plan will not necessarily relate to the prehistoric period as frequently the modern ground level will not relate to previous ground levels (through peat formation, erosion or other developments) which in many cases will have shifted the 'ground section plan' up or down the orthostat. Standing stones should be shown in solid black with fallen stones in outline only. An arrow towards the top of the stone, within the stone outline, may indicate the direction of fall if this can be suggested.

4.2. Objective 2. An accurate depiction of the ground surface (in its present day form, of course) upon which the orthostatic setting is built.

Such surfaces are frequently adjusted by levelling (either by cutting or building or both) and settings may be embanked or encircled by a ditch, or may enclose or be related to cairns, barrows or other structures. While I shall return to the complex problems of cairn survey in due course,

Drizzlecombe stone rows. (Photo: Alex Gibson)

at this stage the necessity exists to record in detail the ground surface to be sure to record any such adjustments. Sections through the site are not enough to give a complete record and the only feasible approach is to conduct a contour survey of the site and a reasonable '*cordon sanitaire*' around it. The size of this *cordon* must be left to the judgement of the fieldworker but must extend far enough to bring the monument into relationship with the general lie of the ground in the locality. This must involve survey of at least 10m out from the stone setting and sometimes much more. The survey should be conducted to furnish contours at no more than 10cm intervals. Such contour survey will, of course, allow sections to be reconstructed by the researching scholar between any two points across the site. The surveyor can decide whether he or she can publish the stone setting and contour survey superimposed, or whether the superimposed version should be accompanied by a plan of the stone setting *simpliciter* if the combined version is so 'busy' as to impair an immediate assessment of the stone setting's actual form. The contour survey must be tied to local OD (Ordnance Datum), an exercise rendered daily more difficult by the loss of benchmark indicators. It may be at this point, especially in the Highland Zone where benchmarks are few and far between, that global positioning equipment will come into its own although it is hard to believe that even the most currently sophisticated GPS will allow <u>survey</u> of stone settings to be carried out to a sufficiently accurate degree.

4.3. Objective 3. To portray the skyline features and other visible geographical features (and to furnish elevation drawings of orthostats) that may reflect upon, and indeed control, the siting of the orthostatic setting in question.
    By way of introduction I am reminded of an excavation I conducted in Eskdale in the mid-

1980s. Not far from the site was the nascent (at that time) Buddhist monastery 'Samye Ling' which serves as a centre and refuge for monks who have escaped from Tibet as well as, of course, a retreat for western 'converts'. The Lama of the monastery was persuaded to visit us. He came, courteously (and wisely) refused a cup of excavation tea, and responded to my questions as to why Eskdale had been chosen as their final refuge. His answers were revealing. Only at a site where the mountain mass was 'enough', only where the river 'flowed in the right direction', was it appropriate to build the monastery. In fact, there were more than a thousand 'reasons' why a site should be chosen – they included factors reflecting detailed aspects of vegetation, geomorphology, relief, drainage and meteorology which were held to foster an appropriate atmosphere for meditation. This discussion immediately brought to mind the location of many henges as well as stone circles which seem consistently to be associated with riverside dispositions, raised skylines and other land features which suggest that it was important for them to overlook the near neighbourhood while being overlooked from afar.

The analysis of these criteria must, of course, form a vital aspect of the study of these monuments and to this end we have to add the requirement for information relating to foresight–backsight possibilities associated with celestial observation.

These matters ought now to be addressed by routine survey to enable the gradual construction of a database containing the information relating to topographical situations of all monuments of this class. The record should comprise two components.

1. On plan.

At scales which will vary with circumstances, originating from the centre of the stone setting in a series of segments can be constructed indicating the depth of view commanded from the monument around the entire circumference of its prospect. Areas of 'dead ground' will appear as breaks in the segments and points of particularly deep perspective may be indicated by arrows with 'horizon' indicated (in the case, for example, of the sea) or with locations given of the terminal point of the prospect. Current but impermanent obstacles to vision such as buildings, trees and so on should be ignored and the prospect reconstructed as if in a vegetationless landscape. This exercise should be conducted on the ground but a supporting record can be created by all-round prospect photography.

2. In elevation.

At the same scale as the ground plan a panorama should be created with the centre of the setting as its viewpoint. In the case of a simple setting it will be possible to display the elevation of each orthostat against the panorama behind. In the case of some complex settings, like multiple stone rows, that may not be feasible and elevations of each row will have to be undertaken with the panorama from the centre of the setting shown separately.

There will be rare sites, notably linear settings, where the panorama visible at each end will differ notably from that viewed from the centre and, indeed, from the other end. Where such variation occurs then panoramas at different and extreme points should be recorded.

4.4. Objective 4. To record elements of a stone setting no longer visible but concealed beneath (for example) vegetation or peat.

I am unaware of any instance of the successful use of geophysical means to establish the existence of standing stones buried by peat although resistivity survey would presumably offer the prospect of success if the peat was of some depth and bedrock did not lie directly beneath it, thus allowing contrasting masses for registration. Using geophysical survey to establish the position of stone-sockets where stones have been removed is, of course, well known.

In the relatively common upland situation where stones have been inundated in peat, probing is a readily available, simple and effective method of locating buried orthostats. Surveying arrows and other metal points should be eschewed in favour of bamboo wands lm in length and painted with 'luminous' orange or yellow paint. In addition to their greater length and cheapness, bamboo canes are biodegradable if lost and will not deface the buried stones that they come into contact with.

Probing is an operation that requires patience and <u>plenty</u> of canes. It should take place on a grid, prestrung on the ground, the grid reflecting the size of orthostat being sought but normally of no larger than 0.5m intervals. Each stone must be probed and contacted on four sides to ensure its verticality and then 'shaped' by further probings. Bedrock, erratics and fallen stones will all happily serve to confuse the fieldworker and only clearly defined vertical or fallen stones should be plotted. Once located, such 'lost' orthostats should be differentiated as less completely known than their visible peers – either by hatched infill if a reasonable 'shape' has been ascertained or by a small cross marking their assessed centre point.

4.5. Objective 5. To record cairns and other features associated with the orthostatic setting either by direct stratigraphical association or by propinquity.

The recording of cairns is a difficult matter to which there would appear to me to be no ideal solution. The problem lies in the ability of the surface of the cairn to reveal information as to the sequence of its construction, of its robbing, or of its previous exploration. As a consequence it is desirable to record the detailed morphology of the surface of the cairn and to this extent a simple stipple infilled outline with orthostatic components shown is not enough. The problem is resolved for the surveyor where nature has engendered a substantial and prolonged cover on the cairn so as to 'smooth' the surface with a thin layer of humus which, however, may well not completely conceal the evidence indicated above. In instances of this kind the appropriate form of record must be contour survey at vertical intervals of, normally, not more than 10cm.

The problem still remains, however, of cairns where no such 'smoothing' effect has occurred, which remain as a jumble of stones with their interstices – often treacherously deep – yet where, impressionistically, some form can be seen to exist in their surface morphology which hints at structural (or destructional) complexity. Contour survey is really quite impossible in these circumstances where in order to achieve any meaningful result the degree of 'adjustment' 'selection' and 'interpolation' of points would rob the result of any objectivity or checkability. 'Stone by stone' drawing indicating vertical height differentiation by shading and spot height insertion is certainly a technique that we would not reject were the site under excavation. Yet in the context of archaeological field survey this scale of recording is impracticable in terms of its ergonomic implications. Furthermore it is unlikely in my experience that any cairn will be <u>totally</u> exposed in this form, thus invalidating the 'totality' of this approach. I myself have experimented with the illustration of the morphology of cairn surfaces with hachures, but, while I believe that information of value was transmitted, the result is not beautiful nor do hachures, intended as they are for earthwork illustration, create any realistic impression of the true nature of the material under study.

The complex stony cairn remains a problem of surveyed illustration which may only be completely resolved by a combination of techniques to illustrate as much recoverable archaeological information as possible.

Damage at Cerrig yr Helfa stone row. (Photo: Alex Gibson)

4.6 Objective 6. The description of the monument and of the constraints of survey.

The date(s) of survey and any constraints upon survey should be described. The latter will, of course, include vegetation (in detail) but may also include weather and visibility. The geology of each stone should be described as well as its colour. In order to accomplish this stones should be numbered logically from North to South and the number of stones as thus registered recorded. The numbering should be included on the original archive plan and only if necessary transmitted to the published plan (i.e. if comment in text demands it). Stones should be searched for decoration or, indeed, for obvious fossil inclusions and a photographic record made of these. Where stones are split along natural laminations in the rock and appear as multiple orthostats their individual points should be recorded but their original unity noted.

Finally constraints on access to the site, from the point of view of land ownership and of health and safety, should be clearly set out.

5. Publication of the result

The essence of publication is the transmission of all essential information and the precise source location of all other relevant material. Publication should also always seek to separate as far as possible that which is interpretation from those that are, in so far as they can be, objectively recorded data. I have suggested above a fairly demanding process of recording and propose to indicate below in tabular form the precise allocation of production to publication and archive. It must be made quite clear in the published account that all the items that exist in the archive that are not necessarily produced in the published account. Under no circumstances should

Table 18.1 Summary

Objective	Publication	Archive	Remarks
Objective 1. An accurate survey of the stone setting.	Yes. With very large sites it may be necessary to publish separate sector plans as well as an overall plan to allow the ground section plan of each stone to be assessed.	Yes. With all survey notes, readings, memoranda and comments.	The published scale should, where at all possible, allow the ground section plan of each stone to be clearly assessed. Published scale should be visual rather than notational. North point indicating dated magnetic bearing should be of sufficient length to allow satisfactory use of a protractor from the published plan. The plan frame as published should represent limit of survey or less — otherwise limit of survey should be shown.
Objective 2. An accurate depiction of the ground surface.	Yes where possible. There may be circumstances where this plan is combined with that pertaining to Objective 1. This plan should anyway include all the information on the Objective 1 plan and should only be produced separately if the bulk of information leads to obfuscation.	Yes, as above.	Where probing or other activity has taken place due to e.g. peat formation, an attempt should be made to recreate the original contour of the site by probing on a grid and measurement.
Objective 3. To portray skyline features and other visible geographical features and to furnish elevation drawings of orthostats seen from the inside of the setting.	Yes. A separate numbered plan may be necessary in the case of complex or exceptionally numerous settings. It may prove necessary to break panorama into a series of 'strips' to respect page size — if so A–B, B–C, C–D etc should be indicated on Objective 1/2 plan as directional points.	Yes. Backed by a separate numbered plan in archive. All photographic cover in negative form (appropriately numbered from north) should be deposited with the archive. For archive purposes film should be monochrome although duplicate colour coverage should also be taken.	Orthostats drawn in elevation should be numbered according to site scheme. Numbering from northernmost stone, left to right, or clockwise if a circle. North point should be indicated by clear vertical arrow. The panorama should not only include skyline horizon but other major geographical features (rivers, crags, intervening relief, etc.).

Objective			
Objective 4. To record elements of a stone setting no longer visible.	Yes. As adjunct to Objective 1/2.	Yes. Degrees of certainty may be expressed on original survey drawings or in the notes.	Methods must be clearly described. Methods should avoid any damage to buried features. Detected orthostats (or fallen stones) should be numbered in sequence with other orthostats -- numbers suffixed 'N' (non–visible)
Objective 5. To record cairns and other features associated with the orthostatic setting.	Yes. It may be necessary, in addition to inclusion of these details as an adjunct to Objectives 1/2, to publish a larger scale detailed plan of some of these features, e.g. cists.	Yes. Conventions and annotations to clarify portrayal of detail.	Stratigraphical relationships must be sought and described. It ought explicitly to be stated where such relationships are *not* visible.
Objective 6. The description of the monuments and of the constraints of survey.	Yes. Fully set out in published account.		
Objective 7. Interpretation only to be produced separately if the bulk of information leads to obfuscation.	Yes. Reconstruction detail or superimposed information relating to lines of sight, azimuths, tracking devices, etc. should NOT be included with Objective 1/2 information but MUST be set out on a separate drawing.	Yes. Here should be recorded names of all survey party, daily diary, etc. Yes. Draft interpretations should be included and minor uncertainties unsuitable for inclusion in the published account must be included here.	Ephemeral 'diary' detail is of considerable archive interest and should not be expunged. The archive should be deposited with the most suitable record depository (in Scotland, NMRS) and its accession number given in the published account. Interpretational information should be clearly segregated from the Objective 6 'descriptive' information. Having said this, very simple interpretative information on an otherwise uncluttered plan may, for reasons of economy, be built into the Objective 1/2 plan, but this is not an ideal solution.

interpretational material be included upon basic plans (relating to Objectives 1, 2 and 3) and 'overlay' grids, azimuth information etc., unless of the very simplest, should be restricted to a separate plan or elevation. It must not be allowed to obfuscate the objectively recorded data.

The above recommended procedure will result in the following published output:

PLAN 1/2 relating to Objectives 1,2,4 and 5. If in the nature of a particular exercise the volume of information on this plan becomes confusing then Objective 2 information should be shown against a separate plan of the orthostatic setting = PLAN 2.

ELEVATION 3 relating to Objective 3. A separate plan may be necessary in very complex settings to allow the numbering of each stone. Normally this enumerative exercise can be included in PLAN 1 above.

PLAN 4 associated features (Objective 5) will again appear on PLAN 1, but detailed depictions may require this further = PLAN 4.

PLAN 5 Interpretation: to include all 'superimposed' information that may assist with the interpretation/explanation of the site.

i.e. A maximum of five illustrations for each site with a likely outcome in most instances of two, plus one for interpretation (but see 'Remarks' in table on pp. 216–17).

I am aware that this represents a quantum leap in the work involved in the recording of such sites. That leap is, in my view, demanded by the multi-disciplinary clientele that such recording now serves. Cultural Resource Managers rightly require an accurate, date-lined condition statement. Those with a wider view whether into the terrestrial or celestial 'catchment zone' of such sites require yet further information. While, of course, there are those who require an absolutely accurate and three dimensional view of the site for purely archaeological research. To all of these potential (and actual) clients I reiterate that I suggest the above approach as a way forward, and I anxiously await response from all sectors as to that which I have suggested which is *de trop*, and to that which (God forbid!) requires further input.

To Aubrey I say that those who, by a life-time of devoted work, bring together a range of scholastic endeavour and develop an holistic view of these quite extraordinary sites, must be honoured by the elevated standard of recording that their effort has so clearly rendered essential. To suggest a standard for survey at orthostatic monuments, not in the hope of producing an agreed standard (!), but of stimulating a debate that might lead to that much to be desired objective, is, I hope, a fitting tribute.

H.A.W. BURL:
A BIBLIOGRAPHY

1962. 'Stone circles again', *Current Archaeology*, 12, 27–8.

1970. 'Henges: internal features and regional groups', *Archaeological Journal*, 126, 1–28.

———. 'The recumbent stone circles of NE Scotland', *Proceedings of the Society of Antiquaries of Scotland*, 102, 56–81.

1971. 'Two "Scottish" stone circles in Northumberland', *Archaeologia Aeliana*, 49, 37–51.

1972. 'Stone circles and ring-cairns', *Scottish Archaeological Forum*, 4, 31–47.

——— (with N. Jones). 'The excavation of the Three Kings stone circle, Northumberland', *Archaeologia Aeliana*, 50, 1–14.

1973. 'Dating the British stone circles', *American Scientist*, 61, 167–74.

1974. 'The recumbent stone circles of north-east Scotland', *Proceedings of the Society of Antiquaries of Scotland*, 102 (1969–70), 56–81.

———. 'Torhousekie stone circle', *Transactions of the Dumfriess & Galloway Natural History and Archaeological Society*, 49, 24–34.

1975. 'The early prehistoric monuments', in L. MacLean (ed.) *The Hub of the Highlands*, 65–77. Edinburgh.

1976. 'Circles in time', *Archaeology*(USA), 29, 242–9.

———. *The Stone Circles of the British Isles*. Newhaven & London: Yale University Press.

1977. 'Intimations of Numeracy in the Neolithic and Bronze Age Societies of the British Isles', *Archaeological Journal*, 133, 9–32.

——— (with P. Freeman). 'Local units of measurement in prehistoric Britain', *Antiquity*, 51, 152–4.

1979. *Prehistoric Stone Circles*. Princes Risborough: Shire.

———. *Rings of Stone*. London: Frances Lincoln (Weidenfeld).

———. *Prehistoric Avebury*. Newhaven & London: Yale University Press.

1980. 'A word in time: folk stories and stone circles', *Sangreal*, 3, 5–13.

———. 'Prehistoric stone circles on Machrie Moor', *Arran Naturalist*, 4, 21–6.

———. 'Science or symbolism: problems of archaeoastronomy', *Antiquity*, 54, 191–200.

——— (with A. & A.S. Thom). *Megalithic Rings: Plans and Data for 229 Sites*. BAR no. 81.

———. 'By the light of the cinerary moon: chambered tombs, astronomy and death', in C. Ruggles & A. Whittle (eds) *Astronomy and Society in Britain During the Period 4000–1500 BC*, 243–74. BAR no. 88. Oxford: British Archaeological Reports.

———. 'The recumbent stone circles of Scotland', *Scientific American*, 245, 50–6.

———. *Rites of the Gods*. London: J.M. Dent & Sons.

1982. 'Holes in the argument: Stonehenge and the Aubrey Holes', *Archaeo-astronomy Bulletin*, 4 (4), 19–25.

———. 'Pi in the sky', in D. Heggie (ed.) *Archaeoastronomy in the Old World*, 141–69. Cambridge: Cambridge University Press.

———. 'John Aubrey's *Monumenta Britannica*, a review article', *Wiltshire Natural History and Archaeological Magazine*, 77, 163–6.

1983 (with J. Michell). 'Living leys or laying the lies?', *Popular Archaeology*, 4 (8), 13–18.

———. *Prehistoric Astronomy and Ritual*. Princes Risborough: Shire.

———. *Prehistoric Stone Circles*. 2nd edn. Princes Risborough: Shire.

1984. 'Stonehenge et les autres cercles de pierres Britanniques', in J. Vlaeminck & M. Delcourt-Vlaeminck (eds) *Au Temps de Stonehenge*, 41–5. Tournai.

1985 (with C.L.N. Ruggles). 'A new study of the Aberdeenshire recumbent stone circles; 2: interpretation', *Journal for the History of Astronomy*, 8, S25–S60.

———. *Megalithic Brittany: A Guide to Over 350 Ancient Sites and Monuments*. London: Thames and Hudson.

———. 'Stone circles: the Welsh problem', The 9th Beatrice de Cardi Lecture. Report no. 35, 72–82. London: Council for British Archaeology.

———. 'Report on the excavation of a neolithic mound at Boghead, Speymouth Forest, Fochabers, Moray, 1972 & 1974', *Proceedings of the Society of Antiquaries of Scotland*, 114, 35–73.

——. 'Geoffrey of Monmouth and the Stonehenge Bluestones', *Wiltshire Natural History and Archaeological Magazine*, 79, 178–83.

1987. *The Stonehenge People*. London: J.M. Dent & Sons.

——. *Guide des Dolmens et Menhirs Bretons. Le Megalithisme en Bretagne*. Paris: Editions Errance.

1988. '"Without Sharp North . . ." Alexander Thom and the great stone circles of Cumbria', in C.L.N. Ruggles (ed.) *Records in Stone: Papers in Memory of Alexander Thom*, 175–205. Cambridge: Cambridge University Press.

——. 'The sun, the moon and megaliths: archaeoastronomy and the standing stones of Northern Ireland', *Ulster Journal of Archaeology*, 50, 7–21.

——. *Prehistoric Stone Circles*. 3rd edn. Princes Risborough: Shire.

——. *Four-posters. Bronze Age Stone Circles of Western Europe*. BAR no. 195. Oxford: British Archaeological Reports.

—— (ed.). *From Roman Town to Norman Castle. Essays in Honour of Philip Barker*. Birmingham: University of Birmingham.

1989. 'Coves: structural enigmas of the Neolithic', *Wiltshire Natural History and Archaeological Magazine*, 82, 1–18.

1990 (with A. & A.S. Thom). *Stone Rows and Standing Stones: Britain, Ireland and Brittany (2 vols)*. BAR no. S560. Oxford: British Archaeological Reports.

1991. 'The Heel Stone, Stonehenge: a study in misfortunes', *Wiltshire Natural History and Archaeological Magazine*, 84, 1–10.

——. 'The Devil's Arrows, Boroughbridge, North Yorkshire: the archaeology of a stone row', *Yorkshire Archaeological Journal*, 63, 1–24.

——. *Prehistoric Astronomy and Ritual* (rev. edn). Princes Risborough: Shire.

——. *Prehistoric Henges*. Princes Risborough: Shire.

——. 'The Bluestones again', *Current Archaeology*, 125, 238–9.

——. 'Megalithic myth or man the mover?' *Antiquity*, 65, 297.

1992. 'Two early plans of Avebury. A review article', *Wiltshire Natural History and Archaeological Magazine*, 85, 163–72.

1993. *From Carnac to Callanish. The Prehistoric Stone Rows and Avenues of Britain, Ireland and Brittany*. Newhaven & London: Yale University Press.

1994. 'Stonehenge: slaughter, sacrifice and sunshine', *Wiltshire Natural History and Archaeological Magazine*, 87, 85–95.

——. 'Long Meg and Her Daughters stone circle, Penrith, Cumberland', *Transactions of the Cumberland and Westmorland Archaeological Society*, 94, 1–11.

1995. *A Guide to the Stone Circles of Britain, Ireland and Brittany*. Newhaven & London: Yale University Press.

1996. '"Calanais" meets the olde tea-shoppe', *British Archaeology*, 19, 14.

1997. 'The sarsen horseshoe inside Stonehenge: a rider', *Wiltshire Natural History and Archaeological Magazine*, 90, 1–12.

——. *That Great Pyrate*. Port Talbot: Alun Books.

BIBLIOGRAPHY

Agrell, S.O. & Langley, J.M. 1958. 'The dolerite plug at Tievebulliagh, near Cushendall, Co. Antrim', *Proceedings of the Royal Irish Academy*, 59 B, 94–127.

Ainsworth, S. & Barnatt, J. 1997. 'A scarp-edge enclosure at Gardom's Edge, Baslow, Derbyshire', *Derbyshire Archaeological Journal*.

Albuquerque e Castro, L., de Veiga Ferreira, O. & Viana, A. 1957. 'O dolmen pintado de Antelas', *Comunicaçoes dos Servicos Geologicos de Portugal*, 38, 325–46.

Aldhouse-Green, S. 1996. 'The Caergwrle Bowl: a votive prehistoric boat model', in S. Aldhouse-Green (ed.) *Art, Ritual and Death in Prehistory*, 22–3. Cardiff: National Museums and Galleries of Wales.

Allason-Jones, L. 1996. *Roman Jet in the Yorkshire Museum*. York: The Yorkshire Museum.

Allason-Jones, L. & Jones, D.M. 1994. 'Jet and other materials in Roman artefact studies', *Archaeologia Aeliana*, 22, 265–72.

Allen, J.R. & Anderson, J. 1903. *The Early Christian Monuments of Scotland*. Edinburgh: Society of Antiquaries of Scotland.

Andersen, N.H. 1988. 'The neolithic causewayed enclosures at Sarup, on south-west Funen, Denmark', in C.B. Burgess *et al.* (eds), 1988, 337–62.

Andrews J. & Dury A. 1952. *A Map of Wiltshire 1773*. Reprinted by Wiltshire Archaeological and National History Society, Records Branch VIII.

Angell, I.O. 1978. 'Megalithic mathematics, ancient almanachs or neolithic nonsense?' *Bulletin of the Institute of Mathematics and its Applications*, 14, 253–8.

Anisimov, A.F. 1963. 'The Shaman's tent of the Evenks and the origin of the shamanistic rite', in H.N. Michael (ed.) *Studies in Siberian Shamanism*, 84–123. Arctic Institute of North America. Anthropology of the North.

Annable, F.K. & Simpson, D.D.A. 1964. *Guide Catalogue of the Neolithic and Bronze Age Collections in Devizes Museum*. Devizes: Wiltshire Archaeological and Natural History Society.

Ashbee, P. 1984. *The Earthen Long Barrow in Britain* (2nd edn). Norwich: Geo Books.

Ashmore, P.J. 1986. 'Neolithic carvings in Maes Howe', *Proceedings of the Society of Antiquaries of Scotland*, 116, 57–62.

Ashmore, P. 1996. *Neolithic and Bronze Age Scotland*. London: Batsford.

Atkinson, R.J.C. 1951. *Excavations at Dorchester, Oxon: vol.1*. Oxford: Ashmolean Museum.

Baillie, M.G.L. 1986. 'The central post from Navan Fort: the first step towards a better understanding of the Early Iron Age', *Emania*, 1, 20–1.

Baillie, M.G.L. 1990. 'Checking back on an assemblage of published radiocarbon dates', *Radiocarbon*, 32 (3), 361–6.

Bailloud, G., Boujot, C. Cassen, S. & Le Roux, C.-T. 1995. *Carnac: Les Premières Architectures de Pierre*. Paris: CNRS Editions.

Ballard, C. 1994. 'The centre cannot hold. Trade networks and sacred geography in the Papua New Guinea Highlands', *Archaeology in Oceania*, 29 (3), 130–48.

Barber, I.G. 1996. 'Loss, change and monumental landscaping; towards a new interpretation of the "classic" Maaori emergence', *Current Anthropology*, 37 (5), 868–80.

Barclay, A., Gray M. & Lambrick G. 1995. *Excavations at the Devil's Quoits, Stanton Harcourt, Oxfordshire. 1972–3 and 1988*. Thames Valley Landscapes: vol. 3: The Windrush Valley. Oxford: Oxford Archaeological Unit.

Barclay, G.J. 1982. 'The excavation of two crop marks at Huntingtower, Perthshire', *Proceedings of the Society of Antiquaries of Scotland*, 112, 580–3.

Barclay, G.J. 1983. 'Sites of the third millennium BC to the first millennium BC at North Mains, Strathallan Perthshire', *Proceedings of the Society of Antiquaries of Scotland*, 113, 122–281.

Barclay, G. J. 1989. 'Henge Monuments: reappraisal or reductionism', *Proceedings of the Prehistoric Society*, 55, 260–2.

Barclay, G. 1990. 'The clearing and partial excavation of the cairns at Balnuaran of Clava, Inverness-shire, by Miss Kathleen Kennedy, 1930–31', *Proceedings of the Society of Antiquaries of Scotland* 120, 17–32.

Barnatt, J. 1978. *Stone Circles of the Peak: a Search for Natural Harmony*. London: Turnstone Books.

Barnatt, J. 1982. *Prehistoric Cornwall: the Ceremonial Monuments*. Wellingborough: Turnstone Press.

Barnatt, J. 1986. 'Bronze Age remains on the East Moors of the Peak District. Derbyshire', *Derbyshire Archaeological Journal* 106, 18–100.

Barnatt, J. 1987. 'Bronze Age settlement on the gritstone East Moors of the Peak District of Derbyshire and South Yorkshire', *Proceedings of the Prehistoric Society* 53, 393–418.

Barnatt, J. 1989. *Stone Circles of Britain: Taxonomic and Distributional Analyses and a Catalogue of Sites in England, Scotland and Wales.* BAR British Series no. 215. Oxford: British Archaeological Reports.

Barnatt, J. 1990. *The Henges, Stone Circles and Ringcairns of the Peak District.* Sheffield Archaeological Monographs 1. Sheffield: Sheffield University Press.

Barnatt, J. 1996a. 'Barrows in the Peak District: a review and interpretation of extant sites and past excavations', in J. Barnatt & J. Collis (eds) *Barrows in the Peak District: Recent Research.* Sheffield: John Collis Publications.

Barnatt, J. 1996b. 'Moving beyond the monuments: paths and people in the Neolithic landscapes of the Peak District', in P. Frodsham (ed.) *Neolithic Studies in No-Man's-Land; Papers on the Neolithic of Northern England from the Trent to the Tweed,* 43–60. *Northern Archaeology,* 13/14.

Barnatt, J. (forthcoming). *Taming the Land: Peak District farming and ritual in the Bronze Age.*

Barnatt, J. & Pierpoint, S. 1983. 'Stone circles: observatories or ceremonial centres', *Scottish Archaeological Review* 2 (2), 101–14.

Barnwell, E.L. 1873. 'The Treiorwerth tumulus', *Archaeologia Cambrensis,* 4, 195–7.

Barrett, J.C. 1994. *Fragments From Antiquity: An Archaeology of Social Life in Britain, 2900–1200 BC.* Oxford: Blackwell.

Barrett, J., Bradley, R. & Green, M. 1991. *Landscape, Monuments and Society.* Cambridge: Cambridge University Press.

Barrett, J. & Kinnes, I. (eds). 1988. *The Archaeology of Context,* Sheffield: John Collis Publications.

Becker, H. 1996 'Kultplätze, Sonnentempel und Kalenderbauten aus dem 5. Jahrtausend vor Chr. – die mittelneolithischen Kreisanlagen in Niederbayern', Arbeitshefte Band 59. Munich: Bayerischen Landesamt für Denkmalpflege.

Behrens, H. 1981 'The first "Woodhenge" in Middle Europe', *Antiquity* 55, 172–8.

Benn, G. 1880. *The History of the Town of Belfast, with an Accurate Account of its Former and Present State.* Belfast: Marcus Ward.

Berridge, P. 1994. 'Cornish axe factories: fact or fiction', in N. Ashton & A. David (eds) *Stories in Stone,* 45–56. Lithic Studies Society, Occasional Paper 4. London: Lithic Studies Society.

Binchy, D.A. 1958. 'The Fair of Tailtu and the Feast of Tara', *Eriu* 18, 113–38.

Block, R.A. 1990. 'Models of Psychological Time', in R.A. Block (ed.) *Cognitive Models of Psychological Time,* 1–35. New Jersey: Hillsdale.

Boelicke, U. 1996. 'Das neolithische Erdwerk Urmitz', *Acta Praehistorica et Archaeologica* 7/8, 73–121.

Boujot, C., & Cassen, S. 1993. 'Neolithic funerary structures of the west of France', *Antiquity,* 67, 477–91.

Boyd Dawkins, W. 1901. 'On the cairn and sepulchral cave at Gop, near Prestatyn', *Archaeological Journal,* 58, 322–41.

Boydston, R.A. 1989. 'A cost-benefit study of functionally similar tools', in R. Torrence (ed.) *Time, Energy and Stone Tools,* 67–77. Cambridge: Cambridge University Press.

Braasch, O. 1996. 'Zur archäologischen Flugsprospektion', *Archäologisches Nachrichtenblatt* 1, 16–19.

Bradley, R. 1982. 'Position and Possession', *Oxford Journal of Archaeology,* 1.1, 27–38.

Bradley, R. 1984. *The Social Foundations of Prehistoric Britain.* London and New York: Longman.

Bradley, R. 1990. *The Passage of Arms.* Cambridge: Cambridge University Press.

Bradley, R. 1991. 'Ritual, time and history', *World Archaeology,* 23, 209–19.

Bradley, R. 1992. 'The excavation of an oval barrow beside the Abingdon causewayed enclosure, Oxfordshire', *Proceedings of the Prehistoric Society,* 58, 127–42.

Bradley, R. 1993. *Altering the Earth: the Origins of Monuments in Britain and Continental Europe.* Monograph Series 8, Edinburgh: Society of Antiquaries of Scotland.

Bradley, R. 1996. 'Excavations at Clava', *Current Archaeology,* 13, 136–42.

Bradley, R. 1997. 'Architecture, imagination and the Neolithic world', in S. Mithen (ed.) *The Prehistory of Creative Thought.* London: Routledge, forthcoming.

Bradley, R. & Chambers, R. 1988. 'A new study of the cursus complex at Dorchester on Thames', *Oxford Journal of Archaeology,* 7, 271–89.

Bradley, R. & Edmonds, M. 1993. *Interpreting the axe trade: production and exchange in Neolithic Britain.* Cambridge: Cambridge University Press.

Bradley R., Entwhistle, R. & Raymond, F. 1994. *Prehistoric Land Boundaries on Salisbury Plain. The Work of the Wessex Linear Ditches Project.* English Heritage Archaeological Report 2, London: HBMCE.

Bradley, R. & Ford, S. 1986. 'The siting of Neolithic stone quarries – experimental archaeology at Great Langdale, Cumbria', *Oxford Journal of Archaeology,* 5, 123–8.

Bradley, R. & Gardiner, J. (eds). 1984. *Neolithic Studies,* BAR British Series no. 133. Oxford: British Archaeological Reports.

Bradley, R., Meredith, P., Smith, J. & Edmonds, M. 1992. 'Rock physics and the stone axe trade in neolithic Britain', *Archaeometry,* 34, 323–33.

Bray, D.A. 1987. 'The image of Saint Brigit in the early Irish Church', *Etudes Celtiques* 24, 209–15.

Breun Olsen, A. & Alsaker, S. 1984. 'Greenstone and diabase utilization in the Stone Age of Western Norway:

technological and socio-cultural aspects of axe and adze production and distribution', *Norwegian Archaeological Review*, 17, 71–103.

Brewster, T.C.M. 1984. *The Excavation of Whitegrounds Barrow, Burythorpe*. Wintringham: John Gett Publications.

Briard, J. 1984. *Les Tumulus d'Armorique* (L'Âge du Bronze en France 3) Paris: Picard.

Briard, J. 1987. *Mythes et Symboles de l'Europe Pré-Celtique: les Religions de l'âge du Bronze 2500–800 av. JC*. Paris: Errance.

Briard, J. & Fediaevsky, N. 1987. *Megalithes de Bretagne*. Brest: France Ouest.

Buck, C.E., Kenworthy, J.B., Litton, C.D. & Smith, A.F.M. 1991. 'Combining archaeological and radiocarbon information: a Bayesian approach to calibration', *Antiquity*, 65, 808–21.

Buckley, V. 1988. 'Ireland's "Stonehenge" – a lost antiquarian monument rediscovered', *Archaeology Ireland*, 2 (2), 53–5.

Burgess, C.B. 1986. '"Urnes of no small variety": collared urns reviewed', *Proceedings of the Prehistoric Society*, 52, 339–51.

Burgess, C., Topping, P., Mordant, C. & Maddison, M. 1988. *Enclosures and defences in the Neolithic of Western Europe*. BAR International Series no. 403. Oxford: British Archaeological Reports.

Burgess, C.B. 1976. 'Meldon Bridge: a neolithic defended promontory complex near Peebles', in C.B. Burgess & R. Miket (eds) *Settlement and Economy in the Third and Second Millennia BC*, 151–79. BAR British Series no. 33. Oxford: British Archaeological Reports.

Burl, H.A.W. 1969. 'Henges: Internal Features and Regional Groups', *Archaeological Journal*, 126, 1–28.

Burl, H.A.W. 1970. 'The recumbent stone circles of NE Scotland', *Proceedings of the Society of Antiquaries of Scotland*, 102, 56–81.

Burl, H.A.W. 1976. *The Stone Circles of the British Isles*. London: Yale University Press.

Burl, H.A.W. 1979. *Prehistoric Avebury*. London & New Haven: Yale University Press.

Burl, H.A.W. 1980. 'Science or symbolism: problems of archaeoastronomy', *Antiquity*, 54, 191–200.

Burl, H.A.W. 1981a. *Rites of the Gods*. London: Dent.

Burl, H. A. W. 1981b. 'By the light of the cinerary moon: Chambered tombs and the astronomy of death', in C.L.N. Ruggles & A.W.R. Whittle (eds) *Astronomy and Society in Britain During the Period 4000–1500 BC*, 243–74. BAR British Series no. 88. Oxford: British Archaeological Reports.

Burl, H.A.W. 1982. 'Pi in the sky', in D.C. Heggie (ed.) *Archaeoastronomy in the Old World*, 141–69. Cambridge: Cambridge University Press.

Burl, H.A.W. 1983. *Prehistoric Astronomy and Ritual*. Princes Risborough: Shire (Shire Archaeology 32) [reprinted with updated bibliography 1997].

Burl, H.A.W. 1985a. *Megalithic Brittany: a Guide to over 350 Ancient Sites and Monuments*. London: Thames and Hudson.

Burl, H.A.W. 1985b. 'Stone circles: the Welsh problem', 9th Beatrice de Cardi Lecture, *CBA Report 35*, 72–82.

Burl, H.A.W. 1987a. 'The sun, the moon and the megaliths', *Ulster Journal of Archaeology*, 50, 7–21.

Burl, H.A.W. 1987b. *Stonehenge People: Life and Death at the World's Greatest Stone Circle*. London: Dent.

Burl, H.A.W. 1988a. *Four-posters. Bronze Age Stone Circles of Western Europe*. BAR British Series no. 195. Oxford: British Archaeological Reports.

Burl, H.A.W. 1988b. 'Without Sharp North . . . Alexander Thom and the great stone circles of Cumbria', in C.L.N. Ruggles (ed.) *Records in Stone: Papers in Memory of Alexander Thom,* 175–205. Cambridge: Cambridge University Press.

Burl, H.A.W. 1991a. 'The Devil's Arrows, Boroughbridge, North Yorkshire', *Yorkshire Archaeological Journal*, 63, 1–25.

Burl, H.A.W. 1991b. *Prehistoric Henges*. Princes Risborough: Shire.

Burl, H.A.W., 1993. *From Carnac to Callanish: the Prehistoric Stone Rows and Avenues of Britain, Ireland and Brittany*. London: Yale.

Burl, H.A.W. 1995. *A Guide to the Stone Circles of Britain, Ireland and Brittany*. New Haven and London: Yale.

Burl, H.A.W. 1997. 'The sarsen horseshoe inside Stonehenge', *Wiltshire Natural History and Archaeological Magazine*, 90, 1–12.

Burman, R. 1981. 'Time and socioeconomic change in Simbo', *Man* (n.s.) 16, 251–67.

Burton, J. 1984. 'Quarrying in a tribal society', *World Archaeology*, 16 (2), 234–47.

Bussell, G.D. 1976. *A Preliminary Neutron Activation Analysis of Ornaments of Jet and Similar Materials from Early Bronze Age Sites in North Derbyshire and Yorkshire*. Unpublished MA thesis: University of Bradford.

Bussell, G.D., Pollard, A.M. & Baird, D.C. 1982. 'The characterisation of Early Bronze Age jet and jet-like material by X-ray fluorescence', *Wiltshire Archaeological and Natural History Magazine*, 76, 27–32.

Butler, J. 1991a. *Dartmoor: Atlas of Antiquities, vol. 1: the East*. Torquay: Devon Books.

Butler, J. 1991b. *Dartmoor: Atlas of Antiquities, vol. 2: the North*. Torquay: Devon Books.

Butler, J. 1993. *Dartmoor: Atlas of Antiquities, vol. 4: the South-east*. Torquay: Devon Books.

Butler, J. 1994. *Dartmoor: Atlas of Antiquities, vol. 3: the South-west*. Torquay: Devon Books.

Capelle, T. 1995. *Anthropomorphe Holzidole in Mittel und Nordeuropa*. Lund: Scripta Minora.

Case, H. 1973. 'A ritual site in north-east Ireland', in G. Daniel & P. Kjaerum (eds) *Megalithic Graves and Ritual*, 173–96. Moesgard: Jutland Archaeological Society.

Chadwick, N. 1966. *The Druids*. Cardiff: University of Wales Press.

Chandler, A. 1970. *The Amesbury Turnpike Trust*. Monograph 4: South Wiltshire Industrial Archaeological Society.

Chapman, R., Kinnes, I. & Randsborg, K. (eds). 1984. *The Archaeology of Death*. Cambridge: Cambridge University Press.

Charlesworth, D. 1961. 'Roman jewellery found in Northumberland and Durham', *Archaeologia Aeliana* (4) 39, 1–37.

Chippindale, C. 1994. *Stonehenge Complete* (rev. edn). London: Thames and Hudson.

Churcher, I. 1985. *Form and function, comparisons and contrasts. A survey of stone circles in southern Leinster.* Unpublished BA dissertation, University of Durham.

Čižmař, M. 1989. 'Pseudoanthropomorphes latènezeitliches Schwert mit Zeichen aus Lysice (Mähren CCSR)', *Acta Musei Moraviae Casopis Moravkého Muzea* 74, 69–72.

Clare, T. 1986. 'Towards a reappraisal of henge monuments', *Proceedings of the Prehistoric Society*, 52, 281–316.

Claris, P. & Quatermaine, J. 1989. 'The Neolithic quarries and axe-factory sites of Great Langdale and Scafell Pike: a new field survey', *Proceedings of the Prehistoric Society*, 55, 1–25.

Clark, G. 1994. *Space, Time and Man: a Prehistorian's View*. Cambridge: Cambridge University Press.

Clark, J.G.D. 1952. *Prehistoric Europe: the Economic Basis*. London: Methuen.

Clarke, C. 1996. *North Ballachulish Moss*. Unpublished Data Structure Report no. 293, Centre for Field Archaeology, University of Edinburgh.

Clarke, D.L. 1970. *The Beaker Pottery of Great Britain and Ireland*. Cambridge: Cambridge University Press.

Clarke, D.V., Cowie, T.G. & Foxon, A. 1985. *Symbols of Power at the Time of Stonehenge*. Edinburgh: HMSO.

Cleal, R.M.J., Walker, K.E. & Montague, R. 1995. *Stonehenge in its Landscape: Twentieth-Century Excavations.* Archaeological Report 10. London: English Heritage.

Clevis, H. & de Jong, J.J. 1993, 1994, 1995. *Archeologie en Bouwhistorie in Zwolle, 1 – 2 – 3*. Zwolle: Gemeente Zwolle.

Clevis, H. & Verlinde, A. 1991. *Bronstijdboeren in Ittersumerbroek*. Zwolle: Gemeente Zwolle.

Clough, T.H.McK. 1988. 'Introduction to the regional reports: prehistoric stone implements in the British Isles', in T.H.McK. Clough & W.A. Cummins (eds), 1988, 1–11.

Clough, T.H.McK. & Cummins, W.A. (eds). 1979. *Stone Axe Studies*. CBA Research Report no. 23. London: Council for British Archaeology.

Clough, T.H.McK. & Cummins, W.A. (eds). 1988. *Stone Axe Studies vol. 2*. CBA Research Report no. 67. London: Council for British Archaeology.

Cody, E. 1981. 'A hill-fort at Ballylin, County Limerick, with a note on Mooghaun, County Clare', *Journal of the Royal Society of Antiquaries of Ireland*, 111, 70–80.

Coe, M.D. 1987. *The Maya* (4th edn). London: Thames and Hudson.

Coffey, G. 1896–8. 'On a cairn excavated by Thomas Plunkett M.R.I.A., on Belmore Mountain, Co. Fermanagh', *Proceedings of the Royal Irish Academy*, 4, 659–66.

Coleman, S. & Elsener, J. 1955. *Pilgrimage Past and Present. Sacred Travel and Sacred Space in the World Religions*. London: British Museum Press.

Coles, B.J. 1990. 'Anthropomorphic wooden figures from Britain and Ireland', *Proceedings of the Prehistoric Society*, 56, 315–33.

Coles, B.J. 1993. 'Roos Carr and Company', in J. Coles, V. Fenwick & G. Hutchinson (eds) *A Spirit of Enquiry*, 17–22. Occasional Paper no. 7. Exeter: WARP.

Coles, F.R. 1900. 'Report on stone circles in Kincardineshire (North) and part of Aberdeenshire, with measured plans and drawings, obtained under the Gunning Fellowship', *Proceedings of the Society of Antiquaries of Scotland*, 34 (1899–1900), 139–98.

Coles, J. & Coles, B. 1996. *Enlarging the Past*. Monograph 11. Edinburgh: Society of Antiquaries of Scotland.

Collins, A.E.P. 1954. 'Excavations at the Giant's Ring, Ballynahatty', *Ulster Journal of Archaeology*, 17, 44–60.

Collins, A.E.P. 1957. 'Excavations at the Giant's Ring, Ballynahatty', *Ulster Journal of Archaeology*, 20, 44–50.

Collins, A.E.P. 1976. 'Dooey's Cairn, Ballymacaldrack, County Antrim', *Ulster Journal of Archaeology*, 39, 1–7.

Collins, A.E.P. & Waterman, D. 1955. *Millin Bay. A Late Neolithic Cairn in Co. Down*. Belfast: HMSO.

Conant, K.J. 1959. *Carolingian and Romanesque Architecture 800–1200*. Harmondsworth: Pelican.

Condit, T. 1993a. 'Ritual enclosures near Boyle, Co Roscommon', *Archaeology Ireland*, 7 (1), 14–16.

Condit, T. 1993b. 'Travelling earthwork arrives at Tara', *Archaeology Ireland*, 7(4), 10–12.

Condit, T. 1995. 'Avenues for research', *Archaeology Ireland*, 9 (4), 16–18.

Condit, T. & Gibbons, M. 1988a. 'A henge-type monument at Castletown, Co. Waterford', *Decies*, 37, 5–8.

Condit, T. & Gibbons, M. 1988b. 'Two "little-known" hillforts in Co Kilkenny', *Decies*, 37, 47–54.

Condit, T. & Gibbons, M. 1991. 'A glimpse of Sligo's prehistory', *Archaeology Ireland*, 5 (3), 7–10.

Connolly, C. 1938. *Enemies of Promise*. London: Routledge & Kegan Paul.

Connolly, M. 1996. 'The Passage tomb of Tralee – a megalithic tomb at Ballycarty, Co. Kerry', *Archaeology Ireland*, 10 (4), 15–17.

Cook, A.B. 1914. *Zeus: A Study in Ancient Religion*. Cambridge: Cambridge University Press.

Cook, G.T., Hold, A.G., Naysmith, P. & Anderson, R. 1990. 'Applicability of "New Technology" Scintillation Counters (Packard 2000 CA/LL and 2260 XL) for 14C Dating', *Radiocarbon*, 32 (2), 233–4.

Cooney, G. 1993. 'Lambay: an island on the horizon', *Archaeology Ireland*, 26, 24–8.

Cooney, G. 1996. 'Lambay Island', in I. Bennett (ed.) *Excavations 1995*, 26–7. Dublin: Wordwell.

Cooney, G. & Grogan, E. 1994. *Irish Prehistory: A Social Perspective*. Dublin: Wordwell.

Cooney, G. & Mandal, S. 1995. 'Getting to the core of the problem: petrological results from the Irish Stone Axe Project', *Antiquity*, 69, 969–80.

Cooney, G., Mandal, S. & O'Carroll, F. 1995. 'Stone axes as icons: approaches to the study of stone axes in Ireland', in E. Grogan & C. Mount (eds) *Annus Archaeologiae*, 23–36. Dublin: OIA/OPW.

Creighton, J. 1995. 'Visions of power: imagery and symbols in late Iron Age Britain', *Britannia* 26, 285–301.

Cunliffe, B. 1995a. *Iron Age Britain*. London: Batsford.

Cunliffe, B. 1995b. *Danebury: an Iron Age Hillfort in Hampshire. Vol. 6: A Hillfort Community in Perspective*. CBA Research Report no 102. London: Council for British Archaeology.

Cunnington, M.E. 1929. *Woodhenge*, Devizes: Simpson & Co.

Curle, J. 1911. *A Roman Frontier Post and its People: The Fort of Newstead in the Parish of Melrose*. Glasgow: Glasgow University Press.

Curtis, M.R. & G.R. 1994. *Callanish: the Stones, and Moon, and the Sacred Landscape*. Callanish.

Damerow, P. 1991. 'Indrukken in klei. Het begin van het getal', *Natuur en techniek* 59, 9, 697.

Danaher, K. 1972. *The Year in Ireland*. Cork: Mercier Press.

Daniel, G. 1967. *The Origins and Growth of Archaeology*. Harmondsworth: Penguin.

Darvill, T. 1996. *Prehistoric Britain from the Air: A Study of Space, Time and Society*, Cambridge: Cambridge University Press.

David, A. 1977. 'Mesolithic stone beads from Wales', *Bead Study Trust Newsletter*, 29, 5–6.

Davidson, J.L. & Henshall, A.S. 1989. *The Chambered Cairns of Orkney*. Edinburgh: Edinburgh University Press.

Davies, O. 1936. 'Excavations at Dun Ruadh', *Proceedings of the Belfast Natural History and Philosophical Society*, 1, 50–75.

Davies, O. 1938. 'Excavations at Carnagat', *Ulster Journal of Archaeology*, 1, 217–19.

Davies, O. & Mogey, J.M. 1946. 'Large Prehistoric Enclosures in Ireland', *Ulster Journal of Archaeology*, 9, 21–3.

Davis, M. 1993. 'The identification of various jet and jet-like materials used in the Early Bronze Age in Scotland', *The Conservator*, 17, 11–18.

Day, W. & Savory, H.N. 1972. 'The excavation of a Bronze Age burial mound at Ysgwennant, Llansilin, Denbighshire', *Archaeologia Cambrensis*, 121, 17–50.

Déchelette, J. 1913. *La Collection Millon: Antiquités Préhistoriques et Gallo-romaines*. Paris: Leroux.

Devignes, M. 1992. 'Aspects fondamentaux de l'art mégalithique peint Ibérique', lecture given at Dublin Megalithic Art Symposium, 1992.

Dietrich, B.C. 1988. 'A Minoan Symbol of Renewal', *Journal of Prehistoric Religion* 2, 12–25.

Dilke, O.A.W. 1987. *Mathematics and Measurements*. London: British Museum Press.

Doody, M. 1993. 'The Bruff aerial photographic survey', *Tipperary Historical Journal*, 1993, 173–80.

Drack, W. 1954–5. 'Ein Mittelatèneschwert mit drei Goldmarken von Böttstein (Aargau)', *Zeitschrift für Schweizerische Archäologie und Kunstgeschichte* 15, 193–235.

Dumézil, G. 1973. *Gods of the Ancient Northmen* (trans. of *Les Dieux des Germains*, 1959). Berkeley & Los Angeles: University of California Press.

Dunning, G.C. 1943. 'A stone circle and cairn on Mynydd Epynt, Brecknockshire', *Archaeologia Cambrensis*, 97, 169–94.

Duval, P.-M. & Pinault, G. 1986. *Recueil des Inscriptions Gauloises (RIG)* Vol. III. Les Calendriers (Coligny, Villards d'Héria), XLVe Supplément à Gallia. Paris: CNRS.

Edmonds, M. 1993a. 'Interpreting causewayed enclosures in the past and the present', in C. Tilley (ed.) *Interpretative Archaeology*, 99–142. Oxford: Berg.

Edmonds, M. 1993b. 'Towards a context for production and exchange: the polished stone axe in earlier Neolithic Britain', in C. Scarre & F. Healy (eds) *Trade and Exchange in Prehistoric Europe*, 69–86. Oxbow Monograph 33. Oxford: Oxbow Books.

Edmonds, M. 1995. *Stone Tools and Society*. London: Batsford.

Edmonds, M., Sheridan, A. & Tipping, R. 1992. 'Survey and excavation at Creag na Caillich, Killin, Perthshire', *Proceedings of the Society of Antiquaries of Scotland*, 122, 77–112.

Ellis Davidson, H.R. 1969. *Scandinavian Mythology*. London: Paul Hamlyn.

Eluère C. 1982. *Les ors préhistoriques*. (L'âge du bronze en France 2). Paris: Picard.

Eogan, G. 1983a. 'Bryn Celli Ddu', *Antiquity*, 57, 135–6.

Eogan, G. 1983b. *The Hoards of the Irish Later Bronze Age*. Dublin: University College, Dublin.

Eogan, G. 1984. *Excavations at Knowth (1)*, Dublin: Royal Irish Academy Monographs.

Eogan, G. 1986. *Knowth and the Passage-tombs of Ireland*. London: Thames and Hudson.

Eogan, G. 1994. *The Accomplished Art: Gold and Gold-working in Britain and Ireland during the Bronze Age (c. 2300–650 BC)*. Monograph 42. Oxford: Oxbow Books.

Eogan, G. & Roche, H. 1993. 'Neolithic Ritual at Knowth?', *Archaeology Ireland* 7 (4), 16–18.

Eogan, G. & Roche, H. 1994. 'A grooved ware wooden structure at Knowth, Boyne Valley, Ireland', *Antiquity*, 68, 322–30.

Eogan, G. & Roche, H. 1997. *Excavations at Knowth (2)*, Dublin: Royal Irish Academy.

Ericson, J.E. 1984. 'Towards the analysis of lithic production systems', in J.E. Ericson & B.A. Purdy (eds) 1984, 1–9.

Ericson, J.E. & Purdy, B.A. 1984. *Prehistoric Quarries and Lithic Production*. Cambridge: Cambridge University Press.

Espérandieu, E. 1907–1966. *Recueil Général des Bas-Reliefs de la Gaule Romaine et Pré-Romaine*. Paris: Leroux.

Evans, C. 1988. 'Excavations at Haddenham, Cambridgeshire: a "planned" enclosure and its regional affinities', in C.B. Burgess *et al.* (eds) 1988, 127–48.

Evans, E.E. 1938. 'Doey's Cairn, Dunloy, County Antrim', *Ulster Journal of Archaeology* , 1, 59–78.

Evans, E.E. 1953. *Lyles Hill*. Belfast: HMSO.

Evans, E.E. 1966. *A Guide to Prehistoric and Early Christian Ireland*. Batsford, London.

Evans, J. 1872. *The Ancient Stone Implements, Weapons and Ornaments of Great Britain*. London: Longmans.

Fahy, E.M. 1962. 'A recumbent-stone circle at Reanascreena South, Co. Cork', *Journal of the Cork Historical and Archaeological Society*, 67, 59–69.

Ferguson, J. 1980. *Greek and Roman Religion: A Source Book*. New Jersey: Noyes Press.

Fitzpatrick, A.P. 1996. 'Night and day: the symbolism of astral signs on later Iron Age anthropomorphic short swords', *Proceedings of the Prehistoric Society* 62, 273–98.

Fleming, A. 1978. 'The prehistoric landscape of Dartmoor, Part 1: South Dartmoor', *Proceedings of the Prehistoric Society* 44, 97–123.

Fleming, A. 1983. 'The prehistoric landscape of Dartmoor, Part 2: North and East Dartmoor', *Proceedings of the Prehistoric Society* 49, 195–241.

Fleming, A. 1988. *The Dartmoor Reaves: Investigating Prehistoric Land Divisions*. London: Batsford.

Fleure, H.J. & Neeley, G.J.H. 1936. 'Cashtal yn Ard, Isle of Man', *Antiquaries Journal*, 16, 373–95.

Forrer, R. 1909–12. 'Ausgrabungen auf der keltisch-römischen Siedlungstätte des Wasserwalden bei Stambach-Zabern', *Cahiers d'Archéologie et d'Histoire d'Alsace* 1, 28–34.

Fox, A. 1964. *South-West England*. London: Thames and Hudson.

Frazer, J.G. 1926. *The Worship of Nature*. London: Macmillan.

Fredsjö, A., Nordbladh, J. & Rosvall, J. 1975. *Rock-carvings: Kville Härad, Bottna*. Goteborg, Antiquarian Society/Archaeological Museum.

Frolov, B.A. 1977/8. 'Numbers in palaeolithic graphic art and the initial stages in the development of mathematics', *Soviet Anthropology and Art* 16, 142–66; 17, 41–74, 61–113.

Galliou, P. 1974. 'A propos de deux pendentifs gallo-romains du Musée Archéologique de Nantes', *Annales de Bretagne* 81, 259–83.

Gantz, J. 1981. *Early Irish Myths and Sagas*. Harmondsworth: Pelican.

Garton, D. 1987. 'Buxton', *Current Archaeology*, 9, 250–3.

Garwood P. 1991. 'Ritual tradition and reconstitution of society', in P. Garwood, D. Jennings, R. Skeates & J. Toms (eds) *Sacred and Profane*, 10–32. Monograph 32.Oxford: Oxford University Committee for Archaeology.

Gell, A. 1992. *The Anthropology of Time*. Oxford: Berg.

Gelling, P. & Davidson, H.E. 1969. *The Chariot of the Sun and other Rites and Symbols of the Northern Bronze Age*. London: John Dent.

Gericke, H. 1992. *Mathematik in Antike und Orient*. Wiesbaden: Fourier Verlag.

Gerloff, S. 1975. *The Early Bronze Age Daggers in Great Britain and a Reconsideration of the Wessex Culture*. München: C.H. Beck'sche.

Gerloff, S. 1993. 'Zu Fragen mittelmeerländischer Kontakte und absoluter Chronologie der Frühbronzezeit in Mittel- und Westeuropa', *Prähistorische Zeitschrift*, 68 (1), 58–102.

Gibbons, M. 1990. 'The archaeology of early settlement in County Kilkenny', in W. Nolan & K. Whelan (eds), *Kilkenny: history and society*. Dublin: Geography Publications.

Gibson, A.M. 1992. 'Possible timber circles at Dorchester on Thames', *Oxford Journal of Archaeology*, 11.1, 85–91.

Gibson, A.M. 1993. 'The excavation of two cairns and associated features at Carneddau, Carno, Powys, 1989–90', *Archaeological Journal*, 150, 1–45.

Gibson, A.M. 1994. 'Excavations at the Sarn-y-Bryn-Caled cursus complex, Welshpool, Powys, and the timber circles of Great Britain and Ireland', *Proceedings of the Prehistoric Society* 60, 143–223.

Gibson, A.M. 1995. 'Walton', *Current Archaeology*, 12, 444–5.

Gibson, A.M. 1996. 'A neolithic enclosure at Hindwell, Radnorshire, Powys', *Oxford Journal of Archaeology* 15 (3), 341–8.

Gibson, A.M. (forthcoming). 'Excavation and survey in the Radnor Valley, Powys, Wales'.

Giddens, A . 1981. *A Contemporary Critique of Historical Materialism*, London: MacMillan.

Glob, P.V. 1974. *The Mound People*. London: Faber & Faber.

Godwin, H. 1975. *History of the British Flora*. 2nd edn. Cambridge: Cambridge University Press.

Gray, H. St G. 1903. 'On the excavations at Arbor Low 1901–2', *Archaeologia*, 58 (2), 461–98.

Green, M.J. 1984. *The Wheel as a Cult-Symbol in the Romano-Celtic World*. Brussels: Collections Latomus.

Green, M.J. 1991. *The Sun-Gods of Ancient Europe*. London: Batsford.

Green, M.J. 1992. *Dictionary of Celtic Myth and Legend*. London: Thames and Hudson.

Green, M.J. 1996. *Celtic Art. Reading the Messages*. London: Weidenfeld & Nicolson.

Green, M.J. 1997. *Exploring the World of the Druids*. London: Thames and Hudson.

Green, M.J. (1998, in press). 'God in man's image: thoughts on the genesis and affiliations of some Romano-British cult-iconography', *Britannia* 29.

Green, S. 1985. 'The Caergwrle bowl – not oak but shale', *Antiquity*, 49, 116–17.

Greenwell, W. 1864–6. 'An account of excavations in cairns near Crinan', *Proceedings of the Society of Antiquaries of Scotland*, 6, 336–50.

Griffith, F. 1985. 'Some newly discovered ritual monuments in mid-Devon', *Proceedings of the Prehistoric Society*, 51, 310–15.

Grimes, W.F. 1938. 'A barrow on Breach Farm, Llanbleddian, Glamorgan', *Proceedings of the Prehistoric Society*, 4, 107–21.

Groenman-van-Waateringe, W. & Butler, J. 1976. 'The Ballynoe stone circle', *Palaeohistoria*, 18, 73–104.

Grogan, E. & Condit, T. 1994. 'The later prehistoric landscape of south-east Clare', *The Other Clare*, 18, 8–12.

Grogan, E. & Hillery, T. 1993. *A Guide to the Archaeology of County Wicklow*. Wicklow: Wicklow County Tourism Ltd.

Grundy, G.B. 1918. 'The ancient highways and tracks of Wiltshire, Berkshire and Hampshire and the Saxon battlefields of Wiltshire', *Archaeological Journal*, 74, 69–194.

Guilbert, G. 1982. 'Post-ring symmetry in roundhouses at Moel-y-Gaer and some other sites in prehistoric Britain', in P.J. Drury (ed.) *Structural Reconstruction*. 67–86. BAR British Series no. 110. Oxford: British Archaeological Reports.

Haggarty, A. 1991. 'Machrie Moor, Arran: recent excavations at two stone circles', *Proceedings of the Society of Antiquaries of Scotland* 121, 51–94.

Halsberghe, G.H. 1972. *The Cult of Sol Invictus*. Leiden: Brill.

Hamlin, A. & Lynn, C. (eds). 1988. *Pieces of the Past*. Belfast: HMSO.

Hamming, C. 1991. 'Dijkdoorbraken en kleidelven in de vijf marken', *Bronstijdboeren in Ittersumerbroek*, 9–23. Zwolle: Gemeente Zwolle.

Harding, A. 1981. 'Excavations in the prehistoric ritual complex near Milfield, Northumberland', *Proceedings of the Prehistoric Society*, 47, 87–135.

Harding, A.F. & Lee, G.E. 1987. *Henge Monuments and Related Sites of Great Britain*. BAR British Series no.175. Oxford: British Archaeological Reports.

Harding, J. 1995. 'Social histories and regional perspectives in the Neolithic of lowland England', *Proceedings of the Prehistoric Society* 61, 117–36.

Harris, W. 1744. *The Antient and Present State of the County of Down*. Dublin: Edward Exshaw.

Hartnett, P. 1957. 'Excavation of a passage grave at Fourknocks, Co. Meath', *Proceedings of the Royal Irish Academy*, 58C, 197–277.

Hartwell, B., 1988. 'Air Photography and Fieldwork at the Giant's Ring', *Organisation of Irish Archaeologists Newsletter*, 7, Autumn, 22.

Hartwell, B. 1991a. 'Ballynahatty – a prehistoric ceremonial centre', *Archaeology Ireland*, 5 (4), 12–15.

Hartwell, B. 1991b. 'Recent air survey results from Navan', *Emania*, 8, 5–9.

Hartwell, B. 1994. 'Late neolithic ceremonies', *Archaeology Ireland*, 8 (4), 10–13.

Hartwell, B. 1995. 'The prehistory of the Giant's Ring and Ballynahatty townland', *Lisburn Historical Society Journal*, 9, 1–9.

Hawkes, J. 1962. *Man and the Sun*. London: Cresset.

Hayen, H. 1987. 'Peatbog archaeology in Lower Saxony, West Germany', in J.M. Coles & A.J. Lawson (eds) *European Wetlands in Prehistory*, 117–36. Oxford: Clarendon Press.

Hedges, J. & Buckley, D. 1978. 'Excavations at a neolithic causewayed enclosure, Orsett, Essex', *Proceedings of the Prehistoric Society* 44, 219–308.

Heggie, D.C, (ed.). 1982. *Archaeoastronomy in the Old World*. Cambridge: Cambridge University Press.

Hemming, E. 1991. *The Shaman's Burial from Upton Lovell: a Reassessment*. Unpublished BA dissertation, University of Exeter.

Hemp, W. 1930. 'The chambered tomb of Bryn Celli Ddu', *Archaeologia*, 80, 179–214.

Henshall, A.S. 1963. *The Chambered Tombs of Scotland, vol. 1*. Edinburgh: Edinburgh University Press.

Henshall, A.S. 1972. *The Chambered Tombs of Scotland, vol. 2*. Edinburgh: Edinburgh University Press.

Henshall, A.S. 1979. 'The pottery from Quanterness', in A.C. Renfrew *Investigations in Orkney*. Society of Antiquaries of London Research Report no. 38, 75–9, figs 33–4. London: Society of Antiquaries of London.

Henshall, A.S. 1993. 'The Grooved Ware', in G. Barclay & M. Russell-White (eds) 'Excavations in the ceremonial complex of the fourth to second millennium BC at Balfarg/Balbirnie, Glenrothes, Fife', *Proceedings of the Society of Antiquaries of Scotland*, 123, 94–108.

Henshall, A.S. & Mercer, R. 1981. 'Report on the pottery from Balfarg', in R. Mercer 'The excavation of a late Neolithic henge-type enclosure at Balfarg, Markinch, Fife', *Proceedings of the Society of Antiquaries of Scotland*, 111, 63–171.

Herity, M. 1974. *Irish Passage Graves*. Dublin: Irish University Press.

Herity, M.J. 1982. 'Irish decorated Neolithic pottery', *Proceedings of the Royal Irish Academy*, 82 C, 247–404.

Hicks, R.E. 1975. *Some Henges and Hengiform Earthworks in Ireland: Form, Distribution, Astronomical Correlations, and Associated Mythology*. Unpublished PhD thesis, University of Pennsylvania.

Hill, J.D. 1995. *Ritual and Rubbish in the Iron Age of Wessex*, BAR British Series Report no. 242. Oxford: British Archaeological Reports.

Hill, J.D. 1996. 'Hillforts and the Iron Age of Wessex', in T.C. Champion & J. Collis (eds) *The Iron Age in Britain and Ireland. Recent Trends*, 95–116. Sheffield: J.R. Collis Publications.

Hindle, B.P. 1993. *Roads, Tracks and their Interpretation*. London: Batsford.

Hobsbawm, E. 1983. Introduction, in E. Hobsbawm & T. Ranger (eds) *The Invention of Tradition*, 1–14. Cambridge: Cambridge University Press.

Hobsbawm, E. 1994. *The Age of Extremes*. London: Michael Joseph.

Hodder, I. 1992. *Theory and Practice in Archaeology*. London: Routledge.

Højlund, F. 1981. 'The function of prestige weapons in the reproduction of New Guinea Highlands tribal societies', *Oral History, Institute of Papua New Guinea Studies*, 9 (3), 26–51.

Hope Taylor, B. 1977. *Yeavering: An Anglo British Centre of early Northumbria*. London: HMSO.

Hoskin, M.A., Allan, E. & Gralewski,R. 1995. 'Studies in Iberian archaeoastronomy: (3) Customs and motives in Andalucia', *Archaeoastronomy*, 20 (*Journal for the History of Astronomy*, 26), S41–8.

Houlder, C. 1968. 'The henge monuments at Llandegai', *Antiquity*, 43, 216–21.

Houlder, C. 1976. 'Stone Axes and henge monuments', in G.C. Boon & J.M. Lewis (eds) *Welsh Antiquity*, 55–62. Cardiff: National Museum of Wales.

Howell, J.M. 1983. *Settlement and Economy in Neolithic Northern France*. BAR International Series no. S157. Oxford: British Archaeological Reports.

Hughes, H. 1908. 'Merddyn Gwyn barrow, Pentraeth', *Archaeologia Cambrensis*, 8, 211–20.

Hunt, J. 1967. 'Prehistoric burials at Caherguillamore, Co. Limerick', in E. Rynne (ed.) *North Munster Studies*, 20–42. Limerick: Thomond Archaeological Society.

Hunter, F.J., McDonnell, J.G., Pollard, A.M., Morris, C.R. & Rowlands, C.C. 1993. 'The scientific identification of archaeological jet-like artefacts', *Archaeometry*, 35 (1), 69–89.

Hunter, J.R. & MacSween, A. 1991. 'A sequence for the Orcadian Neolithic', *Antiquity*, 65, 911–14.

Hutton, R. 1996. *The Stations of the Sun: The History of the Ritual Year in Britain*. Oxford: Oxford University Press.

Huysecom, E. 1986. 'La question des bouteilles à collerette: identification et chronologie d'un groupe méridionale répandu de l'Ukraine à la Bretagne', *Revue archéologique de l'Ouest*, Supplement no. 1, 195–215.

International Study Group. 1982. 'An inter-laboratory comparison of radiocarbon measurements in tree rings', *Nature*, 298, 619–23.

Jeunesse, C. 1996. 'Les enceintes à fossés interrompus du Néolithique Danubien ancien et moyen et leurs relations avec le Néolithique récent', *Archäologisches Korrespondenzblatt* 26 (3), 251–61.

Johnson, M. 1993. 'Notes towards an archaeology of capitalism', in C. Tilley (ed.) 1993, 327–56.

Johnson, N. & Rose, P. 1994. *Bodmin Moor; an Archaeological Survey, vol. 1: The Human Landscape to c. 1800*. Truro and London: Cornwall Archaeological Unit, English Heritage (Archaeological Report no. 24) and Royal Commission on the Historical Monuments of England (Supplementary Series no. 11).

Johnson, S.A. 1990. 'The Neolithic and Bronze Age activity at Dun Ailinne', *Emania*, 7, 26–31.

Jones, A. 1997. 'On the earth colours of Neolithic death', *British Archaeology*, 22, 6.

Jong, J.J. de & Wevers, H. 1994. 'Cirkels en zonnekalenders in Zwolle-Ittersumerbroek', *Archeologie en Bouwhistorie in Zwolle*, 2, 75–95. Zwolle: Gemeente Zwolle.

Jope, E.M. 1952. 'Porcellanite axes from factories in north-east Ireland: Tievebulliagh and Rathlin. Part 1. Archaeological survey', *Ulster Journal of Archaeology*, 15, 31–55.

Joussaume, R. 1985. *Dolmens for the Dead: Megalith Building Throughout the World*. London: Batsford.

Kalb, P. 1997. 'Megalith-building, stone transport and territory markers: evidence from Vale de Rodrigo, Evora, S. Portugal', *Antiquity*, 66, 392–5.

Keeling, D. 1983. 'A group of tumuli and a hill-fort near Naul, County Dublin', *Journal of the Royal Society of Antiquaries of Ireland*, 113, 67–74.

Kenworthy, J. 1977. 'A reconsideration of the "Ardiffery" finds, Cruden, Aberdeenshire', *Proceedings of the Society of Antiquaries of Scotland*, 108 (1976–7), 80–93.

Kilbride Jones, H.E. 1935. 'An account of the excavation of the Stone Circle at Loanhead of Daviot and of the Standing Stones at Cullerlie, Echt, . . . Aberdeenshire', *Proceedings of the Society of Antiquaries of Scotland*, 69, 168–222.

Kinnes, I. 1979. *Round Barrows and Ring-ditches in the British Neolithic*, London: British Museum Occasional Papers.

Kinnes, I. 1988. 'The Cattleship Potemkin', in J. Barrett & I. Kinnes (eds), 1988, 2–8.

Kinnes, I. 1992. 'The archaeology of the archaeology of death', *Archaeological Revue from Cambridge*, 11, 11–17.

Kinnes, I.A., Gibson, A., Ambers, J., Leese, M. & Boast, R. 1991. 'Radiocarbon dating and British Beakers', *Scottish Archaeological Review*, 8, 35–68.

Kinnes, I.A. & Longworth, I.H. 1985. *Catalogue of the Excavated Prehistoric and Romano-British Material in the Greenwell Collection*. London: British Museum Press.

Knowles, M.C. 1904. 'Kitchen middens – Co. Clare', *Journal of the Limerick Field Club*, 2, 35–42.

Krupp, E. C. 1994. *Echoes of the Ancient Skies: the Astronomy of Lost Civilizations*. Repr. Oxford: Oxford University Press.

Kruta, V. 1991. 'Celtic Writing', in S. Moscati, O.-H. Frey, V. Kruta, B. Raftery & M. Szabó (eds) *The Celts*, 491–7. London: Thames and Hudson.

Lacy, B. 1983. *Archaeological Survey of Co. Donegal*. Lifford: Donegal County Council.

Lanting, J.N. & Waals, J.D. van der. 1972. 'British beakers as seen from the Continent: a review article', *Helinium*, 12, 20–46.

Lawlor, H.C. 1919. 'The Giant's Ring', *Proceedings of the Belfast Natural History & Philosophical Society*, 1917–18, 13–28.

Leask, H.G. 1945. 'Stone Circle, Castleruddery, Co. Wicklow', *Journal of the Royal Society of Antiquaries of Ireland*, 75, 266–7.

Lecerf, Y. 1986. 'Une nouvelle intervention archéologique au Camp du Lizo en Carnac (Morbihan)', *Revue Archéologique de l'Ouest*, 3, 47–58.

L'Helgouac'h, J. 1965. *Les Sépultures Mégalithiques en Armorique*. Rennes: Université de Rennes.

L'Helgouac'h, J. 1966. 'Les sépultures mégalithiques à entrée latérale en Armorique', *Palaeohistoria*, 12, 259–81.

L'Helgouac'h, J. 1970. 'Le monument mégalithique du Goërem à Gâvres (Morbihan),' *Gallia-Préhistoire*, 13, 217–61.

L'Helgouac'h, J. 1986. 'Les sépultures mégalithiques du Néolithique final: architectures et figurations pariétales: comparaisons et relations entre Massif armoricain et nord de la France', *Revue Archéologique de l'Ouest* (Supplement 1, Colloque de Caen), 189–94.

Le Provost, F., Giot, P.-R. & Onnée, Y. 1972. 'Prospections sur les collines de St-Nicholas-du-Pelem (C-d-N), du Chalcolithique à la Protohistoire', *Annales de Bretagne*, 79, 39–48.

Le Roux, C.-T. 1979. 'Stone axes in Brittany and the Marches', in T.H.Mc. Clough and W.A. Cummins (eds) *Stone Axe Studies* (CBA Research Report 23), 49–56. London: Council for British Archaeology.

Le Roux, F. 1961. 'Etudes sur le festiaire celtique: Samain', *Ogam* 13, 485–506.

Le Rouzic, Z., 1965. 'Inventaire des monuments mégalithiques de la région de Carnac', *Bulletin de la Société Polymathique du Morbihan*, Numéro spécial.

Linckenheld, E. 1927. *Les Stèles Funéraires en forme de Maison chez les Médiomatriques et en Gaule*. Strasbourg/Paris: Société d'Edition 'Les Belles Lettres'.

Lohof, E. 1991. *Grafritueel en Sociale Verandering in de Late Bronstijd in NO Nederland*. Amsterdam: Instituut voor Prae- en Protohistorie.

Longworth, I.H. 1984. *Collared Urns of the Bronze Age in Great Britain and Ireland*. Cambridge: Cambridge University Press.

Loveday, R. 1985. *Cursus and Related Monuments of the British Neolithic*. Unpublished PhD thesis: University of Leicester.

Loveday, R. 1989. 'The Barford ritual complex: further excavations (1972) and a regional perspective', in A. Gibson (ed.) *Midlands Prehistory* BAR Report no. 204, 51–84. Oxford: British Archaeological Reports.

Lurker, M. 1974. *The Gods and Symbols of Ancient Egypt*. London: Thames and Hudson.

Lyle, E. 1990. *Archaic Cosmos: Polarity, Space and Time*. Edinburgh: Polygon.

Lynch, F.M. 1971. 'Report on the re-excavation of two Bronze Age cairns in Anglesey: Bedd Branwen and Treiorwerth', *Archaeologia Cambrensis*, 120, 11–83.

Lynch, F.M. 1984. 'Report on the excavations of a Bronze Age barrow at Llong, near Mold', *Journal of the Flintshire Historical Society*, 31, 13–28.

Lynch, F.M. 1986a. 'Excavation of a kerb circle and ring cairn on Cefn Caer Euni, Merioneth', *Archaeologia Cambrensis*, 135, 81–120.

Lynch, F.M. 1986b. *Museum of Welsh Antiquities, Bangor: Catalogue of Archaeological Material*. Bangor: University College of North Wales.

Lynch, F.M. 1991. *Prehistoric Anglesey* (2nd edn). Llangefni: the Anglesey Antiquarian Society.

Lynch, F.M. 1993. *Excavations in the Brenig Valley, a Mesolithic and Bronze Age Landscape in North Wales*. Cambrian Archaeological Monograph 5. Aberystwyth: Cambrian Archaeological Association & Cadw: Welsh Historic Monuments.

Lynn, C.J. 1977. 'Trial excavations at the King's Stables, Tray Townland, Co. Armagh', *Ulster Journal of Archaeology*, 40, 42–60.

Lynn, C.J. 1986. 'Navan Fort: A Draft Summary of D.M. Waterman's excavations', *Emania*, 1, 11–19.

MacAdam, R. & Getty, E. 1855. 'Discovery of an ancient sepulchral chamber', *Ulster Journal of Archaeology*, First Series, 3, 358–65.

Macalister, R.A.S. 1931. *Tara. A Pagan Sanctuary of Ancient Ireland*. London: Scribner.

MacCana, P. 1970. *Celtic Mythology*. London.

MacNeill, M. 1962. *The Festival of Lughnasa*. Oxford: Oxford University Press.

MacSween, A. 1995. 'Grooved Ware from Scotland: aspects of decoration', in I. Kinnes & G. Varndell (eds) *Unbaked urns of rudely shape: Essays on British and Irish Pottery for Ian Longworth*, 41–8. Monograph 55. Oxford: Oxbow Books.

Madsen, T. 1988. 'Causewayed enclosures in south Scandinavia', in C.B. Burgess *et al.* (eds), 1988, 301–36.

Mallory, J.P. 1988. 'Trial excavations at Haughey's Fort', *Emania*, 4, 5–20.

Mallory, J.P. 1990. 'Trial excavations at Tievebulliagh, Co. Antrim', *Ulster Journal of Archaeology*, 53, 15–28.

Mallory, J.P. 1993. 'A neolithic ditched enclosure in Northern Ireland', *Actes du XIIe Congrès International des Sciences Préhistoriques: Bratislave, 1–7 Septembre 1991*, 415–17. Bratislava: UISPP.

Mallory, J.P. & Hartwell, B. 1984. 'Donegore', *Current Archaeology*, 92, 271–4.

Manby, T. 1979. 'Flint and stone axes in Yorkshire', in T.H.McK. Clough & W.A. Cummins (eds) *Stone Axe Studies*, 65–81. London: Council for British Archaeology.

Mandal, S. 1996. 'Irish stone axes, rock and role of the petrologist', *Archaeology Ireland*, 38, 32–5.

Mandal, S., Cooney, G., Grogan, E., O'Carroll, F. & Guinan, B. 1991/2. 'A review of the petrological techniques being utilised to identify, group and source Irish stone axes', *Journal of Irish Archaeology*, 6, 1–11.

Mandal S., Cooney, G. Meighan, I.G. & Jamison, D.D. 1997. 'Using geochemistry to interpret porcellanite stone axe production in Ireland', *Journal of Archaeological Science*, 24, 757–63.

Manning, C. 1976. *The Royal Inauguration Sites of Ireland.* Unpublished MA thesis, University College, Dublin.

Margary, I.D. 1973. *Roman Roads in Britain* (rev. edn). London: John Baker.

Marshack, A. 1972. 'Cognitive aspects of Upper Palaeolithic engraving', *Current Anthropology* 13, 445–77.

Martlew, R.D. & Ruggles, C.L.N. 1996. 'Ritual and landscape on the west coast of Scotland: an investigation of the stone rows of northern Mull,' *Proceedings of the Prehistoric Society*, 62, 117–31.

McInnes, I. 1968. 'Jet sliders in late neolithic Britain', in J.M. Coles & D.D.A. Simpson (eds) *Studies in Ancient Europe* 137–44. Leicester: Leicester University Press.

Megaw, J.V.S. 1970. *Art of the European Iron Age.* New York: Harper and Row.

Meighan, I.G., Jamison, D.D., Logue, P.J.C., Mallory, J.P., Simpson, D.D.A., Rogers, G., Mandal, S. & Cooney, G. 1993. 'Trace element and isotopic provenancing of north Antrim porcellanites: Portrush-Tievebulliagh-Brockley (Rathlin Island)', *Ulster Journal of Archaeology*, 56, 25–30.

Mercer, R.J. 1978. 'The Castle Fraser (Balgorkar) stone circle: a further note', in H. Gordon Slade, 'Castle Fraser: a seat of the antient family of Fraser', *Proceedings of the Society of Antiquaries of Scotland*, 109 (1977–8), 273–7.

Mercer, R.J. 1981. 'The excavation of a late neolithic henge-type enclosure at Balfarg, Markinch, Fife, Scotland, 1977–8', *Proceedings of the Society of Antiquaries of Scotland* 111, 63–171.

Mercer, R.J. 1986. 'The Neolithic in Cornwall', *Cornish Archaeology*, 25, 35–80.

Mercer, R.J. 1993. 'Secretary's Report', *Monuments on Record: Annual Review 1992–3*, 6–13. Edinburgh: RCAHMS.

Mérimée, P. 1836. *Notes d'un voyage dans l'ouest de la France.* Paris.

Meyer, M. 1995. 'Bemerkungen zu den jungneolithischen Grabenwerken zwischen Rhein und Saale', *Germania* 73, 69–94.

Michon, J.A. 1985. 'The Compleat time experiencer', in J.A. Michon & J.L. Jackson, (eds) *Time, Mind and Behavior*, 20–52. Berlin: Springer-Verlag.

Michon, J.A. 1990. 'Implicit and Explicit Representations of Time', in R.A. Block (ed.) *Cognitive Models of Psychological Time*, 37–58. New Jersey: Hillsdale.

Mikalson, J.D. 1975. *The Sacred and Civil Calendar of the Athenian Year.* Princeton: University Press.

Minahane, J. 1993. *The Christian Druids: on the Filid or Philosopher-poets of Ireland.* Dublin: Sanas Press.

Mitchell, F. 1992. 'Notes on some non-local cobbles at the entrances to the passage-graves at Newgrange and Knowth, County Meath', *Journal of the Royal Society of Antiquaries of Ireland*, 122, 128–45.

Moore, H. 1986. *Space, Text and Gender*, Cambridge: Cambridge University Press.

Moore, M. 1987. *Archaeological Inventory of County Meath.* Dublin: Stationery Office.

Moore, M. 1995. 'A Bronze Age settlement and ritual centre in the Monavullagh Mountains, Co. Waterford, Ireland', *Proceedings of the Prehistoric Society*, 61, 191–244.

Mordant, C. & D. 1988. 'Les encientes néolithiques de la Haute-Vallée de la Seine', in C.B. Burgess *et al.* (eds), 1988, 231–54.

Mount, C. 1994. 'Aspects of ritual deposition in the late neolithic and beaker periods at Newgrange, Co. Meath', *Proceedings of the Prehistoric Society*, 60, 433–43.

Nagy, P. 1992. 'Technologische Aspekte der Goldschale von Zürich-Altstetten', *Jahrbuch der Schweizerischen Gesellschaft für Ur- und Frühgeschichte* 75, 101–16.

Nash-Williams, V.E. 1950–2. 'The Roman gold-mines at Dolaucothi (Carms)', *Bulletin of the Board of Celtic Studies*, (6) 1, 20–44.

Needham, S. (forthcoming.) 'Chronology and periodisation in the British Bronze Age' [in Proceedings of conference on radiocarbon dating, Verona, 1995].

Newman, C. 1993a. 'Sleeping in Elisium', *Archaeology Ireland*, 7 (3), 20–3.

Newman, C. 1993b. 'The show's not over until the fat lady sings', *Archaeology Ireland*, 7 (4), 8–9.

North, J.D. 1996. *Stonehenge: Neolithic Man and the Cosmos.* London: HarperCollins.

O'Catháin, S. 1995. *The Festival of Brigit, Celtic Goddess and Holy Woman.* Dublin: DBA Publications.

O'Connor, P.J. 1992. *Living in a Coded Land*. Newcastle West: Oireacht na Mumhan.

O'Donovan, P.F. 1985. 'A henge at Garryard', *North Munster Archaeological Journal*, 27, 75–7.

O'Donovan, P.F. 1995. *Archaeological Inventory of County Cavan*. Dublin: Stationery Office.

O'Keefe, J.D. 1994. *A Geophysical Resistivity Survey at the Ballynoe Stone Circle, Co. Down*. Unpublished Field Project, Dept of Archaeology, Queen's University, Belfast.

O'Kelly, C. 1969. 'Bryn Celli Ddu. A reinterpretation', *Archaeologia Cambrensis*, 118, 17–48.

O'Kelly, C. 1983. *Newgrange, Co. Meath, Ireland. The Late Neolithic /Beaker Period Settlement*. BAR International Series no. S190. Oxford: British Archaeological Reports.

O'Kelly, M.J. 1982. *Newgrange: Archaeology, Art and Legend*. London: Thames and Hudson.

O'Kelly, M., Lynch, F. & O'Kelly, C. 1978. 'Three passage graves at Newgrange, Co. Meath', *Proceedings of the Royal Irish Academy*, 78C, 249–352.

Ó Nuallain, S. 1984. 'A Survey of Stone Circles in Cork and Kerry', *Proceedings of the Royal Irish Academy*, 84 C, 1–77.

O'Rahilly, T.F. 1946. *Early Irish History and Mythology*. Dublin: The Dublin Institute for Advanced Studies.

Ó Ríordáin, S.P. 1935. 'Recent acquisitions from Co. Donegal in the National Museum', *Proceedings of the Royal Irish Academy*, 42C, 145–91.

Ó Ríordáin, S.P. 1950. 'Excavations of Some Earthworks on the Curragh, Co Kildare', *Proceedings of the Royal Irish Academy*, 53 C, 249–77.

Ó Ríordáin, S.P. 1951. 'Lough Gur Excavations. The Great Stone Circle (B) in Grange Townland', *Proceedings of the Royal Irish Academy*, 54 C, 37–74.

Ó Ríordáin, S.P. 1953. *Antiquities of the Irish Countryside*. London: Methuen.

Ó Ríordáin, S. & L'Eochaidhe, 0. 1956. 'Trial excavation at Newgrange,' *Journal of the Royal Society of Antiquaries of Ireland*, 86, 52–61.

Orme, B.J. 1981. *Anthropology for Archaeologists*. London: Duckworth.

Oswald, A. 1991. *A Doorway into the Past: Roundhouse Orientation and its Significance in Iron Age Britain*. BA Dissertation, Department of Archaeology, University of Cambridge.

Page, R.I. 1995. *Chronicles of the Vikings*. London: British Museum Press.

Palmer, R. 1976. 'Interrupted ditch enclosures in Britain: the use of aerial photography for comparative studies', *Proceedings of the Prehistoric Society*, 42, 161–86.

Parker Pearson, M. 1993. *Bronze Age Britain*. London: Batsford/English Heritage.

Parker Pearson, M. 1996. 'Food, fertility and front doors in the first millennium BC', in T.C. Champion & J. Collis (eds) *The Iron Age in Britain and Ireland: recent trends*, 117–32. Sheffield: J.R. Collis Publications.

Parkin, D. 1992. 'Ritual as spatial direction and bodily division', in D. de Coppet (ed.) *Understanding Rituals*, 11–25. London: Routledge.

Patrick, J. 1974. 'Midwinter sunrise at New Grange', *Nature*, 249, 517–19.

Patton, M. 1991. 'An Early Neolithic axe factory at Le Pinacle, Jersey, Channel Islands', *Proceedings of the Prehistoric Society*, 57, 51–9.

Patton. M. 1992. 'Megalithic transport and territorial marker: evidence from the Channel Islands', *Antiquity*, 66, 392–5.

Patton, M. 1993. *Statements in Stone: Monuments and Society in Neolithic Brittany*. London: Routledge.

Pearson, G.W. & Stuiver, M. 1986. 'High precision calibration of the radiocarbon time-scale, 500–2500 cal bc', *Radiocarbon*, 28 (2B), 839–62.

Pearson, G.W., Pilcher, J.R., Baillie, M.G.L., Corbett, D.M. & Qua, F. 1986. 'High-precision 14C measurement of Irish oaks to show the natural 14C variations from cal AD 1840–5210 cal BC', *Radiocarbon*, 28 (2B), 911–34.

Peatfield, A. 1994. 'After the 'Big Bang' – what? or Minoan symbols and shrines beyond palatial collapse', in S.E. Alcock and R. Osborne (eds) *Placing the Gods: Sanctuaries and Sacred Space in Ancient Greece*, 19–36. Oxford: Clarendon Press.

Pederson, C. 1982. 'The present position of archaeoastronomy' in Heggie (ed.), 1982, 265–74.

Péquart, S.-J., Péquart, M. & Le Rouzic, Z. 1927. *Corpus des Signes Gravés des Monuments Mégalithiques du Morbihan*. Paris: Picard.

Pétrequin, P. & Pétrequin, A-M. 1993. *Écologie d'un Outil: la Hache de Pierre en Irian Jaya (Indonesie)*. Monographie du CRA 12. Paris: CNRS.

Piccini, A. 1992. *Behind the Green Door: Rath and Cashel Entrance Orientation and its Significance in Early Historic Ireland*, MA Dissertation, Department of Archaeology & Prehistory, University of Sheffield.

Piggott, S. 1948. 'The excavations at Cairnpapple Hill, West Lothian', *Proceedings of the Society of Antiquaries of Scotland*, 82, 68–123.

Piggott, S. 1956. 'Excavations in passage grave and ring cairns of the Clava group', *Proceedings of the Society of Antiquaries of Scotland*, 88, 173–207.

Piggott, S. 1958. 'Segmented bone beads and toggles in the British Early and Middle Bronze Age', *Proceedings of the Prehistoric Society*, 24, 227–9.

Piggott, S. 1962. 'From Salisbury Plain to South Siberia', *Wiltshire Archaeological and Natural History Magazine*, 58, 93–7.

Piggott, S. 1968. *The Druids*. London: Thames and Hudson.

Piggott, S. 1989. *Ancient Britons and the Antiquarian Imagination*. London: Thames and Hudson.

Plicht, J. van der & McCormac, F.G. 1995. 'A note on calibration curves', *Radiocarbon*, 37 (3), 963–4.

Plicht, J., Jansma, E. & H., Kars, H. 1995. 'The "Amsterdam Castle": a case study of wiggle matching and the proper calibration curve', *Radiocarbon*, 37 (3), 965–8.

Pollard, A.M., Bussell, G.D. & Baird, D.C. 1981. 'The analytical investigation of Early Bronze Age jet and jet-like material from the Devizes Museum', *Archaeometry*, 23 (2), 139–67.

Pollard, J. 1992. 'The Sanctuary, Overton Hill, Wiltshire: a re-examination', *Proceedings of the Prehistoric Society*, 58, 213–26.

Pollard, J. 1995. 'Structured deposition at Woodhenge', *Proceedings of the Prehistoric Society*, 61, 137–56.

Pritchett, W. Kendrick. 1963. *Ancient Athenian Calendars on Stone*. Berkeley/Los Angeles: University of California Press.

Pryor, F. 1988. 'Earlier Neolithic organised landscapes and ceremonial in lowland Britain', in J. Barrett & I. Kinnes (eds), 1988, 63–72.

RCHM. 1979. *Stonehenge and its Environs*. Edinburgh: RCHAM.

Raftery, B. 1972. 'Irish hill-forts', in C. Thomas (ed.), *The Iron Age in the Irish Sea Province*, 37–58. London: Council for British Archaeology.

Raftery, B. 1976. 'Rathgall and Irish hillfort problems', in D.W. Harding (ed.), *Hillforts – later prehistoric earthworks in Britain and Ireland*. London: Council for British Archaeology.

Raftery, B. 1994. *Pagan Celtic Ireland*. London: Thames and Hudson.

Raftery, B. 1996. *Trackway Excavations in the Mountdillon Bogs, Co. Longford, 1985–1991*. Irish Archaeological Wetland Unit, Transactions vol. 3. Dublin: Crannog Publications.

Raftery, J. 1971. 'A Bronze Age hoard from Ballytegan, Co. Laois', *Journal of the Royal Society of Antiquaries of Ireland*, 101, 85–100.

Ralston, I. 1980 'The Green Castle and the promontory forts of North-East Scotland', *Scottish Archaeological Forum*, 10, 27–40.

Ramm, H. 1980. 'Native settlements East of the Pennines', in K. Branigan (ed.) *Rome and the Brigantes*, 28–40. Sheffield: Sheffield University Department of Prehistory & Archaeology.

Raybould, M. 1997. *A study of inscribed material from Roman Britain: an inquiry into some aspects of literacy in Romano-British society*. PhD Dissertation, University of Wales College, Newport.

Renfrew, A.C. 1973a. *Before Civilization: the Radiocarbon Revolution and prehistoric Europe*. London: Penguin.

Renfrew, C. 1973b. 'Monuments, mobilisation and social organisation in Neolithic Wessex', in C. Renfrew (ed.) *The Explanation of Culture Change: Models in Prehistory*. London: Duckworth.

Renfrew, C. 1976. 'Megaliths, territories and populations', in S.J. de Laet (ed.) *Acculturation and Continuity in Atlantic Europe mainly during the Neolithic Period and the Bronze Age*. Bruges: de Tempel.

Renfrew, A.C. 1979. *Investigations in Orkney*. Edinburgh: Edinburgh University Press.

Renfrew, A.C. 1984. *Approaches to Social Archaeology*. Edinburgh: Edinburgh University Press.

Renfrew, C. (ed.) 1985. *The Prehistory of Orkney*. Edinburgh: Edinburgh University Press.

Renfrew, A.C. (ed.) 1990. *The Prehistory of Orkney* (reprinted edn). Edinburgh: Edinburgh University Press.

Renfrew, A.C. 1994. 'The archaeology of religion', in C. Renfrew & E. Zubrow (eds) *The Ancient Mind, Elements of Cognitive Archaeology*, 47–54. Cambridge: Cambridge University Press.

Renfrew, C. & Bahn, P. 1991. *Archaeology. Theories, Methods and Practice*. London: Thames and Hudson.

Renfrew, A.C., Harkness, D.D. & Switzer, V.R. 1976. 'Quanterness, radiocarbon and the Orkney cairns', *Antiquity*, 50, 194–204.

Richards, C. 1990. 'Postscript; the Late Neolithic settlement complex at Barnhouse Farm, Stenness', in Renfrew (ed.), 1990, 305–16.

Richards, C. 1992. 'Doorways into another world: the Orkney-Cromarty chambered tombs', in N. Sharples & A. Sheridan (eds) *Vessels for the Ancestors*, 62–76. Edinburgh: Edinburgh University Press.

Richards, C. 1993. 'Monumental Choreography: architecture and spatial representation in Late Neolithic Orkney', in C. Tilley (ed.) *Interpretative Archaeology*, 143–78. Oxford: Berg.

Richards, J. 1990. *The Stonehenge Environs Project*. Archaeological Report no. 16. London: English Heritage.

Richards, J. 1991. *Stonehenge*. London: Batsford/English Heritage.

Ritchie. J. 1919. 'Notes on some stone circles in central Aberdeenshire', *Proceedings of the Society of Antiquaries of Scotland*, 51 (1916–17), 30–47.

Ritchie. J. 1920a. 'Notes on some stone circles in the south of Aberdeenshire and north of Kincardineshire', *Proceedings of the Society of Antiquaries of Scotland*, 53 (1918–19), 64–75

Ritchie. J. 1920b. 'The stone circle of Broomend of Crichie', *Proceedings of the Society of Antiquaries of Scotland*, 54, 154–71.

Ritchie, J., 1927. *Some Antiquities of Aberdeenshire and its Borders*; Collected papers with an introduction by his son James Ritchie. Edinburgh: privately printed.

Ritchie, J.N.G. 1976. 'The Stones of Stenness, Orkney', *Proceedings of the Society of Antiquaries of Scotland*, 107, 1–60.

Ritchie, J.N.G. 1985. 'Ritual monuments', in C. Renfrew (ed.) *The Prehistory of Orkney*, 118–30. Edinburgh: Edinburgh University Press.

Ritchie, J.N.G. 1988. 'The Ring of Brodgar, Orkney', in C.L.N. Ruggles (ed.) *Records in Stone. Papers in Memory of Alexander Thom*, 336–50. Cambridge: Cambridge University Press.

Ritchie, P.R. 1968. 'The stone implement trade in third millennium Scotland', in J.M. Coles and D.D.A. Simpson (eds) *Studies in Ancient Europe*, 117–36. Leicester: Leicester University Press.

Ritchie, P.R. 1992. 'Stone axeheads and cushion maceheads from Orkney and Shetland: some similarities and contrasts', in N. Sharples and A. Sheridan (eds) *Vessels for the Ancestors*, 213–20. Edinburgh: Edinburgh University Press.

Rhŷs, J. 1901. *Celtic Folklore, Welsh and Manx*. Oxford: Oxford University Press.

Robinson, T. 1996. 'Listening to the landscape', in T. Robinson, *Setting Foot on the Shores of Connemara and Other Writings*, 151–64. Dublin: Lilliput Press.

Romilly Allen, J. 1901. 'Two Kelto-Roman finds in Wales', *Archaeologia Cambrensis* (6) 1, 20–44.

Ruggles, C.L.N. 1984. *Megalithic Astronomy. A New Archaeological and Statistical study of 300 Western Scottish Sites.* Oxford: Oxford University Press.

Ruggles, C.L.N. 1997. 'Astronomy and Stonehenge', *Proceedings of the British Academy*, 92, 203–29.

Ruggles, C.L.N. 1998. *Astronomy in Prehistoric Britain and Ireland*. New Haven: Yale University Press.

Ruggles,C.L.N. 1999. 'Palaeoscience', in G. Cimino (ed.) *History of Science*, Enciclopedia Italiana, Rome, vol. 1 (forthcoming).

Ruggles, C.L.N. & Burl, H.A.W. 1985. 'A new study of the Aberdeenshire recumbent stone circles, 2: interpretation', *Archaeoastronomy*, 8 (*Journal for the History of Astronomy* 16), S25–60.

Ruggles, C.L.N. & Hinge, P.D. 1991, 'The North Mull project (2): the wider astronomical potential of the sites', *Journal of the History of Astronomy*, 22, S52–S75.

Ruggles, C.L.N. & Martlew, R.D. 1989. 'The North Mull project (1): excavations at Glengorm, 1987–8)', *Journal of the History of Astronomy*, 20, S137–S149.

Russell-White, C.J., Lowe, C.E. & McCullagh, R.P.J. 1992. 'Excavations at three Early Bronze Age burial monuments in Scotland', *Proceedings of the Prehistoric Society*, 58, 285–323.

Salzman, M.R. 1990. *On Roman Time: the Codex Calendar of 354 and the Rhythms of Urban Life in Late Antiquity*. Berkeley: University of California Press.

Sandars, N.K. 1968. *Prehistoric Art in Europe*. Harmondsworth: Penguin.

Sanden, W. van der. 1996. *Through Nature to Eternity*. Amsterdam: Batavian Lion International.

Saunders, N.J. and Gray, D. 1996. '*Zemis*, trees and symbolic landscapes: three Taíno carvings from Jamaica', *Antiquity*, 70, 801–12.

Savory, H.N. 1980. *Guide Catalogue of the Bronze Age Collections*. Cardiff: National Museum of Wales.

Scott, E.M., Baxter, M.S. & Aitchison, T.C. 1984. 'A comparison of the treatment of errors in radiocarbon dating calibration methods', *Journal of Archaeological Science*, 11 (6), 455–66.

Scott, E.M., Baxter, M.S., Harkness, D.D., Aitchison, T.C. & Cook, G.T. 1988. 'The comparability of results across a sub-section of radiocarbon laboratories', in Slater & Tate (eds), 1987, 581–9.

Scullard, H.H. 1981. *Festivals and Ceremonies of the Roman Republic*. London: Thames and Hudson.

Sharples, N. 1991. *Maiden Castle. Excavations and Field Survey 1985–6*. English Heritage Archaeological Reports no. 19. London: HBMCE.

Shee, E. 1974. 'Painted megalithic art in western Iberia', *Actas do III Congresso Nacional de Arqueologia, Porto 1973*, 105–23.

Shee-Twohig, E. 1981. *The Megalithic Art of Western Europe*. Oxford: Oxford University Press.

Shepherd, I.A.G. 1973. *The V-bored Buttons of Great Britain*. Unpublished MA Thesis, University of Edinburgh.

Sheridan, A. 1985/6. 'Megaliths and megalomania: an account, and interpretation, of the development of passage tombs in Ireland', *Journal of Irish Archaeology*, 3, 17–30.

Sheridan, A. 1986. 'Porcellanite artifacts: a new survey', *Ulster Journal of Archaeology*, 49, 19–32.

Sheridan, A. 1995. 'Irish Neolithic pottery: the story in 1995', in I. Kinnes & G. Varndell (eds) *Unbaked Urns of Rudely Shape*, Monograph 55, 3–22. Oxford: Oxbow Books.

Sheridan, A., Cooney, G. & Grogan, E. 1992. 'Stone axe studies in Ireland', *Proceedings of the Prehistoric Society*, 58, 389–416.

Sheridan, J.A., Hunter, F.J. & Saville, A. 1995. 'Organic artefacts from the collections of the National Museums of Scotland', in R.E.M. Hedges, R.A. Housley, C. Bronk Ramsey & G.J. van Klinken, 'Radiocarbon dates from the Oxford AMS system: Archaeometry datelist 20', *Archaeometry*, 37 (2), 423–5.

Sherratt, A. 1976. 'Resources, technology and trade; an essay in early metallurgy', in I. Longworth, G. Sieveking & K. Wilson (eds) *Problems in Social and Economic Archaeology*, 557–81. London: Duckworth.

Sherratt, A. 1990. 'The genesis of megaliths: monumentality, ethnicity and social complexity in Neolithic north-west Europe', *World Archaeology*, 22 (2), 147–67.

Sherratt, A. 1991. 'Sacred and profane substances: the ritual use of narcotics in later Neolithic Europe', in P. Garwood,

D. Jennings, R. Skeates and J. Toms (eds) *Sacred and Profane: Proceedings of a Conference on Archaeology, Ritual and Religion*. Monograph 32, 50–64. Oxford: Oxford Committee for Archaeology.

Sherratt, A. 1996. 'Why Wessex? The Avon route and river transport in later British prehistory', *Oxford Journal of Archaeology*, 15, 211–34.

Sherratt, A. 1997. *Economy and Society in Prehistoric Europe: Changing Perspectives*. Edinburgh: Edinburgh University Press.

Simek, R. 1993. *Dictionary of Northern Mythology*. (English edition of *Lexicon der germanischen mythologie*, 1984.) Cambridge: Brewer.

Simpson, D.D.A. 1989. 'Neolithic Navan?' *Emania*, 6, 31–2.

Simpson, D.D.A. 1993. 'Dun Ruadh – a real Irish Henge', *Archaeology Ireland*, 7 (2), 14–15.

Simpson, D.D.A. & Gibson, A.M. 1989. 'Lyles Hill', *Current Archaeology*, 114, 214–15.

Simpson, D.D.A., Weir, D.A. & Wilkinson, J.L. 1994. 'Excavations at Dun Ruadh, Crouck, Co. Tyrone', *Ulster Journal of Archaeology*, 54–5, 36–47.

Slater, E.A. & Tate, J.O. (eds). 1987. *Science and Archaeology*. BAR British Series no. 196. Oxford: British Archaeological Reports.

Smith, A.H.V. & Owens, B. 1983. 'The Caergwrle Bowl: its composition, geological source and archaeological significance – an addendum', *Report of the Institute of Geological Science*, 83/1, 24–7.

Smith, I. 1965. *Windmill Hill and Avebury*. Oxford: Clarendon Press.

Soffe, G. & Clare, T. 1988. 'New evidence of ritual monuments at Long Meg and her Daughters', *Antiquity*, 62, 552–7.

Sparey Green, C. 1994. 'Observations on the site of the "Two Barrows", Fordington Farm, Dorchester, with a note on the Conquer Barrow', *Proceedings of the Dorset Natural History & Archaeological Society*, 116 , 45–54.

Spriggs, M. & Anderson, A. 1993. 'Late colonisation of East Polynesia', *Antiquity*, 67, 200–17.

St Joseph, J.K. 1980a. 'Air reconnaissance: recent results 49', *Antiquity*, 54, 47–51.

St Joseph, J.K. 1980b. 'Air reconnaissance: recent results 50', *Antiquity*, 54, 132–5.

Stanley, W.O. 1865. 'Antiquities and works of art exhibited' (Proceedings at meetings of the Archaeological Institute), *Archaeological Journal*, 22, 74.

Stanley, W.O. 1868. 'On the remains of ancient circular habitations in Holyhead Island', *Archaeologia Cambrensis*, 14, 385–433.

Stanley, W.O. 1875. 'Presaddfed urns', *Archaeologia Cambrensis*, 6, 126–8.

Startin, W. 1978. 'Linear pottery culture houses: reconstruction and manpower', *Proceedings of the Prehistoric Society* 44, 143–60.

Startin, W. & Bradley, R. 1981. 'Some notes on work organisation and society in prehistoric Britain', in C. Ruggles & A. Whittle (eds) *Astronomy and Society in Britain during the period 4000–1500 BC*, 289–96. BAR no. 88, Oxford: British Archaeological Reports.

Steinsland, G. 1992. 'Scandinavian paganism', in E. Roesdahl & D.M. Wilson (eds) *From Viking to Crusader*, 144–51. Uddevalla: Nordic Council of Ministers.

Stevenson, R.B.K. 1955. 'Pins and the chronology of brochs', *Proceedings of the Prehistoric Society*, 21, 282–94.

Stevenson, R.B.K. 1981. 'The Museum, its Beginnings and its Development. Part II: the National Museum to 1954', in A.S. Bell (ed.) *The Scottish Antiquarian Tradition. Essays to Mark the Bicentenary of the Society of Antiquaries of Scotland and its Museum, 1780–1980*, 142–211. Edinburgh: John Donald.

Stout, G. 1991. 'Embanked enclosures of the Boyne region', *Proceedings of the Royal Irish Academy*, 91 C, 245–84.

Stout, G. & Stout, M. 1992. 'Patterns in the past: County Dublin 5000 BC–1000 AD', in F.H.A. Aalen & K. Whelan (eds), *Dublin City and County: From Prehistory to Present*, Dublin: Geography Publications.

Strathern, M. 1969. 'Stone axes and flake tools; evaluations from two New Guinea Highlands societies', *Proceedings of the Prehistoric Society*, 35, 311–29.

Stuiver, M. & Pearson, G.W. 1986. 'High precision calibration of the radiocarbon time-scale, cal AD 1950–500 cal BC', *Radiocarbon*, 28 (2B), 805–38.

Stuiver, M. & Pearson, G.W. 1993, 'High precision bidecadal calibration of the radiocarbon time-scale, cal AD 1950–500 cal BC and 2500–6000 cal BC', *Radiocarbon*, 35 (1), 1–24.

Stuiver, M. & Reimer, P.J. 1993. 'University of Washington Quaternary Isotope Lab Radiocarbon Calibration Program Rev 3.0.3', *Radiocarbon*, 35, 215–230.

Sweetman, P.D. 1976. 'An earthen enclosure at Monknewtown, Slane, Co. Meath', *Proceedings of the Royal Irish Academy*, 76 C, 25–72.

Sweetman, P.D. 1985. 'A Late Neolithic/Early Bronze Age pit circle at Newgrange, Co. Meath', *Proceedings of the Royal Irish Academy*, 81C, 195–221.

Sweetman, P.D. 1987. 'Excavation of a Late Neolithic/Early Bronze Age site at Newgrange, Co. Meath', *Proceedings of the Royal Irish Academy*, 87C, 283–98.

Sweetman, P.D., Alcock, O. & Moran, B. 1995. *Archaeological Inventory of County Laois*. Dublin: The Stationery Office.

Tacon, P.S.C. 1991. 'The power of stone: symbolic aspects of stone use and tool development in western Arnhem Land, Australia', *Antiquity*, 65, 192–207.

Tacon, P.S.C. 1994. 'Socialising landscapes: the long-term implications of signs, symbols and marks on the land', *Archaeology in Oceania*, 29 (3), 117–29.

Tassell Graves, E. van. 1965. 'Lugus, the commercial traveller', *Ogam*, 17, 167–71.

Taylor, C. 1979. *Roads and Tracks of Britain.* London: Dent.

Thom, A. 1966. *Megalithic Sites in Britain.* Oxford: Oxford University Press.

Thom, A. 1967. *Megalithic Science in Britain.* Oxford: Oxford University Press.

Thom, A. 1971. *Megalithic Lunar Observatories.* Oxford: Oxford University Press.

Thom, A. & A.S. & Burl, A. 1980. *Megalithic Rings. Plans and Data for 229 Monuments in Britain.* BAR British Series no. 81. Oxford: British Archaeological Reports.

Thom, A. & A.S. & Burl, A. 1990. *Stone Rows and Standing Stones I, II,* BAR International Series no. 560. Oxford: British Archaeological Reports.

Thomas, J. 1991. *Rethinking the Neolithic.* Cambridge: Cambridge University Press.

Thomas, J. 1993a. 'The politics of vision and the archaeologies of landscape', in B. Bender (ed.) *Landscape; Politics and Perspectives,* 19–48. Oxford: Berg.

Thomas, J. 1993b. 'The hermeneutics of megalithic space', in C. Tilley (ed.), 1993, 73–98.

Thurnam, J. 1869, 'On Ancient British barrows', *Archaeologia,* 42, 161–244.

Thurnam, J. 1872. 'On Ancient British barrows', *Archaeologia,* 43, 285–544.

Tilley, C. (ed.). 1993. *Interpretative Archaeology.* Oxford: Berg.

Tilley, C. 1994. *A Phenomenology of Landscape.* Oxford: Berg.

Toal, C. 1995. *North Kerry Archaeological Survey, Dingle.* Dublin: The Stationery Office.

Topping, P. 1992. 'The Penrith henges: a survey by the Royal Commission on Historical Monuments of England', *Proceedings of the Prehistoric Society* 58, 249–64.

Toth, N., Clark, D. & Ligabue, G. 1992. 'The last stone axe makers', *Scientific American,* 261, 66–71.

Turville-Petre, E.O.G. 1964. *Myth and Religion of the North.* London: Weidenfeld & Nicholson.

Vendryes, J. 1924. 'Imbolc', *Revue Celtique,* 41, 241–4.

Verlinde, A. 1993. 'Bronstijdbewoning in Zwolle-Ittersumerbroek.' *Archeologie en Bouwhistorie in Zwolle,* I, 33–49. Zwolle: Gemeente Zwolle.

Victoria County History of Derbyshire, 1905.

Waddell, J. 1985. 'Rathcrogan in Connacht', *Emania,* 5, 5–17.

Waddell, J. 1991–2. 'The Irish Sea in Prehistory', *Journal of Irish Archaeology,* 6, 29–40.

Waddell, J. & Barton, K. 1995. 'Seeing beneath Rathcroghan', *Archaeology Ireland,* 9 (1), 38–41.

Wailes, B. 1990. 'Dun Ailinne: a summary excavation report', *Emania,* 7, 22–5.

Wainwright, G.J. 1979. *Mount Pleasant, Dorset: Excavations 1970–71,* Research Report 37. London: Society of Antiquaries.

Wainwright, G. J. 1996. 'Debating the stones of contention', *The Times,* 20 June 1996, 37.

Wainwright, G.J. & Longworth, I.H. 1971. *Durrington Walls: Excavations 1966–68,* Research Report 29. London: Society of Antiquaries.

Wainwright, G.J. 1969. 'A review of Henge monuments in the light of recent research', *Proceedings of the Prehistoric Society,* 35, 112–33.

Wainwright, G.J. 1989. *The Henge Monuments.* London: Thames and Hudson.

Wait, G.A. 1985. *Ritual and Religion in Iron Age Britain,* BAR British Series no. 149. Oxford: British Archaeological Reports.

Wait, G.A. 1995. 'Burial and the Otherworld', in M.J. Green (ed.) *The Celtic World,* 489–511. London: Routledge.

Wallis, W.D. & R.S. 1955. *The Micmac Indians of Eastern Canada.* Minneapolis: University of Minnesota Press.

Ward, G.K. & Wilson, S.R. 1978. 'Procedures for comparing and combining radiocarbon age determinations: a critique', *Archaeometry,* 20, 19–31.

Warner, R.B. 1986. 'Preliminary schedules of sites and stray finds in the Navan Complex', *Emania,* 1, 5–8.

Warrilow, W., Owen, G. & Britnell, W. 1986. 'Eight ring-ditches at Four Crosses, Llandysilio, Powys, 1981–5', *Proceedings of the Prehistoric Society,* 52, 53–87.

Waterbolk, H.T. 1995. 'De prehistorische nederzetting van Zwolle-Ittersumerbroek'. *Archeologie en Bouwhistorie in Zwolle,* 3, 123–73. Zwolle: Gemeente Zwolle.

Watts, S., Pollard, A.M. & Wolff, G.A. 1997. 'Kimmeridge jet – a potential new source for British jet', *Archaeometry,* 39 (1), 125–43.

Way, A. 1866. 'Notice of ancient relics found at Llangwyllog in Anglesey', *Archaeologia Cambrensis,* 12, 97–111.

Way, A. 1867. 'Notices of relics found in and near ancient circular dwellings explored by the Hon. W.O. Stanley, MP in Holyhead Island', *Archaeological Journal,* 24, 243–64.

Webster, J. 1995. 'Sanctuaries and Sacred Places', in M.J. Green (ed.) *The Celtic World,* 445–64. London: Routledge.

Weiner, J.F. 1991. *The Empty Place.* Bloomington: Indiana University Press.

Weir, D. 1987. 'Palynology and the environmental history of the Navan area', *Emania,* 2, 34–43.

Welfare, H. & Swan, V. 1995. *Roman Camps in England: The Field Archaeology.* London: HMSO.

Welinder, S. & Griffin, W.L. 1984. 'Raw material sources and an exchange network of the earliest farming society in central Sweden', *World Archaeology,* 16 (2), 174–85.

Westrop, T.J. 1886. 'Magh Adhair, County Clare, the place of inauguration of the Dalcassian kings', *Proceedings of the Royal Irish Academy*, 20, 55–60.

Whitlock, D. (ed.). 1961. *The Anglo-Saxon Chronicle*. London: Eyre & Spottiswoode.

Whittle, A.W.R. 1991. 'A late Neolithic complex at West Kennet, Wiltshire'. *Antiquity*, 65, 256–62.

Whittle, A.W.R. 1992. *Excavations at West Kennet near Avebury, 1992*, privately circulated.

Whittle, A., Atkinson, R.J.C., Chambers, R. & Thomas, N. 1992. 'Excavations in the Neolithic and Bronze Age complex at Dorchester on Thames, Oxfordshire', *Proceedings of the Prehistoric Society*, 58, 143–201.

Williams, B. 1990. 'Notes and Queries', *Emania*, 7, 45.

Williams, J.Ll. 1994. 'Graiglwyd axe factory excavation, Penmaenmawr', *Archaeology in Wales*, 33, 36–8.

Williams, R. 1989. *People of the Black Mountains*. London: Chatto & Windus.

Wilson, D. 1851. *The Archaeology and Prehistoric Annals of Scotland*. Edinburgh: Sutherland and Knox.

Woodman, P.C. & O'Brien, M. 1993. 'Excavations at Ferriter's Cove: an interim statement', in E. Shee-Twohig & M. Ronayne (eds) *Past Perceptions*, 25–34. Cork: Cork University Press.

Woodward, A.B. & Woodward, P.J. 1996. 'The topography of some Bronze Age cemeteries in Bronze Age Wessex', *Proceedings of the Prehistoric Society*, 62, 275–91.

Woodward, P.J., Davies, S.M. & Graham, A. 1993. *Excavations at Greyhound Yard and the Old Methodist Chapel, Dorchester, 1981–84*, Monograph 12. Dorchester: Dorset Natural History and Archaeological Society.

Woodward, P. & Smith, R. 1987. 'Survey and excavation along the route of the south Dorchester bypass 1986–7: an interim note', *Proceedings of the Dorset Natural History & Archaeological Society*, 109, 79–86.

Wroe, P. & Mellor, P. 1971. 'A Roman road between Buxton and Melandra Castle, Glossop', *Derbyshire Archaeological Journal*, 91, 40–57.

INDEX